INTRODUCTION TO MODERN
POLISH LITERATURE

INTRODUCTION TO MODERN POLISH LITERATURE

An Anthology of Fiction and Poetry

edited by

ADAM GILLON *and*
LUDWIK KRZYZANOWSKI

SECOND EDITION

with a New Poetry Section
edited by

ADAM GILLON *and*
KRYSTYNA OLSZER

HIPPOCRENE BOOKS
New York

Acknowledgment is made to the following authors, translators and publishers who have granted permission to reprint selections included in this anthology:

Zofia Kossak, Maria Kuncewicz, Czeslaw Milosz, Joseph Wittlin, Kazimierz Wierzynski, Alexander Janta, Kazimierz Brandys, Tadeusz Rozewicz, Zbigniew Herbert, Adolf Rudmicki;

Watson Kirkconnell, Paul Mayewski, Magdalena Czajkowska, R. M. Montgomery, Adam Czerniawski, Clark Mills, Victor Contoski;

Gerald Duckworth & Co. Ltd.—for excerpts from *A Polish Anthology,* translated by M. A. Michael;

Frederick Ungar Publishing Co.—for an excerpt from *For Your Freedom and Ours;*

Alfred A. Knopf, Inc.—for a chapter from *Homo Sapiens* by Stanislaw Przybyszewski;

ZAIKS (Polish Authors' Association)—for permission to the editors to translate "The Trial" by Jerzy Andrzejewski;

Harcourt, Brace & World, Inc.—for Chapter V, of Witold Gombrowicz's *Ferdydurke;*

Poland, Illustrated Magazine—for permission to reprint stories by Schulz, Konopnicka, Prus, Zeromski, Nalkowska, Orzeszkowa, Parandowski, Hlasko and Dabrowska;

A. A. Wyn, Inc.—for Chapter XVIII of Maria Kuncewicz's *The Stranger;* Roy Publishers, Inc.—for Chapter II of Zofia Kossak's *The Covenant* and Adolf Rudnicki's story "The Great Stefan Konecki" from *Ascent to Heaven.*

The Charioteer Press, Washington, D.C., for poems "Oh! Oh! Should They Take Away My Stove" and "To—" by Miron Bialoszewski from *The Revolution of Things,* 1974;

Hounslow Press, Toronto, Canada, for the poem "Après le Déluge" by Waclaw Iwaniuk, from its volume *Dark Times,* 1979;

Mr. Cogito Press, Forest Grove, Oregon, for the poems "Tongue, This Wild Meat" and "Caute" by Ryszard Krynicki, from *Mr. Cogito,* Vol. V, No. 1, Winter 1979-80;

Poetry East, Charlottesville, Virginia, for the poem "Incantation" by Czeslaw Milosz, from No. 3, 1980;

Footprint Magazine (1980), Somerville, N.J., for the poem "In One Breath" by Stanislaw Baranczak;

The Polish Review, New York, for the poems "You Who Have Wronged" by Czeslaw Milosz; (Vol. XXVI, No. 2, 1981), "He Chews Raw Rye" by Anna Swirszczynska; (Vol. XXIII, No. 3, 1977). "Psalm" and "Utopia" by Wislawa Szymborska (Vol. XXIV, No. 3, 1979);

Echo, Chicago,Illinois, for an excerpt of "Wind From The Sea" by Tymoteusz Karpowicz, from No. 5, September-December 1980.

Distributed in the United Kingdom by
ORBIS BOOKS (LONDON) LTD
66, Kenway Road, London SW5 ORD

Hippocrene Books, Inc.
171 Madison Avenue
New York, N.Y. 10016

Library of Congress Catalog Card No. 81-86230
ISBN 0-88254-516-7

Printed in the United States of America

Preface to the Second Edition

The recent social and political developments have stirred great interest in Poland throughout the world. This revised, augmented edition of *Introduction to Modern Polish Literature* is an attempt to assist readers in their quest to know and understand the Polish people.

The limited scope of this anthology made it impossible for us to include drama and fiction. We have restricted our new material to selections of poetry written in Poland and abroad. The Polish poets of the last two decades reflect the changing moods of the nation. We have attempted to give the public a variety of styles, from the romanticism of war-time poetry by Krzysztof Baczynski to the classicism of Wislawa Szymborska and the linguistic experiments of Stanislaw Baranczak or Ewa Lipska. The language of the new poets, deceptively simple at first glance, is scrupulously crafted and ingenious. The themes of contemporary Polish verse are drawn from the political realities of the country. The ideas and values expressed by the poets, however, transcend parochial or topical elements. They are often universal and have won widespread recognition, best expressed by the recent award of the Nobel prize for literature to Czeslaw Milosz.

ADAM GILLON and KRYSTYNA OLSZER
Editors of the New Poetry Section

Table of Contents

II POETRY 355

III NEW POETRY 481

Introduction

The aim of this anthology is to offer the American reader a fairly representative selection of Polish fiction and poetry, written during the past seven decades. The scope of this volume made it impossible to include many excellent writers. Other reasons for leaving out important authors were the absence or dearth of good translations or the difficulty of obtaining originals of works recently published in Poland. The editors had to translate a number of works never before rendered into English and provide new translations where the old cnes were found inadequate.

The editors are glad to offer this volume at the present time because no comprehensive anthology of modern Polish prose and poetry in English translation is available in the United States or other English-speaking countries, and also because Poland is now celebrating the millennium of her unbroken continuity as a nation and of her allegiance to the Western cultural heritage. Because of the vicissitudes of Poland's history, we cannot speak of her uninterrupted statehood, but we are certainly entitled to emphasize her continuous national, cultural and literary development.

I

From Beginnings to Romanticism

Faced at the inception of her recorded history in the second half of the tenth century with a choice between the Western Christian culture of Rome and the Eastern Christianity of Byzantium, Poland decided in favor of Latinity. This spiritual orientation made her distinct from many other Slavic nations to which she was related by race and language, but who were moulded by Byzantine influences and traditions.

Thus the Poles do not fit into the popular notion of a "Slav spirit" which imputes to the Slavic nations characteristics that properly belong to the Russians. Joseph Conrad pointed this out when he wrote: "Between Polonism and Slavonism there is a complete and ineradicable incompatibility . . . The Poles, whom superficial theorists are trying to force into the social and psychological formula of Slavonism, are in truth not Slavonic at all; in temperament, in feeling, in mind, and even in unreason, they are Western, with an absolute comprehension of all Western modes of thought."

If a proof of the Polish identification with the cultural legacy of the West were needed, it is supplied by representatives of another great Slavic nation, Russia. They argued that centuries-long experience had demonstrated the profound difference and incompatibility of Latinity and Slavdom. Having adopted Christianity from Rome, Poland had sold her Slavic soul. Wherever Slavdom comes in contact with Latinity it withers and decays. The tragic element of Poland's history lies in her complete submission to Latinity and therefore she was doomed to ruin. Because, in the words of Ivan Aksakov, "it is Russia's mission to realize Slavic brotherhood in liberty. Any Slavic people that betrays this joint mission, that turns away from its brothers and renounces them, renounces its own existence and must perish! Such is the unshakable law of the history of the Slavs."

The epithet "Judas" with which the poet Theodore Tiutchev designated the Poles, illumines Poland's embattled situation between East and West. On the one hand she is considered a betrayer of Slavdom; on the other she sees herself in the role of an outpost of the West. In his brilliant study, *Russia, Poland and the West,* Professor Waclaw Lednicki elaborates this phenomenon as follows:

> Poland's geographical situation, her political development and activities, her cultural traditions made her a missionary of the West; she was preserving and spreading the ideas of Western civilization. For these reasons, after centuries of fighting for this civilization, although having been so often betrayed by Europe, Poland's ties with the West resulted in a particularly deep and indestructible attachment to Europe, to her ideals, concepts and beliefs. In a sense, therefore, Poland has always been more Western in her feelings than the most ·thoroughly Western nations. This tense Europeanism is generally characteristic for every Polish intellectual.

As an organized state entity Poland appeared on the European historical stage comparatively late and thus the Poles labored under a handicap that has been defined as cultural juniority.

The beginnings of Polish literature were modest. Latin was generally used as the literary language and it was in Latin that the first monuments, such as chronicles and lives of saints, were written. In the period of Humanism, Polish authors gave luster to original Latin verse and the names of Clemens Janicki and Matthew Sarbiewski have an honorable place in the culture of Humanist Europe. Latin was also the language of the first extensive history of Poland by Jan

Dlugosz in the second half of the fifteenth century, which far surpassed the early twelfth-century chronicle of Gallus Anonymus and the early thirteenth-century work of Vincent Kadlubek. Progressive social and political ideas were eloquently expressed—still in Latin—by Andrew Frycz Modrzewski in his *De Republica Emendanda;* and it was in that language that Nicholas Copernicus wrote his works among which the epoch-making *De revolutionibus orbium coelestium* is the most noteworthy.

The Revolutions of the Celestial Bodies was published in 1543, a year memorable in the annals of Polish culture by the appearance of Nicholas Rey's *A Short Discourse among the Squire, the Bailiff and the Parson,* a satire on contemporary social and religious conditions, written in Polish. It is this date which is traditionally considered the beginning of modern Polish literature and, significantly, it is a Protestant that is its "father." For, though relative latecomers in the assemblage of European nations, the Poles shared in all the great religious, intellectual and cultural movements of the West. It was under the impact of the Reformation, and of the religious controversies that it engendered, that the use of the native language spread and literature in the vernacular developed. Not the racy and vigorous Rey, but Jan Kochanowski (1530–84) is the foremost writer of Renaissance Poland. This essentially lyrical poet created in his *Laments,* occasioned by the premature death of his daughter Ursula, the greatest poetic cycle of the sixteenth century. By then Polish had become a literary medium of beauty, richness and power which is evident also in the philosophical poetry, reminiscent of the "metaphysical" poets of seventeenth-century England, of Nicholas Sep Szarzynski. To the great Humanist tradition belong also the *Pastorals,* containing vivid scenes from Polish life, of Szymon Szymonowicz who also excelled as a Latin poet.

Simultaneously prose reached artistic excellence. Among its masters, special mention must be made of the inspired Jesuit preacher, Peter Skarga, whose fame rests on the Lives of Saints, but above all on his *Sermons Before the Diet,* an impassioned denouncement of the ills of the Polish state and the shortcomings of its leading class. It would be impossible not to mention the great debt that Polish language and style owe to the classic translation of the Bible by the Jesuit Jacob Wujek (1599), which followed several Protestant versions and whose role in Poland is comparable to that of the Authorized Version in England.

The following century witnessed the flowering of epic poetry inspired by the military events of the period with its almost continuous warfare with the Ottoman Empire and Muscovy, and by the belated reception of Tasso's *Gerusalemme Liberata* in the translation of the great Jan Kochanowski's nephew, Peter. Representative of this trend are Samuel Twardowski and Waclaw Potocki, while the brothers Christopher and Lucas Opalinski must be mentioned as satirists. Vespasian Kochowski is especially notable for his *Polish Psalmody* expressing both a devout Catholic faith and profound patriotism. The influence of French and Italian literature is evident in the conceit-filled verse of the colorful diplomat and lyricist Andrew Morsztyn who was also the translator of Corneille's *Cid*. A colorful picture of the mores of this turbulent age is provided by the *Memoirs* of Jan Chryzostom Pasek who may be likened to his English contemporary, Samuel Pepys.

The seventeenth century, though inferior in comparison with the Golden Age, still maintained a reputable level, but the first half of the eighteenth, the so-called Saxon period, must be considered a time of political decay and intellectual stagnation.

But signs of slow improvement became apparent in the far-ranging activity of the Piarist priest, Stanislaw Konarski (1700–1773), who, guided by the ideas of the French Enlightenment, paved the way for a reform of education, government and literary style. He is honored as the one who "dared to be wise" and his reforming zeal led to the foundation of the forward-looking *Collegium Nobilium,* whose beneficial influence was manifested during the impressive cultural and political revival in the reign of Poland's last king, Stanislas Augustus Poniatowski.

That renascence was also stimulated by the establishment in 1773 of the Commission of National Education as the supreme secular agency engaged in the preparation of textbooks and a reform of the school system on all its levels. The political reform movement which culminated in the adoption of the Constitution of May Third, 1791, was promoted by such thinkers as Stanislaw Staszic and Hugo Kollataj, while historiography is represented by the *History of the Polish Nation* of Bishop Adam Naruszewicz, also a poet of note, who managed to bring his ambitious undertaking only to the end of the fourteenth century.

The most many-sided representative of this brilliant period was Bishop Ignacy Krasicki, author of fables, epic poems, satires and novels. Another fabulist, inspired by La Fontaine, was Stanislaw Trembecki who achieved excellence by using an expansiveness of expression in contrast to Krasicki's conciseness. The sentimental school had among its adherents Franciszek Karpinski whose religious hymns and patriotic poems have assured him a respectable position in Poland's literary annals.

An event of far-reaching consequence was the opening, in 1765, of the first public theater in Warsaw. Though many of the new playwrights were imitators and adapters of French models rather than original dramatists, their contribution to the development of the

Polish stage cannot be overlooked. Special mention must be made of the original "political" comedy, *The Deputy's Return*, by Julian Ursyn Niemcewicz (1757–1841), a prolific writer who cultivated many other literary genres and played an important role in the cultural life of post-partition Poland. He is also an important link in Polish-American relations as a friend of Jefferson, member of the American Philosophical Society and author of an extensive diary describing the early post-revolutionary United States.

The political obliteration of the country was not, as might have been thought, tantamount with the nation's spiritual and cultural death. Paradoxically enough, the period of political enslavement coincided with the greatest flowering of Polish Romantic poetry. Adam Mickiewicz (1798–1855), a student at the University of Wilno, was the first to come out with a Romantic manifesto that resembled the preface to *The Lyrical Ballads.* In 1820 he wrote his famous "Ode to Youth," in which the poet heralded the dawn of liberty. Two years later he published *Ballads and Romances,* a reflection of the Polish-Lithuanian folklore. Mickiewicz was inspired by the anguish of an unrequited love, by Russian persecution and his subsequent imprisonment. He was then exiled to Russia and it is during his stay there that he produced his exquisite *Crimean Sonnets* and *Farys*—written under the influence of the spread of Orientalism which flourished in the European literatures of the period. The young poet won the admiration of a great fellow-poet in Russia—Pushkin.

Like other Polish poets of the Romantic era, Mickiewicz followed the vogue set by Byron. His verse tale *Konrad Wallenrod* (1828) has a mysterious, Byronic hero, and its background is the ancient wars between Lithuania and the Knights of the Teutonic Order. But the main theme is also the problem of loyalty and patriotism.

Mickiewicz was permitted to leave Russia before the uprising of 1830, and his travels in Europe inspired the third part of *Forefathers' Eve* (the second and fourth parts were published in 1823; the first was fragmentary), which appeared in 1832. The protagonist of this great poetic drama is the Gustav of Part IV who is reborn as the new Konrad, to suffer for his nation and to challenge the Spirit of God for an explanation of man's inhumanity to man. The drama shows the transformation of a lyrical lover into an inspired patriot and national poet; it also represents a "Messianic" vision of Poland.

This vision was more fully explained in his *Books of the Polish Nation and of the Polish Pilgrimage* (1832), written in beautiful biblical prose, for the edification of his fellow Poles in exile. Mickiewicz became a great fighter for Poland's independence and a worthy representative of Polish culture in Europe, especially in his role of professor of Slavic literatures at the Collège de France.

But perhaps his greatest claim to fame is *Pan Tadeusz* (1834), the first great national epic in Polish literature. It originally appeared in Paris, and its scene is Lithuania on the eve of Napoleon's invasion of Russia in 1812. The plot is based on a story of a family feud among the country gentry. The regional characters become universal under Mickiewicz's skillful treatment, and his native Lithuania symbolizes the whole of Poland. The classical purity of the poet's style, the richness of his imagery, the humor and serenity make *Pan Tadeusz** one of Poland's great masterpieces.

Juliusz Slowacki (1809–1849) was Mickiewicz's rival. He too began to write under the influence of Byron, from whom he took the lonely and misanthropic hero. Slowacki's work also resembles that of Shelley, especially in his political liberalism and poetic technique. He was chiefly an émigré writer, at first scorned by his fellow exiles, but later accepted as one of Poland's great Romantic poets. He disagreed with Mickiewicz's Messianic views, and in a dramatic poem, *Kordian* (1834), he attacked *The Forefathers' Eve*.

Slowacki is an outstanding lyricist (e.g., in his *In Switzerland*, 1839) and a fine dramatist. He was greatly influenced by Shakespeare. Two of his dramas dealing with legendary early Polish history, *Balladyna* and *Lilla Weneda*, are modelled on *King Lear*, *Macbeth* and *A Midsummer Night's Dream*. His historical play, *Mazeppa*, resembles *Othello*; *Horsztynski* has Hamletian *motifs*.

Slowacki also shows the influence of Victor Hugo and Calderon. Although he ridiculed Mickiewicz's Messianism, Slowacki himself eventually turned to a mystical interpretation of Poland's tragedy. Unlike Mickiewicz, however, he continued to write great poetry after embracing his new faith. His *Anhelli* (1838) is a symbolic half-allegory which parallels Mickiewicz's *Books of the Polish Nation and of Polish Pilgrimage*, and which actually is a presentation of the émigré community as a group of Polish exiles in Siberia.

In *The Genesis from the Spirit* (1844), he applies the doctrine of evolution to the Polish problem.

It is interesting to note that Slowacki rather than Mickiewicz served as a model for the literary modernists in Poland at the beginning of the 20th century, and this is due, no doubt, to the unbelievable poetic range and variety of his output.

Zygmunt Krasinski (1812–1859), though not equal to Mickiewicz and Slowacki in the mastery of form, is the author of a work of genius, *The Undivine Comedy* (1835), a profound social drama prophetically depicting the revolution which was to come only a century later.

---

* An English verse translation by Watson Kirkconnell appeared in 1962 in New York and Toronto. A prose version of the epic by George R. Noyes is available in the Everyman's Library.

Under the guise of allegory, the struggle of a Greek against the over-lordship of Rome, the drama *Iridion* (1836) takes up a problem similar to that of Mickiewicz's *Konrad Wallenrod:* the moral aspect of an enslaved nation's striving for freedom. The "Messianic" theme, so characteristic of the Polish Romantics who sought an explanation for Poland's sufferings, finds fullest elaboration in the poem *Dawn,* with its vision of Poland's mission and ultimate resurrection. *The Psalms of the Future* reflect the poet's anxiety about the intensified social struggle in his time, which might lead to a fratricidal conflict in Poland. The poem *Resurrecturis* emphasizes Krasinski's faith but insists on the preservation of the purity of moral ideas. Though his reputation underwent several fluctuations, Krasinski's work remains a permanent feature in Poland's literary heritage.

Cyprian K. Norwid (1821–1883) was a contemporary of the three great Romantics. He continued the tradition of Romantic philosophy, bringing to it a remarkably modern social interpretation. His complex and varied works were read and appreciated by a few discriminating readers during his lifetime, and his influence was felt only at the beginning of this century. Norwid has many affinities with the Great Three. His narrative poem *Quidam* recalls Krasinski's *Iridion,* and his mystery plays *Wanda* and *Krakus* remind one of Slowacki's dramas.

Yet Norwid's psychological drama *Cleopatra,* which probes the Queen's early love for Caesar, cannot be read without thinking of Shaw's *Caesar and Cleopatra.* Similarly, his imagery and versification anticipate some of the French symbolist poets.

Norwid was also a talented painter and sculptor, and he left a rich legacy of aesthetic criticism on several forms of art. Both in his theories and his poetic diction Norwid resembles the allusiveness of the modernists, whose work he influenced to a considerable measure.

II

Modern Fiction and Poetry

The two tragic insurrections against the Russian Tsarist government of 1831 and 1863 profoundly influenced modern Polish literature. While the former had left the Poles with hopes for a restored, independent country, a dream that was sustained by the many admirers of Napoleon in Poland, the latter produced a reaction against political aspirations and a period of painful self-analysis. The Romantic dream, many responsible thinkers realized, was no longer feasible or even desirable in a land plagued by economic and social backwardness. The theories of Comtist Positivism stirred the minds of university students who, upon reaching maturity, decided that a new creed was needed to enable Poland's growth—based not on Romanticism but on the slogan, "Work from the Foundations," on the ideals of work and realism and the quest for scientific truth.

Poland's Positivism was a social as well as literary movement whose main spokesman was the *Weekly Review,* founded in Warsaw in 1866. The Positivists extolled the virtues and the nobility of work, advocated the emancipation of women and favored educational reforms that would enable the peasant and the working man to obtain some schooling. The Positivist writers examined the sober realities of their country's economic and social life, and turned away from the Romantic dream of independence. It was only natural that prose and journalistic fiction would predominate over poetry while the mood of Positivism was upon the country.

Joseph I. Kraszewski (1812–1887) did for the novel what Norwid had done for poetry—he bridged the gulf between the era of Romanticism and that of Realism. His was truly a gigantic output; in the course of sixty years of literary production, Kraszewski turned out some six-hundred volumes: novels, poems, critical essays, dramas, political and philosophical treatises. Kraszewski was the pioneer of Polish fiction despite the many stylistic lapses, caused by his prolificness.

Many writers learned from him and followed his example, but only a few became outstanding novelists. Of these, Boleslaw Prus (pseudonym of Alexander Glowacki, (1847–1912) was the most striking figure, and perhaps also the most eloquent representative of Positivism. Like Kraszewski, Prus was a many-sided writer whose work included journalism, essays, novels and short stories.

In his novel, *The Doll,* Prus depicted many social strata of the Warsaw he knew. Its very theme—an energetic and somewhat romantic businessman spurned by an aristocratic girl and her impoverished family—is typical of the new mood of the Polish fiction.

Yet one must be wary of simplifications. The Romantic tradition in Poland did not die easily (if at all), and even during the heyday of Positivism it could be found in some writers, e.g., in Wladyslaw Lozinski's romantic biographies, and, for that matter, in Prus's novel as well. The works of Henryk Sienkiewicz (1846–1912), especially his historical novels, depart from the Positivist program, in their romantic portrayal of Poland's heroic past, even though their purpose was to "lift up the hearts"; and some of his stories point out the injustices and inequities of the present (as in his touching account of a talented peasant boy, Yanko, whose love of music is thwarted by society). A winner of the 1905 Nobel prize, Sienkiewicz became the spell-binding weaver of glorious yarns and his characters have become a byword in countless Polish homes. Although he was later criticized for his lack of social insight, he represents a lasting phenomenon in Polish letters, a passionate lover of life and a creator of unforgettable fictional personages, among them a great humorous character, Zagloba, (from his *Trilogy*) who can truly be called a Polish Falstaff.

Eliza Orzeszkowa has brought the Polish novel closer to the European Realistic tradition and has justly been compared to George Elliot and George Sand. Her novels, like Prus's, reflect the Positivist preoccupation with social problems and her range is very wide indeed; she writes of women's suffrage, their psychological adjustment to society (*Waclawa's Memoirs, Martha*), of the Jewish question (*Meir Ezofowicz, Eli Makower*), of the peasant question (*Dziurdziowie, The Churl*), of landed gentry and other social types (*On the Banks of the Niemen*).

The movement toward Realism is unmistakable. The little man, the clerk, the peasant, the Jew, and even the worker enter the novel as protagonists in their own right. Moreover, a sober note of self-examination pervades the modern novelists and short story writers, in their critical evaluation of the past, their realistic appraisal of the present and their ardent quest for a better future.

Stefan Zeromski (1864–1925) combines Orzeszkowa's critical view of society with Prus's compassionate view of humanity and with Sienkiewicz's inspired patriotism. He, too, is a product of the post-insurrectional period, a Romantic-Realist, a historian of Poland's past and present, a passionate fighter for a better, wiser, happier Poland. He writes of human anguish in its manifold manifestations, of romantic heroism, of social injustice, of "homeless men" dedicated to the ideal of improving their society and their nation, blending nationalism with a modern approach to life. But he is also a supreme poet, a grand master of a new Polish prose, rich with lyrical cadences, humor, epic sweep and dramatic power. His *The Ashes* is a more modern artistic version of Sienkiewicz's *Trilogy*—a moving historical novel suffused by lyricism which was beyond the older man. Although in some of his works Zeromski is a naturalist, his lyricism and poetic style, often tinged with archaisms, render his works Neo-Romantic.

The peasant plays an important part in twentieth-century fiction, and he appears as a hero in the works of Selma Lagerlöf, Hamsun, Pearl Buck, Ignazio Silone, Nexö, Gorky, Bates, Vittorini, to mention a few. It is significant that the winner of the Nobel prize for the year 1909 was Selma Lagerlöf, whose novel *Jerusalem* portrayed the

Swedish peasant. And in 1920, the Norwegian, Knut Hamsun, won the prize for the novel *Growth of the Soil*. In 1924 the Polish novelist Wladyslaw Reymont (1867–1925) was the winner, and his major achievement was a four-volume novel, *The Peasants* (1902–1909), a renowned epic of the soil. Reymont is at once a Naturalist and an Impressionist, and his masterpiece gives a lasting portrait of the Polish peasant, his strengths and weaknesses, his dignity as well as his prejudices. Perhaps the measure of its universality may be gauged by the fact that this novel has been translated into many European and Oriental languages.

Poland's traditional close ties with Western Europe were impaired after the 1863 uprising and the country was cut off from the mainstream of European thought and art. This lasted for some two decades, when European influences began once again to seep into the country's intellectual blood stream. The European influence was clearly felt in the movement called Young Poland, which began in Austrian Poland, especially in Cracow. The Young Poland group began by a restoration of poetry to its rightful place, especially lyrical poetry that resulted in a movement called "Tatraism" (after the southern mountains, the Tatras), which inspired poets like Adam Asnyk and Kazimierz Tetmajer.

This native mood was considerably altered by the winds of European trends with the arrival on the literary scene of Ludwik Szczepanowski, who founded the Cracovian journal, *Life*, and later, Stanislaw Przybyszewski, who came from Berlin and took over the editorship of the journal. Thus "Satanism" triumphed over the native "Tatraism," hailing the doctrines of "art for art's sake" and declaring the writer to be free from all moral responsibility. Similar theories were promulgated by a Warsaw journal, *Chimera*, founded in 1901 by Zenon Przesmycki (who wrote under the pseudonym, Miriam). The European malady of *fin de siècle* invaded Poland. The novels of Waclaw Berent and Gabriela Zapolska gave a stern chronicle of this period, satirized by the noted dramatist of the day, Jan August Kisielewski who owed his artistic allegiance to Bahr and Schnitzler.

The Western influences gave rise to a first-rate critic and translator, Tadeusz Zelenski (Boy), who founded the celebrated literary café, Little Green Balloon, and a dramatic poet of genius, Stanislaw Wyspianski.

The latter gave to Polish literature a new conception of drama, that drew heavily on European drama from Aeschylus to Materlinck. His *The Wedding* (1901) is an original and brilliant folk play whose symbolism is both national and universal. Of equal originality was the work of Jan Kasprowicz who wrote of the peasant's freshness and virility.

There was, of course, Futurism, but it fell on deaf ears as far as the general public was concerned. It had arrived at an inopportune time and it never coalesced into a revolutionary literary movement, as in the West. The Italian Futurism was primarily an exotic import. The Russian Futurism and Dadaism, with their nihilism and archaism, could not flourish in a society which only began building its own country, and since the national Futurists were generally unsuccessful in lending an original Polish interpretation to the Western movements, they were doomed to early extinction. It is interesting to note that one of the more original Futurists was Adam Wazyk (who became a noted figure after World War II and whose "A Poem For Adults" appears in parts below). His poems *Eyes and the Mouth* are based not on reality but spring from a sophisticated poetic sensibility. The pioneers and best representatives of this movement were Jerzy Hulewicz, Jan Stur, Emil Zegadlowicz and Zenon Kosidowski. While inconsequential in itself, the short-lived Polish Futurism did affect the technique of later poets and prose writers, particularly through its quest for "the essence of life."

Another important literary group was *Skamander*, whose appearance coincides with Poland's new-won independence. The founders of *Skamander* wanted to break with the shackles of nationalism and the bondage of patriotic themes. They aimed at self-cognition and at universality, without formulating any clear-cut ideological or esthetic programs. They reacted to the fact of independence and it was the nature of their reaction that gave them a distinctive quality—an elemental manifestation of the new realism; their poetry was an expression of the general emotional and cultural reaction to the growing awareness of new social and political conditions, rather than a specific comment on the new conditions themselves. It was, as one critic put it, not a spiritual expression of the times, but more of an echo of the heart-beat surging within them. Their main achievement lies in their having produced a body of lyrical poetry, the joyful acceptance of contemporaneity. No other literary group could boast such an array of poetic talent: Jan Lechon, Julian Tuwim, Kazimierz Wierzynski, Antoni Slonimski, Jaroslaw Iwaszkiewicz—each of these names represents a separate entity and each has made his distinctive individual transition from the past to the new present.

Another movement, developed in Poznan around a periodical called *Spring*, revealed some connections with German Expressionism. Joseph Wittlin (1896–   ), who was initially a member of this group and later developed independently, wrote a series of moving *Hymns* (1920) which described the terrors and sufferings of war.

Of course, there was a wave of Realism throughout postwar Europe; but where the European literary Realism had been practiced

since the middle of the 19th century, in Poland it came into its own
only now, and it was still regarded as a somewhat strange phenomenon. After generations of the Romantic tradition in Poland, it was not
easy for the writer of the twenties to get used to the idea that the
age-long dream for independence had finally arrived. Dreams had
turned real, and the new, *real* Poland was not quite what the Romantic
dreamers had expected her to be. Ironically, the long traditions of
Romantic and patriotic writing were responsible for a disillusioning
shock, now that "the ideal had reached the pavement" (C. K. Norwid's
"Chopin's Grand Piano"). The creative writer lacked the grandiose,
Messianic themes of the nineteenth century and he had to concentrate
on everyday reality. The Romantic vision was no more, and it was
replaced by economical, political and cultural problems. It was no
longer possible to spin heroic yarns of Poland's ancient grandeur, as
Sienkiewicz had done, nor to extol the ideal of freedom, as countless
Romantic and Neo-romantic poets and novelists had done. Freedom
had become a fact, and out of a conflicting maze of political movements and social needs the young State forged ahead, often stumbling
perilously in its progress.

It is small wonder, therefore, that the post-war Polish literature
seemed to grope for the *mot juste* of its existence, uncertain of itself,
yet animated by a powerful drive and backed by a profusion of
literary talent. Some "negative" trends were clearly in the making:
No longer was the writer preoccupied with Konradian individualism
and patriotic expression of heroism and self-sacrifice; he turned his
eyes at the world about him and took a closer look at the countryside, the city dwellings, the slums and the apartment houses; everyday
existence in all its sundry aspects became the *motif*, and the Positivist
creed was pushed to its logical limits of full realism. The "little men,"
the "unknown soldiers," in other words, the non-heroic heroes, commanded the attention of the novelist, and he chose his plots to illumine
the average human condition. He also sought for deeper social meanings, asked more perturbing questions about social justice, even at the
risk of alienating a large section of his reading public (as Zeromski
in his "socialist" novel *Early Spring*, 1925).

The novels of Zofia Nalkowska (1885–1954) are excellent examples
of Realism, seasoned with a rich dose of psychology. Her books are
studies of the feminine psyche that rival Flaubert's *Madame Bovary*
(e.g., *Teresa Hennert's Love Affair*, 1923), and her short stories have
been compared to the work of La Bruyère and Chamfort. She is not
the only outstanding woman novelist of the independence period.
Zofia Kossak-Szczucka (1890–   ) continued the tradition of the Polish historical novel, but although she may lack Sienkiewicz's genius for
invention and poetic imagination, she is a much more thorough social

observer than the author of the famed *Trilogy*. Moreover, her characters are more penetratingly portrayed and she succeeds in an artistic fusion of history with human psychology. Her *Blessed are the Meek* (about St. Francis of Assisi) received universal recognition. The *Crusaders* has the best virtues of Stendhal as well as Sienkiewicz—it is a prophetic book, a poignant and dramatic account of history; its style, as Jan Lechon suggested, is almost no style—it is free from embellishment of any kind and yet the total impact of the novel is overpowering because of psychological revelation and a graphic chronicling of facts.

Two other significant women novelists are Maria Kuncewicz (1897–) and Maria Dabrowska (1892–). The former's masterly studies of neuroticism and social adjustment won her an acclaim far beyond the borders of Poland, e.g., with her works *The Stranger, The Conspiracy of the Absent, The Forester, The Olive Grove.* Dabrowska's masterpiece is *Nights and Days* (1932–1934), a chronicle in four volumes and an epic of everyday existence.

During the late twenties and thirties the Polish novel gained momentum and the prose writers showed great affinity with European literature. Joseph Wittlin's *Salt of the Earth* (1935), translated into thirteen languages and widely acclaimed, is a tale of a simple soldier, a moving portrait of a "little man" in the imperial Austrian army. It is a work that can be favorably compared with the best of English or American fiction. Ferdinand Goetel's literary methods (*From Day to Day*) seem to anticipate James Joyce. Bruno Schultz's stories are Kafkaesque commentaries on the bewildering modern world, and Witold Gombrowicz's *Ferdydurke* (1938) is the predecessor of the modern anti-novel in French fiction. Juliusz Kaden-Bandrowski creates an original style of his own in the Realist-Impressionist tradition (*Black Wings* cycle of novels).

The prose literature of independent Poland indicates richness, versatility and a pronounced Western character. In fact, all important Western novels were translated into Polish; and among them the translations of Joseph Conrad's works by Aniela Zagorska have an independent merit of their own, and have greatly influenced the Polish novelists. Similarly, Boy Zelenski's translations of classical and modern French literature moulded the literary taste of the period.

The ravages of World War II in Poland stopped all normal channels of creative writing, but they failed to stop it completely. Thus, although the country suffered terrible losses, particularly among the educated layers of society, writers continued to work in the underground. And those who wrote little or who matured under the German occupation, used their war experiences in the work done immediately after the end of the war. It is small wonder that the Polish literature of the late forties and fifties (both in Poland and in exile) reflects the upheaval the country has undergone, in its preoccupation with themes of persecution, underground struggle, political tensions and the problems of survival in a hostile world.

Novelists like Jerzy Andrzejewski and Adolf Rudnicki, poets like Jastrun, Broniewski and Wittlin, depict the terrors of the last war. But in the present-day Poland new problems have forced themselves upon the writer, and he has begun to examine the new conditions, sometimes affirmatively, sometimes critically. Konstanty Galczynski, for example, returned to Poland after some years in Europe and, although his poetry was both strikingly original and popular with the readers, he failed to win official recognition by the regime. Some writers decided to break with the government and chose exile in the West, e.g., Marek Hlasko, the controversial young novelist and short-story writer, and Czeslaw Milosz, poet, essayist and novelist. Others, like Mieczyslaw Jastrun, Adam Wazyk, Tadeusz Rozewicz, Kazimierz Brandys, Jerzy Zawieyski and Zbigniew Herbert, continue to live in Poland, producing good poetry and fiction.

When one looks at the major works of the past seventy years, it becomes obvious that no precise distinctions can be drawn between the pre-war and the post-war writers, recent theories of Socialist Realism notwithstanding. For, as of today at any rate, the character of Polish literature has not been drastically changed, except in its emphasis on war and post-war problems. Both pre-war and post-war works reveal the Poles' passionate sense of nationality, their experience of exile and oppression, their prejudices as well as their love of freedom.

PART ONE

Fiction

Wladyslaw Reymont

(1867–1925)

A recipient of the Nobel prize in 1924 (for his novel *The Peasants*),
Wladyslaw Stanislaw Reymont was born in Kobiele Wielke, near Radon,
of humble parents. One of ten children, he suffered greatly in his childhood, spent on an impoverished farm, finally setting out for Warsaw,
where he lived in abject poverty during his first two years in the city.
He made his literary debut with short stories and articles. His first
collection, *Encounter* (1897), was marked by Naturalism and his excellent
knowledge of peasant psychology.

Reymont's first novel *The Comedienne* (1896) and its sequel *Ferments*
(1897) have established him as a story-teller with a great future and a
special talent for mass portraiture. *The Promised Land* (1898) further
develops the Impressionistic technique of the earlier novels, and it paints
a grim picture of Lodz, the industrial debaser of man. Condemning urban-
ization and industrialization, Reymont turned to peasant life, and his
The Peasants (1902–1909) proved a masterpiece of Polish literature and
is considered the best peasant epos in world literature. Reymont depicts
the peasant class without embellishing its prejudices and vices, but he
also reveals its strength and its deep-seated traditions. The novel is composed of four volumes, *Autumn, Winter, Spring,* and *Summer,* and it has
been widely translated.

His other novels are: *The Dreamer* (1910), *Vampire* (1911), *The
Year 1794* (1914–1919).

Three Selections from *The Peasants*

1. BORYNA'S WEDDING*

The sun had rolled over from the south, shedding pale autumn light,
so that the earth glistened as if with dew, and the windows gushed
forth with flames; the pond shone, shimmered, the water in the roadside ditches gleamed like window panes—and the whole world was
soaked in the light of dying autumn and its last cooling breath.

Deaf, speechless quiet wrapped the golden earth. The day was
slowly burning down and dying. But the village of Lipce was as noisy
as a fair.

No sooner had the Vesper bells rung than the village band
spilled out from the mayor's house onto the road. First came the

---

* The titles for the three selections supplied by the translators.

fiddles, paired off with the flute, followed by the drums-and-bells and the bass-viol, decked out with ribbons, all capering merrily.

Behind the band marched both matchmakers and the best men —six of them. They were young fellows, handsome and supple like pine trees, slim-waisted, broad-shouldered, great dancers all, loud-mouthed, unyielding brawlers,—the choicest peasant stock.

They strode massively down the middle of the road, shoulder-to-shoulder, so that the ground rumbled under their feet, so joyous and dressed up for the wedding; the bright sun reflected the gaiety of their striped trousers, the red jackets, the cluster of ribbons upon their hats, and their white coats flowing in the wind like wings.

Their sharp shouts and merry songs filled the air, as they tapped their feet boisterously and marched with such abandon as though a young forest had been torn off the ground and borne aloft by a gale.

The band was playing the Polonaise, as they trooped from house to house to invite the wedding guests. Some brought vodka drinks outside, some asked them to come in, others responded with singing —and everywhere people in their Sunday best stepped out to join them and to march together and sing in unison under the brides-maids' windows:

> Come ye out bridesmaids, come out little Kate,
> For the wedding you'll be late—
> There the fiddles and bass-viol will not stay still,
> Everyone will eat and drink his fill.
> Oy ta dana dana, oy ta dana da!

Their mighty shouting resounded in the village and the gay voices echoed even in the fields, down to the forest edge and drifted into the wide world.

People came out in front of their houses, into their orchards and yards, and some, though not invited, joined the merry-makers, to feast their eyes and ears so that before the party reached the wedding scene almost the entire village had surged about them, milling, pressing and slowing them down, preceded by a vociferous crowd of children.

They brought the guests to the wedding house, heralded their entry with a burst of music, and turned back to fetch the bridegroom.

Witek, in a be-ribboned jacket, had marched lustily with the best men, and now he sallied forth. "Master, the musicians and the best men are coming!" he cried into the window and ran to Kuba.

The band struck up with gusto on the porch, and Boryna came out immediately, threw the door wide open, welcoming them, inviting them inside; but the mayor and Simon took his arms and led him straight to Yagna, for it was time for church.

He strode briskly, and it was amazing he looked so young: his hair cropped, his face clean-shaven, dressed for the wedding. He was uncommonly handsome, and as he was well-set and broad-shouldered and his face bore the stamp of dignity, he could be noticed from afar; he joked and chatted with the farmhands, and mostly with the smith who kept pressing near him.

He was ushered ceremoniously into the house of Mrs. Dominik; the people fell back, and he was led into the main room noisily, with music and song.

But Yagna wasn't there yet; she was being dressed by the women in a locked, closely guarded chamber, for the young fellows pushed against the door, tried to cut slits in it, teased the bridesmaids and were answered by screams, laughter and shouting.

The mother and her sons received the guests, offered them vodka, seated the elders on benches and kept an eye over everything. Such a throng of people had come that it was hard to pass through the main room, and they stood in the halls, even in the front yard. Not ordinary guests, they! Oh, no. Farmowners only, of the best families and the wealthiest, and all of them the kinsfolk and close friends of the Borynas and the Paczes or acquaintances who had driven over from distant villages.

No Klemb or any of the Wincioreks, those one-acre paupers, were there, nor that hireling trash that stuck with old Klemb. No dainties for dogs, and no honey for hogs!

Soon the door of the chamber was opened, and the organist's and the miller's wives led Yagna into the main room, whereupon the bridesmaids clustered about her in a circle, resplendent and pretty like a bunch of flowers, and Yagna the tallest and most beautiful rose stood in the center, all in white, in velvet, plumes and ribbons, in silver and gold—resembling the image carried in processions. Her appearance brought sudden silence to the room so stunned and amazed was everybody. Hey! There was no fairer in all Mazovia!

Presently the best men let go at the top of their lungs:

Strike up, O fiddler, and announce!
And, Yagna, ask your parents' pardon—
Sound off, O flutist, and announce!
And Yagna, ask your brother's pardon!

Boryna stepped forward, took her hand; they knelt, and the mother blessed them with the sacred image and sprinkled them with

holy water. In tears, Yagna embraced her mother's knees, and then
the knees of others, asked forgiveness and bid everyone good-bye.
The women took turns, gathering her into their arms, all crying, and
Josephine's sobs were the most heart-rending because she remembered
her dead mother.

They filed out in front of the house, arranged themselves in
proper order and started out on foot, for the church was nearby.

The musicians went in front and played with all their might.
Next came Yagna, led by the best men—she strode, her gait exuberant, smiling through the tears which still glistened in her eyes. She
was radiant like a flower in bloom, drawing all eyes to herself. Her
hair was braided over her forehead; and she wore a tall crown of
gold spangles, of peacocks' eyes and rosemary sprigs; and from it
flowed onto her shoulder long multi-colored ribbons that trailed
behind her like a rainbow. Her white skirt was amply gathered at
the waist; her bodice was of sky-blue velvet, laced with silver; her
blouse had puffed sleeves, and abundant frills under her neck,
overcast with dark-blue thread. Strings of corals and ambers were
wound about her neck, falling down on her bosom.

Behind her the bridesmaids were escorting Matthew. As the mighty
oak follows the slender pine in the forest, so did Matthew tower behind
Yagna, his hips swaying, casting his glances on both sides of the road.
After them came Mrs. Dominik with the matchmakers, the blacksmith,
the miller and their wives, Josephine, the organist's wife and the
notables. At the end of the procession streamed the whole village.

The sun was setting, and it hung over the forests, red, enormous
and flooding the whole road, the pond and the houses with a scarlet
hue, and they marched in this blaze slowly, in a dazzling array of
those ribbons, peacock feathers, flowers, red trousers, orange skirts,
kerchiefs, white cloaks—as if a field, strewn with blossoming flowers,
were moving and swaying slowly against the wind—and singing, for
the bridesmaids repeatedly intoned in their highpitched voices:

> The wagons clatter, the wagons fly,
> And my Yagna, for you they cry . . .
> > Hey!
> Their songs so sadly ring,
> To cheer you up, they sing . . .
> > Hey!

Mrs. Dominik cried all the way and gazed at her daughter as if
she were a picture, not hearing a word of what people were saying to
her. In church Ambrose was lighting the candles on the altar. In the

vestibule the guests straightened their clothes, formed pairs and proceeded toward the altar for the priest was already coming out of the
vestry.

The wedding was performed speedily because the priest was in a
rush to make a sick call. And when they were leaving church the
organist began to play such mazurkas, obertases, kuyaviaks that people's feet beat the measure, and many were on the point of breaking
into song but fortunately they contained themselves in time.

Their return was disorderly, with every man going as he pleased,
noisy too, for the best men and the bridesmaids wailed in song as if
they were being skinned.

Mrs. Dominik hurried home first, and when the party arrived, she
greeted the couple on the threshold with the sacred image, bread and
salt, and then she welcomed and embraced everybody once more, and
invited them inside.

The band struck up in the hall, and every man who entered would
grab the first woman closest to him, and in dignified steps would lead
her in the Polonaise to the dancing floor. There, like a shimmering,
many-colored serpent, the couples moved around the room, coiled,
circled, gravely turned back, stomped decorously, swayed gracefully
and flowed, weaving in and out; and these dancing couples, one behind the other, head to head were like an undulating field of full-
grown rye, thick with cornflowers and poppies, Yagna and Boryna
in the lead.

The lights on the mantelpiece trembled, the house shook, and it
seemed that the crowd and the dancers' powerful motion would pull
the house apart. They danced a good while before they were through.
The band now began to play the first dance for the bride, as was the
custom of old. The people pressed in a dense crowd against the walls
and filled all corners; the young men formed a big circle in which
Yagna began dancing. Her blood tingled in her veins, her blue eyes
shone, and her white teeth gleamed in her flushed face; she danced
indefatigably, changing her partners all the time, for she had to give
a round to everyone.

The musicians fiddled away until their hands grew faint, but
Yagna seemed to have only begun; her face grew crimson; she whirled
with such abandon that her ribbons fluttered behind her, slapping
the onlookers' faces, and her petticoats, blown up by her impetuous
movements, appeared to fill the whole room. This pleased the farmhands greatly, and they pounded the tables with their fists and shouted
lustily.

Only at the end did she choose her bridegroom; Boryna, who had
been getting ready for it, leaped toward her like a lynx, seized her by
the waist, whirled her around powerfully, and cried to the players:

"A mazur, boys, and give it the works!"

The band blasted away, stirring the people to a pitch of excitement.
Boryna drew Yagna to himself more tightly, threw his coat tails over
his arms, adjusted his hat, tapped his heels and set off, swift as the
wind!

Ah! How he danced! He whirled her about, stepped back, kicked
his heels, cutting slivers off the floor; and crying out in glee from
time to time, he tore across the room with Yagna until they seemed
to merge into each other—a human spindle turning end over end—
radiating singular power.

The band kept playing furiously, ceaselessly in the Mazovian
manner....

People thronged in the doorway, in the corners, and watched in
silent amazement Boryna's unflagging pace; some no longer able to
control their urge to dance, beat out the rhythm; others, more eager,
seized their girls and, paying no heed, joined the dancers.

Yagna, though a strong girl, soon weakened and slumped in
Boryna's arms. Only then did he desist and led her to the inner chamber.

"My, are you a strong one!" the miller cried, hugging Boryna,
"you're my pal, say, let me be a godfather at the first christening."
Soon they got very chummy as the music fell silent and the feast
began. . . .

                              *   *   *

Slowly they started to file behind the tables and take their seats
on the benches. The bride and bridegroom sat at the head of the
table, and on either side the notables, according to each man's rank,
property and seniority, down to the bridesmaids and the children;
there was hardly enough space for everybody even though the tables
were lined along three walls. The best men remained standing in order
to serve the food, and so did the players. The noise subsided as the
organist stood to deliver a prayer—and only the blacksmith repeated
the words after him, since he was reputed to understand Latin; then
they toasted each other's health, and drank to hardy appetites.

The cooks and the best men began to carry in huge steaming bowls,
filled with food, singing:

> We carry chicken broth and rice
> And choicest fowl for you to slice!

And bringing in the second dish:

> Peppered salty tripe we carry,
> Eat away now, and be merry!

The musicians sat near the fireplace and softly played various tunes for the diners' pleasure. The guests ate decorously, taking their time, almost in silence, for hardly anyone uttered a word, and only the sound of their smacking lips and the scraping of spoons against the plates could be heard in the room. And when they had eaten somewhat, and their hunger abated, the blacksmith passed the bottle around and conversation picked up across the tables.

Yagna scarcely ate anything, and in vain did Boryna urge her, hugged her and coaxed her like a child, but she could not swallow even a morsel of meat, so fatigued and hot was she, and merely sipped cold beer, and her eyes wandered about the room as she listened to Boryna's whispers.

"Are you happy, Yagna, dearest? My pretty one! Don't you fear, my little one, I'll take care of you like your mother. . . . You'll be a lady. . . . I'll take a servant for you, so that you don't work too hard . . . you'll see!" he spoke softly, and gazed into her eyes amorously, ignoring the people who were beginning to poke fun at him:

"Like a cat falling upon bacon . . ."

"She's a tasty dish . . . all right. . . ."

"The old fellow's squirming and preening like a rooster!"

"He'll have a whale of a time, the old son of a gun!" cried the mayor.

"Like a dog frisking on a cold winter day," muttered old Simon spitefully.

They roared with laughter, and the miller almost fell over the table and pounded his fist with merriment.

Now the cooks intoned again:

Tasty porridge! Sit you still!
Let the starvelings eat their fill.

"Lean over, Yagna, I'll tell you something," the mayor said, bending behind Boryna's back, for he was sitting beside him, and pinched her hip. "Better ask me to be godfather," he exclaimed uproariously and eyed her hungrily, for he took a great liking to her. She blushed deeply, and at this the women burst out laughing and started to joke and tease her and offer advice on how to handle her man.

"Heat the quilt before the fireplace in the evening . . ."

"Especially feed him fat dishes, to keep him hearty . . ."

"And flatter him, snuggle up to him often . . ."

"Be gentle with him, so he won't notice where you lead him . . ." they spoke one after another, as women will do, when they have had one too many, and their tongues begin to wag.

The whole room shook with laughter, and they let their tongues run away with them, until the miller's wife began to lecture them to have regard for the girls and the children; also the organist argued that it was a great sin to spread scandal and to set a bad example . . .

2. THE LOVERS

. . . They stole into the orchard, passing under the drooping boughs, and quickly, fearfully, like frightened fawns, ran behind the barns, into the darkened snows, into the starless night and into the impenetrable stillness of frozen fields.

The night gathered them in; the village was gone, the hum of human voices suddenly subsided; even the softest sounds of life faded, so that clasping each other's waist they were oblivious to all the world, and they clung to each other closely, somewhat stooped, joyful and afraid, silent yet full of song; with all their beings they drifted into this world, steeped in grey blueness and silence.

"Yagna!"

"Yes?"

"Are you here?"

"I sure am."

That was all they said as they paused sometimes to catch their breath.

Their voices were muffled by the fearful pounding of their hearts and the powerful cry of a secret joy; they looked into each other's faces all the time, their eyes flashed like burnt-out, silent lightnings, and their lips pressed together with thunder-like force and with such a hungry, devouring fire that they rolled with ecstasy, grew breathless, and it was a wonder their hearts did not burst; the ground rushed from under their feet, and they flew as if into a fiery abyss, and looked about with eyes blinded by passion; they rose and ran again, not knowing whither and how, only farther into the very deepest night, until they reached those twisted humps of shadows. . . .

Another furlong . . . and yet two more . . . farther . . . deeper . . . until everything, the whole world, and the very memory of it disappeared from their eyes, until they were lost completely in oblivion as though in an unremembered dream, and only perceived by their souls, as if in that wondrous dream, which they experienced while awake a moment in that room at the Klembs'; the dream in which they appeared still drowning in the luminous line of quiet, mystical words, in which they were still filled with the enchantments of wonderful tales, sacred fears, deepest amazements, ecstasies and unfulfilled longings!

Still enveloped in the magic rainbow of wonders and dreams, they floated as if in a procession of those marvels, evoked a moment ago; they passed through fabulous lands, through those more-than-human scenes—all those becomings, all the miracles, all the profound depths of astonishments and enchantments. Phantoms swayed in the shadows, wandered across the skies, grew with every glance of their eyes, sailed through their hearts, so that at times they held their breath, numb with fear, their bodies clinging to each other, speechless, gazing into the bottomless, turbulent domain of their dream, until their souls blossomed with ecstasies, and they sank to the bottom of wonderment and oblivion.

And then, returning to consciousness, their astonished eyes wandered long into the night, scarcely knowing whether they were alive, whether those wonders were indeed happening to them, whether all this was a dream or an illusion....

"You're not afraid, Yagna?"

"Why, I'd follow you everywhere, even unto death!" she whispered hotly, snuggling up to him fiercely ...

"Have you waited for me?" he asked after a while.

"And how! Anybody comes into the hall, and I'd jump out of my skin ... that's why I came to the Klembs ... for this ... I thought you'd never come ...

"But when I came in you pretended not to see me ..."

"Silly ... did you want me to look so that they would find us out? But I got such a pain in the pit of my stomach that it's a wonder I didn't fall off the stool ... I had to drink some water to come to ..."

"My dearest ..."

"You were sitting behind me, I felt, but I was scared to look at you, scared to speak to you ... but my heart beat so, beat so that people must have heard it ... Jesus, I almost screamed with happiness! ..."

"I thought I'd find you at the Klembs and that we'd go out together..."

"I wanted to run home, but you forced me ..."

"Didn't you want it, Yagna?"

"Fiddlesticks ... I often wanted it to happen that way ... often ..."

"You did so! You did ..." he whispered passionately.

"Of course, Antek! All the time ... all the time. ... Out there behind the stile it's no good ..."

"True ... here nobody can catch us. ... We're alone ..."

"Alone! ... and this darkness ... and ..." she whispered, falling on his neck, and embracing him with all the frenzy of her love ..."

. . . .

Now the wind over the fields ceased, only a slight breeze caressed their burning faces as if with soothing whispers.

Neither bright stars, nor the moon could be seen, and the sky hung low,—a turmoil of dark and ragged clouds resembling a grizzly herd of oxen moving through an empty and bare expanse. The world loomed through waves of grey smoke, and it seemed woven of mists, of darkness quivering everywhere and of writhing murk.

A deep, uneasy, scarcely felt murmur trembled in the air, floated forth as if from the forests sunk in the night, or from the clouds that soared continually like flocks of wild white birds pursued by hawks.

The night was dark and painfully agitated, dull and full of strange motion, full of fear, impalpable tremors, fearful noises, lurking phantoms and of sudden unexplained and terrifying transformations. Sometimes, all of a sudden, from under the coils of darkness shone the spectral pallor of the snows or strange icy, moist, festering glimmers crawled tortuously across the shadows; and again the night would appear to shut her eyelids and the dusk fell with a black unfathomable downpour, and the whole world was lost so that one's eyes, unable to perceive anything, would glide helplessly into the very depths of terror, and one's soul would grow numb, overcome by the dull deadness of the grave. At times the curtains of shadows would be torn asunder, burst as if rent by a thunderbolt, and through the terrifying rifts in the clouds one could see in the depth the dark blue fields of the starry, serene sky.

And again from the fields or from the huts, from the sky or from the farthest distances—one could hardly know wherefrom—there came sounds like trembling scattered voices, gleams like lost echoes, the ghosts of sounds and things long dead, and now roaming the wild; these sounds floated in a mournful procession, disappearing no one knows where, as the lights of dead stars.

But the lovers were blind to everything; a storm rose within them and raged, growing every minute, rolling from heart to heart in a torrent of burning and unuttered desires, of flashing glances, of painful tremors, of sudden anxiety, of ardent kisses, of words tangled, chaotic and dazzling like uncontrolled thunderbolts; of moments speechless like death, of tenderness and also such enchantment that they choked in their embraces. They crushed each other in their arms until it hurt; they practically clawed at each other with their nails, as if intent on the delight of torment; and their clouded eyes no longer saw anything, not even themselves.

And thus swept by love's tempest, blinded to everything, frenzied, oblivious, fused into each other like two burning torches, they flew into that impenetrable night and into the void solitude so that they might give themselves to each other unto the death, to the very bottom of their souls, consumed by the eternal hunger of desire.

They could no longer speak; only unconscious cries were torn out from their very innards, only strangled whispers gushed forth fitfully like flames—vague and maddening words, glances boring to the very marrow, glances numb with frenzy, as that of clashing gales; till finally they were seized with such a terrible quiver of lust that they closed with savage whining and fell . . . completely unconscious . . .

The whole world trembled and reeled with them into a fiery abyss . . .

"I'm losing my mind . . ."
"Don't scream, quiet, Yagna . . ."
"But I must . . . or I'll go mad!"
"My heart is bursting!"
"I'll burn up, for God's sake let go . . . let me breathe . . ."

. . . .

"Oh Jesus, I'll die . . . !"
"My only one in the world!"
"Oh Antek, my love . . ."

Even as the life-giving saps hidden in the ground wake up every spring and spreading through eternal desire, surge to each other across the world, from one end of the earth to the other, coursing through the skies, until they find one another, merge and in a sacred mystery begin to transform before our amazed eyes into springtime, a flower, a human soul, or the rustling of green trees . . . so they, too, pressed to each other through endless longing, through days of torment, through gray, long and empty days until they found each other and with the same, uncontrollable cry of desire fell into each other's arms, closing as powerfully as two pine trees uprooted by the storm and crushed against one another in a desperate embrace, rock, wrestle and reel in a deadly contest, till both crash to their merciless death . . .

And the night shielded them and wove her veil about them so that their desiring might be fulfilled. . . .

3. DISENCHANTMENT

All Boryna's love passed like last year's spring which nobody remembers, and there remained only a vivid recollection of her betrayal, a festering shame and regret, and implacable anger. Yagna, too, was considerably changed. Her life was hard, inexpressibly miserable. She had not, however, admitted her guilt, but her punishment affected her more painfully than it would have other women, because she was more sensitive, had been pampered as a child and she was much more delicate than others.

And she suffered, Lord! How she suffered!

Indeed, she tried to spite the old man in everything, never yield-

ing unless she was forced; she defended herself as best she could, but
this yoke weighed more heavily and painfully upon her neck and she
could expect no rescue anywhere. How many times she wanted to
return to her mother! But the old woman refused, even threatening to
tie her up and send her back to her husband by force!

What, then, could she do? She could not live like other women who
spare themselves no pleasure with young fellows and willingly suffer
domestic hell, fighting every day with their men and every day going
to bed reconciled.

No, that was not for her; her life grew more and more insupportable,
and an unspoken longing—she knew not for what—filled her soul.
True, she paid Boryna spite for spite, but she suffered continual fear,
and felt so hurt and resentful that she often cried throughout the night
until her pillow was wet with tears; and sometimes those days of arguments and quarrels became so hateful to her that she was ready to run
away anywhere.

But where could she go? Whither?

The world was wide open before her, but so terrifying, so impenetrable, so alien and indifferent that she froze in terror—as a bird
caught by little boys and placed under a pot. Little wonder therefore
that because of all this she was drawn to Antek, although her love now
came from fear and despair; for after that dreadful night, when she had
run away to her mother's, something within her had broken and dried
that she could no longer yearn for him with her whole soul as before;
and no longer could she run to him at every beckoning with joy and
a pounding heart; she went only from a sense of compulsion—because
here in her hut it was miserable and boring, and to spite the old man,
and because she imagined that her great old love might come back. In
her heart of hearts, however, she harbored a bitter resentment against
him, blaming him for everything that had befallen her, for her sorrows,
disappointments and her whole hard life; and she also harbored the
even more painful, more quiet and unspoken regret that he was *not*
the man she had fallen in love with; it was a violent cutting pain of
disappointment and disillusionment. For at first, he had appeared to
her as a different man, one whose love lifted her to the skies, whose
kindness overwhelmed her, and who was the dearest being in the world
and so different from others in everything—and now he seemed like
any other man; worse, for she feared him even more than Boryna. He
frightened her with his gloom and suffering and especially with his
rancor. She was afraid of him as if he were a forest outlaw, and indeed
the priest himself scolded him in church; the whole village shied away
from him and people pointed him out as the worst man; there
emanated from him such a dread of mortal sin that often, listening to
his voice, she grew numb with fear; because she imagined that the

Evil One took possession of him and that all hell was about him. At such times she felt as frightened as when the priest admonishes the people and threatens them with eternal torment.

Not for a moment did it occur to her that she, too, was responsible for his sins. Not at all! When she occasionally thought of him, it was only to contemplate his change, for she could not reason clearly. But she felt this change so acutely that she became more and more indifferent to him. Sometimes she would grow rigid in his arms as if suddenly struck by a thunderbolt, yielded to him for how could she resist such a monster . . . And, after all, she was a young woman, full-blooded, strong, and his embraces were so violent that he almost strangled her; therefore, despite all her thoughts about him, she would still give herself to him with equal vehemence, with the thrust of the earth eternally thirsty for warm rain and sunshine. But no more did her soul fall to his feet from uncontrollable passion; no more was she blinded by the feeling of happiness so great that it could lead to the threshold of death; no longer could she reach total oblivion. No, at such times she would think of her house, her chores, and about a new way to spite her husband; and sometimes she even wished that he would release her as soon as possible and go away.

She thought of all this as she was letting the water out of the potato-pots into the yard, working reluctantly, only under compulsion; she was listening keenly for her husband and looking out for him in the yard. And while Pietrek worked assiduously, digging into the frozen earth and mud, she barely moved her hoe, working so that Boryna might see her; as soon as he entered the house she put her apron over her head and cautiously stole behind the stile near the Ploszko barn.

Antek was already there.

"I have been waiting a whole hour for you," he whispered reproachfully.

"You didn't have to wait, if you had gone elsewhere," she snapped at him resentfully, looking about her, for the night was fairly clear, the rain ceased and only a cold dry wind blew from the forests and rustled in the orchards.

He drew her to himself firmly and began kissing her face.

"You reek of liquor like a barrel!" she whispered, turning from him in disgust.

"Is that so? I stink because I took a drink?"

"Well, not *you*, just the liquor," she said more softly.

"I was here yesterday. Why didn't you come out?"

"It was so cold . . . and I've got plenty of work."

"Sure, and you've got to tickle the old man and cover him up with a quilt," he hissed.

"Well, isn't he my husband!" she said harshly and irascibly.

"Don't you provoke me, Yagna!"

"If you don't like it, don't come, I shan't cry for you."

"You don't care to come out to me, do you?"

"Not when you scold me like a dog all the time . . ."

"Yagna, I have so many troubles that it isn't any wonder when a harsh word slips out now and then; it is not because I am angry, no . . ." he whispered humbly, and hugged her tenderly. But she stood stiffly, sulking, and when she returned his kisses it was of necessity, and when she spoke it was no more than a word, and all the while she looked around, eager to go home.

He was quite aware of this and was stung as if a nettle had been put behind his shirt. He whispered in a timid reproach:

"You weren't always in such a rush . . ."

"I'm scared. Everybody's home, they might be looking for me."

"Sure. In the old days you were not afraid to stay out all night . . . You have changed so completely."

"Don't talk nonsense. Why should I have changed?"

They grew silent in a close embrace, and sometimes they pressed to each other more eagerly, drawn together by a sudden desire, hungrily seeking each other's lips, carried away by a common wave of memories, by the harm they had done each other, by self-pity—and a profound yearning to become one. But they could not manage, for their souls drifted apart far away, and they failed to find soothing words of caress, for in their hearts still rankled bitter reproaches, so vivid that their arms involuntarily dropped to their sides, and they became cool to each other and stood like two cold pillars; only their hearts pounded and the words of tenderness and consolation hung about their lips—words they wanted to speak but were unable to utter.

"Do you love me, Yagna?" he whispered.

"Didn't I tell you this plenty of times, don't I come out to you whenever you want me to?" she replied, evasively, pressing her hip against him, for a strange sorrow took possession of her soul and filled her eyes with tears, and she wanted to cry before him and ask his forgiveness that she no longer was able to love him; but he soon noticed this, for her voice chilled him to the marrow, and he shook with pain and his heart was full of unrestrained resentment.

"You lie like a dog; everybody deserted me, and you're in a hurry to join them. You love, indeed, like that mad dog who might bite and who is hard to chase away; sure enough! I can see through you, all right, I know you well. If they wanted to hang me you'd be the first to come out with a rope; if they wanted to stone me, you'd cast the first one . . ." he spoke rapidly.

"Antek, dearest . . ." she groaned, terrified.

"Keep quiet until I've had my say," he cried menacingly, raising his fists. "I'm speaking the truth. And since it's come to this, it's all the same to me; it's all the same."

"I must be off, they're calling me," she stammered, and she wanted to run, greatly frightened, but he caught her hand, so that she could not move, and he spoke in a hoarse voice, charged with malice and hatred:

"And another thing, since your stupid head doesn't grasp it, that if I've gone to the dogs it's on account of you, because I loved you, you see, because of this! Why did the priest rebuke me and drive me out of the church like an outlaw if not for you! Why did the whole village shy away from me as if I was a leper, if not for you? I have suffered it all, yeah, borne it all; nor did I complain when my own father gave you so much of the land that belongs to me . . . And now, *you* loathe me, and you twist like an eel, cheat, run away, fear me and look at me like all the rest, as if I was the worst murderer.

"You need another man, eh? You'd like to have the young fellows run after you like the dogs in spring, you . . ." he shouted in a frenzy and cast upon her head all the wrongs he had to endure so long, blaming her for everything, cursing her for all that he had suffered, until he could speak no more; he was seized with such a fury that he flew at her with his fists, but he took hold of himself in the last moment, and only pushed her against the wall and strode away briskly.

"Jesus, O Antek!" she cried out loud, having understood suddenly what had happened, but he did not return, and she ran after him desperately, blocked his way, hung on his neck; he tore her from himself like a leech, threw her to the ground and ran off without a word. Yagna fell, sobbing as if the whole world had collapsed upon her.

After a long while she came to herself, still unable to understand everything, but she felt deeply that a wrong was done to her, that such a terrible injustice was committed, that her heart was bursting with pain, and she choked inwardly and wanted to scream with all her strength to the whole world: "I am not guilty, not guilty!"

She continued to call him although his steps could be heard no more; she called into the night—in vain.

A deep sense of penitence, a heart-felt sorrow and that dull, oppressive, dreadful fear that he might not return to her, and the old love suddenly revived within her—all these laid heavily upon her the burden of disconsolate sadness, so that not caring any more, she wept loudly on her way to the hut.

Translated by ADAM GILLON
and LUDWIK KRZYZANOWSKI

Henryk Sienkiewicz

(1846–1916)

A Nobel prize winner and one of the best-known Polish novelists abroad, Henryk Sienkiewicz was born in the village of Wola Okrzejska in 1846. He completed his university studies in Warsaw in 1870. While still at school, he wrote poetry and prose, but he began his literary work as a journalist contributing to the Positivist journal, *Weekly Review*. In 1876, Sienkiewicz went to the United States for a few years. He lived in Modjeska's famous Polish "Brook Farm" in California. While in the United States, he wrote a series of "Travel Letters" which were published in *The Polish Gazette*.

His American experiences provided inspiration for some of his stories, notably "The Lighthouse Keeper" (1882) (which we present below). Upon his return to Poland, Sienkiewicz devoted himself to literature. He began with *Humorous Pieces from Worszyllo's Portfolio* (1872), which followed the Positivist vogue; next came a collection of short stories satirizing social conditions in Polish villages, entitled *Charcoal Sketches* (1877). "Yanko the Musician" (1879), a sentimental tale of a poor peasant boy who vainly dreamed of owning a violin, gained wide popularity both in Poland and abroad.

When Sienkiewicz turned to the writing of historical novels, he broke with the program of Positivism, which demanded a utilitarian approach and frowned on the sentimental and idealized view of the past. But his trilogy of historical novels took the public by storm even though the critics battled as to its merits; the three parts were: *With Fire and Sword* (1884), *The Deluge* (1886), and *Pan Michael* (1887–1888). The novels portrayed the heroic days of Poland in the seventeenth century, as it waged wars against the Cossacks, Tatars, Swedes and Turks.

Sienkiewicz is a great master of the seventeenth-century language and simple tale of adventure, but he lacks subtlety of psychological characterization. His protagonists are uncomplicated men who are presented as men of steadfast courage and capable of supreme sacrifice and blind, unreasoning love. The magnitude of his fictional canvas, his skill in handling involved plots, the picturesque vividness of his narrative and, last but not least, his humor have made Sienkiewicz the most outstanding historical novelist of his time. Sienkiewicz received the Nobel prize in literature in 1905.

His other important historical novels are *Quo Vadis* (1896—which was translated into English along with the Trilogy), and *The Knights of the Cross* (1900). *Quo Vadis* is a romance of ancient Rome under Nero. According to some critics, it was the most widely read nineteenth-century novel in the world. Two million copies of the book in various languages were sold shortly after its publication, and it has been reprinted many times since. (There are several film adaptations of the novel.) *The Knights of the Cross* describes the Polish and Lithuanian struggle against the Teutonic Order in the fifteenth century, a novel which Sienkiewicz found most difficult to write, perhaps because in this work his adventurous plot is complicated by many social conflicts among the gentry, the magnates, the clergy, the burghers and peasants.

After his historical novels, Sienkiewicz turned to contemporary matters and wrote two renowned novels, *Without Dogma* (1891) and *The Polaniecki Family* (1895), imbued with conservative ideology. These books were also translated into a number of languages and saw many editions abroad, but the critics agree that their author lacks psychological insight and that his forte was the historical novel.

After the outbreak of World War I, Sienkiewicz went to Switzerland where he directed a program of aid for Poland. He died in Vevey on November 16, 1916, after he abandoned work on a novel of Napoleonic times. In 1923, his remains were brought to Poland for a solemn burial in Warsaw.

The Lighthouse Keeper

I

It happened once that the lighthouse keeper in Aspinwall, not far from Panama, disappeared without trace. Since he was lost in a storm, it was assumed that the unfortunate man must have come close to the very edge of the rocky islet on which the lighthouse stood, and was washed away by a breaker. This assumption was the more probable, for on the next day his boat, usually anchored in the rocky inlet, could not be found. Thus the position of a lighthouse keeper became vacant, and it had to be filled as soon as possible, because the lighthouse was quite important both for the local traffic and for the ships sailing between New York and Panama.

Mosquito Bay has many banks and sandbars, among which navigation is difficult even at daytime; it is almost impossible at night especially in fog that frequently hangs over these warm tropical waters. At that time the lighthouse is the sole guide for the numerous vessels.

The task of finding a new lighthouse keeper fell to the United States consul stationed in Panama, and it was a troublesome undertaking first, because a successor had to be found within twelve hours; and second, he had to be a most reliable person, and therefore the candidate must be screened carefully. Moreover, there were no applicants for the job.

Life in the lighthouse is usually hard and does not in the least appeal to the southern people who are easy-going and prize their freedom to roam at will. A lighthouse keeper is almost a prisoner. Except for Sundays he is not allowed to leave his rocky islet. The boat from Aspinwall brings him food supplies and water once a day, where-upon the boatmen leave at once, and the one-acre islet is deserted. The keeper lives in the lighthouse, and keeps it in order. During the day he signals the weather by hoisting flags of many colors, as the barometer indicates, and in the evening he lights the beacon. This would not be an arduous task were it not that to get to the lights at the top of the tower, one had to walk up over four hundred winding and very high steps, and on occasion the keeper must make this trip several times a day. On the whole, this is a monastic life; worse, it is a hermit's existence. Little wonder, therefore, that Mr. Isaac Falcon-bridge had quite a problem to find a permanent replacement for the lost keeper; and it is easy to see his joy when most unexpectedly a successor appeared on that very day.

He was an old man, of seventy or more, but hale, erect, of a military bearing. His hair was completely white, his complexion dark as that of a Creole; but his blue eyes suggested that he was not a man of the South. His face was depressed and sad, but honest. Falconbridge liked him at first sight. He only had to interview the man; hence the follow-ing conversation ensued:

"Where do you come from?"

"I am a Pole."

"What have you been doing up till now?"

"Wandering from place to place."

"A lighthouse keeper should stay in one place."

"I need a rest."

"Have you served at any time? Do you have any certificates of honorable government service?"

The old man drew from his breast pocket a faded silk rag, resem-bling a strip of a tattered flag, unfolded it and said:

"Here are the certificates. This cross I received in the 1830 Polish uprising. The second is from the Carlist war; the third is the French legion; the fourth I got in Hungary. Afterwards I fought in the States against the South, but they gave no crosses there—so here's the paper."

Falconbridge took the document and began to read.

"Hm! Skawinski? This is your name? Hm! Two flags captured single-handedly in a bayonet attack . . . You were a brave soldier!"

"I can be an honest lighthouse keeper."

"You have to climb the tower several times a day. Are your legs strong?"

"I crossed the plains on foot."

"All right! Are you familiar with maritime service?"

"I served on a whaler for three years."

"You've tried various professions."

"The only thing I have not found is peace."

"Why?"

The old man shrugged his shoulders. "Such is my lot."

"Still, aren't you too old to be a lighthouse keeper?"

"Sir," the candidate said in a voice that suddenly betrayed emotion, "I am very tired, too many knocks . . . You see, I've been through a lot. This job is one I wanted to get more than anything else. I'm old, I need peace. I've got to tell myself: 'Here you stay put, this is your port.' Ah, Sir! This depends on you alone. Such a job may not come my way again. What luck that I was in Panama . . . I implore you . . . In God's name, I am like a ship which if it does not make the harbor will go down . . . If you want to make an old man happy . . . I swear I am honest, but . . . I've had enough of this roaming."

The old man's blue eyes expressed such a profound plea that Falconbridge, whose heart was simple and kind, was moved.

"Well," he said, "I'll take you. You are the lighthouse keeper."

The old man's face shone with inexpressible joy.

"I thank you."

"Can you go to the lighthouse today?"

"Yes, sir."

"Good-bye, then . . . One more word: any failure in service will mean dismissal."

"All right."

That same evening, when the sun had rolled to the other side of the isthmus, and a night without twilight followed a sunny day, the new keeper was apparently manning the station, for the lighthouse was casting its beams of bright light on the waters as usual. The night was utterly calm, quiet, truly tropical, suffused with light mist, forming a great rainbow of color, its edges soft and indistinct. The sea was rough, for the tide was rising.

Skawinski stood on the balcony, near the huge beacons, appearing from below like a black dot. He tried to collect his thoughts and to grasp his new situation. But his mind was too much under pressure to reason clearly. He experienced the feeling of a hunted animal that finally has eluded its pursuers on some inaccessible rock or cave. At last the time of peace had come for him. A sense of security filled his soul with untold delight. Here upon this rock he could simply mock his old wanderings, his old misfortunes and failures. He was indeed like a ship whose masts, ropes and sails had been broken by a gale, and which had been tossed from the clouds down to the sea bottom, struck by the waves, spitting foam, and which nevertheless had made the harbor. The images of that gale passed now quickly through his mind in contrast to the quiet future that was about to begin. Some of his strange vicissitudes he had himself narrated to Falconbridge, but he had not mentioned a thousand other adventures. It was his misfortune that whenever he pitched his tent somewhere and kindled a fire to settle permanently, some wind would pull out the stakes of his tent, blow out his fire, and drive him on to ruin. Looking now from the lighthouse balcony on the illumined waves, he recalled all that he had been through. He had fought on four continents—and in his wanderings he had tried almost all occupations. Diligent and honest, he often made some money and always lost it despite all expectations and utmost caution. He had been a gold-digger in Australia, a diamond prospector in Africa, a government rifleman in the East Indies. When he once started a farm in California he was ruined by drought; he tried to trade with savage tribes in the interior of Brazil; his raft was smashed on the Amazon; he himself, defenseless and almost naked, wandered in the forests for several weeks, living on wild fruit, constantly risking death from the jaws of wild beasts. He set up a smithy in Helena, Arkansas—and it was burnt in the big fire of the entire city. He then fell into the hands of Indians in the Rocky Mountains, and miraculously was rescued by Canadian trappers. He served as seaman on a ship plying between Bahia and Bordeaux, and later as a harpoonist aboard a whaler; both vessels were shipwrecked. He owned a cigar factory in Havana, and was robbed by his partner at a time when he was ill with the vomito. At last he arrived in Aspinwall—and here was to be the end of his ill-luck. For what else could overtake him on this rocky islet? Neither water, nor fire, nor men. Actually, Skawinski had not suffered much harm from men. He had met good people more often than evil ones.

It appeared that all the four elements conspired against him. Those who knew him said he had no luck and thereby explained everything. In time he himself became a bit of a maniac. He believed that some powerful and spiteful arm pursued him everywhere, on all continents and oceans. However, he disliked speaking about this; only sometimes, when he was asked whose arm it could be, he would point mysteriously to the North Star and say it came from there . . . Indeed, so uncannily constant was his adversity that it might easily unsettle anyone's mind, especially that of the man who was its victim. But Skawinski had an Indian's patience, a great, quiet power of resistance which comes from true honesty. In his day, he had received several bayonet wounds in Hungary, because he had refused to reach for the stirrup and cry for quarter, by which means he would save himself. In the same way he would not surrender to misfortune. He crawled up against the mountain, industriously as an ant. Pushed down a hundred times, he would calmly resume his journey for the hundred and first time. In his own way, he was quite odd. This old soldier, forged in God knows what fires, steeled and battered by hardships, had a child's heart. During an epidemic in Cuba, he contracted the disease because he had given away all his quinine, of which he had had a considerable supply, without having left a grain for himself.

There was another remarkable quality about him—that after so many disappointments he was always trustful and never lost hope that all would turn out well. In the winter he grew more cheerful and foretold great events. He awaited them eagerly and the thought of them sustained him throughout whole years . . . But the winters passed, one after another, and they merely whitened his head. At last he grew old, began to lose his energy. His patience turned more and more to resignation. His old calm gave way to sentimentality and this hardened soldier waxed tearful at the slightest provocation. He was also subject to fits of nostalgia, caused by any circumstances: the sight of swallows, gray birds resembling sparrows, the snow on the mountains, or some tune that recalled a similar song heard long ago . . . At length, he was possessed by one idea: the idea of rest. It overwhelmed him completely and swallowed all other desires and hopes. The eternal wanderer could no longer dream of anything more desirable or precious than some quiet corner in which he could rest and await a peaceful end. Perhaps, because some caprice of his fate had so tossed him over all the seas and lands that he could hardly catch his breath, he imagined that the greatest human happiness was not to wander. To be sure, he deserved such modest measure of happiness, but he was so used to failure that he thought of this as people dream of something beyond their reach. He dared not hope for it.

And now, unexpectedly, within twelve hours he had obtained a position as if chosen for him out of all the jobs in the world. No wonder then, that when he lighted his beacon that evening, he was dazed and asked himself whether it was real and dared not say "yes." Meanwhile, reality spoke to him with irrefutable proofs; thus he passed hour after hour on the balcony. He gazed, took in everything, convinced himself. It seemed that he was looking at the sea for the first time in his life.

The lens of the beacon cast into the darkness an enormous cone of light, beyond which the old man's eye was lost in the distance, totally black, mysterious and awesome. But this distance seemed to run towards the light. The mile-long waves rolled out of the darkness, gleaming, rose-colored in the light of the beacon. The tide was swelling more and more, and it flooded the sandy bars. The enigmatic speech of the ocean issued from the depths ever more powerful and loud, sometimes resembling the roar of cannons, and sometimes the rustling of immense forests, or the remote chatter of human voices. In time it subsided. Then his ears would detect deep sighs, then sobs, and again menacing outbursts. Finally, the wind swept the haze away, but

drove in black, ragged clouds, which obscured the moon. From the
west it began to blow more violently. The waves leaped ferociously
against the lighthouse cliff, and licked its base with foam. In the distance a storm was growing. On the dark, swirling expanse shone a few
green lanterns, hung from the masts of ships. These green dots rose
high, fell, and swayed right and left. Skawinski came down to his
room. The storm began to howl. Outside, people on those ships were
fighting with night, darkness and waves; but in the room it was peaceful and quiet. Even the sounds of the storm scarcely penetrated the
thick walls, and only the measured tick-tack of the clock lulled the
weary old man to sleep.

II

Hours, days, and weeks went by . . . Sailors claim that sometimes,
when the sea is raging, a voice from the night and darkness calls them
by their names. If the sea's infinity can call thus, perhaps, when a man
grows older, another infinity also calls on him, darker and more mysterious; and the more fatigued he is by life, the more welcome he finds
these calls. But in order to hear them one needs rest. Besides, old age
likes to isolate itself, as if with a foreboding of the grave. The lighthouse was such a half-grave for Skawinski. Nothing is more monotonous than such an existence in the tower. Young men, when they accept
it, leave the service after a while. The lighthouse keeper is usually a
man no longer young, morose and self-centered. If by chance he leaves
his lighthouse and returns to the world of men he walks among them
like a man awakened from a deep slumber. The tower lacks all minute
impressions which, in ordinary life, guide men in relating all things to
themselves. Everything the lighthouse keeper comes in contact with
is immense and devoid of clearly defined forms. The sky is one whole-
ness, and water another, and between these infinities rests the solitary
human soul! It is a life in which there is never-ending meditation, and
nothing rouses the keeper out of this meditation, not even his duties.
One day is like another, like two rosary beads, and the sole variety
is provided by the changes of weather. Yet Skawinski felt happier than
at any time in his life. He rose at dawn, took his meal, polished the
lenses of the lamps, and then, sitting on the balcony, gazed into the
distant sea, his eyes ever hungry for the sights before him. On the
gigantic turquoise background he could usually see flocks of swollen
sails, shining in the rays of the sun so brightly that his eyes blinked
from the dazzling light; sometimes the ships making use of the so-
called trade winds, passed in a long line, one after the other, like a
chain of seagulls or albatrosses. The red buoys, marking the way,
swayed in a light, gentle motion; amidst the sails an enormous greyish

plume of smoke appeared every afternoon. It was the steamer from New York, carrying passengers and goods to Aspinwall, with a long, foamy wake trailing behind it.

From the other side of the balcony Skawinski saw clearly Aspinwall with its busy port, its forest of masts, boats of all sizes, and a little farther away, the white houses and the turrets of the town. From the height of the lighthouse the houses appeared like seagull nests, and the boats as beetles, and the people moved like tiny dots on a white stone wharf. In the morning, a light eastern breeze brought a confused hum of human life, over which rose the whistle of steamers. In the afternoon came the hour of the siesta. Traffic in the port ceased; the gulls hid in the crevices of the cliffs, the waves weakened and became somewhat lazy; and then the lighthouse reigned over the land and the sea, and nothing marred the stillness. The yellow sands from which the waves had receded glistened like golden stains on the expanse of the waters; the tower was sharply outlined against the azure sky. The flood of sunbeams poured from the sky onto the water, the sands and the cliff.

The old man was then overcome by some indolence, full of sweetness. He felt that the rest he was enjoying was perfect, and when he thought that it would last, he lacked nothing. He was filled with dreamy happiness, and, since a man easily adapts himself to a better fortune, he gradually gained faith and confidence. For he thought—if people build houses for invalids, why could not God finally provide for His own invalid? Time passed and he grew stronger in this conviction.

The old man got used to the tower, the beacon, the cliff, the sandbars and the solitude. He also became acquainted with the gulls that hatched in the rocky crevices, and that gathered on the lighthouse roof. He usually threw them the remnants of his food, so that they soon grew tame, and when he fed them afterwards, he was surrounded by a veritable storm of white wings, and the old man walked among them like a shepherd among his sheep.

At low tide he set off for the low, sandy bars, on which he collected tasty clams and beautiful pearl shells of the nautilus, which the ebbing waters had left on the sand. At night, by the light of the moon and the lighthouse, he went fishing among the jagged rocks where the fish were in abundance.

At last he came to love his cliff and his treeless islet, grown over with tiny stumpy plants that oozed sticky resin. The view of the distant horizon compensated him for the poverty of his islet. In the afternoon hours, when the air gew very transparent, he could see all the isthmus down to the Pacific, covered with luxurious vegetation. It seemed to Skawinski in such moments that he was looking at one gigantic garden. Coconuts and bananas in huge clusters seemed to form rich, tufted bouquets, right behind the houses of Aspinwall. Farther on, between Aspinwall and Panama could be seen a huge forest, and over it hung in the morning and at dusk a reddish haze of vapors,—a truly tropical forest, flooded at the bottom with stagnant water and tangled with lianas,—a humming wave of gigantic orchids, palms, milk-trees, iron-trees, and gum-trees.

Through his telescope the old man could see not only the trees and the thickly spread banana leaves but also crowds of monkeys, big marabous and flocks of parrots, that soared at times like a rainbow cloud over the forest. Skawinski knew intimately such forests, for after the shipwreck on the Amazon he had wandered for several weeks among similar vaults and thickets. He knew how many dangers and how much death lay hidden under their wonderful, smiling surface. During the nights which he had spent in those woods he heard the sepulchral voices of howlers, the roar of jaguars at close range; he saw gigantic snakes hung like lianas on trees; he knew those somnolent forest lakes, full of cramp-fish and swarming with crocodiles; he knew under what a yoke man lives in that impenetrable wilderness, in which single leaves can be ten times his size, and which teem with blood-thirsty mosquitoes, tree-leeches, and enormous poisonous spiders. He had come to experience and suffer all this himself; hence he was capable of taking that much more pleasure from the sight of those forests whose beauty he observed and admired from his height, while he was shielded from their treacherousness.

His tower protected him from every evil. He left it only occasionally on Sundays. He then put on his navy-blue keeper's uniform with silver buttons, pinned his medals on his chest, and bore his white head with a certain pride when on leaving church he heard the Creoles say among themselves: "We have a decent lighthouse keeper; even if he's a Yankee, he isn't a heretic." But he returned to his islet as soon as the Mass was over, and he returned in a happy frame of mind, for he still had no trust in the mainland. On Sunday he also read the Spanish newspaper which he bought in town, or *The New York Herald,* which he borrowed from Falconbridge, and eagerly scanned their pages for news from Europe. Poor old heart! At the lighthouse tower and on the other hemisphere it was still pining away for his country . . .

Sometimes, too, when the boat with his daily food and water came to his islet, he went down for a chat with the guard, Johns. Later, however, he apparently began to shy away from people. He ceased to visit the town, to read the papers and to come down for political debates with Johns. Whole weeks went by thus, without his seeing anybody or being seen. The only signs that the old man was alive were the disappearance of the supplies left on the shore, and the lighthouse beacons lit every evening with the regularity of the sun rising over the waters in those parts. It seemed that the old man had grown indifferent to the world. This was caused not by nostalgia but rather just this— that even nostalgia had turned into resignation. To the old man the whole world was now encompassed by the islet. He had become accustomed to the idea that he would not leave the tower till his death, and he simply forgot that there existed anything else beside it. At the same time he became a mystic. His gentle blue eyes turned into the eyes of a child, always fixed on some object and as if glued to the distance. His constant isolation and his simple and great environment caused the old man to lose the sense of his own identity; he was ceasing to be an individual, and was increasingly becoming merged in the things which surrounded him. He did not attempt to rationalize this; he felt it unconsciously. At last it seemed to him that the sky, the water, his cliff, the tower and the golden sand-bars and the swollen sails and the sea-gulls, the ebb and flow of the tide were one great unity, one immense mysterious soul; while he himself was drowning in that mystery, sensing that soul which lives and becalms itself. He sank and was rocked, grew oblivious to everything and in that limitation of his own individual existence, in that waking, half-sleep, he found a peace so great it almost resembled half-death.

III

But the awakening came.

One day, when the boat brought water and food supplies, Skawinski went down an hour later from the tower, and noticed that besides the usual cargo there was one more package. On the package were United States stamps and a distinct address: "Skawinski, Esq." written on the coarse canvas.

The intrigued old man cut the canvas and saw books; he took one in his hand, examined it and put it back, his hands trembling violently. He covered his eyes as if he did not believe them; it seemed to him as if he were dreaming—the book was Polish. What could it mean? Who could have sent him the book? At the first moment he failed to remember that in the beginning of his lighthouse career he had read once in the *Herald*, borrowed from the consul, about the founding of a Polish society in New York, and that he had at once sent to that society half of his monthly wages, which were not much use to him on the tower. The society reciprocated by sending him the books. They came in a natural way; but at the first moment the old man could not get the connection. A Polish book in Aspinwall, on his tower, in his solitude, was to him an extraordinary thing, a breath from the night, that something was calling him by name with a voice very dear old days; a miracle. Now it seemed to him, as to those seamen in the but almost forgotten. He sat for a while with closed eyes, and was almost certain that when he opened them, the dream would disappear.

No! The package, cut open, lay before him, distinct in the bright afternoon sun, and on it was the book he had opened. When the old man extended his hand toward it once again, he heard in the stillness the beating of his own heart. He glanced; this was verse. On the cover stood printed in large letters the title, and below it the author's name. That name was not strange to Skawinski; he knew that it was a great poet's, whose works he had even read after 1830 in Paris. Later, when he fought in Algiers and Spain, he had heard from his compatriots about the ever-growing fame of the great bard; but the rifle had become so much a part of Skawinski that he hardly took a book in hand. In 1849 he left for America, and in the adventurous life which he led he scarcely ever met a Pole, or ever came across a Polish book. With all the greater anticipation, therefore, and with a heart pounding more rapidly, did he turn the title page. It seemed to him now that on his solitary rock something solemn was about to occur. Indeed it was a moment of great peace and stillness. The clocks of Aspinwall had struck five in the afternoon. Not a cloud marred the brilliant firmament; only a few gulls were coursing through the sky. A great calmness lay upon the ocean. The waves on the shore murmured softly, gently spreading across the sands. The white houses of Aspinwall and the splendid clusters of palms smiled in the distance. Truly there was something solemn in the air, something calm and grave. Suddenly, amid that calm of nature, the old man read aloud in a trembling voice, so that he might understand better:

> O Lithuania, my fatherland,
> Thou art like health; what praise thou shouldst command
> Only that man finds who has lost thee quite.
> Today I see, and limn, thy beauty bright
> In all its splendor, for I yearn for thee.

Skawinski's voice failed. The letters began to jump before his eyes; something broke in his chest and rose like a wave from his heart higher and higher, muffling his voice and strangling his throat . . . In a moment he took hold of himself and read on:

> O holy Virgin, who dost oversee
> Bright Czenstochowa and in Wilno shinest
> Above the Ostra Gate! Thou who inclinest

To shelter Nowogrodek with its folk
In faithfulness. When I, in youth, bespoke
Thy help, by miracle thou didst restore
My failing health; when my sad mother bore
Me to thy seat, my deathlike eyes I raised;
Walked to the threshold of thy shrine amazed;
And thanked God for the health brought back to me—
So by a miracle thou wilt decree
That we regain our country.

The surging wave overpowered his will. The old man broke out sobbing and threw himself on the ground; his milk-white hair mingled with the sand on the shore. It was nearly forty years since he had last seen his country, and God knows how many years had elapsed since he had heard his native speech; and now that speech had come to him by itself; it had crossed the ocean to find him a solitary on another hemisphere—so loved, so dear, so beautiful! In the sobs that shook him there was no anguish but only a suddenly aroused, immense love that shut out everything else . . . With those great tears he simply asked forgiveness of that beloved, distant country for having grown so old, having become so much a part of the lonely rock and having so forgotten that even his homesickness had begun to fade away. But now it had "come back as if by a miracle"—therefore, his heart was breaking. Minutes passed but he remained lying motionless. The sea-gulls flew over the lighthouse, screaming as if anxious about their old friend. The time in which he fed them with the remnants of his food had arrived; therefore, some of them swooped down from the roof of the lighthouse towards him; then more and more of them came, and they began to peck him and to flap their wings over his head. The rustling of their wings wakened him. Having wept his fill, his face now reflected a certain peace and radiance, and his eyes were as if inspired. Unthinkingly he gave all his food to the birds, which fell upon it with an uproar, and he picked up the book again. The sun had passed already behind the gardens and the virgin forest of Panama, and was sinking slowly beyond the isthmus to the other ocean, but the Atlantic was still full of brightness; there was still enough light and he continued to read:

. . . Meanwhile bear
To those treed hills my spirit of despair,
To those green meadows, stretching far and wide . . .

The dusk at length obliterated the letters on the white page; a twilight brief as an eye's twinkle. The old man leaned his head against the rock and closed his eyes. And then "She who defends bright Czenstochowa" took his soul and carried it to "those fields painted with various grain." The sky was still burning with long red and golden strips, and through that brightness he drifted towards his beloved countryside. The pine woods rustled in his ears, the native rivers murmured.

He sees everything as it was. Everything asks him: "Do you remember?" He remembers! And he sees wide fields, the balks, the meadows, the forests and the villages! It is night! At this time his lighthouse illumines the darkness of the sea; but now he is in his native village. The old head droops on his breast, and he is dreaming. Images move before his eyes rapidly and a little chaotically. He does not see his home, for it was razed by war; he does not see his father and mother, for they died when he was a child; but otherwise the village remains as though he had left it yesterday; a row of huts with lights in the windows, the dike, the mill, two ponds facing each other, and resounding all night with a chorus of frogs. Once in this village of his he stood on guard all night; now that past rushes at him in a sequence of visions. He is a lancer again, and he stands watch; from afar the tavern looks on with flaming eyes and resounds and sings and roars amid the stillness of the night with the stamping of feet and the voices of fiddles and bass-viols. "U-ha! U-ha!" It is the uhlans that strike sparks with their taps, and he feels lonely there on the horse. The hours drag on lazily, and at last the lights go out; now, as far as the eye can reach, there is an impenetrable mist; evidently, the fog rises from the meadows and shrouds the whole world in a whitish cloud. One might say a veritable ocean. But no, these are meadows; before long the land-rail will be heard in the darkness, and the bitterns will cry out in the reeds. The night is still and cool, a truly Polish night! In the distance the pine wood soughs without wind . . . like a sea wave. Soon the dawn will cast its pale light upon the east; already the roosters are crowing in the yards. Their cries are taken up from hut to hut; presently the cranes are clamoring from somewhere on high. The uhlan feels fresh and full of zest. People were saying something about a battle tomorrow. Hey! Go he will, like all the others, with shouting and the fluttering of pennants. The young blood wells up within him like the sound of a bugle, although the night breeze cools it. Already it is dawn; it is dawn. The night is growing pale; woods, thickets, a row of huts, the mill, the poplars emerge from the shadows. The wells are squeaking, like the weathervane on the tower. How dear this land is, how beautiful in the rosy glitter of the morning sun. Oh, my only land, my only one!

Quiet! The watchful guard hears someone approaching. They are probably coming to relieve the guard.

Suddenly a voice speaks above Skawinski.

"Get up, old man! What's the matter with you?"

The old keeper opens his eyes and looks with amazement at the man standing before him. The shreds of his dream visions struggle with reality in his mind. Finally the visions pale and disappear. Before him stands Johns, the harbor guard.

"What is it?" Johns asks, "Are you ill?"

"No."

"You didn't light the beacon. You'll be fired from your job. A boat from St. Geromo foundered on the shallows. Fortunately no one was drowned, or you would be tried in court. Get into the boat with me; you'll hear the rest at the consulate."

The old man turned pale; indeed, he had not lighted the beacon that night.

Several days later Skawinski was seen aboard the steamer sailing from Aspinwall to New York. The poor man had lost his job. New roads of wandering opened before him. The wind was once more snatching that leaf, to toss it over lands and seas, to torment it at will. Hence the old man had aged greatly and had become stooped during the last few days; only his eyes shone. He was carrying his book along on his breast, as he set out on the new road of life, and he pressed it with his hand from time to time, as if afraid that it too might be lost to him.

Translated by ADAM GILLON
and LUDWIK KRZYZANOWSKI

Note: Excerpts from Mickiewicz's *Pan Tadeusz* are from the new English version by Watson Kirkconnell, Polish Institute of Arts and Sciences, New York, 1962.

Eliza Orzeszkowa

(1841–1910)

One of the outstanding masters of the Polish realistic novel, Eliza Orzeszkowa was born in Miekowszczyzna near Grodno in 1841. Her father,
Benedict Pawlowski, a former Napoleonic officer, patriotic leader and
wealthy landowner, left a library which enabled Orzeszkowa to acquire an
early intellectual education, making her one of the most educated women
of her time. She was married in her sixteenth year to a well-to-do landowner, Peter Orzeszko. On her husband's estate in Ludwinowo she gathered
a great deal of information about people, and came close to the movement
of democratic youth which organized the insurrection of 1863, and which
shaped her views. During the uprising, she cooperated with the movement.
Her husband joined the ranks, and after the uprising was quelled, he was
exiled to Siberia. Orzeszkowa moved to Grodno where she began her
literary activities. She wrote articles and pamphlets and became one of the
most progressive advocates of social equality, demanding full rights for the
peasants and Jews, and castigating the gentry's smugness and intolerance.

She belonged to the generation of the so-called "Positivists," but she
differed from them in her emphasis on the moral predicament of man, and
in her ambiguous attitude toward the uprising, which she did not condemn
outright. Her work revealed the rise of social awareness, which the Positivists demanded of writers, and her fifty volumes of novels and short
stories are indeed a Polish "Human Comedy," a rich gallery of Poland's
people at the close of the last century.

Her first novels dealt with the problems of women who could not cope
with life, (e.g., *Waclawa's Memoirs* (1871), *Martha* (1873), and *Pan
Graba* (1872). But her interests in the social scene made her write of the
hitherto unknown hero in Polish literature, the little man, the servant, the
small-town Jew, the oppressed, "the bent, the wrinkled, the tired." She
was particularly concerned with the Jewish problem and wrote a treatise
"On Jews and the Jewish Question," and her cycle of Jewish novels (*Meir
Ezofowicz*, 1877, *Eli Makower*, 1875), reflect her condemnation of anti-
Semitism and portray the conflict between the forward-looking and backward elements of the Jewish community.

Dziurdziowie (1884) and *The Churl* (1889) deal with the peasants,
their ignorance as well as their native nobility. Other novels and stories
describe the landed gentry and all other social types of the country. *Nad
Niemnem* (On the Banks of the Niemen, 1886) is regarded as Orzeszkowa's
best novel. It gives a sweeping view of the Polish social scene, stressing the
most important postulates of the Positivist movement against the background of the Polish village: the manor versus the peasant's cabin. The

novel praises the love of labor, the importance of agriculture, respect for knowledge; it scolds light-heartedness, selfishness, and the class prejudices of the landed gentry and aristocracy. But above all, this masterpiece breathes the spirit of life into dozens of men and women, and her descriptions of nature and social customs deserve a comparison with Mickiewicz's *Pan Tadeusz.*

The short story *Powerful Samson* (1878) is typical of Orzeszkowa's preoccupation with the ignorant mind and the elevating effect of art and Idealism upon it. It also shows her use of pathos and the sociological as well as artistic interests of the writer.

Powerful Samson

(Excerpts)

. . . Shymshel, the son of a water carrier or woodcutter, a poor student at a free school, possessed no fortune except the two hundred zlotys collected by public donation. He was, nevertheless, deemed such a good match in the eyes of young girls and their parents that, when his marriage with Tsipa was announced, everyone was astonished at the luck of the little *gizelka* or salesgirl whose old mother carried heavy baskets of fruit in the streets and whose sisters had married cobblers, carpenters, and the like, men of the unrefined trades and low estate. It is true that these cobblers and carpenters owned houses and large workshops, and had steady incomes. Shymshel did not own a house nor did he have a workshop, or an income, but he was educated. Moreover—or therefore—he was so beautiful and delicate.

Shymshel and Tsipa married, possessing a joint capital of thirty rubles. Besides this, Tsipa also had a trousseau, that is three undershirts, two feather beds, two dresses and one quilted jerkin.

They had nothing more at the time of their marriage, and yet somehow they lived twelve years . . . During that time, nine children were born to them. Four died, five lived. No doubt they will have five more; three of them to die and two to grow up, and yet they will love on . . . It may seem strange, or even improbable to you, that a family affluent in such magnificent, or to be more explicit, numerous results could live on a capital of thirty rubles. I myself was greatly astonished at this until I got to know Tsipa a little better.

In appearance she is a little Jewish woman, and as they say, very simple. At twenty-eight she looks more than forty. Her small figure straining forward, her back covered with a quilted jerkin which is humped and shining, not with the richness of the material but with age, she moves through the crowd with short, hurried, and yet shy and seemingly stealthy steps.

She seems to be constantly troubled, numbed, stultified, and only her black eyes, darting frequent flashes, move very quickly in her dark, wilted face. These flashes betray a constant and intent quest, a pursuit for something and at times take on a malicious expression. They are then in perfect harmony with the low forehead covered with uncountable lines running from the thick brows to the edge of the black wig.

But please do not laugh at this small and simple Jewish woman who does not look attractive or wise. She has accomplished something quite important. She has resolved in actual practice a certain social problem which the world has found extremely difficult, namely the question of feminine equality in the right to earn. Tsipa has reached an ideal solution to this question, for her earnings have been supporting her husband and five children for the past twelve years. All her enterprises which led to this objective are founded on the capital of thirty rubles.

With these thirty rubles, which represented the foundation of her family's existence, Tsipa opened a grocery store. However, she did have an additional credit, equal to this sum, promised by the shop in which she had previously worked. The most important task of any kind of enterprise whose aim is to earn a profit is to find customers. Tsipa began to look for customers from the very first day that her shop opened. She is looking for them to this very day, not because she cannot find them, but because having found them she loses them and must look for new ones. She loses them for a variety of reasons, among which the most inferior part is played by certain mysterious activities which Tsipa performs in the evening after the shop is closed, in the right corner of that very shop, between the cupboard, counter and wall. A specific rustle can be heard issuing from that corner as if something were being sealed and then sealed again, as if something were being sifted and poured.

Although these activities, to which the proprietress of the shop devotes herself at this hour, may appear mysterious in the dim light of the lamp that burns on the floor behind the counter, it would, nevertheless, be an exaggeration to ascribe a tragic significance to them. Tsipa does not belong to any kind of Jewish plot to the detriment or for the destruction of the Christian population. She is not preparing in privacy and secret any kind of injurious activity against her *meropia*[1] for I can vouch for it that she does not possess any *meropia* of her own, and I even doubt that she ever in her whole life heard

---

[1] Meropia—victim of exploitation (according to the anti-Semites of Orzeszkowa's time, meropia was designated by the Jewish Community Council).

the sound of that word. She is acting absolutely on her own, and not in compact with her own people. Her *meropia* is a collective being, carrying the names of the buying public, and the powerful authorities that impel her to sift and pour in order to turn high quality goods into mediocre and mediocre into inferior, are the educated husband, the five children and the thirty rubles which are the principal invested in her enterprise. Tsipa's *meropia*, the buying public, seems to possess a sense of taste and an exquisite sense of smell. For scarcely do its members become acquainted with her goods when they soon stop buying, and that after numerous but unfortunately justified reproaches, much shouting and beating. Hence, Tsipa's search for new customers constitutes a chain of never-ending trials and endeavors. Her trials and endeavors are varied: a pleading wail, hand kissing, performing every service that anyone may demand. In order to gain the good graces of the public and to make additional money from time to time, she becomes everything in turn: a public messenger, a letter carrier, an agent for house servants, a go-between for borrowers and lenders, for sellers and purchasers. She is at the shop infrequently, only now and then. Her mother, one of her sisters or a neighbor will replace her while she runs up and down stairs the whole day long, toting heavy bundles under her arm, carrying piles of old clothing on her back, standing humbly on the threshold of houses with a basket in each hand, one with dried fruits and nuts and the other with tea and bottles of wine, quarreling with cooks and janitors who do not want to admit her to her benefactors, softening their severity with a pair of figs or a handful of nuts. At times she grows impatient with persons of her own sex who create an onerous competition for her and induce her by the force of their fists to leave the battlefield. Once, a large piece of the once-velvet collar that had adorned her quilted jerkin remained in the hands of these uncouth representatives of a great idea.

Having lost the magnificence of her dress in this manner, Tsipa wept plaintively . . . This moment of emotion was exceptional with her. On the whole, she never complains of anything, and if sometimes, someone meeting her mournful gaze, asks with more or less sympathy: "Well, Tsipa, are things going very badly with you?" she never even answers in the affirmative but says: "As God wills, so it is." There are some who, knowing Tsipa's situation at home a little better, will say to her as they look at her dark, wrinkled face, so often moist with perspiration and exhaustion and quivering with involuntary, nervous twitches:

"And what is your husband doing all his life? Why doesn't he help you?"

Then the dejected expression leaves Tsipa's face and is supplanted by something resembling anger.

"He has his work!" she answers sullenly. "He cannot help me in trading."

"You are very fortunate, Tsipa, to have such a clumsy husband."

Hearing this Tsipa raises her head:

"If I had ten daughters, I would pray God to give them all the happiness that I have."

●

It now gives me great pleasure to present Shymshel to you, in person this time, of whom you have heard so much from me! I am sure that once you have looked at him, you will confirm Tsipa's statement that he is very beautiful and delicate. He is tall and slim. His hands are as white as those of a woman of great quality and high birth. They are narrow and very shapely, though thin. His face, lean and pale with its long, curly raven-hued beard, possesses a strange purity and delicacy of features and a calm and most kind expression. When he happens to lift his eyes from the book, his face becomes suffused with the light of deep and mysterious dreaminess; it is apparent that those black eyes, with the fiery depths and moist surface, weep at times at the Babylonian enslavement and destruction of Jerusalem, and often gaze upon the flaming hieroglyphics that wreathe the proud head of the archangel of knowledge and upon the diamond teardrop that burns in the eye of the angel of prayer. Something of the calm pride of that angel Sar-ha-Olam[2] and of the strange goodness of Sandalfon[3] is mirrored and remains in Shymshel's fiery and yet mild eyes. If his lips, outlined in a thin and scarcely pink line amidst the black beard, did not belong to an uneducated and simple Jew, they would have infallibly signified a sensitive, nervous, even artistic nature, so exquisite is their shape, so eloquently do they tremble as they move from time to time, and so understanding, yet mild and tender is the smile that appears upon them.

I agree entirely with Tsipa's opinion of her husband's appearance, and discover that by looking at her with eyes which contain something of the light of the angel of knowledge and the angel of pity, one can think, surmise and regret a great deal . . .

If you have taken as great an interest in this Jew as I have, then you may look at him as much as you will and as often as you may wish if you come at the same hour to the same yard. For every day, without fail, he sits of an evening, at a table, his face turned toward the window with the dim lamplight falling on it. He either bends over a book or gazes somewhere on high. At times you will see him with little Esther as she jumps on his knees or with little Lezer, who

---

[2] Sar-ha-Olam—angel of knowledge

[3] Sandalfon—angel of prayer

climbs on his back and buries both hands in his raven hair. He is very happy then. He forgets the slavery in Babylon and Sandalfon, and laughs at his children and presses loud kisses on their cheeks. . . .

We shall not look at him longer now, for the door to the sign-painter's home is opening and a group of dark figures, having come out, moves under the orange hand that seems to threaten their heads, and in noisy talk passes through the yard and enters Shymshel's room.

Let us follow them.

You know the room from my previous description. It is crowded now. Six men have entered. I present them: Itzek—the tinker, Moishe —the sign-painter, Yosel—the furrier, Meyer—the son of Yosel the furrier, and two others I do not know.

It is for these people that Moishe had lighted his house *a giorno*. It is they who had talked so noisily with him. But what do they want from Shymshel? They are bowing with a respect so great that it is immediately apparent that these simple craftsmen feel the learned man's great superiority. Shymshel greets them politely, gently but with a composure befitting his dignity. Yosel, the furrier, steps out of the center of the small group (being either the oldest or the most eloquent), and with some timidity launches upon the subject and says that the whole company has decided . . .

Decided . . . what? Have we guessed? They have decided something. What could they have decided? Naturally, something that is to undermine or painfully wound the Christian world, as the brochure would have us believe. I vow that it was written by a man of great wisdom and adapted to the Polish language by a man of still greater wisdom. It is called: "World Conquest of the Jews."

They (they, a militant nation!) wish to and try to conquer the world, and now they must have decided something that will lead to this aim.

So Yosel, the furrier, says that he and his companions have decided on the day of the nearest Purim . . . to give a play.

Is that all?

Only this.

. . . to give a play for the benefit of the poor . . .

Rebe Shymshel has a beautiful voice for singing, a very beautiful voice. No one else can sing the main part better than he.

The cantor himself has advised them. The cantor, who, as everyone knows sings so magnificently and who knows the voices of the whole community as well as his own.

Rebe Shymshel is a learned man, a very learned man. No one but he can arouse the people's eager sympathy for this undertaking; no one but he can add dignity to it. Rabbi Boruch himself, whose great zeal in caring for the poor is known, begs . . .

What are they to play? They are to perform a play called "Powerful Samson" which Rebe Shymshel knows (for what is not known to the wisdom of Rebe Shymshel?), and in which there is such beautiful singing and such beautiful scenes, that—och!

. . . Shymshel, or Samson, thinks for a long while upon the proposition put to him. The thing they have asked of him is no longer meditation or contemplation, but action, a thing that Shymshel has not yet come in contact with.

Action terrifies him. It will be hard for him to walk, move, try— in a word: to act. And a thing as flighty as giving a play: will not this offend his dignity, will it not lower his authority?

He thinks for a long time, then he rises and says:

"If the cantor says that I have a beautiful voice for singing, and if Rabbi Boruch begs me to do this, and if it is for the poor, then I agree to take part in this."

*

Delilah sat behind a curtain on a Viennese chair. Her azure gown was spread over a large crinoline and a small pink fan was in her hand. She sat and her great childish eyes, which looked out of her face like forget-me-nots in a bouquet of peonies, gazed straight at the audience. Then she rose and came out from behind the curtain. She began to sing.

A very nice bass voice.

She sang that she must lure Samson with her charms in order to extort from him the mystery of his strange strength . . .

Delilah found it a little awkward to move in the long dress and iron hoops. Besides, she was much troubled by the implement in her hand, not knowing what to do with it.

The woolly locks that flowed about her brow and down her back increased the warmth that one feels at the sight of so many eyes riveted to one's face. Her bass voice trembled and fell to so low a register that it was not at all appropriate to a delicate, feminine bosom. Her azure eyes were moist with tears of unutterable suffering.

But this was nothing.

Never in all his life had Shymshel seen so beautiful a woman.

As he walked on stage, did he see the Delilah who was really there? No one knows. However, I did hear afterwards that as Shymshel walked on stage, instead of Meyerek's crimson face, forget-me-not eyes and woolly locks, he saw a snow-white countenance in a garland of gleaming raven braids, gazing at him with eyes shining like two stars.

He saw a musing tear, a passionate fire in those black eyes, and the figure which faced him was tall, lissom and as the heavens are warmed by the eastern sun so it emanated a breath of the sultry raptures of the east.

Never before had Shymshel experienced the sensation that he now felt, nor could he name it. But as he approached the charming apparition which stood before his eyes, and as he began to sing to it, his voice possessed such soft and fervent, plaintive and violent shades that Delilah opened her eyes wide with amazement and when later she was to give him her hand, as the part called for, she did so with evident trepidation.

With a gesture of violent joy Shymshel caught her hand, not the one holding the fan but the other, and drawing Delilah to his bosom, placed a kiss on her lips. Completely frightened by this kiss, Delilah broke away from his embrace and sat down on one of the two Viennese chairs placed in front of the porch of her palace.

Having calmed down somewhat, Shymshel sat on the second chair and the duet began.

Samson's fate was sealed in this duet. He was reticent and not easy to draw out, but Delilah's charms succeeded in overcoming the most determined resistance. Standing before her, in vain did he sing to her in his most convincing, most supplicating voice: *"Dus is nit dein gescheft."* The beguiling seductress knew well that this was an important business for her and so long did she sing in her bass voice (Shymshel heard the most beautiful mezzo-soprano instead of the bass), so long did she open wide her tired childish eyes with the effort (Shymshel saw two black burning diamonds instead) that, worn out by the battle and overcome with love, he grasped his locks with both his hands, and showing them to the sorceress sang out: "My strength is in them."

The Philistines arrived. But what was this? They were the same who had died at Samson's hand in the third act. Having risen from the dead, their wrath against their murderer must have been all the greater. They were waiting for Delilah. They stole to the palace door, peeked through its only window and exchanged mysterious signs. But there she was.

She emerged from behind the curtain and, holding the pink fan in one hand, carried a large strand of long raven hair in the other. The joy of the Philistines was indescribable. The king himself shook Delilah's hand in token of gratefulness. The knights took their swords out of their scabbards, and with a shout of furious vengeance, fell upon Samson as he came out of the palace. Samson had changed. Without the helmet and hair, without the white coat, he fell into the enemy's hands and without much ceremony they blinded him in both eyes.

The curtain fell. A silence of deadly awe fell upon the auditorium; only sobs could be heard in the darkness.

They were right—these compassionate souls—to shed tears. Dressed in his theatrical costume, Samson sat on the bench where the Philistines had placed him. He was deathly white, breathing heavily and his eyes were closed.

"Rebe," Moishe spoke to him, "look at the palace, which you are to topple on the stage . . . Maybe it is too heavy for you . . . We can make it smaller . . ."

But only a hollow moan rattled in Shymshel's chest.

"My enemies have taken the light of my eyes," he whispered in anguish, "I am blind and my eyes will never see the great works of the Eternal."

"*Herstel*"[4] the Philistines said to each other as they exchanged surprised glances. "He thinks that we have really gouged out his eyes."

Suddenly Delilah moved through the dressing-room. Shymshel heard the rustle of her dress and raised his eyelids.

His eyes hurled bolts of anger and despair, a dark flush covered his pale face.

"What have you done to me? What have you done to me? You have ruined me! I have lost my eyes through your great cunning, I have been captured and ruined!"

Shouting these words with increasing violence and force, he clenched his fists and made a rush toward Delilah, who dropped her pink fan in fear and ran into the farthest corner of the dressing-room where she hid behind a long, flowered robe of one of the Judaic Elders. Moishe also shielded her with his wide shoulders, and not daring to lift his hand to the learned man, stretched both his hands in front of him and called in a persuasive voice:

"Rebe! Ay, ay, Rebe!"

Shymshel's wrath lasted but a short while and quickly changed into a deep and gentle grief. He fell on the bench, lowered his hands, closed his eyes and began to moan:

"Oi! Oi! I looked upon your face as on a flower of paradise. Your lips were to my lips like a brook of honey. Your eyes burned like a great flame and all my heart melted before them . . . And you have wronged me so. For I am lost, Delilah."

No longer was anyone paying attention to the plaintive lament of the blinded hero except Delilah, who baring her head of the locks and roses, looked at him with fear.

On the stage stood a palace. Different from the one before. It was composed of two pasteboard pillars joined at the top with a pasteboard cornice. The Philistines were feasting around the pillars. They were happy and singing. For their greater joy, they commanded the blinded prisoner to be brought under the monarch's roof. Samson,

---

[4] *Herstel*—do you hear!

led by two soldiers, stood with his eyes closed. He was not frightened; only mortally sad.

Look closely at him: it would seem that within this one hour his face had become thinner. His pale cheeks seem to have fallen in, and his closed eyes are surrounded by dark circles. One could say that this face has been wasted by passion, love, hatred, despair . . .

The Philistines laughed, mocked him in all sorts of ways, telling him of the destruction and vengeance that they were sowing in his country. And he, a prisoner, a blind, helpless athlete, could no longer defend it . . .

In vain were the Judaic Elders crying there somewhere, in vain did the Judaic women fill the air with their lament, and the most valiant men stain with their blood the seared wastes of Judaic fields . . . Samson would no longer shield his native land with his chest, the strength of which has been taken away, he would not see his arms raised against the enemy with eyes dispossessed of their light . . .

Shymshel listened to the ridicule and triumphant tales of his enemies and slowly began to lift his head . . . Feeling his way, he left the palace with faltering steps, stood on the other side of the pillars and began to sing. How deep and boundless was the pain with which his voice swelled! What great heights it climbed! With what desperate calls and invocations it was filled! He called to Jehovah for strength, for that old strength, which he desired for only a moment, only one moment, for one instant . . . Calling thus, he lifted up his trembling hands and his pale face with its closed eyes and lips, surrounded with a tormented expression.

Standing thus, framed by the pasteboard pillars in the light of the lamp with a long funnel which one of the Philistines held close to his face, he bore the semblance of a martyr, but a martyr who suffered "with the suffering of millions."

This lamp, held close to his face (probably to light the scene), burned his cheek. He thrust it away with an energetic and irate gesture, seized the pillars with both hands, shook them and toppled them upon the Philistines who, too, fell upon the ground with a great noise . . .

They were all killed and Samson was killed.

The inanimate bodies of the dead lay under the palace ruins, and the scarlet, yellow and green colors of their robes shimmered amidst the crushing pillars. The curtain fell and the public broke into phrenetic shouts.

✿

There, through the dark street, lighted by a weak flame of an infrequent street lamp, strode a lonely, slim male figure. As it passed beside the occasional lamp post, the figure glowed with a sheen of the scarlet, gold and diamonds that covered it. When it was engulfed by darkness, its long cloak falling in folds grew white and unfurled like the arms of a phantom. The figure was alone, but by no means sad. The dignified stride indicated lightness and force, and from its chest, once in a muted and once in a loud burst of tone, flowed the magnificent aria of triumph.

Shymshel, having crushed the Philistines and himself under the capsized palace walls, had risen from the dead, had comprehended, had forgotten all the past humiliations and anguish. But not for one single second had he stopped being the "Powerful Samson." True, walking now from one street to another, between the brick walls with the dark or only infrequent windows dimly lit here and there, he ran in his mind through all the great deeds he had performed and was filled with joy and pride.

At times a recollection of the beguiling and faithless Delilah flashed through his mind . . . then longing and regret wrung his heart. Yet quickly he called to mind his native land, Judea, which he had saved from blood, tears afid conflagration; he raised his head high, sang louder and more joyously and trod on the uneven pavement of the dark street as on laurel wreaths . . .

In this manner Shymshel passed the boulevard and entered the side lane. Automatically, out of habit he turned toward his home and without giving a thought to his actions and still singing, he touched the latch of his low door with his hand and stood on the threshold of his room.

He stopped and stood for a few minutes in numb immobility.

In the room, a lamp burned on the table that stood at the window. A foul, yellowish smoke curled upward from its long cylinder. Farther the gray, low walls, beds with feather covers, old clothing, torn and dirty, strewn over the floor and chest, several smaller and larger human figures lying here and there in slumber had created a chaos in the dim light which was completely incomprehensible to his eyes and mind. He understood after a few minutes—and awakened.

. . . He lowered his head and looked at his clothes.

A strange smile appeared on his lips.

Samson's white cloak fell over his knees and feet in soft folds, the scarlet robe radiated a golden luster in the light of the lamp, the beads of his necklace covered his chest with the sparkle of rubies, emeralds and silver, and on his forehead he felt the soft touch of the crest that hung from the knight's helmet. He smiled strangely for a long while, until lifting his arms he slowly removed the golden helmet with the crest from his head. He placed it on the table and gazed at it with

flaming eyes from which after a while two large tears rolled down
his pallid cheeks.

"Farewell, powerful Samson, great among men! You have taught
me that there are heroic deeds in this world, a great love toward
people, beautiful Delilahs and . . . small, weak, unhappy Shymshels."

He had learned that never had he been great, or wise, or happy
. . . and he wrung his hands with such vehemence that the bones
cracked in their joints, and then he placed them on the back of his
neck and began to unclasp his necklace of rubies, emeralds, and silver.
He unfastened it and took it off and held it in both hands, stretched
in front of him. From beyond that net of shining strings gleamed his
black eyes, brimming with large tears.

"Farewell, powerful Samson, great among men . . ."

He then raised his eyes and his hands holding the necklace dropped
to his knees. He saw before him a picture of which he at first did not
know the meaning. Before him the gloomy depth of the room was
strewn with six pairs of lively, glistening points. These points were
human eyes and they shone at various levels and at various distances
from each other, but the human figures to which they belonged were
completely hidden in the dark. The six pairs of eyes were staring at
Shymshel's face and expressed admiration, wonder and joyful astonishment. As he lowered his hands which held the necklace to his knees,
these points, black, blue, gray, but all burning with a shining luster,
began to move toward him. Above, at the highest point, he noticed
two other lights. They were golden like two ducats and a monotonous,
loud purr issued from the spot from which they shone.

It was the gray cat which sat high in the opening of the oven, looking at the master of the house and purring. Lower, was the family
group, asleep when Shymshel had arrived, but which awoke later
and, sitting on the floor, each in the place where the awakening had
found him gazed at the radiant costume of husband and father . . .

Thus they all sat and had been looking for some time, holding
their breath in order not to startle the vision in crimson and gold
which seemed like an apparition from their dreams. Tsipa was first
to slip out of the gloom, furtively, very quietly, crawling rather than
walking toward her husband's knees.

She sat down again as she reached his knees, lifted her dark,
wrinkled face enclosed by the rim of a black round cap worn at night
instead of the wig, laced her hands over the quilted skirt with the
blue stockinged feet showing from under it, opened her mouth and
looked at his face with eyes suffused with the honey of tenderness.

Behind her the fiery-haired heads of little Mendel and Esther
emerged out of the gloom. Enoch strained forward his wan, thin
face, above which appeared a crumpled rim of a hat pushed to the

back of his head. Liba stood up behind all of them with her braid undone to half its length, holding little Lezer in her arms.

All were silent.

And Shymshel was silent for a long while, looking in turn at the figures that now surrounded him closely.

Then his eyes encompassed them all, and quickly hiding his face in both his hands, he was shaken with a loud wailing.

Crying thus he said:

"My poor children! Oh, my poor, poor little fish, my diamonds. What am I to do for you? What can I do for you? I myself am so poor, weak, small and so—ignorant, and so—stupid. And you will always be poor, small and ignorant and stupid."

Suddenly he stopped crying and moaning and sprang up from the stool. Standing at the window, he gazed deep into the darkness. He stood thus for a while until he saw again . . . a great and long band of gold which against the dark backdrop of night formed a golden ladder, its rungs filled with angels and at the peak, weaving garlands, the white, the merciful angel of prayer, crowned with suffering.

Shymshel turned toward his family and snatched little Lezer from Liba's arms . . .

Had someone stood in the cramped dark yard outside the window in which the dim lamp was shining, he would have seen a singular scene:

At the back of the gloomy room, at its farthest corner, still shone the golden eyes of the cat as if suspended in mid-air. Closer, the thin, wan faces of Liba and Enoch, their lips opening in astonishment, rose out of the gloomy background. Closer still little Esther and Mendel stood holding hands, their wide-open blue eyes almost hidden by the great masses of fiery locks that fell on their brow. Near them Tsipa in the round cap that clung to her head, frightened and saddened at her husband's weeping folded her dark hands over her bosom; and closest of all, just by the window, a tall Jew with tousled, black hair, wearing a scarlet robe that shone with gold embroidery, bending over the table, holding in both his outstretched hands the two-year-old child in a gray shirt. Almost touching it to the window pane, and sending his beseeching, tearful look somewhere high above, he cried in a loud voice:

"Sandalfon! Sandalfon! Pray that Jehovah make him a 'Powerful Samson!'"

Translated by KRYSTYNA CEKALSKA

Maria Konopnicka

(1842–1910)

Although primarily a poetess, Konopnicka is also one of the most gifted short-story writers of Polish literature. She was born in Suwalki in 1842 and educated in Warsaw. Outside the schools she learned several foreign languages and acquired a considerable poetic erudition. Her first volume of poems was published in 1881, and she continued to write prolifically until her death. Her output includes poems, short stories, critical studies, children's books and translations of foreign authors. In 1882 she edited the journal *Swit* (Dawn). In 1890 she was expelled from Warsaw by an administrative decree. She spent a number of years abroad in Munich, France, Switzerland and Italy. In 1902, her sixtieth birthday and twenty-fifth anniversary of her literary work were celebrated in Cracow and in Lwow by public ovations. She spent the rest of her life in the Sub-carpathians in a summer cottage which was the nation's gift to her greatest woman poet.

Konopnicka's literary work coincided with the period in which the labor and peasant movements began to organize and there was an enhanced awareness of social problems. The main themes of her poetry and prose deal with the little man's plight. She is indignant about the misery she sees about her, and she puts her poetic gift at the service of the people whose lives she observed closely. Without didacticism, she preaches the cause of the oppressed, allowing their simple stories to speak for themselves.

Konopnicka's numerous poetry collections reflect her versatility; they are rich in color and thematic variety. A great number of her poems have been set to music and have become popular as folk tunes.

Many of her poems are motivated by her sociological and moral earnestness, but there are also numerous pure lyrics which are considered outstanding by the critics. The latter are divided in their appraisal of Konopnicka's modern peasant epic, "Mr. Balcer in Brazil" (1909); some regard it highly, while others feel it lacks the genuine epic quality. Her stories, however, need no critics to prove their vitality. They are still being published and widely read, and some, like "German Boys," "Our Jade," "Smoke," "Urcanowa" and "Township Charity" are often cited as masterpieces of the genre. These stories are beautifully put together and, as all of her work, they reveal the author's warm sympathy for suffering mankind.

Still Life

I am sorry, extremely sorry, but I am not able to tell you what he looked like, the way he stood up or walked about, how he moved his hands or his head, or he stooped or kept himself erect, nor can I say anything about the sound of his voice or the color of his eyes. Not because I wish to keep all this a secret, but because I made his acquaintance at a time when he was exceptionally still, with his head motionless, his eyes closed, his hands folded, and not a sound, not a breath left in his chest. He lay in his coffin.

It was a plain pine-wood coffin, varnished black, with a flat tin cross nailed to the lid, and four candles, right and left of it, stuck in heavy pewter candlesticks that were the property of the chapel of the hospital. They were lighted at the very last moment, just as the hearse, drawn by a single horse, rattled over the rugged pavement and stopped in front of the chapel. The driver climbed down from his seat to unbutton the edges of the black cloth covering the wooden bottom of the vehicle that had been pinned up to prevent them from being frayed. The gate of the hospital squeaked, and out came the janitor; the hearse driver went up to him, accepted some of his snuff, made use of it with due deliberation, sneezed, wiped his nose and mustache with the sleeve of his funeral coat, and they began to chat. The funeral horse took advantage of this, lowered his head, nodded a couple of times, narrowed his bloodshot eyes, and fell asleep.

Meanwhile the little chapel bell set in with its raucous, monotonous rattle, the attendants opened the chapel door from the inside, and a handful of passers-by who had stopped at the sight of the hearse and waited at the sidewalk opposite, hastily entered. There were some nine or ten of them. An old beggar wrapped in a well-worn uniform coat, the janitress of the third house upstreet, the washerwoman from across the street, a cobbler's apprentice carrying a last, a bunch of kids, a gentleman with his collar raised and a misanthropic grin on his face, who had stepped out of the corner bar, and finally a barefoot, weather-beaten peasant in a coarse linen garb, his mud-stained hands pressing a discolored cap tightly against his bare chest.

The women crossed themselves as they entered, drew nearer to the coffin and knelt down sighing loudly, indifferently; the men stopped at the threshold, answered the old man's time-honored greeting with the traditional "forever and ever," and took a pinch of snuff from him. As for the children, they immediately swarmed out noisily to every corner, touching with their fingers the candlesticks, the black wooden box on which the coffin was standing, and the walls on whose dead-white surface danced the yellow reflections of the gently flickering lights of the four thin tapers. The little bell continued its tuneless, raucous buzzing.

Suddenly a squat, sturdy nun entered through the side door leading to the hospital passage; she bent a knee before the crucifix on the main wall, but rose immediately and turned towards the door with a rapid, almost soldierly movement. Following on her heels, in came two attendants; they, too, knelt down, crossed themselves and stood up ready to get hold of the coffin and take it out.

Quite obviously, this was a place where no time was wasted on any idle loitering. If you must be born, get born; if you must die, die; and if you want to be buried, let's get over with it, for there are ten others waiting—being born and dying.

One could read all this in the keen gray eyes of the nun that kept gazing at the entrance door with impatience.

Meanwhile the people stirred and moved up to kiss the hand of the reverend sister: children first, then the adults. Only the peasant remained standing at the threshold, a dull, empty stare in his wide-open eyes.

"Who's it that died, Reverend Sister," asked the janitress.

"Oh, just one of those folks," replied the nun casually, waving her hand with the wide sleeve, without as much as looking at the woman. Indeed. Where hundreds are dying, what does one of them matter?

"Any kids left behind?" the janitress continued her inquiry.

"Oh, certainly, some three or four . . ."

The nun shrugged as though pitying the blindness of those who die leaving children behind; yet her eyes did express some concern over the fate of those three or four.

The janitress and the washerwoman heaved a sigh and nodded.

At that very moment, three children stumbled against the high threshold and came into the chapel. They seem to have walked a long way, for their faces looked very hot and sweaty.

The oldest, a girl about ten, wearing a gray threadbare little frock, a flat hat with a black ribbon and shoes that were rather down on their heels, was holding two boys by their hands; the younger one, aged about five, was waddling precariously on his little bowlegs, hardly able to keep pace with his sister. Both boys were holding bast hats in their hands, their hair stood up like a brush, and they wore wide black ruffles round their neck that contrasted sadly with the colored patches on their spencers and trousers. The coarse shoes on their bare tanned feet stamped ahead noisily.

"Come on, come on, hurry up, now," urged the nun standing by the coffin. "Why do you come so late? And where's that grandmother of yours?"

She didn't wait for an answer and pulled at the girl's sleeve.

"Kneel down here and say your prayers: three times 'Our Father,' three 'Aves,' and three 'Last Prayers,' But hurry up."

The boys gazed at the nun with frightened eyes; deep color rose to the sallow cheeks of the girl, her lips trembled, her eyes filled with tears.

"That the daughter?" asked the janitress in a low voice.

"Yes, the oldest daughter."

"They still got their mother?"

"No, they haven't; she died here last autumn."

"What did he die of?" inquired the washerwoman.

"Heaven knows, my dear. Consumption, or something. He coughed and coughed, and then he died."

"Was he an artisan?" asked the gentleman with the raised collar, fingering his yellowish beard.

"Him, an artisan?" said the nun, with a shrug. "A messenger's what he was."

"Well, children, are you ready?" she turned to the three kneeling youngsters.

The girl was still holding her brothers' hands, staring at the coffin; heavy, glistening tears were rolling down upon her little gray dress.

The orphans jumped up as at a command.

"Well, there's no use waiting any longer. If the grandmother hasn't shown up yet, she is obviously not coming at all. Get busy and carry it out."

The pall bearers standing near the coffin reached for it.

Just then there was some shuffling at the door, the tapping of a cane probing the way ahead for the old legs of an old, half-blind woman; she came along all by herself, her white, sightless eyes wide open, her thin, desiccated arm outstretched groping.

"The grandmother, it's the grandmother," they whispered near the threshold, and the little group stepped back to make way for her.

"Come on, little grandmother, come on, give me your hand," said the nun eagerly, wishing to lead the blind woman to the coffin.

But the old woman waved her away with her bony hand.

"No, no, I don't need anyone. I can see everything. I can manage all right, I see everything. Are you there, Kazia?" she asked in the same breath, in a cold hard voice.

The little girl let go of the boys' hands, walked up to her grandmother and kissed her hand.

"They've put the lid on already, have they?"

"Yes, grandma, they have ..." and the girl burst out in irrepressible sobbing.

"Well, they gotta open it again. Let'em open it. I've brought this here along to put under his head ... If he's gotta be buried let him be buried with ..."

With trembling hands she unfolded a piece of percale with some braid stitched on around it, and cheap little ribbon bows in the four corners.

"This gotta be put under his head ... Let'em open the coffin ..."

She opened her sightless eyes even wider and walked straight towards the coffin till her hands touched it; then she took one step back and murmured something dejectedly.

"Kazia," she cried out again, but her voice broke suddenly, and her sunken lips continued to move without a sound.

The nun beckoned to the pall bearers. One of them slipped down the lid that had not yet been nailed on.

That was when I saw the wax-colored face of the deceased with a hard, gloomy expression frozen on it. His hands were folded on his chest, with a brightly colored picture stuck between them, and his legs, stretched out painfully, seemed to be taking a rest, at last, after all those long, long errands he had had to run delivering a letter here, a parcel there . . .

The people drew nearer and stood on tiptoe.

The other pall bearer slipped his hands under the body and half raised it.

"Put it in, Missus, he's heavy," he told the old woman.

But she didn't let go of her kerchief.

"If you think I'll let anyone . . . It's my job, I'm his mother," she mumbled, her heavy cane knocking at the steps of the platform. "How could I let anyone else . . . It's me that's borne him. It's me that'll tuck him in now he's dead . . ."

But she couldn't climb those steps. Perhaps it was her strength that failed her, perhaps the steps were too shaky to offer sufficient support; anyway, she couldn't make it.

"Kazia, give me a hand, Kazia," she ordered in a different tone.

The girl ran up and put her arm round her waist.

"This way, grandma, there . . ." she said, directing the blind woman's hands, "here's his head, right here . . ."

"Hurry up now, put it down, Missus! Put it down, I say!" cried the pall bearer impatiently.

The old woman did not seem to hear him. She dropped her cane on the floor and was arranging her son's last resting place with her bony hands fumbling inside the coffin.

"You were so afeared you'd have a hospital funeral, sonny," she murmured in a low voice, "see now you've got your own private funeral sonny, not a hospital funeral, no . . . And you won't have to lie in any common hold with others . . . Don't you be afeared . . . You got a coffin all to yourself, it's paid for, not just borrowed; and your own plot in the churchyard, too, the rent's all paid . . . Twenty years' rent, sonny, to lie in consecrated ground . . . You got a hearse, you got four candles, you got everything. I spent fifteen rubles, sonny, just for you, not for myself. I've kept nothing for myself, nothing, sonny. Now that you've gone before me, what use would it be to me?"

There was grief and pride in her voice. Her gray head kept trembling.

The people around sighed. The nun, both hands shoved deep into her sleeves, recited the Pater Noster aloud.

"Are you through, at last, or aren't you?" yelled the pall bearer furiously, and without waiting any longer, he let the body fall back onto the blind woman's hands.

"Oh, oh," she broke into a moan and bent over the coffin. "Oh, oh, take me with you, Joseph, take me home . . . to the eternal home."

Her gray head was shaking convulsively, and big, heavy tears rolled down her cheeks and fell on her son's chest. There was a moment of silence, broken only by the sobbing of the woman. The children looked around terrified. The nun began to recite the Ave.

Then the blind woman drew herself up and stood erect.

"Kazia," her voice had regained its former harshness, "pick up the kids, hold them up here; let'em say good-by to their father."

The girl lifted the smaller boy with a big effort and held him up to the coffin.

"Kiss your father's hand, Manny," she told him, breathing hard. But the little fellow was scared and turned his face away from the coffin.

"Go on, kiss it, do as you're told," insisted his sister holding him up in the air.

The grandmother stretched out her hand, felt for her grandson's head and pressed it down to touch the folded hands of the dead man.

"Julie," said the girl, letting the little one down, "It's your turn now to say good-by to father."

The older boy climbed up by himself, stood on tiptoe and kissed his father's sleeve.

Grandmother pressed his head down, too, against the father's chest.

"Look and remember," she said, "that, though your father's died at the hospital, he got his own funeral . . . got his own coffin and everything else. Now, don't you ever forget that!"

"God almighty," the impatience of the pall bearer was rising, "if there was that much fussing over everyone, there wouldn't be time to handle half of what's passing through our hands!"

The girl pulled her grandmother away, and down came the hammer; a score of blows, and the lid was on.

"How about the plate? Where's the plate?" asked the old woman with a start.

They fetched the plate from a corner.

She passed her hand over the coffin and pointed to a place:

"Right here, nail it on right here. And the cope's got to show on the outside."

By "cope" she meant the piece of percale whose edges were left to show a bit.

"Kazia," she added, "you watch them nail it on straight. It's all been paid for. . . . And the ribbon's got to show, too."

Two blows of the hammer sufficed to nail the tin plate to the coffin. It read:

> Joseph Szczeptek
> Town Messenger
> lived to be 43

One could hardly expect more detailed information on meeting a person for the first time.

"Lift it! A bit further to the right. No, not that way, this way. Now, higher up. That does it!" the pall bearers shouted alternately, then the coffin was on its way out.

The old beggar moaned and began to recite the Prayer for the Dead in a loud voice. He counted on due appreciation.

The old woman started fumbling nervously in her pockets.

But she couldn't find anything.

"I'm sure there was still something left, a grosz or maybe two," she mumbled.

I approached and held out my hand to the girl, offering her some silver coins.

She understood, picked up two coins without a word and handed them to her grandmother.

"Here you are, grandma . . ." she said.

The blind woman threw back her head and stretched her arm out toward the beggar.

"Here you are," she said, "for Joseph's soul. And don't you ever go round telling you've had to pray for nothing. If there's a funeral, let things be done in a proper way."

Then she walked out of the chapel slowly, carrying her head high, feeling her way with her cane.

On The Road—A Greek Vignette

On his way to Syracuse, Timon of Athens encountered a powerful man, almost godlike in build, bearing on his shoulders a small sack that was almost empty, yet bending to the ground under its weight. A strange and laughable sight.

"What are you carrying thus, Hercules?" asked Timon scornfully.

The man stopped; catching his breath with difficulty, he wiped his brow with the back of his enormous hand and replied:

"The most unbearable of burdens."

"Is that so?" laughed Timon. "Then it must be Clitias' manner of speech!"

Clitias was known throughout Athens for his stuttering and awkward way of speaking.

"You are mistaken," replied the man, "his speech is like a feather that could easily be carried in the beak of a sparrow flying to build a nest under your roof."

"Ho, ho," laughed Timon, "you seem to be a stranger here, you have never been to the Agora! But if your sack is so very heavy it must needs be laden with the pride of Trasiculus?"

"That's not it, either," replied the Syracusan, straightening his back with an effort. "Trasiculus with all his pride is but a vesicle that I should be quite ready to carry around Helicon three times on the tip of my finger, were it not for his evil smell of mush that would compel me to wash my hands in seven waters."

"Ha, ha, ha," laughed Timon, "I see you are quite an orator. Now then, if it is not the pride of Trasiculus, might it be the virtue of your Syracuse women who are said to have such big teeth that every husband must knock them out with his fist before he takes the first kiss."

"He would be unwise to do that," said the wanderer, "for no woman has teeth larger than are needed to obey the law of decency and hold her tongue where it belongs. As for their virtue, I have seen adolescents play with it in the streets of Syracuse, and I must admit, it was one of the finest disks ever tossed about by the deft hand of a Greek."

"Oh, you venomous giant!" exclaimed Timon gaily.

But then he suddenly turned serious and said:

"Perhaps, then, it is the reign of your tyrant, the great Dionysius, that you are carrying?"

"Once again you are mistaken, my friend," retorted the Syracusan. "If his reign were as heavy as my sack, believe me, it would cease to exist tomorrow, and Dionysius would no longer be the great Dionysius. Demos has a peculiar gristle back of his neck that he will let no one touch. On that gristle men, stronger than you and I, have broken their teeth."

"You intrigue me," said Timon, drawing nearer. "I know that nowadays philosophers go round the market places, sowing their wisdom, so that it may grow on the stones. One of those bearded men of Athens recently said that the heaviest thing in Greece is the tears of the helots. Perhaps it is those tears that you are carrying in your sack, brother?"

"What I bear is heavier even than the tears of the helots," said the man.

"What is it, then, in the name of Zeus?" cried Timon, his eyes blazing.

"The laughter of the helots, gleaned in the market place of Syracuse," replied the man. And he continued on his toilsome way, bending under his heavy burden.

Translated by ILONA RALF SUES

Boleslaw Prus

(1847–1912)

Boleslaw Prus (pseudonym of Alexander Glowacki), the Balzac of Polish literature, was born at Hrubieszow in 1847. When he was sixteen, he participated in the uprising of 1863, and was injured by a shell and badly burned. He was later released from Russian imprisonment, his eyesight permanently impaired by the shell wound.

He was educated in Warsaw and Pulawy, his main interest being sociology and economics. In 1872 he took a job in the Warsaw factory of Lilpon and Rau which manufactured railroad cars. But he soon turned to journalism, and his articles surveyed many sore spots of national life. His "Weekly Chronicles" made him famous but while he continued to write articles for various magazines, he turned to short stories and novels, reaching the heights of excellence in fiction as well as in journalism.

Prus was the most representative writer of Polish Positivism, but he never became dogmatic. He was primarily concerned with social and cultural progress, and in his short stories and novels he realistically portrayed many facets of his society. In *The Returning Wave* (1880), he depicted the life of industrial workers of Lodz; in *The Outpost* (1886), the fate of the peasant struggling to hold his land against the German; in *The Doll* (1890)—which is his acknowledged masterpiece—a shopkeeper hero spurned by an impoverished, aristocratic girl; in *The Emancipated Women* (1893), a new generation of Polish women; in *The Pharaoh* (1895), he presented under an Egyptian disguise, the social and political ills of Poland, and in *The Children* (1909), he revealed the terrible plight of the Polish people during the period of reaction following 1905.

The "Chronicles" of Prus contained a great deal of material that was later encompassed in his short stories and novels. Prus became one of Poland's outstanding short-story writers, displaying great variety in subject matter and structure. His best-known story is perhaps "The Vest" which appeared in English translation. (His novels *The Outpost* and *The Pharaoh* have also been published in English.) There are several collections of his stories, *From the Legends of Ancient Egypt* (1888) being one of them.

Prus' fiction, as well as his journalism, provides a true panorama of nineteenth-century Poland. His many-sidedness, the richness of his characterizations, his profound understanding of the social scene, and his epic style have invited comparison with Tolstoy; his kindly but not always painless humor reminds one of Chekhov.

Prus was a quiet, bespectacled little man, who for the greater part of his life suffered from agoraphobia, and scarcely moved outside the city limits of Warsaw. He tried to overcome his weakness by taking a trip through Europe, but, unlike the German character of "In the Mountains" (reprinted here), he could not rid himself of dizziness by the application of the principle "like is cured by like."

From Legends of Ancient Egypt

Behold, how futile are human hopes in the face of the order of the world; behold, how futile in the face of the judgment which the Eternal One has written in fiery signs across the heavens. . . .

The centenarian Ramses, powerful ruler of Egypt, was dying. A strangling demon who sucked his heart's blood, the strength of his arms and at times even the consciousness of his brain, had fallen upon the breast of this sovereign at whose voice millions had trembled for half a century. He, the great Pharaoh, lay like a felled cedar on an Indian tiger skin, his feet covered with the triumphal cape of an Ethiopian king. Stern even toward himself, he called the wisest of physicians from the temple of Karnak and said:

"I know that you have powerful drugs which either kill or heal immediately. Prepare one suitable to my illness and let it end once and for all . . . one way or another."

The physician hesitated.

"Consider, Ramses," he whispered, "that since you descended from the heavens above, the Nile has overflowed a hundred times. Could I administer to you a drug that is precarious even for the youngest of your warriors?"

Ramses sat up in bed.

"I must be very ill indeed," he shouted, "when you, priest, have the courage to give me advice. Be silent and do what I tell you. For Horus, my thirty-year-old grandson and heir, is alive. And Egypt cannot have a ruler who is unable to mount a chariot and carry a spear."

When the priest offered the dreadful medicine with a trembling hand, Ramses quaffed it off as a thirsty man drinks a cup of water. Then Ramses summoned the most illustrious astrologer from Thebes and ordered him to tell frankly what was written in the stars.

"Saturn is in conjunction with the moon," the wiseman replied, "which portends death to a member of your dynasty, Ramses. You have done wrong to drink the medicine today. For vain are human plans in the face of the judgment the Eternal One inscribes upon the heavens."

"It is only natural that the stars foretell my death," replied Ramses. "And when will this take place?" He turned to the physician.

"Before sunrise, Ramses, you will either be as hale as a rhinoceros, or your sacred ring will be on the hand of Horus."

"Bring Horus," Ramses said in a weakening voice, "to the Hall of the Pharaohs; there let him await my last words and the ring so that there be not a moment's pause in the conduct of the government."

Horus wept (for his heart was full of pity) at the approaching death of his grandfather; but because there could be no pause in the conduct of the government, he went to the Hall of the Pharaohs surrounded by a large number of servants.

He sat on the porch from which marble steps descended to the river below, and, filled with undefined sadness, gazed at his surroundings.

Just then, the moon, beside which glimmered Saturn, the star of evil omen, was tinting the metallic waters of the Nile with a golden hue, painting the shadows of the great pyramids on the meadows and gardens, and lighting the whole valley for several miles around. Despite the late night, lamps burned in the huts and buildings, and the people poured out under the open skies. Crowds of boats moved along the Nile as on a festive day; countless throngs were undulating in the palm groves, on the water's edge, in the market places, on the streets and beside the palace of Ramses. Yet it was so quiet that the rustle of water reeds and the wailing howl of hyenas in search for prey reached the ears of Horus.

"Why are they gathering thus?" Horus asked one of the courtiers, pointing to the endless field of human heads.

"They wish to greet you, Sire, as the new Pharaoh and to hear from your lips of the beneficences you intend to confer upon them."

And this was the first time that the heart of the Prince was lapped by the pride of greatness as the steep shores are lapped by the running sea.

"And what do those lights mean?" Horus inquired further.

"The priests have gone to the grave of your mother, Zephora, in order to bring her body to the catacombs of the Pharaohs."

Grief for his mother was reawakened in the heart of Horus. The severe Ramses had had her remains buried among the slaves because she had been charitable towards them.

"I hear the neigh of horses," said Horus listening intently. "Who is riding out at this hour?"

"Sire, the Chancellor ordered the messengers to repair for your teacher, Jetron."

Horus sighed at the memory of his beloved friend whom Ramses had banished from the country for instilling in the soul of the grandson loathing for war and pity for the downtrodden people.

"And the light beyond the Nile?"

"With that light," the courtier answered, "the faithful Berenice greets you from the cloister prison. The High Priest has already dispatched the Pharaoh's boat for her; and when the sacred ring flashes on your hand, the heavy cloister gates will open and she will return to you, loving and yearning."

Hearing these words, Horus asked no more; he became silent and covered his eyes with his hand.

Suddenly he hissed with pain.

"What is it, Horus?"

"A bee has stung me in my leg," the pale Prince replied.

The courtier examined his leg by the greenish light of the moon.

"Praise be to Osiris," he said, "that it was not a spider, for at this hour its venom is deadly."

Oh! how futile are human hopes in the face of unalterable judgment. . . .

Just then the commander of the army entered and bowing before Horus said:

"The great Ramses, feeling that his body is growing cold, has sent me to you commanding thus: 'Go to Horus, for I will not be long of this earth, and carry out his will as you have been carrying out mine. Though he ordered you to yield Upper Egypt to the Ethiopians and to conclude a brotherly alliance with this enemy, obey him when you see my ring on his hand. For the Immortal Osiris speaks through the mouths of the rulers."

"I will not yield Egypt to the Ethiopians," said the Prince, "but I will make peace because I grieve for the blood of my people; write an edict directly and hold riders in readiness so that, when the first fires light in my honor, they may be ready to run toward the noon sun and carry grace to the Ethiopians. . . . And write a second edict that, from this hour until the end of time, never is a prisoner to have his tongue pulled out from his mouth on the field of battle. I have spoken. . . ."

The commander fell on his face and then retired to write down the commands, whereas the Prince instructed the courtier to examine his wound again for it caused him great pain.

"Your leg is somewhat swollen, Horus," said the courtier. "To think what would have happened if a spider had stung you instead of a bee. . . ."

Now, the Chancellor of State entered the hall, and bowing to the Prince, said:

"The mighty Ramses, seeing that his sight is failing, sent me to you with the following command: 'Go to Horus and blindly carry out his will. Even though he order you to release the slaves from their chains and to distribute all the land to the people, you are to do it when you see my sacred ring on his hand, for the immortal Osiris speaks through the mouths of the rulers!"

"My heart does not go so far," said Horus, "but prepare an edict directly saying that fees and taxes for land tenure are to be lowered by a half and that slaves are to be granted three days' rest from labor, also that without court sentence they are not to be beaten on their backs with a stick. Also write an edict recalling from banishment my teacher, Jetron, who is the wisest and noblest of all Egyptians. I have spoken. . . ."

The Chancellor fell on his face, but before he could retire to write the edicts, the High Priest entered.

"Horus," he said, "at any moment the great Ramses may depart for the country of shadows, and Osiris will weigh his heart on an infallible scale. When the sacred ring of the Pharaohs flashes on your hand, command and I shall obey you, though you should want to destroy the miraculous temple of Amon, for Immortal Osiris speaks through the mouths of the rulers."

"I shall not destroy," replied Horus, "but build new temples and increase the treasuries of the priests. I demand only that you write an edict for the ceremonial transfer to the catacombs of the body of my mother, Zephora, and a second edict . . . for the release of my beloved Berenice from the cloister prison. I have spoken. . . ."

"Your deeds are wise," the High Priest replied. "Everything is prepared for the execution of these orders, and I shall write the edicts anon; when you touch them with the ring of the Pharaohs, I shall light this lamp to announce favors to the people and freedom and love to your Berenice."

The wisest physician of Karnak entered.

"Horus," he said, "your pallor does not surprise me, for Ramses, your grandfather, is dying. The mightiest of the mightiest could not withstand the power of the medicine I did not wish to administer. Only the deputy of the High Priest has remained with him to take off his finger the sacred ring when he dies and give it to you as a sign of unlimited power. But you are growing paler, Horus," he added.

"Examine my leg," Horus groaned and fell on the golden chair, the arms of which were carved in the form of hawks' heads.

The physician kneeled, examined the leg and moved back in horror.

"Horus," he whispered, "you have been bitten by a very poisonous spider."

"Am I to die? . . . at such a moment? . . . Horus asked in a scarcely audible voice.

Then he added:

"Will this happen soon? . . . tell me truthfully. . . ."

"Before the moon hides behind that palm. . . ."

"Ah so . . . And Ramses, will he live long? . . ."

"Do I know? . . . The ring may be on its way to you now."

Just then, the ministers entered with the edicts.

"Chancellor," Horus called, catching him by the hand, "if I were to die now, would you carry out my commands? . . ."

"Horus, may you live to the age of your grandfather," the Chancellor replied. "But, were you to stand before the judgment of Osiris directly after him, every one of your edicts will be executed with the sacred ring of the Pharaohs."

"With the ring," Horus repeated, "but where is it?"

"One of the courtiers told me," the Commander whispered, "that the Great Ramses is breathing his last."

"I sent word to my deputy," the High Priest added, "to remove the ring as soon as Ramses' heart stops beating."

"Thank you . . ." said Horus, "I grieve . . . Oh, how I grieve. . . . But all of me shall not die. . . . My blessings, peace and happiness shall remain after me and . . . my Berenice shall regain her freedom. . . . Is it far from me now? . . ." he asked the physician.

"Death is a thousand soldier's paces from you," the physician answered sadly.

"Do you hear, is anyone coming thence? . . ." asked Horus.

Silence.

The moon was approaching the palm and touched its first leaves; the fine sand rustled softly in the hourglass.

"How far? . . ." Horus whispered.

"Eight hundred paces," the physician replied. "I do not know whether you will succeed in touching all the edicts with the holy ring Horus, even were they to bring it to you directly. . . ."

"Give me the edicts," said the Prince, hearkening for hurried steps from Ramses' chambers. "And you, physician," he turned to the doctor, "tell me how much life remains so that I may ratify at least those instructions most dear to me."

"Six hundred steps," the physician whispered.

The edict on the reduction of fees for the people and labor for the slaves fell to the ground from Horus' hand.

"Five hundred . . ."

The edict on peace with the Ethiopians slipped from the knees of the Prince.

"Is someone coming? . . ."

"Four hundred," replied the physician.

Horus became thoughtful and . . . the order concerning the transfer of Zephora's body fell.

"Three hundred . . ."

The same fate befell the edict on recalling Jetron from banishment.

"Two hundred . . ."

Horus' lips became livid. His stiffened hand threw to the ground

the edict forbidding the pulling out of tongues of captured prisoners.
He kept only . . . the order freeing Berenice.

"One hundred . . ."

The tapping of sandals was heard amidst a deathly silence. The
deputy of the High Priest ran into the hall. Horus put forth his hand.

"A miracle! . . ." the new arrival exclaimed. "The Great Ramses
has regained his health. . . . He has risen from his bed and wants
to leave at sunrise to hunt lions. . . . He summons you, Horus, as
a sign of grace, to accompany him. . . ."

Horus' dying gaze turned toward the Nile where the light glimmered in Berenice's prison and two tears, tears of blood, rolled down
his cheeks.

"Do you not answer, Horus?" the surprised messenger asked.

"Do you not see that he is dead?" whispered the wisest physician
of Karnak.

Behold, human hopes are futile in the face of the judgment which
the Eternal One inscribes in fiery signs across the heavens.

Translated by KRYSTYNA CEKALSKA

In The Mountains

"My dear Sir," said a friend of mine, an odd fellow. "My dear Sir, the
homeopaths follow an excellent principle: 'like cures like.' For even
the usual practitioners treat smallpox with smallpox and Pasteur wants
to cure rabies with rabies. But why give such examples? . . . Let me
tell you about an experience I witnessed, whereby a man cured himself of an imaginary fear by means of real danger."

After this introduction, my friend lit a cigar and continued:

"I saw the Alps for the first time when I came to Thusis twenty
years ago. A few days after my arrival in the town, I set forth for a
little walk in company with a number of others. But on this occasion
I experienced such fear that, discouraged, I left Thusis immediately,
and for the next few years I could not stand the sight of mountains.
Six of us set out on the trip: two of us Poles, a German, an Englishman and two French ladies; we were all staying at the same hotel. We
did not take a guide because the Englishman knew the region, and
the peak we were to climb seemed as visible and easy as a chair in the
middle of the room. True, through the binoculars I saw several creases
running across the length and width of the mountain slope, but because they were no bigger than a furrow, I gave them no further
thought. I was even rather surprised that we started out at nine in the
morning for a short walk. Not wishing to admit that I hadn't the

slightest knowledge of the mountains, I made no comment, and during the trip behaved like a tourist who had at least walked the Himalayas. This attitude won general respect and especial affection from the German.

Naturally, I reciprocated in kind, for he was an unusually charming man. But he had one defect: he suffered from dizziness.

We had a gay time along the way: all of us, even the Englishman, romped like children. Only I was serious, and from every incline the German looked back and quoted excerpts from Virgil. He said that this was the best distraction from things one did not wish to see."

"Does your head swim here too?" I asked.

"Yes," he answered quickly, "but . . . let's not talk about it, because then I wouldn't take another step."

I became silent, and my German friend recited Virgil louder and glanced behind him more and more often. Once he even caught me by the hand and whispered in my ear:

"Your composure, Sir, is a source of courage to me. Were it not for you, I should have stopped on the way or . . . broken my neck. . . ."

Cold sweat covered my forehead because my spirit was in quite a different state from what my poor companion thought it to be.

I was especially deeply troubled by the fact that, despite the two hours' journey, the mountain we were to climb was not any closer; it seemed to me that it continued to be about a mile from us. But my dismay reached its peak when suddenly the mountain we were approaching disappeared and, instead, I saw a great mass of earth and rocks which began somewhere far below us and ended, it seemed, just below the stars.

The cliff we were climbing had the form of a huge staircase with steps a few hundred paces high. Every time I stood under one of these steps, I thought that at last this was the peak. However, after climbing fifteen minutes, I would find that we were not on the top, but on a new step or small field beyond which another step arose—and thus without end.

Meanwhile, the road was becoming wilder. The forest, grass, brush and even the soil disappeared. We walked on a layer of stones which gradually grew larger and slipped from under our feet with increasing ease. Giant mountain tops arrayed in plumes of clouds or ravines exuding a bluish mist surrounded us in growing numbers.

Occasionally, the mountain creases smoothed out; the huge steps and terraces disappeared and instead, I saw a slanting wall which slipped from under my feet to run steeply toward the sapphire forest slumbering a full verst deep. Once, when I forgot for a moment that I was on the mountain, it seemed to me that I was standing in a plain which suddenly sloped under my feet so that one part of it rose to

the sky while the other fell away somewhere to the depths of the earth.
My head swam and in order not to fall, I caught hold of the arms of the
German who was in front of me. He quickened his pace and we found
ourselves in a less steep spot.

"Thank you . . ." he whispered, clasping my hand tightly. "I feel
better now. . . . You saved my life. . . ."

I was stunned. Meanwhile, the ladies ahead of us were adjusting
their shawls and dresses which, according to them, were not arranged
aesthetically.

"What dreadful heat!" one of them exclaimed.

"Such an uncomfortable road!" lamented her companion.

After a quarter of an hour of easier going, the cliff we were ascend-
ing ended. I saw that we were surrounded on all sides by snow-
capped or bare mountain tops, that there was nothing, or rather only
the air, between them and us. I do not know why at that moment
I felt a calm pride and unreasonable rapture.

"We are at the top," said the Englishman, and bowing to the
ladies, he lit a cigar.

"What a beautiful view!" both ladies cried.

Then they drew mirrors out of their pockets and began to arrange
their somewhat disheveled hair.

"Two o'clock!" my compatriot announced in Polish. "Our dinner
has gone to the devil and perhaps supper too. . . ."

The German, meanwhile, sat down and, lowering his face to the
ground, began to recite Virgil.

"Do you see Thusis, Sir?" I asked him. "It looks like a few grains
of peas."

"No, I don't. I'm not looking at anything," he answered. "Moreover, I don't know if I'll be able to climb down. . . ."

The Englishman noticed the pallor of the German's face, shook
his head and handed him a flask of brandy. The poor, ailing man
took a drink and relaxed a little.

We had been sitting about a quarter of an hour, when a rather
cold wind began to blow. I was looking toward Thusis when I noticed a
strange phenomenon. In the deep gorge at our feet the blue mist
turned a brighter hue, then became sky blue, still lighter and finally
completely white. Then it quickly began to fill all the valleys so that it
seemed that we were surrounded by a sea of milk on which the mountain peaks floated. And not only did they float, but gradually they
began to submerge and sink. I clearly discerned a motion between
the fog and the mountains, but became terrified when I noticed that
the peak on which we stood had begun to fall. . . . I could have sworn
that we were dropping into the cloud below us, toward which we were
swiftly approaching.

"What does it mean?" one of the ladies asked the Englishman.

"The fog is rising," he replied somewhat pensively. "We must descend," he added.

"So we are not falling, but the fog is rising toward us . . ." I thought, greatly relieved.

But clouds have swift wings. We had not yet arisen from our seats, when the fog engulfed us on all sides and though it was day, it became so dark that we could not see a few paces ahead. We felt the dampness on our hands and faces; then it began to rain, then to rain and snow and finally the snow fell as thickly as during a winter storm at home.

Despite this, we walked on, holding each other's hands. The road was safe and the Englishman knew it very well. From time to time the slippery stones would give way underfoot and then—amid hearty laughter we would slide down a few feet. The German laughed the loudest. He was in excellent humor from the moment the fog veiled the mountain declivity and the chasm from his view.

In one of our stumbles we slid not the two or three feet, but about thirty feet downward. The ladies had begun to scream: "Oh! Oh!" —when we slowed down and felt the hard rock underfoot.

The German, greatly satisfied, was the first to rise, and extending his stick, wanted to move on. But the Englishman stopped him.

"Permit me," he said, "to get our bearings."

He groped his way for a few paces and soon vanished in the fog. "Ho! ho . . ."

"Would you like to use a compass?" my countryman asked.

"But of course. Show it to me," the Englishman replied, impatiently snatching the small compass my countryman used to adorn his watch chain.

The Englishman looked, turned the compass and his head, and finally clicked his tongue.

"We must stay here until the fog lifts," he said, smiling to the ladies.

Then he whispered to us:

"We've gone astray. We're on a different side of the mountain. . . ."

"How high are we?" asked the German.

"Perhaps half way down, but . . . I don't know."

"Maybe there's a ravine here somewhere?" the German asked.

"I'm not sure of that either," the Englishman replied. "At any rate, the ridge of this rock is very steep."

The ladies sat sullenly.

"What a pity we didn't bring our thermos of chocolate," one of them remarked.

It was already past four o'clock when a strong side gust of wind uncovered the horizon for a moment.

A shudder ran through me. I saw that we were sitting on a ledge several feet wide. Behind us rose a sloping cliff covered with slippery stones over which it was now impossible to climb, and in front of us —a mile below—a valley. . . .

There was no way to descend toward the valley from the ledge because, in this place, the rocky face of the mountain fell almost vertically.

"When do we go on?" one of the ladies asked.

"When the fog moves," replied the Englishman.

"And if it doesn't disappear by night?"

"We'll spend the night here."

"You're joking. . . ."

"Not at all," he replied solemnly. "We have fallen into a trap and we must be patient."

"Then, gentlemen, give some kind of signal," the other interjected. "The region is not uninhabited, perhaps someone will hear us. . . ."

"That's exactly what we intend to do. . . ."

My countryman had a revolver which he shot in the direction of the valley. But the noise was so weak that I doubted if anyone had heard it.

Meanwhile, the fog had become denser. The ladies enveloped themselves in their shawls and sat sadly while the German, with signs of great agitation, paced back and forth.

Suddenly, he seized my hand and led me aside. His face wore a wild expression.

"Sir," he said in a changed voice, "I know that we are sitting on the edge of an abyss and though I do not see it, the very thought makes my head swim so that . . . I can't stand it any longer. . . ."

"What will you do then?" I asked in amazement.

"I'll jump. I'd rather die than suffer so . . . I'm warning only you; it's best the others should know nothing. . . ."

"Have you gone mad?"

"Yes . . . I feel that I am mad. . . ."

At that moment, the Englishman approached us and before I had realized it, he had seized the madman. He wanted to tie the German's hands and said in a low voice to me:

"Throw a kerchief over his head. . . ."

But the unfortunate man wrested free, pushed both of us away and ran left along the ledge.

After a while we heard a heavy thud and a smothered rumble of rolling stones. . . .

"What's going on there?" one of the ladies called on hearing the noise.

"Nothing," answered the Englishman in a hollow tone. "Our friend is trying to climb up. . . ."

Then he whispered to me:

"Not a word about this or the rest will follow him. In this situation madness is contagious. Frightful situation. . . ."

He took a long gulp of brandy, offered me some and then . . . in a pleasant tenor voice intoned an aria from an operetta. The gloomy French women brightened and began to sing with the Englishman. Even my compatriot forgot his dinner and joined them in an off-key bass voice, constantly making mistakes in the melody.

Astonished and terrified, I alone remained silent. The singing on the brink of the abyss revealed to me the superhuman courage of the Englishman but also the horror of the situation.

"Sing!" one of the ladies called to me. "That's the best remedy for boredom and cold."

"It may also draw the attention of the mountaineers," the other added.

The three of them then began a new and gayer aria. This time my compatriot bellowed unceremoniously in Polish:

"The devil take you, you Englishman, you and your mountain! If I weren't afraid of the Swiss I'd eat you instead of my veal for dinner."

The Englishman politely turned his pale face toward the Pole and waved his hand in time to the tune.

Suddenly we heard a voice from below. The Englishman sprang to his feet and ran toward that part of the ledge from which the German had hurled himself.

"Hey-ho!" a voice called from below.

"Hey-ho!" we answered in a chorus.

The ladies kissed each other out of joy.

"I did not kill myself!" called the voice. "Come down this way! . . . The road is excellent!"

To our amazement, we recognized the voice of our German.

"You can jump off the ledge, gentlemen! It is barely a few feet high. . . . But you must carry the ladies down in your arms!" the German shouted.

"Thank God!" my countryman called. "I'll at least eat supper today!"

And he jumped straight into the fog.

Again we heard the rumble of stones and the lamenting voice of my countryman.

"Heaven help him and his road! I must have sprained a leg. . . ."

Then we heard a conversation below. Evidently, he had already met the German.

We all descended in turn despite the protestation of the ladies who by no means wanted to be in the arms of the Englishman. But finally they thought better of it: the rock here created a kind of shelf three to four feet high, from which one could descend only by jumping or with the aid of another person.

After leaving the fatal ledge, we found ourselves on a steep slope strewn with stones from top to bottom. Thus, the four of us holding each other's hands: the ladies in the middle and the Englishman and I on the ends, we did not walk but skidded noisily at high speed. Below and a little to the side we saw two shadows sailing in the fog: they were my compatriot and the thwarted suicide—the German. Despite our great speed, we skidded for nearly a couple of minutes over the steep mountain slope. But the lower we fell, the less dense the fog became. When we were in the middle of the slope we finally saw the valley with its few shepherds' huts.

When we all met on the meadow a quarter of an hour later, the Englishman took the German's arm and said to the ladies:

"Do you know, ladies, that an hour ago this man wanted to kill himself?"

Abashed, the suicide walked away and the French women, seeing the seriousness with which the Englishman spoke, began to laugh. Even my compatriot considered it an excellent joke. But when we told them what had happened, one of the ladies burst into tears and the other became hysterical.

Actually, we owed our lives to the temporary insanity of our companion. For the ledge hung over an abyss, and one could descend to the valley without danger to his life only in the one spot from which the German had jumped.

The remainder of his adventure was quite simple.

When he had hurled himself from the rock, he had landed on a layer of stones, and wanting to put an end to his dizziness, rushed blindly ahead. In a few minutes he passed through the fog and saw a safe road. Then, recovering from his fright, he climbed again with some difficulty in order to lead us down.

"And what do you say to this, Sir?" concluded my friend. "Since that experience, the German completely rid himself of dizziness. . . . He even became a member of the Mountain Climbers' Club, and today we often see his name on the list of tourists who climb the highest peaks."

Like cures like.

Translated by KRYSTYNA CEKALSKA

Stefan Zeromski

(1864–1925)

Although once named for the Nobel Prize, Stefan Zeromski is not too well known abroad because of the "Polish" character of his works. This outstanding novelist and dramatist was born at Strawczyna in the Kielce district of Russian Poland in 1864. He was raised in the shadow of the disastrous 1863 uprising, which loomed large in his fiction. He was educated in the Russian Gymnasium in Kielce—an experience he later used for his novel *Sisyphean Labors,* which has been called the *Nicholas Nickleby* of Polish fiction. Tragic circumstances in his family and tuberculosis made Zeromski leave Kielce before he finished his studies at the Gymnasium. He spent the next few years taking veterinary courses in Warsaw, serving a term in the Citadel for participation in conspiratorial activities, and tutoring in the country estates. He then traveled in Western Europe, and served as assistant librarian of the Polish National Museum in Rapperschwill on Lake Zurich (1892–1896). After returning to Poland in 1897 he worked as a librarian in Warsaw, and in 1904 turned to writing as a full-time occupation.

His first stories appeared as early as 1889, but recognition came with the two volumes of stories: *Tales* (1895) and *Ravens Will Tear Us to Pieces* (1896). Although Zeromski is a lyricist in style and sentiment, the stories were a shocking portrait of social ills in the country. This preoccupation with injustice and suffering produced his first masterpiece *Homeless People* (1900), a poignant novel about the frustrations of a Polish intellectual, who is inspired by a Promethean dream of improving the lot of his countrymen, and who falls victim of his own idealism. This book and his many other novels are marked by a highly poetic style, which sometimes becomes epic. Another acknowledged masterpiece of Zeromski is *The Ashes* (1904), a historical novel about the Napoleonic era of "heroic conflict," as he called it. His other more important novels are: *The Faithful River* (1913), *History of a Sin* (1908), *The Wind from the Sea* (1922), *The Fir Forest* (1925).

Several generations of Poland's youth were brought up on Zeromski's books, which encompassed Poland's history as well as its contemporary times. His novel *Early Spring* (1925) caused a storm of controversy which abated only with the death of the writer who was given a state funeral. Zeromski has been called a demonic artist, like Dostoyevsky, Strindberg or Beethoven, with the qualification that his demons were perhaps too clearly of Polish origin.

During his last years Zeromski mastered the dramatic form; his comedy *The Quail Fled from Me into the Millet* (1924) is both a successful picture of his own generation and an impressive feat of dramatic compactness.

Dream of a Sword

You went out into the darkest autumn night, where roared the gale and lashed the wind, while we, a nation of twenty millions, in our bedrooms, chambers, garrets, and subterranean kennels all slept the stony sleep of slaves. You went out stripped, like a smuggler, to the waist. On your shoulders you bore the parts of a printing press. You were loaded with leaflets that announced the deliverance of our bodies and our souls. In your left hand you grasped a pole with which you groped in the dark for the sentry guarding the frontiers of our land, and in your right you held a revolver, ready to shoot. Thus you crossed the border streams. You came into our country bare and with bleeding feet. In that night Independence was brought to this land of the poor in spirit, this night, too, was brought the declaration of the rights of the holy Proletariat, which the greater power of the rich had trodden underfoot. You brought us then priceless scrolls of Polish law from the sunken graves of the emigrants. You brought us "a second string" torn from the lyre of the immortals. Having stepped on to your native soil you followed the groans of the people. Your signpost was the moaning of the working man. Those of whom the Fatherland knew not, those by whose toil the world was fed, were found by you, lifted up, summoned and united into a comrades' camp of men who fight for freedom.

Who today will count the flaming brows that the frost of Siberia has chilled to steel? Whose understanding shall wade through the immensity of suffering that Polish Socialism has borne in chains? Who shall measure the length of the road it has trodden out in the snows, across the frozen furrows and the swamps of exile? Its name and unstained honor are today decried by the Polish journalist, who lives by trampling on the fires of idea. Aping the torturer, he debases the chivalrous shade of the soldier to the level of the specter of the scoundrel·who follows in his track and seizes the booty. Your steps, soldier, ring with a yearning echo in the recesses of the people's heart, as an echo resounds in the forest. As an echo in the dimness of the forest they die away. Yet you yourself are the people, and your blood seeps into the people. From the clotted puddles of blood, from those virgin recesses, are growing up wondrous legends such as Poland has not yet known. In people's souls are stirring dreams of the plume of fame.

For alone the Polish Muse will not desert you, will not decry you, soldier! She alone will not take fright at your dreams and deeds. Even if your cause were lost, she will keep her faith in you. She will see and bear in mind your days and nights, your pains, efforts, toil, and death. She will lay your head, bashed by the butts of the soldiery, on a pillow of the most wondrous verse, that in years to come she will take from the splendor of our ancient tongue. With a cloak of dignity, woven of the most wondrous colors of her art, she will cover your naked body that knows no belt of gold or robe of red, when the people of Lodz dig it up from the common pit, to give it the only thing the people can give, a pinewood coffin.

Into your hands grown stiff, hands that are powerless only in death, she will lay her golden dream, the dream of so many generations of the young, the dream of a knightly sword.

(Written in the year 1905.)[1]

Translated by M. A. MICHAEL

Dawn

They did not notice when the light of the candles paled and the objects in the room grew more distinct. In through the open window flowed a brisk chillness. The boughs and their branches, the twigs with leaves scarcely unfolded, grey with the frost of early morning, lay motionless in the emptiness of the windows, enfolded in unbreakable sleep. Yet now and then a cold, moist breeze came from off the water to hang among the branches of Spanish jasmin and huddled into their moist leaves, so as to fall asleep for a while beneath their roof on a slippery, barely sprouting branch and rest in a tonic morning snooze. Out of the misty distances emerged the gentle soft voice of a water-hen.

Day was breaking.

In the frames of the windows stretched the quiet blue, and in it dark veins began to sketch in the distant hills and the belts of trees in the valleys. High in the cloudless sky, like a lily, the morning star—that gable ornament—was shining its last. The dawn, coming in a rusty blaze from away beyond the earth, had already enfolded the fringe of the world.

Peter said:

"You have not even seen, Raphael, what it is like here with me. Come and look. The dawn's already here."

The two stood in the open window.

Lower down, just beyond the garden fence, you could see through the branches a sleeping pond. From the surface of its waters, which

---

[1] The year of a Socialist revolution in Russian-occupied Poland, as in Russia itself. The large manufacturing town of Lodz was the scene of bitter fighting.

were a pale cerulean, like steel that fire has blued, smoked wondrous-colored mists. The kindred of earth and heaven were leaving the water for the sky, parting from it with sorrow, like a soul when it discards its body. Yet, before they left, they stood above it as though sunk in prayer. It seemed then to those who saw it, that this moment should last forever, that just this was eternity, that just such is infinity. But a brightness approaching from afar sprinkled the shadows with hyssop, and at its sovereign signal the water remained alone there below, while the mists forsook its breast. They folded in their wondrous trailing raiment, unfolded transparent wings and, swooning, writhing in grief, vanished into the blue. There, where the dawn had not yet reached, in the depths of the alders, their blue sisters dreamed their yestereve-begun, still-nightly dream. Different were the trees among them: they had light blue leaves and their trunks appeared to be growing out of a snowy cloud. The distant sandbanks at the shallow water's edge were rosy, like the cheeks of a wakened child. Beyond the pond, on the flat-topped rise, stood an emerald tilled field, like a motionless shield, a-glisten with a crop of spring rye, that with its own life had already begun to turn into a living field.

Peter put his left arm round Raphael's waist, and Raphael shyly clasped his brother. They fell silent. Motionless they watched out that dawn, gazing at the wondrous waters, at the inexpressible color of the heavens that were gradually beginning to flame, at their live reflection in the motionless depths. It was so quiet that each could hear how the life that was in them flowed in the other.

From *The Ashes*, Vol. I.
Translated by M. A. MICHAEL

In the Mountains

The hounds had moved off into the forest.

The echo of their music grew fainter and fainter until finally it was drowned in the silence of the woods. It seemed, at whiles, that two almost imperceptible voices still throbbed among the trees—where, one could not tell. Now it would seem as though from Samson's Woods, now from the direction of Maple or Beech Wood, from Grassy Forest, now again as if from Stay Mountain. . . . When the breeze died away, there fell a silence as bottomless and unbounded as is the blue of the sky that shows between the clouds, and then there was nothing to be heard at all.

Round about stood firs with flattened tops, like tapering spires that have not been carried right to the cross. The bluish trunks gleamed in the darkness. Aged mosses hung down from their enormous branches. With vital roots thrust between the stones right down to the earthen base of the immense ramp of rocks, with the talons of their tortuous arms planted into every pocket of earth and sucking our every drop of moisture, these great firs had already been waving their regal tops among the mists of Bald Mountain for more than one century. Here and there stood one alone, whose branches had withered and stuck out like rungs cut by an axe. Only its top was bright green, with cones upraised, like a stork's nest towered above the expanse. The branches of the spruces, on which lay a heavy layer of snow, drooped towards the ground, bent into arches. Thrust out in their white coverings in every direction, near and far, these shaggy paws, covered with white and lined as if with mother-of-pearl, seemed to be lurking and lying in wait. The joyous green of the youngest terminal needles glistened like unsheathed claws. Every now and then, succumbing to their own weight, sensitive to every sigh of the wind, tiny particles would fall from these snowy wrappings and disappear into the white quilt on the ground with as little traces as drops of rain in the depths of a lake. From the tops floated down a scarcely perceptible powder, so light that it hung long in the air with crystals sparkling before it had sunk to the ground.

Towards midday a gentle thaw began to warm the snow. White clouds, permeated by the luster of the sun, floated across the pale blue expanse. Along the cruciform topmost branches of the spruces the melted ice was turning into huge drops, which on the dark green of the icicles hanging from the lignified moss, from the cracked and rugged bark, threw out sheaves of cold sparks. Lower down, beneath the swarthy shadow of the branches, was the earlier morning chill. Some young dwarf-spruces, reddish brown, but yellowish at the top, bowed by the excessive weight of the snow, held their tall heads to the very ground, unable to tear their frozen branches from it. Elsewhere the roots of stumps torn out of the ground by the harsh gales of the Mountains of the Holy Cross stuck up and formed yawning caverns of fear beneath the drifts.

Raphael stood motionless, leaning against the trunk of a thick beech, and listened intently.

Above him and before his eyes were stout, twisted, frozen branches the color of a perch's scales. Their thin, steel twigs were motionless and the great tree, with twists and coils like a man's taut muscles, seemed to be the very spirit of the frost. The giant beech stood alone, hard and cold, as though it did not belong among the trees. The king of Bald Mountain! Its branches do not tremble before the wind, nor does its trunk bend. Its spreading top, lifted above the woods, looks down from its dominating spur on to the broad valleys to the north and south, surveys the single arm of the mountains. Solitude everywhere, fields, villages . . . Far away, beyond the chain's last eminence, beyond Guardfield, fields stretch across as far as Forest Edge, right to the top of Stony Mountain. The age-old beech remembers from the springs of its youth unbroken forest in the valleys of Wolfden, Marshfields, Birchhill, on the mountains as far as Kielce. In its lifetime the forests of oaks had fallen beneath the axe. The wet, sour, impassable swamps, from which eternal waters oozed, had dried up among the plots of the peasants' clearings. There, where for centuries shaggy dwarf-spruce had grown and rotted, the wind whistles among stalks. The fields of cleared ground had eaten into the very fastnesses of its forest, leprous patches were spreading over the tattered fringe of its coat, from year to year forcing their way higher, up beyond the rock-encumbered tops of Doggers, Merryhill. . . . At the foot of the mountains the stagnant water, nourisher of trees, is drying up, leaving the red earth, that bares its stones to the sun. Only the juniper covers its nakedness and wounds. More and more seldom now do bears rub their shaggy bodies against the trunk of the old beech; more and more seldom comes the great-horned stag to dream in the shade of its branches, and the wolf, the hares' terror, does not so often lie in wait here for the dappled fawns of the roe-deer. No longer do eagles' wings whir above its mighty branches, and the vulture only flies thither from time to time to look from its top in horror and anger at its ruined heritage.

Contrary to the strict rules of the chase, Raphael had walked away from the stance and furtively made his way to the summit on the hill. For a moment he stood there where the forest ended and, seized with a dull fear, looked on the place where witches, hags, and errant spirits of the forest flock together at midnight, where the Evil One himself appears. The smooth sides of huge blocks of quartz sparkled with grains of bright color in the sun, just like frost. Frosted sticks protruded from the snow like weapons forged of crystal. Aged firs cast their shadows over half the cliff.

Returning to his place the young hunter strained his ears. . . . While he thus dispatched hearing to the farthest bounds to reconnoitre, he was tricked into thinking that the forest too was listening with him. The silence was unchanging, deep, deep, in very truth unfathomable. . . .

But, see, out from the confines of the forest there came a sluggish puff of air, a whisper awakened from deep sleep, the plaintive, long-drawn-out exhalation of the caught breath of the forests of Bald Mountain. The tops of the trees bent before it as if in reverence, when that song ineffable flowed into the forest. The sound of it, which was scarcely to be caught from the nothingness, which was like a confession of age-old emotions betrayed in quiet weeping, like a groan without hope, came from the solitudes of the forest a second, a third time and, trick-

ling in quiet hues of sound, died away to nothing in the precipice. It
seemed as if this enchanted song, that had its abode in the trees, was
making some reproach, that it was calling. . . . In the bright air, among
the green tufts of needles, it flowed beneath the heavens. The fastnesses
clasped it in their mysterious arms, the forest took it to itself again,
its own mother, the forest-ancestral-soul, the forest-sister-love. It died
away like a sigh, that melancholy murmur-after-murmur. . . . Where
did it die?

Perhaps on the rubble of the tall cliffs, that, when the waves and
foam of the sea had retired, split into a litter of boulders grown about
with ruddy mosses. Perhaps in the ring of oaks rotted through and
through that, like a body guard, surround the dust of the walls of the
holy temple where centuries before the Serene One graciously received
her offerings. Perhaps on the stony brow, on the hard breasts of the
idol Lelum-Polelum, which, covered by the moss of a thousand winters
and a thousand springs, sleeps in an unknown pit and will sleep on
unknown forever and ever. Perhaps in the tracks of the eternal stag
that carries about the forests in its antlers the spars of the Holy Cross
and appears to man once in a hundred years.

As it approached out of the distance, it seemed to Raphael that
that song of the woods would flow through his body just as it did
through the trees. He forgot where he was and what was happening.
There wound within him a thread of memories ungrasped, intangible,
misted, strangely begging for the alms of remembrance. He was far
from that place, not below the summit of Bald Mountain, at the
stance. He was in the garden of his childhood. The ice and snow-
coverings of everything that was real, melted away. The forgotten
garden at the back of the old manor—spreading apple-trees with
trunks in some places still bound about, like jars, from former graft-
ings; bunches, bouquets of rosy flowers . . . luxuriant gooseberries,
thick red-currants had grown about each path. Above the tall grass,
that a beady dew still covers, young cherry-trees rise snowy-white,
virginal. These, it seems, are little spring clouds, morning cloudlets
that have sailed even hither from the fringes of the sky and, helpless,
have settled down here among the tall poplars and old fences. The
bees hum, the wasps and the flies fill the whole orchard with their
buzzing and, he knows not why, his heart with reverence and dread.
Oh, how dear it was, how happy in this shady orchard of his home!
Beyond the fruit-trees stretch inaccessible thickets, coppices of osier
and water-willows. On the islands, in the midst of the fusty water,
shaggy willows with moldered trunks and a confusion of luxuriant
shoots, sad black alders with blood-red suckers, affright the eye. Frogs
croak in the water that glistens with nenuphar and frog-spawn, and
countless birds whistle. Rustle of leaves, murmur of insects, and

scarcely audible, muffled whispers, swishes, hisses, sighs, or quiet groans, that the body can scarcely feel, as if a tingling and a tickling were passing up and down. . . . A small boy, a healthy, happy chatter-box, merry and gay as a lark, runs about the paths of this garden. He jumps at the heels of his father who carries a loaded gun, his only care not to wet his feet in the dew. Here a ladybird catches his eye as it crawls over a wet leaf, there a snail showing black in the white dew; a ray of sunlight falls on the crimson calyx of a tulip that has just that morning bloomed. . . . Quiet, quiet. . . . In the thickets the voice of a golden thrush sounds sweet and merry as the spring itself, as a child's soul. Then with a clap of thunder a shot rings out and echoes in the trees. His heart grows numb and halts in its course. His whole joyful body trembles. . . . From the height of an elm growing in a corner of the garden the golden thrush falls with fluttering wings and stains the wet grass with blood. Ah, he can still see its spluttering hiss that was choked off as he stretched out his hand towards it. And that sudden fear! Sudden, stabbing fear, joy, vengeance, rapture, and ineffable, childish pain. The bird beats its wings and throws itself from side to side. Rises on its legs. . . . Its eyes have grown dull, yet still strive to see. They look. Something has smudged them, veiled them over. . . .

When was it and where? Had they really been, or had he only dreamed them, those cruel bird's eyes fixed in his memory, like nails driven into wounds that are there at life's very beginning?

But, then, silence ensues, and with it, like clouds on the uplands, other visions come floating.

A wood dark and grim, lit by the light of the moon. Huge snows lie over it, over the black forest. Harness-bells ring out and their echo reverberates in the recesses like an arrogant challenge to battle. The moon queens it in cold space. His eyes cannot tear themselves from its disk, and strange whispers, half-words, at last entire sentences, flow towards him. That is the pitiless light calling him to itself, drawing him up to the heights towards sweet harmony, towards melodies rapturous as those of the woods. . . . His father loves to drive that way, along the little-known forest road. In these fastnesses roamed packs of wolves. So when they drove into the dreary thickets of serried trees, powder was poured into the pans of their two muskets and double-barrelled pistols pulled from beneath their belts. He could still hear the whisper of his mother's prayers. . . . A cold shiver pierces him to the marrow and lifts the hair on his head as if with the chill fingers of a numbed hand. The harness-bells jingle louder and louder the further in they drive, till at last they seem to be ringing like a chime. Four horses rush along a road that no sleigh-runners have grooved. The beat of their hooves scatters the snowdrifts as if they were heaps of the finest flour. Now and then something cracks beneath the sleigh. Mysterious voices can be heard in the woods. The whole forest seethes and clamors with the echoes of the harnessbells. Till, see, the curtain of spruces rolls aside for an instant: from the narrow forest clearing can be seen a hill and on it jagged ruins. The moon lights up the snow and ice that lie on the cornices of the fallen walls, on the sills of the staved-in windows.

Those are the ruins of an Arian church.

How strange, unexpected the grief!

Wherever is this day? Where was it left behind for all eternity?

And that dear spring. . . . After the Easter holidays the return home with his parents from a visit to relations. They drive that same way. The coach slowly trundles over the roots and across the dark marshes through which the track leads. All around is thick, wet forest, a-smoke with steam. Everywhere stagnant water gleams in the darkness under the trees. Slippery black limbs with rotten branches lie in the dark pools in the road. And, see, again the ruins come into view. The horses are reined in. Their parents allow the children to go up to the top of the hill. The elder brother and sisters race each other. . . .

Once a broad carriage-way for landaus, coaches, and iron-tired carriages made its way to this hill, but now even pines are growing up from it. In the ruts stand thick spruces, at the corners have appeared centenarian firs, from the ditch that runs in the center have shot white-stemmed birches. The forest has barred access to the ruins, taken possession of that which had gone into it, and become itself again. There are no longer either windows or doors. No one looks after the banned temple, save the tall clumps of thistles. The wild rose creeps down from the top of the naked buttresses and stretches out barbed, mendicant stems. There, where perhaps the altar had been, where the eyes of the faithful had sought the visible sign, is a black skeleton of bramble. Indefatigable water gnaws at tile and stone, and the moss buries their scattered dust beneath itself. Outside the walls, in the heart of the temple and in the forest, what a multitude of wood-violets! The poor little flowers, grey paupers of the forest, are like drops of the pale sky of northern springs that have fallen to earth from on high and shivered into the shapes of little flowers. What delight, what mysterious, inaccessible delight—something like that forest . . . and how rapacious a something, painful, slippery from the rain and horrible with the echo of each step, in that ruined church! What is within it? What is it that weeps and calls from the earth after the departing child? His eyes cannot part from it, nor his feet tear themselves away. The flowers he had plucked fly from his hands and in his ears he hears the spluttering hiss of that thrush killed in the garden.

A sudden, distant, piercing sound rang out in the forest. A second answered it, plaintive and clear, like a softer tenor. Raphael woke as

from sleep and mechanically raised his gun to his cheek. In an instant
he had come to himself and glued aggressive eyes on the forest. The
dreams took flight. The sun was grilling, the puffs of warm wind grew
stronger, and now and then from the trees huge cakes of sticky snow
would fall to the ground.

The hounds are running, he whispered to himself.

From *The Ashes*, Vol. I.
Translated by M. A. MICHAEL

Forest Echoes

General Rozlucki was sitting sternly on a folding stool. The stool
(portable property of land-surveyor Knopf) was placed right in the
center of a rug taken down from the wall over my mother's bed. On the
other side of the camp fire, on a tree stump solicitously covered with
a blanket, sat the aforementioned land-surveyor Knopf, wriggling and
grimacing in his ankle-length raincoat as in a mobile tent. Close to him
was assistant forestér Gunkiewicz, stuck rather uncomfortably among
the gnarled branches of a wind-felled tree, which the forest guard had
brought along, holding on with infinite care to a tumbler of arrack to
which two spoonfuls of tea had been added for appearance's sake.
Community scribe Olszakowski and the old bailiff Gala, with a copper
medal (for "suppressing the Polish rebellion") pinned to his Polish
rust-colored peasant's greatcoat, sat side by side. My father, an old
hunter, quite at home in the forest, was lounging on the ground. And
I, the undersigned, who had just been honorably promoted from
second to third grade, was all over the place.

General Rozlucki, retired, plenipotentiary of one of the most gen-
erously endowed beneficiaries, had just come to the farm my father
had been renting for many years, to incorporate a large section of
state forest in the estate, in accordance with an ukase on the exchange
of land.

The cutting off of the triangle of forest land was almost completed.
Land-surveyor Knopf, who had been "visiting" us for a week to everybody's dismay, had at last staked out the demarcation line, along
which hired lumbermen had long been chopping down the trees of
the old, dark forest. The plenipotentiary, who had also been staying
with us for the last three days, was in a hurry to turn this additional
land over to my father in the presence of the local authorities. The
two teams of peasants cutting down the trees along the border line
were approaching each other from opposite directions. It was expected
that the transaction would be completed before sunset, but night had

fallen and the work along the line was not quite finished. Nevertheless the general had decided to leave the next day. The officials, too, wished to be done with it. It was therefore agreed to work the night through till the morning, if need be.

A campfire was lit at the edge of the forest. Supper was brought over from the manor two miles away, and we passed our time as best we could, waiting for the last few score fir trees to be chopped down.

Everybody was in fairly good humor. Good old Gunkiewicz, with the two last tufts of hair left on his temples, his scanty goatee tinted black with a cheap dye, had already imbibed at least nine tumblers of tea with arrack, asking anxiously every time I handed him another whether it would not be too much, ". . . for, I believe, this is my third . . ." I kept assuring him, with the authoritative air of someone eminently well skilled in arithmetic (up to decimal fractions), that he was mistaken—whereupon he humbly submitted to my superior knowledge and accepted another tot of arrack.

Community scribe Olszakowski, versed in all things human, and particularly in county and community ways of making easy money (which had already made him "suffer" a term in the Kielce jail), an incontestable genius, who might easily have become minister of the interior or of foreign affairs, or who might even have filled both posts simultaneously, a notorious grafter, extortioner of peasants, exploiter of Jews, past master in circumventing the law and an all-round busybody—was drinking little in deference to the general present, and devoted more attention to the food. But being so omniscient he actually was not in the least impressed by the general and felt quite at ease to let his wit sparkle for the benefit of the little gathering.

Bailiff Gala was chewing and swallowing anything that was presented to him; he was not averse to drinking and mumbled cheerfully. Quite obviously he wholeheartedly enjoyed government service in the woodland and he was quite satisfied with that day's activity.

Even Knopf, that walking gastritis (and enteritis), that shrivelled-up neurasthenic, that creature who should eat nothing but certain easily-digestible foods (non-acid and lean—foods such as no one had ever eaten, or seen, or even known by name in any remote village, and especially not in the Swietokrzyskie Mountains), that bore who could not sleep at night, who could not bear to hear cocks crowing, dogs barking, turkeys gobbling, geese gaggling, or even hens clucking —a veritable Egyptian plague to any sane and robust people working on the land in a country where every one is so fond of dog kennels, where mongrels, hounds, pointers, dachshunds, well—"doggies" in general, of any breed and age, not only howl and bark all night long, but lounge on sofas and couches, where the cocks never stop crowing, and those who stop are at once put to death for being remiss—even Knopf, as I've said, was in fairly good humor that night.

He told us an acrimoniously witty anecdote about his astrolabe (which, according to evil tongues, he was in the habit of dressing up in his own galoshes, trousers and coat, to protect it from the rain). Although the point of his story was ruined by assistant forester Gunkiewicz bursting into laughter prematurely at a moment that wasn't funny at all, Knopf continued to smile—an event which was considered a real phenomenon within a radius of three counties, where it was talked about for several years.

The general, a fairly well preserved old fogy, behaved with the appropriate dignity. During this improvised supper party he practically ignored the bailiff and the scribe, but tolerated their presence without a protest and did not object to their eating chicken and various cold roast meats with a hearty appetite, to their tossing down tumblers of home-made liquor with beer "for a chaser," nor even to their "warming up" with tea and arrack. To Gunkiewicz he addressed a gracious word every now and then, and with Knopf he talked. He himself ate slowly and sipped tea.

The general was a Pole and made a point of speaking Polish even in government offices. His pronunciation bore traces of a Russian accent, but that accent somehow fitted his tall figure, his thick jacket of a peculiar cut, his round cap with its red band and extraordinarily wide peak, his cloth spats and gray mustache curling upwards.

The fire blazed, fed by the forest guard. The dry juniper burned, crackling merrily. From the forest across the evening dew came the thump-thump of falling axes. It resounded through the forests, through the vast Swietokrzyskie fir tree groves, deep into the damp, sleepy, silent wilderness. The echo of the blows sped from mountain to mountain, from grove to grove, towards a bleak distance, into the night, into the fog. Hounded, driven-out, far-away voices trembled somewhere outside the world and called from the beyond. They returned frightened and mute from the distant marshes where no one dare walk, where it "spooks." From time to time one heard amidst the blows of falling axes the ominous creaking of a breaking tree, the rustling and crushing of its mass of boughs and branches, the hollow formidable thunder of falling timber. The echo snatched up the sound and carried it into the dark, distant night, the sorrowful news growing faint and fainter, the heart-breaking message of that blow. The whole forest was breaking down, crumbling, with every tree roaring in testimony of a moment never to be forgotten, calling out of the depth of darkness with living voices.

Red and enormous, the moon emerged from the veils of the forest and went slowly on its way among the dark clouds. The group gathered round the fire fell silent. The air turned chilly. My mount (a gray, bony, half-retired farmstead mare whose mane and tail I had clipped on arriving for my vacation, and whom I tortured with the strap of an old saddle, and forced into perilous gallops) stood somewhere near the fire. One could see her fine head and shoulder-blades, her pensioner's hoofs, and above all her eyes lost in meditation on the blazing fire and the people sitting round it . . .

The general had put down his glass some time before and was sitting up straight with his chest stuck out and one of his legs gracefully stretched out sideways. At times, he turned his head towards the forest. He listened to the sound of the echoes and then turned his head back to its former position.

He turned to Gunkiewicz:

"Assistant Forester, how far is it from here to Suchedniow?" Gunkiewicz put down his tumbler and replied with the proper polite inclination of his camouflaged bald spot that it wouldn't be quite seven miles straight across the fields.

"You know the path round here, don't you?"

Gunkiewicz smiled proudly or condescendingly. He could not find a word vigorous enough to indicate the extent to which he was familiar with every nook round there; hadn't he been assistant forester there for twenty odd years!

"Yes . . ." muttered the general thoughtfully. "And do you know the one leading from Zagnansk to Wzdol? There used to be an inn near that path, right in the forest . . ."

"Zagozdzie—why, it's still there."

"A bumpy path full of roots went from there towards Suchedniow, and another, better one, towards Wzdol, towards Bodzentyn."

"That's right, general."

"You say that inn is still there?"

"So it is. A real thieves' kitchen. Horse-traffickers from every corner of Poland meet under that roof."

"In front of that inn, across the road, on the other side, there was a sand-hill. Big, yellow . . . There were a few birch-trees growing on that hill . . ."

"What a remarkable memory, general! Only one of those birches is still there. And what fine trees they were. That scoundrel of an inn-keeper cut them down. One of the birches was left standing, and even that one simply because there's a cross leaning against it. This the blackguard daren't touch."

"What cross? How did a cross get there?" asked Rozlucki in an animated tone.

"Well, there is a cross, there . . ."

"But what's the reason for placing a cross at that spot, eh?"

"Well, that's the way with crosses, general. Some people put one up, others pass by and raise their hats, and it simply stays there. It's started rotting at the foot, but it's been secured with props on two sides."

"Who put it up?" insisted the general.

"To tell the truth," muttered Gunkiewicz with a shy smile, "to tell the truth, it's me who put up that cross. We've got plenty of wood hereabouts. I took a fine, firm healthy pine. And our carpenter, who is among us now as our bailiff fashioned it . . ."

"Oh, never mind . . . why mention it . . ."

"We dug the tree way deep into the sand, way deep . . ."

"But why precisely at that spot?"

"Because a man lies buried there under that hill, my general."

"A man's buried . . ." repeated the general. "And you had known that man, had you?"

"Well, certainly I knew him; in a forest district like mine one can hardly fail to know a man . . . With miles and miles of woods all round . . . Whoever gets into those woods doesn't bypass my house, or even my bed."

The general bowed his head and kept silent for a long spell. At last he took a silver cigarette case from his pocket and opened it, his hands rather unsteady.

"Well," he said with a cold grin, "do you know that the man buried there was my nephew?"

Land-surveyor Knopf, who until then had been sitting motionless, staring into the fire with lips tightly pressed together and an expression of utter disgust on his face, suddenly gave the general a withering look:

"Rymwid?" he exclaimed.

The general turned towards him:

"Exactly, Rymwid . . . You, too, seem to know something about him . . ."

Knopf's lips twisted a number of times, as if he had just drunk some pure lemon juice; he waved his hands in various directions, blinking his white eyelids. Then, amid a series of hypocritical smiles most insufferable to the eyes, he muttered:

"Well, yes . . . Rymwid . . . of course . . ."

"Rymwid!" repeated the general vehemently, with a sneer. "Lieutenant in my regiment—Rymwid! 'The captain!' Well, he got his due . . ."

"So he was your nephew?" Gunkiewicz asked fearfully, his eyes fairly popping out of his head.

"My own brother's second son, John," said the general pensively. "My brother died on the field of honor during the Sevastopol war, before Malakoff Hill. Major-general, a man of the Nicholaian era. Promoted for his conduct in the Hungarian campaign, awarded medals, an estate in Penza. Dying on the battlefield, he asked me to take care of his two sons. I gave him my word as a brother and a soldier that I would make men out of them, that I would see to it that they made their way in the world. And I kept my word. I did bring them up . . . The older one served in the Caucasus and died there of cholera as staff captain. Peter, unmarried. The younger one, John, served in my regiment after graduating from the cadet school. He married young; she was a Polish girl, née Plaza; they had a baby son when that vile Polish insurrection started. When that vile insurrection broke out, we got orders to transfer. I was lieutenant-colonel at the time. We went to the Opoczno district."

The general lost himself in meditation. Knopf rolled himself a meticulously even cigarette, pushed it carefully into his cigarette holder and busied himself trying to find an ember to light it. The general seemed to be waiting for the moment when the other would at last have lit his cigarette, and when Knopf took his first puff, he said:

"Well, then. That nephew of mine betrayed us. We had barely taken up quarters when he ran away in the dark of night to join the gang. In the morning, Captain Shchukin reported what had happened: John was gone. A note was found on the table of the quarters where we were living, in Sielpia, informing me, as the then commander of three battalions, that 'faithful to his homeland' and suchlike nonsense, he appealed to me, his superior and his uncle, to stain my honor as officer, break my oath and run away to the woods, to join the gang, as he had done. That's how it was, gentlemen."

Knopf was smoking his cigarette cautiously, slowly. He was blowing geometrically perfect smoke-rings and following them with his eyes. Gunkiewicz no longer felt like having any tea. He sat there stunned, staring at the general.

"News reached me of our deserter being chief of staff of one of the gangs. All right, then, 'That's why he went there,' Captain Shchukin, under whom my nephew had served, told me. Service in the army is tough, hard, and thankless, but in the gang service is easy, light. There our lieutenant could be a captain without any great effort. 'If there's anything in those Polish armies that isn't hard to get,' he added, 'it's promotion.'"

Knopf had finished his cigarette; he laughed at Captain Shchukin's joke. The general continued:

"We were constantly on the march, in pursuit of one or other of the gangs. We'd barely get out of the Knoskie woods and reach Suchedniow woods, before they'd have run off deep into the woods towards Bodzentyn. We'd go back, and they'd be at our heels. There was one of their leaders in particular, a colonel or captain called 'Walter,' that fooled us more than the rest. He'd have lots of fires burning as in a camp, while he withdrew to a place quite a distance away, and spent the night without a fire. We arrive with a posse, and surround those camp fires as stealthily as possible, then we attack them at night and find—no one. He'd hear the fracas and come up on us like a brigand: shooting our soldiers, picking them out against the glaring light of the fires, and running back into the woods again. He also made use of some peasants he had seduced: they would lead us at night to those dummy camps."

The village scribe shot an oblique glance at the bailiff and grinned wryly. The bailiff sat up very straight gazing fixedly at the general.

"That's what happened more than once in the Samsonow region . . ."

"Near Gozd . . ." chipped in Gunkiewicz.

"That's right, near Gozd, too."

"Near Klonow . . ." muttered Knopf.

"But the game did come to an end," said the general. "You can get away with a trick once, twice, maybe even three times, but it won't work for ever. It so happened I was marching at the head of a few companies from Zagnansk to Wzdol—in fact, along that road to the inn. I spent the night at the inn and despatched Shchukin with one company to ferret out that man Walter. The rascal wouldn't come out to fight, instead he sits tight in the swamps between Klonow and Bukowa Gora for weeks, so we've got to look for him.

"I had barely fallen asleep that night, when my aide-de-camp, a young fellow, burst in to report 'heavy shooting in the woods!' I was immediately wide awake. The forest was roaring . . . Just as we hear it roar now . . . What a pity . . . What a heartache. I despatched another company as reinforcement for Shchukin. It didn't take more than two hours, and they came marching back. A peasant has led them to the camp, that time to a real one. When they surrounded them and launched a bayonet attack, the majority fought their way out and fled into the forest; many were killed on the spot. Shchukin brought back one taken in hand-to-hand fighting; to put it briefly, it was none other than my nephew, Rymwid. I had received the irrevocable order from my brigadier-general to clear the forest up to Bodzentyn at any cost, including the power of life and death. There was no time to send the prisoners to the prison in Kielce, and besides the forces at my disposal were rather limited. My officers were in a flurry and looked at me, his relative, with severe, questioning eyes.

"I immediately convened a court-martial, for we had to pursue the gang without any loss of time. I presided, with Captain Shchukin and Captain Fedotov on my right, and Lieutenant von Tauwetter and Sergeant Yevseyenko on my left. We went at once into session in the large room of that inn. A tallow candle was burning in the candlestick . . ."

The general spoke faster and faster, less and less distinctly, and using more and more Russian words, phrases, and even whole sentences. He moved to make himself comfortable on his stool and continued:

"They brought him in. Six soldiers, and he in the middle. Short, emaciated, black, ragged. Hair tousled. Barely recognizable . . . I looked at him: Johnny, my brother's favorite son . . . I had brought him up; used to hold him on my knees . . . Stuck in some despicable rags . . . His face, torn open right across by a bayonet thrust, all blue and swollen. As they brought him in, he stopped by the door, waiting. And you, judge, pass your sentence!

"First the usual formal question: who he is. He keeps silent. We all looked at him. A good comrade, beloved colleague, warm-hearted chap, outstanding officer. His face had become insolent, frozen into a sort of a grin which twisted that pleasant, kind and gentle face—as a blacksmith takes a piece of soft iron and twists it once and for all in the fire into a crooked hook.

"The soldiers who guarded him acted as witnesses. They testified that they had captured him in the forest fighting hand-to-hand; they testified that he was him all right, their own Lieutenant Rozlucki. A clear case, what else could there be? The vote . . .

"At that moment, one of the judges on my right, Captain Shchukin, turned to me saying he wanted to ask the accused some more questions. All right, ask your questions. Shchukin rose from his seat, propped himself up on his fists as hard as he could, finally leaned over towards him across the table. The veins on his forehead were bulging; his face grew as dark as earth. He looked fixedly at the accused. We all wondered what else he was going to ask. Still the fellow couldn't utter a single word, for he was a hard man without much education. His nostrils were quivering, his brows knitted. At last he banged the table with his fist and shouted at the accused:

"'Rozlucki, don't you dare stand before us with that insolent air! Don't you dare look at us in this fashion! Did you give your oath or didn't you? What did you do with your oath? Answer me! Did you swear allegiance—yes or no?'"

" 'I did,' he said.

" 'You did!' Shchukin shouted again at the top of his voice, his fists pressed on the table. 'And how did you keep that sacred pledge? You deserted the ranks and went over to the enemy! Is that the truth or isn't it?'

" 'It's true.'

" 'In connivance with others who betrayed your sovereign you have ambushed and attacked his armed forces. You were a leader of the traitors, you gave them the most detrimental directives, you taught them where and how to attack. I have seen you with my own eyes today fighting the soldiers of your own company. I testify here that I have seen Private Denishchuk wounding you with his bayonet. Is this true or isn't it?'

" 'It is true.'

" 'If all this is true, don't you dare look at us—faithful, honest soldiers—with your air of a hero. You are standing here before a tribunal that stands for justice. You own uncle will judge you. Look down and humble yourself, for you are a traitor and a villain.'

"To this he replied:

" 'I am standing before the tribunal of God. As for you, you may judge me according to your standards, if you wish.'

"Shchukin sat down.

"They voted: two votes—Shchukin's and von Tauwetter's—for punishment on the spot; two votes for sending him under escort to the prison at Kielce. It was up to me to tip the scale. And . . . I tipped it . . ." he said in a low voice, nodding.

"They were on the point of taking him out. Yevseyenko moved that he might have a last wish. I gave him the floor. He looked at me with those abysmal eyes, fixedly. We were all standing behind the table. He approached. He stared into my eyes, and I into his. Like the points of the guns . . . I remember his austere words:

" 'In the face of death, I order—and this is my irrevocable last will—that my little son, my six-year-old Peter, be brought up as a Pole, as I was myself. I order that he be told—even if this be against the conscience of his tutor—of everything his father did, up to the very end. I ordered him to work for his country and, if necessary, to die for it without batting an eyelid, without a sigh of regret, as I do. that's all.'

"He saluted us.

"They led him away.

"It was nearly daybreak. I went to the alcove where I should have slept that night. I opened the window. It was dawning. Morning. On the opposite side of the road six soldiers were speedily digging a pit in the sand. I withdrew to the far end of the alcove. I turned my face to the wall. My God! . . .

"When I went back to the window, it was bright daylight. I could see quite clearly. There he was, with twelve soldiers standing on guard, carbines at foot, sitting peacefully on the sand heap, his profile turned towards me. They had taken off his insurgent's jacket. He was in his shirt-sleeves, and his shirt was torn on the chest. In his clenched hands, between his knees, he was holding a snapshot of his son Peter. Head bent forward, hair falling over his forehead, lost in contemplation of the photo.

"Up from behind the corner of the inn marched the platoon of soldiers belonging to his own company. The platoon faced him. Von Tauwetter in command. The soldiers stood with their guns at the ready. They were still. A minute passed, then another, and a third . . . I waited. I waited for Tauwetter to give the command. Not a sound. Silence. He was unable to give the command. The other was still sitting with the eyes on his picture. I had the impression that he had died already, sitting there. For a fleeting moment, I felt relief. He was waiting. Then he raised his head, that seemed to weigh a thousand *puds*. He stood up on the heap of sand. His feet sank into the soft ground, so he readjusted his position once, and then a second time. He turned his head to look behind, brushed back the hair falling on his forehead and looked at the soldiers. Thank God, there it was again, that expression of disdain he had had when facing the court-martial. I watched it spreading slowly over his face, his forehead, his eyes. I felt elated to see it happen, just like that, proudly . . . That he was a Rozlucki . . . I sensed the terrible will power it took to pass through the stage of being an insensate corpse, to be transformed into something quite different.

"He called out in Russian:

" '*Zdarovo, rebiata!*'[1]

" '*Zdravia zhelayem vashemu blagorodiu!*'[2] the soldiers shouted back, as one man.

"Yevseyenko was approaching to blindfold him. He stopped him with a mere glance. The sergeant went away. Then he pressed the little photograph to his heart and shut his eyes. His lips parted in a beautiful sublime smile. I closed my eyes too. I leaned against the wall with my chest. I waited, waited, waited. At last, . . . Rat-t-t-t."

Land surveyor Knopf took off his cap murmuring to himself with parched lips. Gunkiewicz was digging with a stick in the ashes of the campfire as if he wanted to bury the abundant tears of a drunkard rolling down his cheeks.

Silence fell. Echoes were calling one another from mountain to mountain.

Suddenly the village scribe turned to the general and asked:

"Will you permit me to ask a question, General? Where is that little son Peter now, who was then six years old?"

"And what business is it of yours where he is?" retorted the general rudely, in a harsh voice.

"I was just curious to know if the last will and order of that insurrectionist had been carried out."

---

[1] Hi, fellows!

[2] We wish you well, your Honor!

"None of your business, and don't you ever dare ask me that question again!—D'you hear me?"

"I gathered that much right from the start," replied the scribe, looking the old general straight in the eyes with his roguish smile in impudent mockery. "I gathered that much right from the start; that last will of yours, my dear Captain Rymwid, must have given the devil a good and hearty laugh . . ."

Translated by ILONA RALF SUES

Andrzej Strug

(1873–1935)

Andrzej Strug (pseudonym of Tadeusz Galecki) is best known as the writer of Poland's underground struggle against the Tsars. His earliest literary efforts were dedicated to the "underground people" who were fighting for independence and social justice. As a youth, Strug joined the ranks of the underground himself, and later became a prominent member of the Polish Socialist Party—as a soldier, journalist and creative writer.

Although he was one of the first to join the Legions of Pilsudski, after 1926, Strug broke with his former comrades-in-arms and became a leading figure of the opposition.

Representing the Left in Polish postwar literature, Strug attracted the younger generation of writers which regarded him as their leader and was profoundly affected by his writings and personality.

His major novels, *The Underground People* (1908), *Recollections of an Old Sympathizer* (1909) and *Tomorrow* (1909), bring to Polish fiction a different type of hero. "The underground people," related though they are to Zeromski's "homeless people," live far more dangerous lives. They are subjected to brutal imprisonment, forced labor and contemptuous treatment even at the hands of their own people. Their work is ungrateful, brings them no glory, and often their hazardous existence ends in despair and doubt. Masterfully, Strug creates the atmosphere of conspiratorial activities, emphasizing the role of "the little man" and the "unknown soldier." Strug's portrait of these men is not only exciting fiction, it is also an accurate historical account of an important period in Polish history.

In such postwar novels as *The Key to the Precipice* and *Yellow Cross* (which is considered as one of the most important psychological novels of war), Strug pondered and dissected a vast array of political, social and international problems. Strug's funeral gave ample testimony of his enormous popularity in independent Poland, for his coffin was followed not only by state dignitaries and the representatives of arts and sciences but also by huge crowds of simple folk.

The Obituary

Everything took place as had been arranged. There were wreaths, there were crimson ribbons and a crowd of a thousand people. They sang The Red Banner over the grave, and there were encomiums to which the people listened. But the tributes went unfinished. The Cossacks burst into the cemetery and the horses trampled the graves with their hooves . . . A skirmish flared briefly and died and a score or two were arrested . . .

The people are stirred, they have felt the wild wind sweeping through the foul air of their basements. Even after death you are useful.

My task is to chronicle your deeds and bring your unsung name into daylight. They'll stand at the type-form composing the words letter by letter . . . for the wide mourning box beneath the thin little lines of a cross. You must be honored . . . but how?

Let them, the people, know that you existed; and those who knew you, let them understand at last that it was you, you that they knew. No need for secrecy now. You shall have fame. Not a few will be roused, fired by your tale; not a few sustained in suffering. You shall have fame.

                              ❁   ❁   ❁

You took your leave at the worst moment. Was it fair? The task is still great; whom shall we put in your place? Unfair . . . Orphans were left behind. On Wola[1] they ask whither you disappeared: "Did Walter get himself into trouble, or what? Why doesn't he come?"

He got himself into trouble, you folk of Wola, he won't be coming any more. . . .

You could have waited for today—not much, just a brief while of living.

I've a deep sadness for your sorrow, a deep sadness. . . .

Why did you hurry so? It was wrong of you. . . .

                              ❁   ❁   ❁

Listen, brother, listen well, the revolution's on its way, on its way and setting the earth atremble.

They're waking—even there below—waking powerfully, for they've been sleeping powerfully. Won't you believe it?

Listen! It's the truth, it's begun! New days are coming, days we've not seen before. The people look up differently, breathe differently, the enemy has a different fear.

We shall rise out of the earth now, rise with our treasures and reserves, begin to boast with our work. Tomorrow is not far, we'll live to see it.

Listen, brother, listen well. We'll rise from our underground and do a little fighting. Eye him to his eye, measure him, size him up.

Only you will not rise from the earth depths to see that shining day. Wouldn't it have been better to see it? Fill your eyes with the brightness? Swallow the free air?

One sultry evening in the underground you said: "To have to keep

---

[1] The workers' district of Warsaw

your eyes about you all your life, to have to hide, never let a sound escape you—a terrible thing, a shame. . . ."

We swam a long, hard way, lost strength, were sucked under; now we've made it, here's the bank, here, you can touch it . . . but you're at the bottom . . . how will it be on the bright bank without you?

❖ ❖ ❖

Remember?

Student discussions, long papers, quarrels, taking sides, relations broken, renewed, groups, circles, plans, plans, plans, . . .

This fame of ours dragged through the streets of Warsaw, this pride of ours. . . .

Where, when was there ever a Napoleon more certain of ruling the world than we two, then?

The university threw us out, we said: We are destined for higher goals!

Locked up, behind bars, we said: Be brave, the eyes of the world are on us!

They set us free a few months later and we were ashamed to be free, it was a crime.

Into the world, the far world, we followed the rest of them.

Parisian years, the work, the fights, do you recall that noble pride of ours? *Rue des Courcelles.* Behind the barricades, two miserable starved dogs. The last of the borrowed sous had gone for the printing of polemical pamphlets.

London, merciless, terrifying, miserable, unendurable. Remember the misty autumn night we lay lifeless with hunger in the dark, un-heated suburban room?

And that star-studded summer night thick with the odor of pine sap and pasture flowers, when we crept over the border and returned to the fatherland. . . .

The unuttered, unconfessed thought lay in each of us, to swear that never would we leave our land again. . . .

❖ ❖ ❖

Now, after the years, it is hard to believe. How did we endure those days? The Testament is right: Faith lifts mountains and moves them from their place.

Days of hunger, cold and wandering . . . distrust, fear, envy. . . .

We did the work of ten, each of us did, and two of us ate for one. Our schemes tore like cobwebs in the wind and we patched them asking each of the other: Will anything come of it? Darkness, intrigue, betrayals, constant remorse engulfed us. It might have been worse. We were accustomed to fear.

We were lucky somehow. When inevitable disaster faced us we

were saved by a miracle. We were astounded. You said: It's clear that God is on our side.

Do you recall how we fled into that little shop to escape? In the Old City?[2] No time to lose, and like that, instinctively. . . . The shop-keeper said nothing, we said nothing, not a word, there was no time; the police were there, hot on the scent. . . . Tell me, who told her, who taught her? . . . "Two of them ran by here toward Bugaj,[3] I think. . . ." She slipped us out the back way through the gate, again without a word. . . . Is she still alive?

And that Jew at the gate. Remember him? "You gentlemen had better not go upstairs, the police are in the apartment." Who was he? How did he know us? Where did he come from?

We suffered it for the third, tenth, hundredth, thousandth time. Now our tribe has increased and even without us would endure.

Then why couldn't we have left together?

❋   ❋   ❋

You died in a strange bed, they dressed you in a strange coat, strange boots for the coffin.

Listen, what did we ever possess of our own? Not a nook of our own, a moment, a secret of our own. Hardly a thought of such things. . . . Forever dragging ourselves about . . . but always . . . it was a dog's life.

You should have listened, you should have gone somewhere once in your life for a rest. You wouldn't listen to that.

You would have dragged on for another year or two. You would have seen something more, lived to see something—even if only a cleaner sun. And then it would have been easier for you. . . .

We prattled about it always: we would rest when they took us; in prison, in exile we would rest.

But there were moments of loneliness when a word tore out of us: "Let the devil send them for us already!"

To spite us they didn't come. . . . And so you fell, exhausted, like the end horse stumbling in the harness. Rest . . . rest. . . .

❋   ❋   ❋

I'll write your tale with vibrant, palpable words. Something to be long remembered. Great, eternal fame for you, man of the under-ground, man without a name!

Let your name, unfurled, be the pride of thousands, a living signal, a goad, a call to battle.

Let them know you!

---

[2] District of Warsaw
[3] A street in the "Old City."

I have to work now. The copy is ready, waiting only for you. We'll print it up tomorrow. I'll spend the night at the type-form setting up your deeds. A single column was all they allotted you. Your life must fit into that, and your soul. It'll be bright for you in the mourning-box and my tale will be short. I'll prepare it in the night, in the calm and safe night. This long night I'll spend with you alone, dead brother. . . . Setting type to type and reading the words off one by one.

Who knows? Perhaps out of the pain of memory, out of the sorrow of thought, perhaps out of the stillness of the night your shadow will rise and stand before me, quiet and sad, stand for a moment and nod and then drift away. . . .

❋   ❋   ❋

Tomorrow the press will beat the pages off, one by one. The smithy will simmer with work. The quiet, skillful beating of the press, the rustle of papers and the heaps of newsprint rising hour by hour.

Your edition will go into the world by the usual routes. Throughout the Polish land the people will seize it and read it and shed a tear for you, a man's tear in which there is strength and an oath. It will spread through the world, passed from hand to hand, farther and farther until one day a crumpled, wrinkled scrap of it will fall somewhere sometime, borne by chance, blown by the wind, on an unknown road where an unknown man will find it and pick it up. . . .

From *The Underground People.*
Translated by LUDWIK KRZYZANOWSKI

Stanislaw Przybyszewski
(1868–1927)

Novelist, essayist and dramatist, Stanislaw Przybyszewski was born at Lojewo in Kujawy, in German Poland. He studied in Berlin, and served a term in Moabit Prison because of his friendship for a Polish socialist. Throughout his life he remained an outsider and a newcomer. In 1898 he took over the editorship of the Cracow journal *Life,* having made a name for himself in Germany as an advocate of extreme modernism, and a follower of the Scandinavians. His philosophy made him both famous and notorious. It rejected reason and praised intuition and "absolute art."

His novels *Mass for the Dead* (1893), *Satan's Children* (1897) and *Homo Sapiens* (1898) first appeared in German, then in Polish (the latter was translated into English in 1915), and like his dramas, they greatly influenced Polish literature, through their unorthodox treatment of plot and his exalted Neo-Romanticism. The most characteristic of Przybyszewski's postulates was the idea that the function of art is to present the human soul in all its "holy" manifestations; hence in his fiction and drama the inner lives of his heroes are of paramount importance, while the external world is reduced to a bare minimum. The metaphysical motivation has replaced the realistic interpretation of human behavior, which was basic to Polish Positivism.

Przybyszewski influenced Polish literature also by virtue of his editorial position on the *Life* journal and his association with young Polish writers. Of his dramas, the best known are *For Happiness* (1900) and *Snow* (1903), both translated into English.

By the Way

Falk and Marit stopped, slightly embarrassed. From the road he had caught sight of her at the lake and went down to meet her.

"I have keen eyes, haven't I?"

"Yes. I didn't think I could be seen here."

Silence.

The day was drawing to a close, the air was sultry, the sky overcast.

They seated themselves at the water's edge. Falk turned his gaze upon the smooth surface of the lake.

"What a wonderful hush on the lake. Only once before I've felt a hush like it—a super-hush."

"When?"

"When I was in Norway—it was on the fjords. Oh, it was wonderful!

Silence again.

Marit was extremely uneasy.

"How did you get home last night?"

"Oh, very well."

Conversation started and halted, and started and halted again.

"How sultry it is!" Falk observed. "It's much cooler indoors."

They turned toward the house.

Falk made an effort at a more intimate tone.

"I spent the most delightful evening of my life yesterday."

Marit was silent, every now and then throwing him a scared glance.

Falk understood, but her tacit resistance annoyed him. Today he must make a finish. It was inevitable, he felt, yet he was too faint to overcome her resistance.

He must muster up his strength. Oh, he knew himself well. The very second glass would do it. A strength of purpose knowing no obstacles would then leap up in his soul.

"Have you anything to drink in the house? I've swallowed such a lot of dust."

Marit brought a bottle of wine. Falk drank it off quickly, then stretched himself in the arm-chair and fastened his stare upon her.

Marit did not dare to raise her eyes.

"What's the matter? Have you committed a crime, or what?"

There was profound sadness in the look Marit gave him.

"Be kind to-day. Don't repeat what happened yesterday. I suffered so the whole night. Oh, what a terrible man you are!"

"Really? Do you really think so?"

"You mustn't laugh at me. You have robbed me of everything. I cannot pray any more, because I keep thinking of what you told me. I think with your thoughts. You have removed all my shame."

"I can go away."

"Oh, no, no, no, Mr. Falk. Only be kind—do what you want—only not that. Don't ask that of me."

Her face was so tragic that Falk involuntarily felt compassion. "Very well, Marit, I won't. Only don't say Mr. Falk. Call me Eric. We are so near each other already. Our relations are so intimate. Will you call me Eric? Yes?"

Falk stood before her.

"I will try," she whispered.

"Because you see, Marit, I love you to insanity. Whole days I roam from place to place thinking of nothing but you. At night I cannot sleep. What am I to do? I keep drinking, drinking, only to quiet my-self. I stay hours at a time in cafés with those simpletons, listening to their vapid talk—it gives me almost physical pain—then when I leave I feel the same distress, am just as desolate. I know, I know, darling, it's not your fault. I'm not reproaching you. But you are ruining me. . . .

"I know you would do everything for me—ha, ha!—except only one thing, the one thing indeed that is the sure proof of love.

"You may repeat that you love me a hundred times, yet I will not believe it; because love is either real love knowing no limits, no petty shame, is blind, unreasoning, neither high nor low, with neither sin nor merit in it, strong and great as nature itself; or—but there really is no 'or.' There is only one love. That love recognizes not religion or shame. It stands above all the prejudices that fetter mankind. The rest is only whimsy, a palliative for boredom. Ha, ha, ha!"

He stopped before her and laughed his Satanic laugh.

"My dear child, I wanted an eagle to soar aloft with me to the heights of my solitude, and I found a tender, delicate, timid dove. I wanted a wild, proud lioness, and I found a rabbit always afraid of the gaping jaws of a rattlesnake.

"No, no, don't be afraid. I won't do anything to you."

Marit burst into sobs.

"Don't cry, Marit, don't cry. I'll go crazy if you cry. I didn't want to hurt you. But everything in me thrills and urges me toward you, my only, my beloved."

Marit continued to cry.

"Don't cry, don't cry, my darling." He dropped on his knees and covered her hands with kisses.

"Don't cry." He caught her in his arms, kissed her eyes, stroked her face, and more and more passionately caressed and clasped her radiant little head.

"My only, my darling, my, my—"

And she pressed herself to him, flung her arms about his neck, and their lips met in a long wild kiss.

Finally she broke away.

Falk rose.

"Well, now everything is all right. But just smile a little, smile." She smiled.

Falk grew animated. He kept drinking, and told anecdotes, and joked more or less successfully, then fell abruptly into silence.

A dullness and heaviness hung in the room. They glanced at each other solemnly, breathing heavily.

It grew dark. The maid entered and called Marit out. Falk looked after her a long time. He felt a cruel, rapacious desire, with a severity and relentlessness in it as in a rolling stone, which though it knows it will drop into a bottomless pit, yet obstinately keeps on rolling.

The darkness in the room thickened. Dense clouds covered the sky. Each minute the sultriness became more intolerable. Falk got up and paced the room, deep in reflection.

"Won't you come in to dinner?"

He took her arm and drew her close. At table they held a stubborn silence. Conversation, notwithstanding Falk's attempts to keep it up, broke off and always had to be started afresh again. They returned to the drawing-room. After long pondering Falk said:

"Don't be angry with me, Marit, if I stay here later than usual to-night. A storm is coming up. Besides, I can't sleep. It frightens me to be alone—eh?—I'm not in your way, am I?"

Marit seemed to take fire.

For some time they sat in silence. Everybody had gone to bed. It was as if the whole household had died out. In the dull, stifling hush before the storm they could scarcely breathe. The tick-tick of the pendulum almost caused them physical pain.

"Aren't you afraid to be alone in this huge, empty house?"

"Sometimes I'm dreadfully afraid. I feel so lonely, as if I were the only human being in the whole world. I'm ready to sink through the earth with fright."

"But to-day you don't feel lonely?"

"No."

There was a long oppressive silence.

"Marit, have you still got the poems I wrote for you last spring? I'd like to read them."

"They are in my room upstairs. I'll get them."

"No, Marit. I'll go up with you. It is much cosier in your room. I myself am afraid of something here. You know in what a state my nerves are."

"But somebody might hear us going upstairs."

"Don't be afraid. I'll walk so quietly that no one will hear me. Everybody is asleep anyhow."

She still refused her consent.

"Don't be afraid, my sweet, my darling. I won't do anything to you. Absolutely nothing. I'll sit quite still and read my poems."

There was a clap of thunder.

"Very still. And when the storm is over I'll leave without making a sound."

At last they entered her room. He locked the door. They stopped on the threshold as though caught fast. The very air seemed to be panting and coiling itself round their bodies in live rings.

Suddenly Marit felt herself swept up in a mad, thirsty embrace.

Her eyes flashed with all the colours of the rainbow. And in her soul she felt the mad joy of an insane dance over a precipice.

She flung her arms about his neck, hurled herself blindly into the abyss of sinful delight.

Suddenly she started away in fright.

"No. Eric, for God's sake—only not that!"

Her bosom rose and fell. She gasped for breath.

Falk released her from his embrace and came to himself.

A long silence.

"Listen, Marit," he said coldly and sternly. "Now we'll separate. You see how cowardly you are? It's a shame to withdraw now. You are a rabbit, my dear, and I am a kind man. I'm a kind, soft-hearted man. You haven't the courage to tell me, "Go, Eric, go and leave me my clean conscience. Leave me my useless, stupid virginity." No, you haven't the courage to say that. I'm stronger than you. I'm a man, and therefore I go. Good-bye.

"I'm going away. I leave you your religion, your chastity, that absurd Catholic chastity—ha, ha!—your clean, tranquil conscience. I'll deliver you from so-called sin—yes, sin is what your Catholic eunuchs call the most beautiful thing in the world . . . be happy, be very, very happy!"

The storm grew fiercer.

Every moment the window lighted up with greenish zigzag flashes.

Falk turned to the door.

"Eric, Eric, how can you be so cruel, so cruel?"

All the pent-up, long-suppressed torture in her soul suddenly burst in a great storm of weeping.

"Eric, Eric," she cried, choking and gulping her sobs.

In a blind panic Falk caught her in his arms.

"Marit, Marit, I won't go away. I'll stay with you. I haven't the strength to tear myself away from you. It was only a momentary flash of insanity. I thought I'd be able to leave you. But I can't, I can't. I'll never desert you. Marit, my sun, my only happiness."

A great clap of thunder tore the heavy curtain of the air and rolled in the sky in immense reverberations.

Falk's breast was full of an unwonted tenderness, profound, passionate. He took Marit in his arms, rocked her like a child, fondled and caressed her, whispered ardent words of love, all oblivious of everything else in his life.

"I'll give you such happiness—such happiness—"

The rain beat in torrents against the window.

Now they were alone, all alone in the whole world. The rain, the thunder, the tempest cut them off from the rest of humanity. Marit pressed herself close to him.

"How good you are, how good you are, Eric! And you'll never leave me, will you? We'll be happy."

"We'll stay together forever and be happy," Falk said mechanically.

That cruel, rapacious something suddenly sprang into his soul again, that rolling stone moving downward into the pit.

He pressed her with prodigious force and passion.

They heard not the thunder, they saw not the lightning. All round them began to dance and whirl and blend, finally, in a madly careening, gigantic fiery ball.

Falk took her . . .

One suppressed cry, then a gurgling and groaning of insane bliss. The storm ceased. It was already four o'clock in the morning.

"Now you must go away, Eric."

"Yes, I must."

"Go by way of the lake, then climb over the monastery wall, and you'll be on the road. Else you may be seen."

Half way home he was caught in another rainstorm. He ought to take shelter somewhere, he thought, but felt too weak to look for a place. Besides, what matter if he did get a bit wet?

Huge black clouds lowered in the sky again, closing in nearer and nearer to the earth.

A long-drawn, awful peal shook the welkin; the lightning split the sky in two.

Another thunderclap, flashes of lightning one after the other, and a downpour as if the clouds were precipitating themselves on the earth.

In an instant Falk was drenched to the skin. He scarcely heeded it.

Of a sudden he saw a gigantic sheaf of fire tear loose from the sky and divide into seven flashes. That same moment the white willow by the roadside was enveloped in flames. The lightning had rent it from top to bottom.

Life and destruction.

Of course. Where life is, there also must be destruction, annihilation.

Marit, yes, Marit was ruined.

In Falk's mind suddenly flashed the blinding thought that it was he who had ruined Marit.

Why not? I am nature, therefore I create life and destroy it. I pass over a thousand corpses because I must, and I create life also because I must.

I am not only this one I. I am also you and he, God, the world, nature—and something more whereby I know what you are, eternal stupidity, eternal mockery.

I am not a man. I am a superman . . . ha, ha, superman! He burst out laughing at the fantastic word. Yes, a superman, a cruel man devoid of conscience, but great and good. I am nature. I have no conscience, because nature herself has no conscience.

Superman! Ha, Ha! It was a sick laugh.

Superman! Ha, Ha! He went on laughing his sick laugh.

Out of the black sky he saw a fiery column tear itself loose and divide into seven flashes and on its way kill a dove. And it will divide again into a thousand flashes and kill a thousand doves and rabbits, and so it will go on forever, giving birth and killing.

For such is the will of Fate.

For I must do it.

For my instincts demand it.

For I am I. I am a criminal diabolic nature.

And on this account I am to torture myself?

Ridiculous!

Does the lightning know why it destroys? Can it choose its course through the air?

No. It can only know that it struck in this or that spot, that it destroyed this or that object.

I, too, know, and am entering the fact in the records, that I destroyed an innocent dove.

The atmosphere was so permeated with electricity that a sea of fire seemed to be hovering in the air.

Falk walked on, enveloped in the mighty storm—he walked and thought. He walked like a mysterious formidable power—like a demon sent down upon earth, a demon with a whole hell of torments for scattering fresh creative destruction.

He stopped at the ditch. It was running full of water. If he walked round it, he would come out on the road. A little more or less wetness, what was the difference now? Yes, nothing mattered now, nothing, absolutely nothing.

So he forded the ditch. The water reached to his shoulders.

At home, after undressing and going to bed, he fell into a delirium.

From *Homo Sapiens*, Alfred A. Knopf, 1915.
Translated by THOMAS SELTZER

Zofia Nalkowska

(1885–1954)

Daughter of a renowned reformer of geography, Zofia Nalkowska was born in Warsaw and brought up in a refined and scholarly home where she formed a deep and lasting friendship with her parents. Already in her teens, she showed a keen interest in politics, literature and the social conditions about her. Her first novel, *Women* (1906), appeared when she was only twenty-one. It was a typically Positivist work which reflected her interest in psychology, philosophy and economics. The author was imbued with a zeal for bettering the world and ridding it of evil. Moreover, her youthful and also her later novels were refreshing in their portrayal of the eternal feminine, and won acclaim for the writer's limpid style and the realism and the psychological accuracy of her characterization.

Zofia Nalkowska is a rare phenomenon in Polish literature. Her artistic vision of the world remains at a high level no matter what her themes are. The novels *Girls of the Same Age, Narcyza, The House of Women* (1920) and *A Bad Love* all deal with eroticism and its mysterious connection with social complexity. Nalkowska probes into the lives of her women characters: their superficial sensual experiences as well as the shocking spiritual dramas. Such novels as *Teresa Hennert's Love Affair* (1923), *The Jackdaw* (1927), *The Border* (1935), and *Life's Ties* (1948) are often regarded as her three outstanding books in which she excels both as a psychological and sociological novelist. These realistic novels present the writer's generation, its social conflicts before the war and its struggles after the defeat of 1939. Other novels that deal with social causes are *Walls of the World* (1931) and *The Impatient Ones* (1939).

The Jackdaw and *Unwholesome Love* (1928) spread Nalkowska's fame abroad, and two of her plays, *The House of Women* (1930) and *The Day of His Return*, also won recognition in other countries.

Nalkowska wrote two series of short stories, entitled "Characters," one in 1920 and the other in 1947. They follow the tradition of La Bruyère and Chamfort.

Her *Medallions* (1947– from which we present excerpts) is one of the most frequently translated books of Nalkowska. It is a result of the novelist's participation in the work of the International Committee to Investigate Nazi Crimes which conducted a survey of a considerable number of Nazi torture chambers and concentration camps in Poland. (The examination took place while the war was still in progress). The *Medallions* is thus not a work of fiction, but rather a novelist's report on what she heard and saw, a shocking document of our times.

Medallions

(People prepared this fate for people)

Professor Spanner

1

That morning we were there for the second time. It was a bright, fresh May day. A brisk breeze blew from the sea, recalling something out of the past. Beyond the trees of the broad asphalt avenue was the surrounding wall and behind it spread a spacious courtyard. We already knew what we were about to see.

This time we were accompanied by two elderly gentlemen. They had come as Spanner's "colleagues"; they were both professors, both doctors and scientists. One was tall and gray-haired, his face lean and noble; the other was equally large, but stout and heavy besides. His full face expressed good nature and something akin to anxiety.

They were somewhat similarly dressed and not according to our style; in their long, black, woolen spring coats they looked rather provincial. Their soft hats were also black.

The modest little unplastered brick building stood in a corner of the courtyard a little to the side, as an unimportant annex of the large building which housed the Anatomical Institute.

We first walked down to a dark roomy basement. In the oblique light which fell from the distant, high-placed windows the dead lay the same as yesterday. Their creamy-white, naked young bodies, resembling hard sculptures, were in a perfect condition, although they had been waiting many months for the time they would no longer be needed.

Like in sarcophagi they lay lengthwise, one body on top of another, in long concrete tubs with open lids. Their hands were not folded across their chests according to funeral ritual but lay alongside their bodies. And the heads were cut off from their torsos as neatly as though they were of stone.

In one of the sarcophaguses, on top of the dead, lay the headless "sailor" already familiar to us—a splendid youth, huge as a gladiator. The contours of a ship were tattooed on his broad chest. Across the outlines of two smokestacks appeared the inscription to a vain faith: *God with us.*

We passed one corpse-filled tub after another, and both the foreigners walked and looked, too. They were doctors and knew better than we what it all meant. Fourteen corpses would have sufficed for the needs of the Anatomical Institute. Here, there were three hundred fifty of them.

Two vats contained only the hairless heads severed from those other bodies. They lay one on top of another—human faces like potatoes heaped up haphazardly in a pit: some sideways as if pressed into a pillow, others turned face down or up. They were smooth and yellowish, also excellently preserved and also chopped off at the nape as though they were of stone.

In a corner of one of the vats lay the rather small, cream-colored face of a boy who might have been eighteen when he died. Slightly oblique dark eyes were not completely shut but barely covered with the lids. The full lips of the same color as the face assumed a patient, sad smile. Smooth and expressive brows were lifted towards the temples as though in disbelief. In this utterly queer situation which was beyond his understanding he awaited the final verdict of the world.

Farther along there were more tubs with the dead and then vats with people hacked in two, cut up into pieces and skinned. A few corpses of women lay in a single tub set separately at a distance.

We also saw in the vaults a few more empty tubs, barely finished, without the lids. They signified that the stock of dead needed by the living was insufficient, that plans were afoot to expand the whole venture.

With the two professors we later passed to the little red house and saw there on the now cold fireplace a huge vat full of a dark liquid. Someone familiar with the premises lifted the cover with a poker and drew to the surface a dripping human torso, cooked to the bone.

There was nothing in two other vats, but close by, in a row on the shelves of a vitrine, lay skulls and thigh bones, boiled clean.

We also saw a large chest with layer upon layer of finely prepared human skin, cleaned of the fat. Jars of caustic soda stood on the shelf, a cauldron containing mordant was set into the wall; and there was a big oven for burning the scraps and bone.

Finally, on a tall table lay pieces of whitish, gritty soap and several metal molds containing the dried soap.

This time we did not climb the ladder to the attic to see the skulls and bones stacked high on the clay floor. We only passed for a moment in the part of the courtyard where traces could be seen of three completely burned down buildings, the remnants of crematorium-type metal furnaces and a large number of pipes and cable. It was known that the little red house had twice been set on fire. Each time, however, it had been noticed and put out.

We left with the two professors who immediately parted from us and went on their way conducted by someone we did not know.

2

The thin, sallow-faced young man with clear blue eyes who is testifying before the Commission was brought from the prison for the investigation. He has no idea what we want from him.

He speaks deliberately, gravely and sadly. He does speak Polish, though with a foreign accent, slightly rolling his r's.

He says that he is a native of Gdańsk. He had attended primary school, then completed six grades of secondary school. He was a volunteer and a scout. During the war he was taken prisoner, but escaped. He worked at shovelling snow in the streets and then in a munitions factory. He ran away again. All this, more or less, took place in Gdańsk.

When his father was taken to a concentration camp a German came to lodge at his mother's. This German gave him work in the Anatomical Institute. And that is how he came to Professor Spanner.

The professor was writing a book on anatomy and engaged him to prepare the bodies. He was giving a series of lectures at the university, a kind of preparatory course for the students. He had the book published; it was for this book that he worked. His assistant, Professor Wohlmann, worked too—but one cannot say whether also on a book, or just so. . . .

This side wing was finished in 1943 for an Incinerator Plant. At that time Spanner made arrangements to obtain a machine for separating the meat and fat from the bone. Skeletons were to be made from these bones. In 1944, Professor Spanner ordered the students to store the fat from the dead separately. Every evening when the courses were over and the students had departed, the plates of fat were taken away by workers. There were also plates with sinews and meat. Well, they either threw the meat away or burned it. But the people in town complained to the police, so the professor ordered it burned at night because the stench was too great.

The students were also told to remove the skin neatly, next, the fat neatly, then—according to the book of instructions—the sinews down to the bone. The fat removed by the workers from the plates remained lying all winter and then, when the students left, it was converted within five or six days into soap.

Professor Spanner and Senior Assistant von Bergen also collected human skin. They were going to dress it and make something of it.

"The senior assistant, von Bergen, well, he was my direct superior. Dr. Wohlmann was Professor Spanner's deputy. Professor Spanner was a civilian, but he was registered with the SS as a doctor."

The prisoner does not know where Dr. Spanner may now be.

"Spanner went away in January 1945. When he left he told us to work on the fat collected during the semester; he ordered us to make the soap and the anatomy properly, and to keep everything tidy so it looked *human.* He did not tell us to remove the recipe, perhaps he forgot. He said he would return, but didn't. When he left, his mail was sent to the Institute of Anatomy at Halle an der Saale."

Sitting in a chair by the wall and facing the light that streams through the windows, he makes his disposition. He is in full view as he pauses and reflects, eager to tell exactly how it all was, without omitting anything. He is one and there are a score of us: Commission members, local authorities, court officials.

Excess of zeal sometimes makes him incomprehensible.

"What was this recipe?"

"The recipe hung on the wall. The woman assistant, who was from the countryside, brought a recipe for soap and copied it for us. Her name was Koitek. A technical assistant, she too went away, but to Berlin. Besides this there was also a note on the wall. It was written by von Bergen and concerned the thorough cleaning of the bones preparatory to making skeletons. But the bones did not come out right, they were spoiled. Either the temperature was too high, or the liquid too strong." That old trouble still worried him.

"The soap from the recipe was always a success. Just once did it fail to come out right. The last lot, lying on the table in the Incinerator, it's no good.

"The soap was made in the Incinerator. Dr. Spanner himself directed the production with the assistance of von Bergen, the one who used to go for the corpses. Did I ever go with him? Yes, I did, I went only twice. And also once to the prison in Gdańsk.

"The corpses were at first brought from the lunatic asylum, but later these bodies were not enough. Then Spanner wrote to all the town mayors not to bury the dead, that the Institute would send for them. They were brought from the camp at Stutthof, those condemned to death at Koenigsberg, from Elblag, from all of Pomerania. Not until a guillotine had been set up in the Gdańsk prison were there enough corpses. . . .

"They were mostly Polish corpses, but at one time there were also German military men, beheaded in the prison during the celebrations. And at one time four or five dead were brought and the names were Russian.

"Von Bergen always brought the corpses at night."

"What kind of a celebration was this?"

"The celebration was in the prison. The dedication of the guillotine. The chief, Spanner, and other guests were invited. The chief took von Bergen and me along. Why he took me along, I don't know, for I wasn't invited. The guests came by car and on foot. They came to that room. But we did not enter it, we had to wait. We had already seen the guillotine and the gallows. It was at that time that the four German military men condemned to death were there. And people said that a German pastor performed the ceremony of dedication.

"I saw one of the prisoners brought in. His hands were manacled behind his back, his bare feet were quite black, and aside from his trousers, he was naked.

"There was a purple curtain and beyond it another room and the prosecutor. The senior assistant later talked with the executioner and then told us about it. Well, we heard the prosecutor's speech, then a whirring noise and a sort of a stretching, stamping noise like someone running. And the iron struck. The executioner reported that the sentence had been carried out. And we already saw four bodies carried out in an open casket.

"I don't know if a priest was present at the dedication but people said that one of the military men in uniform was a priest.

"At one time von Bergen and Wohlmann brought a hundred corpses from that prison.

"But later Spanner wanted corpses with heads. He also did not want people who were shot; there was too much work with them; they spoiled too soon and stank. For instance, we got a German army man who had been condemned to death. He had a broken leg with a shot wound in it. And he was beheaded as well. Everything all at once. The corpses from the lunatic asylum were with heads.

"Spanner always had a stock of bodies, because if later there weren't enough of them he'd always have to take headless corpses.

"The big headless sailor is from the Gdańsk prison. The bodies were cut in half because they were too big to fit into the cauldrons.

"One man can give maybe five kilograms of fat. The fat was stored in the Incinerator in a stone tub."

"How much?"

He ponders a long while, he wants to be as accurate as possible. "One and a half hundredweight."

Immediately, however, he adds: "At least, so it was at first. But lately there was less. When they had already begun the retreat to the Reich there was maybe a hundredweight. . . .

"No one was supposed to know about the production of soap. Spanner forbade even the students to be told. But they'd look in there, and later one told another, so perhaps they knew. . . . And at one time they even called for students to the Incinerator to help with the cooking. But only the chief, the senior assistant, myself and two German workers had daily access to the production. The finished soap was taken by Dr. Spanner and was at his disposal.

"The finished soap? . . . Well, when it is ready, it's soft at first—

well, so it has to cool. Then we had to cut it. And Spanner locked it up. There was not only the soap there, a machine also stood there. The five of us had access. And if others wanted to enter, they had to ask for the key."

"Why was it secret?"

He ponders this a long time. He wished to reply to the best of his knowledge.

"Maybe Spanner was afraid, or something . . ." he reflects intently. "To my thinking, if somebody, a civilian from the town, heard about it, maybe there'd be a rumpus. . . ."

It might seem that here, too, a purple curtain is hung between us and him. There was no way to get at him.

Someone finally asked: "Did no one tell you that it was a crime to make soap from human fat?"

He replied with complete candor: "No one told me that."

But it gives him food for thought. He does not immediately reply to the questions that follow. Finally he replies without reluctance.

"Of course, various people came to the Institute and to Spanner. Professor Klotz, Schmidt, Rosmann came to see him. At one time the Minister of Health was in the Institute of Hygiene . . . and the Minister of Education, also Gauleiter Förster. They were received by Professor Grossmann, the dean of the whole Medical Academy. Some of them were here when this house had not yet been built, so they only visited the Department of Anatomy to see what it was like, whether there was anything lacking. And though the Incinerator was already there, well, the soap was always removed after four, five days. Can't say if they saw the soap. They might've. And the recipe always hung there during inspection so if they'd read it, they must've known what was cooked there.

"Yes, the chief ordered me to make the soap with the workers. Why me? I don't know. As to Spanner, when he'd lock up the soap like that, I often thought that he was up to some swindle. If he was supposed to be writing his book about soap, he wouldn't have forbidden us to speak about it. Maybe he himself stumbled on the idea of making soap from left-overs? . . . He probably wasn't ordered to make it because then he himself wouldn't have had to look for a recipe. . . ."

No certainty results from these reflections.

"What about the students? . . . Like me, everybody was at first afraid to wash with this soap . . . there was aversion to using it. The smell was bad. Professor Spanner earnestly tried to stop the odor. He wrote to chemical works to send him oils. But one could always tell by the smell that it wasn't the right kind of soap.

"Yes, I told them at home. . . . At first, one of my friends even saw how I shuddered at anyone washing with such soap.

"At home, my mother was also disgusted. But it soaped so well she used it for the laundry. I got used to it, for it was good. . . ."

An indulgent smile appears on his thin, sallow face.

"It can be said that the people in Germany know how to make something out of nothing. . . ."

In the afternoon we called both old professors, medical colleagues of Spanner, to a hearing. The talks were held at their place of work, in an empty room of one of the hospital buildings.

Examined separately, both stated that they knew nothing about a building with a hidden soap factory. They saw it this morning for the first time and the sight horrified them.

Examined separately, both stated that Spanner—a man not more than forty—was an authority in the field of pathological anatomy. Not having known him long and seldom meeting him, they could not say anything about his morals. They only knew that he was a member of the Party.

Each of the deponents sat at a distance from us, in a chair standing by itself, his face wearing a distinctly distressed expression. Each sat there without removing his black coat and holding his black hat on his knees.

Both spoke sensibly and cautiously. Both, when speaking, took everything into consideration. On that May day Gdansk was still full of Germans: ranks of German prisoners-of-war passed down the streets and were showered with flowers by their women. But the authorities were Polish, and Soviet troops formed the garrison.

To the question whether, knowing from his scientific activities, they could suppose that he was a man capable of making soap from the bodies of executed prisoners, each replied differently.

After reflecting a long while, the tall, thin one, with the gray head and noble features, stated: "Yes, I could have supposed that, had I known that he received such orders, for it was well known that he was a disciplined member of the Party."

The other man, the stout, good-natured one with the pink complexion and hanging jowls, also pondered this for a long time. After reflection, having as it were weighed everything in his conscience, he replied: "Well, yes I might have supposed that—because Germany was then suffering from a great shortage of fats. And consideration for the economic situation of the country, for the good of the country, might have induced him to do so."

Translated by JADWIGA ZWOLSKA

Characters

MARCIA OR A YOUNG GIRL

Marcia says: "I don't require that the world admire my virtues. That would scarcely be just. But I do want it to admire my shortcomings." She is neither preoccupied with herself nor does she wish to change. She does what gives her pleasure. Sculpting, painting, embossing leather, playing and singing. She is wise and sensuous. Working without thought of fame, Marcia is not surprised nor is she sad when she is not successful but begins to think how to attain her aim the next time.

She does not disdain others as does Kamil; she even likes people when they catch her interest. Otherwise she is completely indifferent to them. She loves reality and observes it attentively. She likes herself.

She does not understand how anyone can fall in love and suspects that it is all pretense. She observes men with a grave and stern mien and later laughs like a child, even a little unwisely, and lets them kiss her red mouth. But she is frightfully surprised if one of them imagines that she has done this for love and is himself in love with her. Marcia smiles and says: "How can anyone be so stupid?"

ELVIRA OR A YOUNG WOMAN

Elvira says, "As for me, I never hurry." She is probably secure in the thought that everything will fit into her life. She does the things that she finds pleasant and that offer no difficulty. She smiles only when she thinks that something is amusing.

She talks willingly and with deliberation about herself. She likes herself. Slim, calm and pretty, she likes everything that goes on about her. Life does not interest her; it only gives her pleasure.

When she is out in the world, she doesn't think of triumph and adulation but of pleasure. Elvira likes to travel, she likes the theater and music. She is an authority on good food, clothes and literature. But she has no passion. Nor is she interested in new things or new people. She does not desire the things others have. Things that are unattainable are precisely those that she does not care for.

Elvira is not ambitious and she does not care what people say about her. Hiding the things that should be hidden, she is not afraid of indiscretion, does not tremble at the thought of a scandal and does not seek anyone's favor. Nor does she try to prevail upon or charm anyone. Everything is easy for her and turns out well.

Thus she is sweet to her husband, children and lovers. Bestowing upon each his due with untroubled placidity, she is not too concerned whether these things are of the noblest quality.

ZENOBIA

Zenobia is young as she looks into one's eyes and laughs as she did in her youth, with complete trust in others and in herself. Her face is circumscribed with a regular oval; her eyes are bright and when she smiles her fresh lips, colored a shade of Rose Ciel as of yore, flatten out with a certain languid charm against her rounded, too-white teeth.

Her jokes find response and evoke hearty laughter. The willing attention she gives to people, her quick concern in everything that concerns others and her avid kindness win their friendship and sympathy.

All this is so as long as Zenobia looks into one's eyes, as long as she faces one.

But she need only turn her head a little to the side, or the light need only fall on her face from a different angle and her face changes suddenly. Cheeks which were rounded are divided into parts by folds; the line of her chin juts out at a right angle and sags a little. Her profile seems to belong to another woman. The flesh comes away from the bones, limp and flabby under the loose skin.

Seen thus from the side, Zenobia changes into an evil old woman, a bitter, wretched and crafty witch. Her words sound futile; her jokes no longer amuse. Seeing her thus, people exchange quick glances and draw away from her, disappointed.

They wonder: what is she really like? But they find no answer. Some claim that she is completely different, different from herself. And to her face they pay her compliments while in profile they laugh at her.

But, looking in a mirror, Zenobia sees herself only from the front. She knows less about herself than others do. Having confidence in herself and others, she does not use a hand mirror to have a side or back view. She does not know at all that she is young and old at the same time, that she belongs to two epochs, but lives only in certain segments which she strings carefully on the thread of time suspended in fiction.

There are many women like Zenobia. But these things are more noticeable in her than in others.

THEODOSIA OR A SENSITIVE HEART

When the last war broke out, Theodosia and her husband left the beautiful house in which she had been so happy. She concealed her treasures in the walls and cellars and asked a poor, trustworthy woman to watch the objects that could be neither hidden in the walls nor buried, took as many bags as would fit into the baggage compartment of the Buick and departed with a broken heart.

They were not as successful in their escape as others. Not far from the city a group of armed men took away their car, threw the things out into the road and drove off.

Theodosia and her husband, each carrying a small suitcase, continued their journey on foot. They lay with others in the potato field under the low-flying bombers, in the roar and flames of incendiary bombs and the chatter of machine guns. They followed small side paths, ate in peasant cottages, slept in barns. When the peasants refused to hire out their horses and wagons, fearing to leave their homes at such a time, Theodosia would say indignantly that this was Bolshevism.

The further they traveled, the more difficult it was to get food. The urban population had fallen upon its own country like locusts, streaming over the roads, moving, surging, overflowing to one side and another, seeking safety, trying to understand. When the disaster became obvious to everyone, the people began to turn back.

Theodosia and her husband decided to return. They bought whatever they could find, some fatback and grain, hired a horse-cart, its seat padded with hay, and set out on the return journey to their abandoned home.

And in the meantime great changes had taken place under the blue sky.

Crowds of people moved on both sides of the road, returning to their capital which had been captured by the enemy and ruined by heavy siege. Soldiers and officers returned in the same direction, their uniforms in tatters, leaning on canes, often bareheaded, some of them with their feet in bandages and rags instead of shoes.

Everywhere along the road heavy automobiles lay pushed to the side, smashed, their steel sinews contorted, their bones cracked, like carcasses picked clean of meat. Small cannon and trucks lay overturned.

The small mare trotted briskly and the man holding the reins kept repeating as he pointed his whip: "This is our whole wealth."

Farther from the road, rows of burned cottages, ruined houses, blackened and broken trees, trampled fields with big bomb holes and cavities passed slowly by.

In the black squares of burned cowsheds and stables lay the distended and charred carcasses of horses and cows. In the ruins of one cottage without a roof or walls, a peasant woman stood at the untouched stove cooking something in a tall black pot.

The picture of ruin and disaster accompanied them throughout the journey. Theodosia could not hold back her tears at the sight of so much sadness. For she was thinking of her own home. Weeping and trembling she kept repeating, "What will we find at home?" Her husband consoled her kindly.

They journeyed a whole day and at nightfall arrived in their own neighborhood. They had returned exactly a month from the day of their departure. Here, too, they saw a few ruined houses with the rubble on the streets like disgorged bowels. Theodosia covered her eyes at this horrible sight. The cart stopped at last. Theodosia's husband drew her hands from her face. She was speechless when in the darkness she recognized the form of her home standing unscathed, black against the somewhat lighter night sky.

She climbed out of the cart, knelt down on the ground and kissed the step of the porch stairs. The faithful poor woman opened the door and showed them the unscathed rooms which she had watched and guarded as if they were her own. There was no electricity but she found a candle and an oil lamp. They even found a pair of pyjamas for her husband and warm slippers, and the Persian sumak that usually hung on the wall near the couch.

After the dreadful journey and the sights that stretched along the road, her own peaceful walls seemed like heaven to Theodosia.

Overcome by emotion, Theodosia embraced her husband and said tearfully, "Dearest, now I know that there is a God."

Her husband moved away from her in embarrassment.

Blazhey or a Defenseless Person

Blazhey is free from many everyday cares. His mind is not occupied with questions like—what kind of gloves he should buy, which pair of trousers he should wear today, or what pair of shoes he should put on. Following the present style of going bareheaded in the summer, Blazhey does not even wear a hat.

Looking at his handsome, intelligent face, hearing his youthful voice, the passerby thinks with dread and fascination of what he was and must have been before the war.

Blazhey is among us. People pass him on the AB line at the edge of the Cracow Old Market Square, see his incomprehensible figure on one of the squares of Praga (a suburb of Warsaw on the right bank of the Vistula), stop beside his cart on one of the intersections of Piotrkowska Street in Lodz. Blazhey's face appears not much higher than the sideboards of his cart. For he has no legs, neither right nor left, nor does he possess a right or left arm. What is left is not much but it allows him to live. The little that remains, like a fragment of ancient sculpture, is beautiful.

As if everything that we have said here was not enough, Blazhey attracts the attention of others, of his fellow-men, with his peculiar sounds of soft music. There is a small mouth organ attached on a vertical wire to the side of the cart so that it reaches his lips and thus without effort he can play the old army songs.

With his beautiful, human eyes Blazhey looks brightly into the eyes of people, of his fellow-men, who approach him and stop beside his cart. And in a strong human voice he says, "Thank you, madam," or "Thank you, sir." At first the money was placed beside him on the boards of his cart, but now one may drop the money into a special slot box placed there for this purpose.

Smiling, Blazhey says that he travels to various towns, though his family lives in Poznan and that is where he always returns. And he shows his healthy, white teeth in a smile.

There are many people similar to Blazhey but only one who is exactly like him. One can devote a great deal of thought to him. To him and his fate.

Dionysius or an Old-fashioned Man

When Dionysius was young, he was not insensible to the fate of humanity. He saw her striding along the road of evolution and revolution toward what used to be called the bright future of the world. He believed in the day when justice and fraternity would triumph; he believed that the human race was evolving toward perfection.

But all the people he now thinks about are in their graves. From all those in the group and family photographs, the snapshots with friends, he alone is alive. The violence unleashed by the infinite harm and cruelty of the new times has crushed all the convictions of his youth. Dionysius recollects with bitterness the illusions whose influence and charm molded his character.

Thus, instead of justice and fraternity, Dionysius looks upon burned cities, plundered museums, weeps for the murdered, strangled, burned. On the vast battlefields of Europe the wreckages of two wars snarl at each other and shoot at each other in the night.

People whose conscience is burdened with recent plunder and murder enjoy themselves in places where music plays once more. The dread power of history has hurled a curse upon this century.

Dionysius feels that to live in these times is a disgrace. His mind recoils from faith in such a world; he does not wish to accept it as reality.

Dionysius has lost faith in humanity; he only believes in people.

If they should change, if each one would sincerely want happiness, its achievement would be simple.

Unfortunately, each one wants a different happiness. And if people want happiness for someone, then they snarl and shoot at each other in the night.

Dionysius leaves the gloom of his miserable room that stands in the burned-out house, to walk the streets of Warsaw which are marked by the ghosts and skeletons of old buildings. Walking thus, he does not raise his eyes so as not to see the ruins and the fecundity of the hurried, avid and criminal life.

On the square which he passes, a group of foreign youth, side by side with local students and workers, are breaking up the ruins, loading the rubble on trucks, salvaging whole soot-covered bricks from the devastation, stacking them carefully for the future construction of factories and schools.

Dionysius is not aware of this living, vivid, staged metaphor, for he does not lift his eyes nor does he look in that direction. He does not believe in the future though it is at last becoming the present. He does not believe that humanity is composed of people and that they and not the dread and mysterious power of fate makes contemporary history.

He allows the first signs of the era of which he dreamed to pass him by.

Translated by **CHRISTINA CEKALSKA**

Maria Kuncewicz

(1899–   )

Born in 1899 in Samara, Russia, Mrs. Kuncewicz (née Szczepanska) was educated in the universities of Cracow and Nancy and also studied music in the Warsaw Conservatory and in Paris. Already her first book, *Alliance with the Child* (1926) attracted attention by the vivid directness of its intelligent style and the frank treatment of the problem of motherhood. *Face of the Man* (1927) is characterized by the same qualities of sincerity. *Two Moons* (1933) has for its locale the quaint town of Kazimierz on the Vistula in which the author made her home for many years in the interwar period. She spent the years 1940–1955 in England and then took up permanent residence in the United States. Unlike many outstanding Polish writers whose works are unknown outside Poland, Mrs. Kuncewicz, thanks to the translation of her works, has been acclaimed as a writer of note. *The Stranger* is a deft and penetrating study of neuroticism, relentless in its dissection of the diseased mind of an egocentric woman. *The Keys* (1946) is the story of the author's escape from Poland to Rumania, France and finally Great Britain. The special and most significant quality of the book is the imagination with which she encompasses her experience and the ordeal of her nation. *The Conspiracy of the Absent* (1950), a powerful and moving novel beginning midway in World War II, moves back and forth between Poland under Nazi rule and air-raided London. *The Forester* (1955) set against the background of mid-nineteenth century Poland, is a stirring and complicated picture of an alien world, with its young hero, Casimir, who was born of an ethnically mixed stock, waging an inner struggle for a patriotic allegiance. Also in 1955 her play *Thank You for the Rose*, written in English, was produced in London by an avantgarde theatrical group.

Mrs. Kuncewicz's most recent novel is *The Olive Grove* published in New York. She also edited an anthology of Polish prose writers currently living in Poland, *The Modern Polish Mind* (Boston, 1962).

In 1937 she was awarded the Literary Prize of the City of Warsaw and a year later the Golden Laurel of the Polish Academy of Literature. While living in London she founded the International Pen Club Center for Writers in Exile and after moving to New York was president of its American Branch. She is currently Visiting Professor of Polish literature at the University of Chicago.

After Forty Years[1]

Meanwhile Rose suddenly ceased to be in such a hurry to go home, which meant to a room in Wolf Street, with "board" in a "cultured, Christian family."

Adam, as soon as he found himself in the street, began to look about for a taxi.

"We will drive, won't we? You are tired."

She held his arm.

"No need, Adam, I feel very well. And it isn't that I am in a hurry, only that I did not feel like wasting time. What was there still to do at the Paul's? Dinner, certainly, was excellent. Well, I ate and drank. And Martie is coming to me today. And driving in a taxi, it's like in a box—you don't see anything. And it's too stuffy. Let us go in a horse cab."

Presently they got into an old cab. Rose settled on the seat with childish joy.

"There is nothing like a horse cab. I remember Yula, when she married that rich Russian in Taganrog, had splendid harnesses. In winter—three fine horses under a net, the *kalakolchiki* (little bells) tinkled till the whole street was gay with them. In summer a phaeton with two horses shining like new chestnuts, and off they went to the sea to bathe. Or to a far-away farm they drove in a *tarantas*, with a samovar and down pillows for the night out of doors. My aunt was very self-willed and Grandfather used to be frightfully upset by some of the things she did. In the evening he was often sitting, so they said, with another exile, a comrade from the insurrection, playing bezique. Then he moaned: 'What a shame, what a dishonor, my daughter has married a Russian. There will be no rest for me in the grave'. And the comrade agreed: 'Even beyond the grave, brother, you will know no rest.' But where were they to be found—those Poles in Taganrog? When, later on, my father, a Polish legionary's orphan—no longer young, worn out with Czar Nicholas' regime in the corps and by the Crimean campaign—appeared in the town, it was not strange that Grandfather started beating and starving Sophie, my mother (she was fifteen then), to force her to marry that Adolph Zabczynski."

She wandered for some moments, looking sadly at the houses and the sky.

"Well, now, look: Poland. I do not like it very much, Adam," she sighed; "they compelled my mother and me to come here. My mother,

[1] The title of this selection supplied by the editors. Rose is also called "Eva" or "Evelyn."

why, she was in love with a Russian boy, and never grew accustomed to my father, although—God rest his soul—he was a real gentleman, noble and distinguished. But he was melancholy and could not bear people. And I? All the happiness I ever had was Taganrog. Until suddenly Louise declared: Taganrog: that is Asia; my school friends and teachers and the boys who were there (how beautifully Pietia used to play the ocarina!)—they were all enemies and barbarians; that is to say, Russians. Yes, and from day to day she bade me cast away my happy childhood and return to that Poland for which my grandparents longed. For them it was the country of their happy youth. But for me, what was it? Exile. The home of a cross aunt. Ah, Adam . . . When I arrived in Warsaw, which was unknown and strange and unlike anything of which I was fond, if I was angry with anybody, do you know what I called him in thoughts? 'Wretched Pole!' "

Adam put his hands to his ears to keep off these words. He writhed: "Why do you drag that up now? If you called him that in your thoughts, well, you did, and yet you were always a true Pole."

Rose nodded her head doubtfully.

"A true Pole. Remember what you said yourself about me: 'Contrariety and pride brought you back to Poland.' That was the truth. Only through contrariety and pride I wanted to come back to Poland, when I was in Russia. But now . . . now I am driving with you along these streets. They are ugly. There is little that is picturesque or rich in this town of Warsaw. And I feel—what will you say, my dear?—I feel that I could die for it. I should be ready and glad to die for each small brick in this Poland."

He moved uneasily: "Why die? It is better to live, with God in your heart."

The cabman stopped his horses. They had reached their destination.

"It's a pity," said Rose, "it is so pleasant to look at the world when the heart is good. As a matter of fact I have known the world very little."

Adam paid the cabman and rang for the porter, but Rose still hesitated in the doorway.

Scarcely had they gone in and taken off their things than Adam got out his pocket-book and his pencil and put on his spectacles. Thus armed he waited patiently while Rose hung up her coat in the wardrobe. She took rather a long time about it, but at last sat down opposite her husband, breathing heavily. However, she immediately got up again and rang the bell.

"Let us have some coffee."

He looked at her reproachfully.

"Why do you drink black coffee? They forbade you long ago."

She raised her eyebrows.

"Who forbade it? Dr. Gerhardt never said anything to me about coffee."

The coffee was brought in. She arranged the cups and in the midst of these hospitable activities she sat down again.

"I don't know where the sugar is," she whispered. "Can we drink it without sugar? I have no strength to look for anything."

She stroked Adam's back.

"Do you really wish me well? Good health and long life? Tell me, Adam. Only it is not worth while lying, for I shall know anyhow whether you are telling the truth."

He shrugged his shoulders.

"Did I ever lie to you? I never lied, although you never cared whether I did or not."

He bent his head.

"Even for lies, there were but few opportunities for us." Rose nudged his arm.

"Well, Adam, Adam! Don't say that. Why recollect it now? I, you see, wanted—on the contrary—to tell you that I bear no grudge against you. Neither for those long years of ours, nor for today. I have forgiven you everything."

He pushed away his cup and an expression of boredom spread over his features.

"Well, and the accounts? Now, this moment I can give you a hundred zlotys for your journey on condition that next month you repay the same amount to the holiday fund. For we must certainly go to take the waters at Truskawiec; with the Wladyses, the political situation is uncertain, and one cannot count on them. As for the money from your shares, for which you wrote me a power of attorney, I've paid three hundred—as you asked me to do—to the furrier, and here is the receipt."

Rose listened piously for a time; then the attention began to fade from her face. When it came to the receipt she laid her hand on Adam's notebook.

"You don't seriously think that these things are important?"

He started and flushed.

"Certainly they are important. And, anyway, you yourself wanted to do it."

"I did. I often want something and afterwards I am overcome with surprise that I could have wanted such an impossibility."

She broke into a laugh.

"Accounts? Accounts between us . . . but, Adam, forty years of marriage! How many years does one need to count what you owe me and I owe you?"

"Oh, if that is what you meant"—he sighed—"it is a difficult matter. But why did you want to do it today?"

"For my life will end here!" she said.

Adam's reserve vanished in the twinkling of an eye.

"Your life will end? Eva, you're concealing something! You've already been to the doctor? Here? Have they frightened you?"

She shook her head. "Oh, no! Not that. Only that a miracle has happened to me. What I was always expecting has come now."

"What—what has come? What miracle?" he asked feverishly. "At least tell me. No doubt it is some madness. I have seen lately that you've been taken with something again."

She wrung her hands.

"Again? No, not again. It was never like this before. This is completely new."

"But what, Evelyn? Do stop tormenting me with riddles!"

She got up and went to the window. She held the curtain with one hand. Presently she came back tense with excitement.

"No, Adam, don't ask. I want frightfully to tell you and I cannot. You see, surely, that it's not in my power?" She caught his hand in both her own. "Really, what is the good of talking? There always were, and there remain, so many mysteries between us; you for me, I for you, we were always mysteries. And that was not such a bad thing. Only hate was bad. Now I understand that one should not hate mysteries. So, please do respect my last secret."

Adam's face twitched, he hesitated.

"Good!" he sighed at last. "I will not ask. I also know that it is useless to plague myself trying to understand you." He paused and turned pale. "For the rest, I have no right . . . Since we do not live together and you do not ask me about my life."

She got up, suddenly radiant.

"Ah, ah, it is just that! You see you admit it yourself. For a year you have been living at Kwiatkowska's. I understand: it is friendship. She is old, you are old—and both of you are made of the same clay. You like to sit at tea talking about people: 'So-and-so is like this or like that. Someone's son-in-law has embezzled money, someone's wife has eloped'—not gossip, only you feel yourself one family. And afterwards you talk of Poland, of the community . . . which party is right, how things used to be, and how they are now. And you prophesy. And you argue about divine providence, the duties of a citizen and the young generation. After that you tell anecdotes, or go together to a lecture, or to the movies, or to church on Sundays, or to various national celebrations. I understand your Aunt Regina was the same; at your parents' home they used to argue like that and had similar interests—and at Kwiatkowska's it is the same. You love that, you've missed it your whole life—and now you have found it; and you are glad and you feel at peace. Well, life was difficult with me. I did not care for people, I was wild, I cared for music and my sorrow, my yearning and my secrets. You immediately warm the place, wherever you settle; I always wanted to be somewhere else. Your father was a burgomaster, your grandfather was a yeoman farmer; but mine were exiles, wanderers and soldiers of the foreign legions. You and I do not make a pair. I understand and I make no claims upon you. Oh, that is important, you see! At last, at last, I make no claims upon you."

She choked and plucked at her chain.

"What accounts can there be between us if there are no claims?"

He was following with difficulty Rose's rapid speech. His mouth and eyes were almost colorless with age and very grave. He did not contradict and did not interrupt her at all. When her flow of words was checked, he still sat listening to the silence. At last without taking his eyes from his wife's lips, which were quivering after this great effort, he repeated: "You and I do not make a pair, no . . ."

He listened again as though to himself.

"But are there many well-matched pairs in the world? And yet they live a godly life. Everything you said is true. About Kwiatkowska. About our families: And that is true too, that we were mysteries to one another. One thing only is not true: about hate. You hated my mystery, but your mystery . . . your mystery," he dropped his eyelids and added in a scarcely audible voice: "I loved it."

Rose shed tears.

"Oh, God, how dreadful! I know."

He controlled himself quickly and went on:

"You know how very much you surprised and delighted me through the whole of my youth. You know how I have suffered day and night. How I desired to reconcile you. How I succumbed to you. But do you know when I finally lost you? When I counted for nothing with you, Evelyn?"

She did not answer. She looked at her husband with tearful eyes. Then he pressed his fists against the arm of the chair, crouched as though for a leap and said hoarsely:

"It was when, having mastered you once in my life, by hate, I could not continue in hatred for longer than one night."

He choked and his eyes became bloodshot.

"And do you know *when* I really understood it? This morning! You insulted me dreadfully. You told me that I had purposely given my child to death, to hurt you. And you did still worse: you insulted God. Because in that dreadful hour when our son was dying I did not blaspheme as you did, but desired to inspire you with Christian humility—you now, hardened at heart, made God the enemy of man— to hurt me. . . ."

He broke off, his voice failed him. However, he did not yield to his weakness.

"You compelled me today to be angry. I will confess. There was one moment when I desired your death. . . . Oh, Eva"—he folded his hands—"scarcely had that desire passed from my accursed head to my heart, when it faded away. And when you felt ill, I would have given my life for you. But you . . ."

He got up, horror widened his eyes.

"You . . . smiled at me as if you liked my hate."

He lifted his hands and let them fall again. With hunched shoulders he went to the window. On the way he whispered again:

"I understood a great deal this morning."

The reddish October sun threw its rays lower and lower over the roofs, the panes of the third-floor windows opposite glittered like lanterns, the day drew towards its close with a pathos which only the pigeons observed. Busy and excited, they strutted up and down on the cornice of the building cooed and looked questioningly towards the west. Adam wiped his nose. Rose came up and touched his shoulder.

"Adam, forgive me. My heart is torn when I think of your life. But do think also of mine. You say you cannot hate. But that is just your great good fortune. Did you ever consider how hard, how inhuman it was for me to live with my hatred? And why did you—good and wise as you were—why did you not save me, stupid as I was? Why were you afraid of me, Adam? Why?"

He replied in a quivering voice:

"How could I save you from yourself? Only God can save people from themselves, my dear."

She sobbed instead of replying. On the other side of the street the windowpanes and the pigeons still glistened, but in the room dusk began to fall. They stood in silence side by side, sunk in their own thoughts, and both alike helpless. When the windows grew dark, Rose was the first to awaken.

"Oh, why are we talking in such a dreadful way? In any case nothing can be mended now. It can only be ended."

Then Adam turned his face and said:

"Yes, Rose. Before long all will be ended. One thing we can still do: Forgive."

They looked at each other. In the dark their features were invisible—their faces looked indistinct and ghostly, like wisps of fog. They fell into each other's arms and wept together.

From *The Stranger,* Chapter XVII, English
edition, L. B. Fischer, New York, 1945.

Maria Dabrowska

(1892–1965)

Maria Dabrowska (née Szumska) is regarded as the foremost contemporary Polish writer. She was born in Russow, near Kalisz, in 1892. She studied natural sciences, sociology and economics in Warsaw, Switzerland, Belgium, France and England. She also studied the cooperative movement in Finland, then came back to Poland to marry a noted social worker. For some ten years she was a militant advocate of the idea of cooperative movement, then turned to fiction.

Dabrowska's first collection of short stories, *People from There* (1925) was based on her childhood memories, and it immediately established her place in Polish literature. The protagonists of these stories are the under-privileged, homeless and landless peasants, and the shocking picture of their lives is evoked with objective realism and startling authenticity. Her lowly heroes are not without a measure of dignity, and their lot, for all the misery, is not without some affirmative aspects.

Dabrowska's acknowledged masterpiece is the saga of Kalisz, *Nights and Days* (1932–1934), a four-volume chronicle novel, which has been called an epic of every-day life. The book is a family tale about small county squires and ordinary, average people in the period from the 1860's to the outbreak of World War I, narrated with simplicity, in an epic style and in the spirit of wise compassion.

Her other important writings are *The Crossroads* (1937), a survey of the peasant problem in Poland, its sequel, *Hand in Hand* (1939), *Orphan Genius* (1939); also collections of stories: *The Signs of Life* (1936), *The Morning Star* (1955), *The Village and Other Stories* (1957, also published in English in Warsaw). Dabrowska has also written juvenile books, plays, and criticism, and has been a leading publicist. She translated the *Diary* of Samuel Pepys, and assembled her essays on Conrad in a volume *Sketches About Conrad* (1959).

On a Beautiful Summer Morning

On a certain May day in nineteen forty-two, Doctor Alice Swiacka lay down for a brief rest after lunch. She asked to be wakened before five, that is, before her usual visiting hours. At this time the flat, which faced Filtrowa Street and Wielkopolski Square, was steeped in a silence which the city noises accented like an obligato. Alice fell asleep immediately and dreamt that together with Joseph Tomyski and his wife, two friends she seldom saw,—she was walking across the Poniatowski Bridge in winter. It seemed to be after a battle or bombardment, gaps in the bridge had to be avoided; underneath it could be heard the gurgle of water. It was slippery on the bridge, and snowy and dark besides. In spite of this Alice could see very well that the Vistula flowed foamy and turbulent, mightier than ever. But the city above it was practically non-existent—there was not a single light and only a faint outline of the walls. They walked hurriedly in a disagreeable and nervous way, either trying to escape mortal danger or bound towards something terrible. The Vistula, choppy and white with foam for a change, resounded with a roar like a mountain waterfall or the ocean raging in a storm. Shouting above this noise Alice called to Tomyski: "I don't understand why Warsaw does not destroy this river with destruction!" And being worn out she wanted to lean against the bridge railing after uttering these words, and suddenly saw that the railing was broken and she leaned—was practically leaning over a chasm. She endeavored to shout one again, "Why does not Warsaw destroy this river with destruction" but fear shocked her so violently that she awoke.

In a twinkling she mentally repeated the words from the dream, amazed that she could dream such a mutilated sentence, as though it, too, had been struck by a shell. She lay there a minute longer, enjoying the voluptuousness of the afternoon, especially pleasant after that ominous dream. She gazed at the large pink tulips, one of those lovely bouquets which, like votive offerings, adorn the rooms of popular physicians.

Suddenly, something like a crash of thunder ejected her from the couch. That was one of the tulips shedding its petals in the silence onto the glistening varnish of the table. Almost simultaneously was heard the metallic, grating, rhythmic rumble of the tram coming up the street. This dual noise brought Alice Swiacka back to reality. She was afraid that no one woke her, and here it must be almost the receiving hour. She glanced at the wrist of her left hand—no, it was only 4:30. "I slept so little," she saddened. "A pity."

She rose however and, while tying back the white doctor's coat she donned, remembered that the guest room was occupied by her friend, Dr. Sophie Nussen who, fleeing in panic from a blackmailer lying in wait for her, arrived the day before yesterday; that her daughter Wanda's room was the distribution point for several papers of the underground press, and that in the former room of her dead husband lay a 20-year-old English fugitive from a prisoner-of-war camp, ill with typhus. She reflected anxiously that the Englishman had already been with them too long and now there was not the slightest possibility of removing him from the house. On the contrary, due to the illness it was necessary to confide his presence to another doctor since she herself being a gynecologist could not take the responsibility of treating typhus. And he had to be cured. Marrow froze in her bones at the very thought of what to do with the corpse should the youth die. In fairness one really ought to warn Sophie Nussen about the Englishman and the danger in Wanda's room . . . But even this was impossible. The tension of the situation demanded tranquility for all the inmates. A person as frightened as Sophie Nussen could remain here only with the feeling that she was in a very safe place and not involved in any risky folly. Otherwise the state of her nerves could easily snap the mental balance so well achieved that none of the acquaintances, not even her friends (except a few persons whom it was necessary to confide in) suspected that anything went on in this house besides doctoring, raising Wanda's three-year-old Johnny and waiting for the end of the war.

At that same moment the novelist, Joseph Tomyski, his thoughts on the peaceful flat on Wielkopolski Square and Filtrowa, was striding towards it along Polna Street with the intention of taking a short cut through the vegetable plots. He had been entrusted with writing a longer piece on the Germans as the age-old historical menace to European nations. It was to be smuggled abroad to shock the so-called conscience of the world which—according to some circles in the underground work—did not fully realize the threat implicit in German fancied rights. The piece was about finished and required only an afternoon's work. But just today the Tomyskis were warned that the house on Mokotowska Street, where they were living and which had long been under observation, should expect a Gestapo raid. Joseph did not know whether this meant his flat, since the majority of the residents in the house were more or less threatened. He nevertheless considered it wise to find a safer place where he could quietly finish the almost completed script. All the more so since his wife had a heart ailment; the panic she would fall into seeing him sit down at the typewriter that day could harm her. Ludmilla Tomyska was considerably older than her husband but the endangered heart did not age her so much as make her seem rather younger than Tomyski, and given to mawkish considerations.

In these circumstances Tomyski's thoughts immediately and unhesitatingly turned to Alice Swiacka. His former rather friendly relations with her had quite evaporated, but during a dinner, to which his wife and he had been invited about half a year ago, they had met with so much well-being, calm and interest in things other than the war, that he did not doubt the correctness of his choice. He felt as it were a slight resentment toward Alice because of the security in her home even though it was to his advantage. He told himself, "It seems to be going well with her. She's come up in the world, she's lost that sense of risk for which she was formerly distinguished in all circumstances." And then he immediately defended her. "Such a fine doctor. . . . Why shouldn't she consider that in performing her professional duties she fulfills all which a person need do? It is only the abnormal situation which prompts me towards abnormal demands."

Thinking thus, he dropped into a shop on Polna Street for some cigarettes. It was a corner shop which at this moment was crowded with people who arrived for the belated rationed bread. Much to Tomyski's surprise complete silence reigned among the dozen odd people—an unheard of thing among those who crowd for bread. Pushing his way to the counter Tomyski caught sight of a man with a closely shaved head and an impenetrable expression on his flat face, dressed in a gray quilted jacket, sitting near the counter. The man was eating a slice of bread and butter and savoring a piece of sausage. Joseph Tomyski at once recognized in him a Soviet prisoner-of-war. There flashed through his mind the news, recently spread by word of mouth, about Soviet prisoners somewhere in camps near Siedlce who, tortured by hunger and inhuman treatment, threw themselves on the barbed wire and, at the price of the first ranks of dead, escaped into ominous freedom. Was the news true? Who could guarantee it? Tomyski wanted to believe it, since it effaced the dread which Soviet prisoners aroused when they deserted to the service of the Germans. And this man sat there and somehow confirmed the news. People stared at him in silence and settling their business squeezed their way carefully and slowly towards the exit. Absentmindedly the proprietress took the money, gave change and bread, clipped coupons as though in a dream, with eyes lowered. Her helper, a fat, pretty blonde stood alongside, completely motionless, as though incapacitated by the impression to perform any duty. Outside the window one could see time and again the grayish green uniforms and ruddy faces of German officers moving above the bottles of vinegar and packages of ersatz-coffee.

Tomyski waited for quite a while until the place was cleared a little and finally purchased the cigarettes, embarrassed to say that he had asked for a different brand. He handed a few to the man who, having both hands occupied, put the bread down on his knees and silently, without thanking him, took the cigarettes and slipped them into a pocket of his quilted jacket.

Leaving the now nearly empty shop Tomyski heard the proprietress, finally regaining speech, say in a tired voice:

"By Christ, man, eat, and be off with God! You probably don't believe in God. Then go with the devil because they'll bump us both

off, you and me." Tomyski was still able to hear, "What a pickle for
a person to be in!" but the rest he did not catch.

He turned into the vegetable plots that covered the former race
track and, overcome by a vague sort of emotion repeated, not in his
thoughts but nearly in a whisper: "What a shame, what a pity that
they have made us suffer so. . . . And especially now . . . especially
now. . . . What a mistake. . . . This is what is called placing people in a moral situation with no way out. . . ."

These thoughts wandered for a moment through his mind and disappeared as a falling star does without any one knowing what happens
to it.

"A village idyll amidst hell," he now thought, absorbed by the May
charm of the garden plots over which people swarmed, digging in the
yellowish soil dotted with the green of young vegetables, still sowing
something, planting. For the moment death held no threat for this
bending over garden plots; here spring seemed to be just spring; nothing more nor less.

Tomyski carried the lightest of typewriters wrapped in a plainly
tied package, a very common sight in those days of carrying and haul-
ing. It was already close to 4:30, the sky brightened with clear weather,
the sun took on its early evening blush. Young peas, onions, chives
began to glisten like green lights. The increased screech of the black
martins could be heard as they flew lower.

The screeching of the black martins could also be heard over
Filtrowa Street and the Square. But Alice Swiacka did not notice it.
Like the majority of people in town she did not even know the name
of those black streaks of lightning circling in thousands of zigzags
over the city. She was combing her graying hair which rose high over
the smooth forehead and not too young but pleasant face with its slight
nose and blue eyes whose darker stripes were like those seen on the
petals of an iris. Next she devoted herself to a pedantic washing of
hands, foaming them endlessly with soap under the stream of water
running into a shiny wash basin. When she finally began to wipe them
the door of the room opened and a maid with a large immobile face
and dour glance, whose slight squint intensified her expression of
haughtiness or contempt, peered in.

"Well, I was just coming to wake you," she announced not too
agreeably.

"Thank you, my child"—smiled Alice, though the words "my child"
fit no one less than the caryatid standing in the dorway, nor could anyone else have received Alice's smile with greater indifference. As this
conspicuously massive person was about to close the door behind her,
Alice stopped her.

"Helen, have Wanda and Johnny returned yet?"

"They're on the Square. You can see them through the window," came the bored answer.

"What about the patient? Asleep?"

"Who knows? Maybe he's dead?"

With these words Helen left, Alice sighed. That housekeeper was her real worry. Hired a year ago after a few "part-time" ones, and "good" at first, she grew more sullen from day to day, becoming peevish and unpleasant as she began to get acquainted with the situation in the house, especially after the appearance of the Englishman. With difficulty Dr. Swiacka tolerated the presence of this gloomy aversion at home, but she was afraid to fire Helen in these times. She even feared that Helen might decide to leave of her own accord. As long as she was here she probably felt so tied to the disloyalties in the house that even though she were capable of denunciation she would have to weigh this step carefully.

A few weeks ago Alice Swiacka perceived that Helen was quite aware of her apprehension. She refused to accept a new increase, bolstering her refusal with a scornful squint of her lack-luster eyes and saying: "You have enough expenses as it is now. Don't you worry," she added, "I won't go to the Gestapo."

At first Alice did not know whether to take these words for good or evil. Being however quite tormented (this happened at the beginning of the Englishman's illness) and eager for some sort of reassurance, she interpreted them to mean good. But when, after the arrival of Sophie Nussen, Helen, on inspecting her, declared, "I don't like that lady at all," Alice was again frightened. And once more Helen hovered over the house like a cloud from which no one knew what might fall.

Musing on this for an instant, Alice left her surgery in order to look in on the Englishman at the other end of the large, beautiful flat, before the arrival of her patients. As she stood leaning over the sleeping face of the youth, purple with fever, attractive with its long eyelashes and golden lock over the forehead, the bell rang. And while she was checking the patient's pulse Helen came in noisily and announced, "It's the gentleman who was here once for supper."

Alice was happier to see Tomyski than he had expected. Her sympathy for this elderly gentleman, whose fifty years were belied by his smooth face and the supple waistline of a youth, was enhanced by the wealth of feeling she derived from his works. That was why she stretched out both hands towards him and felt rejuvenated with sheer delight.

"So cordial. That's a good sign," thought Joseph, for the moment incapable of disinterested feelings. He immediately explained his problem but out of discretion did not say clearly what it was all about. He was simply writing a novel and, because of the warning received, would not want it to fall accidentally into prejudiced hands. He needed just an afternoon to finish the chapter already begun. While saying this, trying to be casual to the point of neglecting the logic of details, he noticed something like a shadow of indecision and alarm steal across Mrs. Swiacka's face. This slightly embarrassed expression on her face and the delay in answering, a hair's-breadth longer than necessary, produced an unpleasant impression on Tomyski.

"Could she be afraid of such a trifle? That I'll spend an afternoon writing a chapter of a novel in her home?" he wondered, forgetting that it was not a chapter of a novel that he was to write. He was about to withdraw his request, but there was no time, for he had barely wavered, and not a trace of the fleeting embarrassment remained in Alice's face. Neither in the face nor in the words with which she invited him to the quiet library, once the workroom of the late Peter Swiacki, professor of mathematics.

"Dear Joseph," she said, clearing the desk for his typewriter, "this is the quietest room. I think that you will be able to write well here. And if it is comfortable, please come again . . . always, as often as you wish. I shall be proud if one of your works should be created here. . . ."

She broke off and again fell silent with parted lips, with an expression of tense attention, as though listening to the words of half-hearted hospitality, now dying away. . . .

It seemed to Tomyski that Alice still wanted to say something. He waited, friendly but withdrawn, not making the conversation easier for her. After a while he heard her say that humanity may not strive towards the destruction of itself.

"I speak as a naturalist," she was convincing the astonished listener, "No species in nature strives for its own annihilation. Hence all my belief and hope that the world will sober up and people will not permit the extermination of mankind."

"Of course," agreed Tomyski dejectedly. He had no time. He stared at the floor so that Alice would not notice his impatience. He came close to joking: how can a person who contributes to the increase of successful childbirths talk about the extermination of mankind?

But when he raised his head to say this he saw how the doctor's blue, darkly striped eyes were filled with tears.

"Don't be so shocked," she burst out laughing, wiping her nose and eyes now flowing with tears. "It's only my nerves. I had a bad dream today about destruction. But I don't believe in the self-destruction of mankind. And even if . . . We doctors are so familiar with death. Fear and dread are a thousand times worse than death."

"Practically the same words were uttered by Baltasar Gracian. And probably many others before and since. No need to cry," muttered Tomyski awkwardly and timidly.

And she asked: "Gracian?"

"Gracian. A Spanish writer of the 17th century. I have just been reading him, and do you know . . ."

At this point the unsuccessful conversation was cut short, since almost simultaneously two bells were heard, one after another.

"I must go. I should have gone right away, anyhow." Alice sounded concerned. "Don't be shocked," she repeated, "But I'm not even ashamed to cry before you."

Tomyski was not shocked. He was moved. Left alone he continued for a while one of those inspired, fascinating dialogues with his absent hostess, so successful most often after the occasion had passed. However, he quickly ended with this temptation and energetically set to work even though it was not the thing he wished to write. However, it generated that singular kind of satisfaction produced by an accomplishment of things urgently needed even though it diverted one from one's proper mode of life. For people whose only social obligation lies in expressing oneself, such duties resulting from the sudden demands of the moment, despite contrary appearances, are like playing hooky—an agreeable avoidance of sacred responsibilities. Something like that occurred to Tomyski when he paused to light a cigarette. Simultaneously he heard the happy cry of a child: Dr. Swiacka's little grandson had evidently returned with his mother from their walk. His young father, Orchowski, a reserve lieutenant, was with the Polish Army abroad, probably in Scotland. Tomyski did not know him. For that matter he scarcely knew Dr. Swiacka's daughters, this Wanda and the other Barbara, whose husband was an Agricultural Bank administrator of estates somewhere in the country.

"The mother was always very interesting," he thought listlessly, "But this daughter not particularly. As far as I remember the other one was more striking. But then, I don't know. The only somebody in this family was really Alice. That always hurt them. Even that scholarly husband . . ."

The child quieted down. Time and again the doorbell rang in various ways—there was never a shortage of patients here. But on the whole it was rather quiet. Joseph worked better than he did in his own house. He finished before eight and began correcting the text. He came to just as the little clock on the shelf struck 8:30. Hastily he gathered up the papers and tied the typewriter.

"In fifteen minutes," he thought anxiously, "Ludmilla will get frantic thinking I'll not get home before curfew."

He greeted Wanda Orchowska in the hallway. She was svelte, slender as if not yet fully matured. She said nothing.

"Pretty," he conceded "but unsympathetic."

Meanwhile Alice was thanking him for something: her young eyes had so much sparkle in them that suddenly he seemed to see her completely in their blueness.

"You have no idea," she said opening the door for him, "how much talking to you has meant to me. How much it has lifted my spirits. I must see you more often. You and Ludmilla."

"I'd like that," he assured her. He was so befuddled that he forgot to thank her for the favor rendered him. He wanted to return from the stairs but he remembered the curfew hour in time.

"I'll make that a separate visit," he cheered himself. "And we must invite her over."

Getting out of the tram on Polna Street he dropped in once again on friends in Noakowski Street with whom he left the finished manuscript until the day after tomorrow.

At home he told Ludmilla that after his walk through the garden plots he dropped in on Swiacka, where he was delayed a little longer. Ludmilla Tomyski did not notice that he had walked in with the typewriter. She was near-sighted and was not in the habit of noticing details. Joseph extolled Dr. Swiacka's virtues and charm. He resolved that they must find time to renew friendly relations with her, and he tried to kindle the desire in his wife, which was not difficult since Ludmilla, if the state of her heart did not get her down, was ready for everything.

After saying good-by to Tomyski, Alice and Wanda hastened as quickly as possible to the dining room to finish their tea (real tea—received in a parcel from Lisbon) in the company of John Barycz.

Tall, broad-shouldered, blond and kind-faced, Dr. Barycz called to mind a mighty field of grain under a blue sky rather than a dull hospital ward. Only the gray eyes showed a little of the city weariness. He was now slightly nervous about the combined intravenous injection just administered to the Englishman as part of the treatment with which, like all internists, he was clumsy. Besides, he did not hide that the condition of the patient continued to be serious. He barely ventured to state that he thought the blood pressure had stopped falling. However, the appearance of new bedsores pointed to a continuously unsatisfactory circulation. Alice reported to her colleague her observations on the state of the pulse which had improved. A rather good sign was the slight drop in temperature. The patient's age likewise favored his recovery, but would a blood clot form during the period of convalescence? The case was so difficult that one had to reckon with this.

After an exchange of their fears and hopes they remained despondent for a while, reluctant to discuss the thing which bothered them: What to do with the body if the patient should die? But one could not really tell what bothered Wanda, whose youthful face and prominent forehead expressed a peculiar obstinacy and irrelevance to that which concerned the two doctors.

Her small soft lips, like her mother's—the only sign of a sweet maturity in her school-girlish appearance kept compressing and opening as though struggling with the desire to say something unexpected.

Presently, however, Dr. Barycz sighed "Well, time to go." And even though, like most doctors he had a night pass, he prepared to leave. Saying good-by in the hallway he remarked:

"There was shooting in town as I was coming here. Some big action because I heard grenades and machine guns."

The news made her feel shock at the fate of new victims who would fall as a result of German revenge, and joy that the resistance was making itself felt, that it was beginning to frighten the Germans in this country for good. But the joy was very direct. And though Alice Swiacka, as if paying tribute in honor of human feelings, whispered, "Jesus Mary, there'll be new victims," her blue, shining eyes sparkled even more and her attractive face with the slight nose and soft lips became distinctly gayer. Even Wanda came to life. And, as so often occurs during parting, an intensive, hushed conversation developed during the last minutes. The doctor left, favored with the latest radio bulletins.

After locking the door both women went in to the child for a moment who sat on a potty under Helen's eye and monotonously sang:

"Poland is not yet dead as long as we are dying!"*

"Why isn't that child asleep yet?" Wanda became indignant. "He should have been asleep long ago!"

"Do I know why he isn't sleeping? He just doesn't sleep. He won't let me put him to bed." And with the words, "Well, I'm going," Helen left, her face as heavy and expressionless as the wall.

Undressing Johnny, Alice said:

"On such a commonplace occasion the child sings such a paradoxically tragic truth. Because only as long as we are dying . . ."

"You are becoming very melodramatic," interrupted Wanda.

"Wanda . . . melodramatic or not. But we probably have enough reason to understand the situation."

Wanda stared penetratingly with the black eyes of her father. She asked sharply:

---

* The child has unconsciously given an ironic twist to the first line of Poland's national hymn which literally reads: "Poland is not yet dead as long as we are living."

"How then, mother, don't you understand that Allan must not die?
He must not die!" she repeated with emphasis.

Alice observed her daughter amazed, since at this moment it was
not the Englishman she had in mind.

The child already lying down, called from the bed:

"Mamma kiss me! Kiss me! me, me, kiss. Me, mamma kiss."

Wanda bent down over her son. "Mamma has already kissed you.
I have already said good night. You're supposed to sleep. You should
have been asleep long ago."

Both left on tiptoes. Alice seeing that Wanda was making her way
towards the sick room, stopped conspiratorially and slipped back to
her grandson, who was sobbing with despair. They fell into each other's
embrace.

"Granny," wailed the child. "Remember how we kissed on the
square? How we kissed?"

When the child fell asleep Dr. Swiacka went to Sophie Nussen who
was playing patience. In medical vernacular they began to talk about
patients. Sophie looked haggard as a result of the shocks she had
suffered. Nothing about her suggested the Orient or the South yet
there was something—in a sort of northern way—vulnerably Semitic.
Her hair, before she had suddenly turned gray, had been light. Long-
legged, seldom a characteristic of her race, full-breasted with a large
head, a prominent profile and large bulging watery blue eyes, she was
not pretty but terribly interesting. She was one of those magnificent
flowers of the Jewish petty bourgeoisie who, when young, managed
to go abroad and marry foreigners, admirers of *charme Slave,* who
marvel at the softness of Polish women and the gay Polish personality.
Something like this had happened to Sophie in her youth. She, however, was content with a Swiss fiancé during her student days and returning to Poland single, married here. She separated from her husband and did not know his fate; her only son was in the Polish Army
somewhere in the Near East or Africa.

"Ali," she said to her friend, breaking the silence that had suddenly risen between them. "You're somehow not yourself today. Why?
Am I supposed to give you courage? Look at my situation. Sheer madness! But just à little peace in a home like yours and I immediately
recover my energy so that I could climb walls. Can anyone want more?
What more could possibly have been added to the death in our hearts
that you, so cheerful the day before yesterday, are somehow not quite
so today. Do you know?" she turned to her own affairs, "if they finish
me off, then while dying I shall be happy that I experienced this moment in your home. God! How happy you made me! Listen, Alice!
No meeting with the most ardent lover would have given me the belief
in life that your smile did as I walked in. And my heart had already

begun to turn to ice! Darling, appreciate that. Jews in my position are as bitter as wormwood. You can't disarm them with a smile. Only if you die for them are they capable of admitting that you were not an anti-Semite. . . . Come, smile, my brave one. Are you afraid?"

Alice smiled.

"You're hard on the Jews. It's not always the same."

Moving from the couch to the table she took Sophie's delicate hand, clasping the palm in her own, and rested her cheek against the two entwined hands.

"My dear," she began, looking into Mrs. Nussen's protruding, surprised-like eyes. "I'm not afraid . . . Or rather I fear a little for you . . . Because you see . . . All of our houses . . . No, it is not so easy to say. You see, it is their speciality—I mean the Germans, to arrange a moral situation without escape. Because each of our houses . . ."

"Would rather die for Poland than for the Jews"—interrupted Sophie turning red to the roots of her hair.

"Oh Sophie! You too? Everything is different. I thought it was that I deceived you, do you understand? I wanted to warn you so that in case of anything you wouldn't have any resentment. Because you can't even guess that in this house . . ."

"What are you saying?" interrupted Sophie again. "I didn't guess? You wonderful stupid creature, who do you take me for? I have guessed everything. Don't I have an ear and eye? You think that I don't know that something is going on in your house? Don't tell me that your Wanda is only taking care of Johnny. Poor thing, you probably thought: Sophie is like the others, thinks only about her own salvation. You're mistaken. Your drama is mine also. I know that wherever we go we endanger not only people but also causes. Holy causes. Well, that, too, is a moral situation with no way out."

"Without an easy way out," Alice corrected her and herself. "But everything is all right now. It was only the question of your understanding, that you would not be surprised."

"What could surprise me?" asked Sophie with inexpressible sweetness. "Am I not walking after my own funeral? Besides, I have foreseen everything. The little one that brought me . . . she's also such a foolish Polish bit of wonder. No one will ever honor that," she said in passing. "It seems that the little one has already notified people because several times they have let me know that in case of danger they have some 100 per cent 'sure' place. I couldn't go there before because that house was packed with Jews. But they will report . . ."

"Darling," Alice began to laugh, "if it were urgent for me to be rid of you immediately I could give you an excellent house," she thought of the Tomyskis. "I'm afraid it is precisely because of my selfishness that I wanted to have you. Only it bothered me that . . ."

At that moment—it was already 10:30—someone rang the front
bell sharp and long as though it were a fire alarm.

Alice jumped up. "Jesus Mary! They'll wake up the child!"

Everything in the house began to move, but before Alice and
Wanda managed to run into the hallway, Helen had already opened
up. In the kitchen could be heard a man's gasping voice urging—
"Quick, water!"

When they reached the kitchen Helen was tearing off the jacket
from a young boy doubled up and leaning against the table with his
other now sleeveless arm. He was bespattered with blood, his head
was hanging so that the long hair from the forehead fell down in sticky
streams on the table. Helen screamed:

"Please, leave the kitchen, Madame! This is my business!"

Alice regained her professional calm and her face took on a resolute
masculine expression.

"What do you mean?" she was surprised. "He is wounded. Wanda,
go and get Sophie immediately. I'll need her"—she turned to her
daughter. "Thank God," she added briskly, "I thought it was the
Gestapo."

She began to wash the wound, issuing curt, confident instructions
to Helen who, grown suddenly meek, began to listen and help. The
wounds were not dangerous but there was a great loss of blood.

"Is this from the shooting that was heard this evening?" Alice
sought information while performing her duties.

"Yes, I sat in the ruins until nightfall and that's why the loss of
blood. I feel badly," worried the wounded man, "that I rang this way.
But I was dazed. And I have no one but her in town. And the fact
that there's a doctor . . . who will help . . ."

After washing his face Alice recognized Helen's brother who sometimes came to see her. He was very much like her except where she
seemed heavy and unattractive he was youthfully handsome. He was
no more than 18 years old.

"Then you must have known, Helen, that he belonged to an underground organization?"

"Why shouldn't I have known," she responded haughtily. "What
the hell, he kept his gun with me."

"Watch how you speak before the doctor," the wounded boy repri-
manded her. "Please doctor, let me stay till dawn, and then I'll join
the partisans in the woods. I'm not armed. Frisk me. I buried it in the
ruins. I'll tell her," he indicated his sister with his eyes, "where she
should search. She'll bring it out of hell and back to hell again," he
complimented.

The wound on the face was two scratches caused by the grazing of two bullets. It was sufficient to plaster them up so that they looked like the results of a drunken brawl. It was deeper on the shoulder but the bone was not touched. Sophie Nussen gave a glucose injection, repeating with delight, "Sheer madness!" Wanda was clearing away the bloodstained scraps of gauze. Alice gave the boy a glass of wine and a ham sandwich. Bedded down in the doctor's surgery he immediately fell asleep. The child did not wake up.

Alice did not manage to find out how the youth got here. Did the janitor let him in? That bothered her, even though the janitor in that house was all right. But no. The wounded boy probably crawled through the garden plots. He could have come in from the back through the unfenced grounds of the villa on Krzycki Street which was ruined during the siege. She discussed this a while with Sophie who rubbed her hands and nervously trembled.

"Go, lie down"—Alice ordered her as if wholly strengthened by the authoritative charm of a person skilfully performing the tasks of her profession. "Helen, please go to bed, immediately." She turned to the maid who sat over the sleeping brother, covering her face with her hands. She, however, did not succumb to the charm and only uncovering her face announced harshly:

"I'll sit here. Soon as it's dawn I'll take him out. The back way."

"Well, just as you wish," Dr. Swiacka relented as though stepping out of her role. "If something should happen to him please wake me up."

She glanced in on Mrs. Nussen who was already in bed, but with the light still on and smoking a cigarette. Upon seeing Alice she repeated, "Pure madness. Pure like alcohol," she added for emphasis.

"Oh, my dear," exclaimed Dr. Swiacka, rejoicing, "What a load off my heart. I was so afraid of that Helen!"

And she told her of her suspicions. After hearing her out Sophie added with a charming smile: "Darling. You were only afraid that the child would waken."

Alice did not continue the conversation that was interrupted by the night bell. She considered that Sophie was sufficiently, even exceptionally well acquainted with the dangers of the house. Silently she slipped into the child's room where Wanda usually slept. But tonight Wanda was on duty with the Englishman.

Before daybreak Dr. Swiacka was awakened by a squeaking door and the sound of walking on tiptoes. That was Helen showing her brother out. A thought flashed through Alice that she should have kept the boy for about two days. But before she could get out of bed for this purpose, she fell asleep again.

At noon that day the Englishman regained consciousness. And when after a week he was that much stronger that she could talk with him, Alice told him in her bad English that he had had typhus and what course the illness had taken. Then silence followed, only Wanda's soft and full and sweetly mature lips opened and shut alternately in her pouting face. Allan stared long, once at these lips and then at Alice's blue, darkly striped eyes leaning over him. With a trembling hand he managed to move the golden lock off his forehead with such an effort as though it were of stone. With a still greater effort he said:

"There is not a person in England who would do for anyone in the world what you have done for me."

When they remained silent he repeated it once again, more distinctly and slowly.

Alice smiled guiltily.

"In England . . ." she answered, "Oh, in England it would not be necessary. Such a situation can not possibly arise there."

But she expressed this so awkwardly in English that even Wanda shrugged her shoulders. Allan, on the other hand, did not quite understand. Both women, however, felt greatly relieved that everything began to turn out well.

The Gestapo did not come to the building on Mokotowska Street but somehow Tomyski did not find the time to renew his relations with Alice Swiacka as he had promised himself. It was only in the latter half of May that he unexpectedly met Alice at the dentist's. To meet a doctor as a patient at another doctor's office is a thing so amusing that in spite of himself he was gay. Besides, completely irrespective of the feelings which they had for one another, they were mutually glad to meet. Alice seemed to be slightly excited and her lips were exceptionally red. He was even surprised that a person of her age (probably well over 50) could have such alluring, red lips, and he stared at them in spite of himself. She noticed it immediately and, smiling, explained convincingly:

"You probably think I have lipstick on. No, it's my heart. A few sleepless nights because of tachycardia and a skipping pulse beat induces such a reddening of the mucous membrane of the lips. I have been over-tired lately and will have to leave even if for a little while. All three of us will probably go to Barbara's. To my daughter in Podlasie."

They were alone in the large parlor that served as a waiting room. Before Tomyski was able to say something Alice suddenly changed her seat to the easy chair standing close to him. Quickly looking around the room she leaned over, practically to his ear and whispered slowly —"We had an Englishman stay with us."

With a sort of liberating exaltation, as if released from a vow, and no longer able to bear the burden of the secret alone, she told him the history of the typhus case. Joseph listened, not daring to interrupt her or ask any questions. He sighed with relief when he heard that the Englishman was no longer at the Swiackis'.

"He had to move elsewhere although he is not yet fully recovered. The house is closely watched, we received warning from our intelligence. Yes, it was necessary to liquidate this clandestine point and in general clean the house a little. Because, if you please, the Englishman is only part of the story."

"Well, all right," interrupted Joseph; "But you shouldn't speak of this. Why do you tell me?"

"Who then should I tell it to? Who should know all this if not you?" Alice said in surprise as though reprimanding him.

Dropping the subject, she suddenly reminded herself, "Oh yes, do you know what he said when he was already conscious? He said there is not a person in England who would have done for anyone what we did for him."

She stared at Joseph quizzically as though she sought in his face an explanation of the words that disturbed her. He answered after deep thought:

"There occur at times historical situations in which there is only room for ethics of risk and heroism. And there are others in which normal social morality suffices. Who knows," he added with hesitation, "whether a higher civilization will not do away with the need for heroism. Such as our heroism, at any rate."

"Yes," agreed Dr. Swiacka. "Perhaps their civilization does away with the need and even the possibility of such heroism. But its greatness has terrifically increased our ability for heroism. We want somehow to equal so great an ally. And even excel it. With what can we excel it if not the madness of sacrifices? If not with some sort of unselfish generosity?"

"This generosity," he picked up, "with which you have excelled the possibilities of all Englishmen will only increase the difference between them and us. Because of the madness of heroic sacrifice is excused only between equals. Equals in the conscience of both sides," he emphasized.

As he half-whispered the words "both sides," a slight movement started in the neighboring dentist's surgery. The silence of the treatment was interrupted by sounds of conversation and the clatter of dental equipment thrown into the disinfecting tray. Sending the patient to the hallway via another door, a smallish, bright-faced brunette in a white apron appeared on the threshold of the parlor. Inviting Swiacka with a gesture and greeting Tomyski with a nod she said:

"Please doctor."

Alice bade Tomyski, now absorbed in his own problem, a fleeting farewell. He was now ashamed of having been vexed with Alice for becoming so frightened when he came to her with his work. He felt slightly humbled, like a person who thought he was brave when he merely multiplied the dangers then faced by the courage of that woman. He now understood that she had been afraid for him.

"Fool," he thought of himself unkindly.

In order to explain to Dr. Swiacka who had not known his feelings at that time—and a little out of concern for her, he ran next day to the clinic of which Alice was part owner and Chief of Staff. The doctor on duty told him that Dr. Swiacka had already left for the country yesterday.

She must obviously have smelled a rat, he thought.

During the next month Joseph Tomyski was too distracted to be concerned with Dr. Swiacka's fate, being kept busy by a multitude of small or important matters which happened during this long night of occupation. Sometimes he was happy in thinking that Alice came out of such a difficult situation safely. It was only in June that he again faced her case.

One late afternoon he walked along Niepodleglosci Avenue up to Rozana Street where he had a meeting with an editor of a clandestine bulletin for which he wrote. Between Rakowiecka Street and Pilsudski Avenue he unexpectedly met a theater critic, a man younger than he, at whose house he had recently lectured to a group in the underground organized as a Drama School. The critic's name was Jerzy Kochanski. A short, compact man with dark, burning eyes in an oval face and lips quivering as though he were moved, he gave the impression of a person who lives passionately. Tomyski knew him from before the war and liked to talk with him.

They greeted each other with pleasure and after the introductory "What's new?" Kochanski said: "I was just thinking about you and I'm glad that I met you. You know Dr. Swiacka . . ." he lowered his voice.

"I know her very well," Joseph affirmed and grew anxious with alarm. "I didn't know that you knew her."

"I've known her for a long time. A year ago our underground courses were held in her house."

Kochanski looked around. Dusk was falling. The street ran between the garden plots from which the people had already gone. It was empty.

"Well, it's necessary to save that woman," he said suddenly. "Those women," he corrected himself.

Tomyski became numb.

"What's it about?"

"Well please, just listen."

And Kochanski told about the Englishman, mentioning besides this the other dangers of the Swiacki household which Tomyski did not know. He was annoyed that someone besides himself knew even more than he about all this and especially that he spoke about such secrets so plainly. He simply grew tired listening.

"Well, all right," he replied at the end. "I don't understand. Everything that you tell me belongs, after all, to the past. I met Dr. Swiacka a few weeks ago and she told me that the house is clear. Has she already returned from the country?"

"Nothing belongs to the past. Both of them have returned from the country. And since nothing threatening occurred on Filtrowa Street during their absence, they became so confident of their luck that everything began anew."

"How is that? And the Englishman?"

"And the Englishman. During convalescence he developed a clot in the leg. He couldn't stay where they took him. And then you know what his patient is like for a doctor. In a word, he returned. That Jewish doctor also returned. It was necessary to install a radio in the safe house to which someone advised her to go. A question of coincidence. But that's not the point. The thing is that Dr. Swiacka's house continues to be closely watched. They don't believe it. That's what our people are like. You are the only one that can talk some sense into her. She looks up to you. The Englishman is already walking. He can be shifted elsewhere."

"Well all right, I'll reason with her, but I don't know if her daughter will listen to me."

"If she doesn't, her mother will be lost. Dr. Swiacka is valuable in herself. Like a store of arms or something like that. It must be done quickly. The latest by tomorrow."

"I'll do it tomorrow. I'll simply take Dr. Swiacka's baggage to my place."

"It would be better if you didn't endanger your life either. Why make the job easy for the Germans? To destroy the creative intelligentsia is their dream. But, all right," he cut the doubts. "It will be for a short time. In three days at the most the army will take care of the Englishman. And I'll call for Mrs. Nussen."

As they walked towards Polna Street among the potato plots Tomyski added loyally:

"I'm doing this only for Dr. Swiacka. With the Englishman. Because I think Englishmen could bear the fate of prisoners-of-war. As so many of ours. The English are pets of the camps. They lack nothing there, for the whole world does everything and more for them."

"Nothing, except freedom," interrupted Kochanski. "They are less accustomed than we to endure the lack of freedom."

Tomyski recalled the scene in the little store on Polna Street.

"And that certainty that no one will tell him, 'Go, because they'll bump us both off, you and me.' And the conviction that what good would such a Pole be who wouldn't know how to die easily? . . ."

They were by now standing in front of 5 Mokotowska Street where Tomyski lived, and Jerzy Kochanski did not pick up the conversation. Curfew was drawing near and he lived a good bit farther. He thanked Tomyski and arranged to drop in tomorrow afternoon to discuss details of "bringing over the baggage."

Tomyski still asked him:

"And the child. That grandchild of Alice's?"

An angelic smile lit up Kochanski's sharp face.

"Luckily he stayed in the village with his Aunt Barbara," he said tenderly. He had a little daughter whom he adored.

Upon returning home Tomyski immediately revealed everything to his wife.

Ludmilla was not disturbed by Mrs. Nussen, since they had temporarily sheltered this kind of vulnerable guest several times in their home.

With regard to the Englishman, she said:

"I always told you that a real English gentleman can be found only in Poland. Like Dr. Swiacka!"

And then she added:

"Tomorrow we must finish putting away the winter things. We won't be able to do a thing once the house is full of those English."

In spite of the calm of which she always had more than he, Tomyski went to bed in fear of whether Ludmilla would not suffer a heart attack at night. She often received worse matters splendidly and then paid for it with heart ailments. He was especially afraid of a sleepless night, during which she would worry, not about the anticipated guests, but fear about his going to that house on Filtrowa Street.

Of course, he overrated himself. Because as soon as Ludmilla put her pretty head on the pillow he heard the deep regular breathing of sweet sleep.

He himself fell asleep before daybreak. But he rose early and went first to the clinic on Poznanska Street, since he expected to find Dr. Swiacka there in the morning.

It was a beautiful June morning. One of those when the sun and sky seem to be man's allies. Thus, Joseph was thrown off balance when he was told at the clinic that the doctor would come in later because she had had to perform a sudden and difficult operation during the night.

Without delay he took the tram to Filtrowa Street. He jumped off at the end of the square and waiting until the tram left, wanted to cross to the other side but after the first step drew back on the pavement and stood petrified. For at that instant the front door of the corner building opened, and in the train of grayish-green uniforms appeared three persons in Indian file. First came Dr. Alice Swiacka, behind her, her daughter Wanda Orchowska. The third was an elderly lady, unknown to Tomyski, with a magnificent Semitic profile and protruding, surprised eyes. Simultaneously he recognized at the edge of the curb two open cars, the kind usually used by the Gestapo. Dr. Swiacka and her daughter were bareheaded, and looking straight ahead did not see him. They were calm and Dr. Swiacka was even smiling.

While the women entered the first car another couple of armed Germans came out of the building between whom was a youth with a head of glistening curls. Finding himself in the car, this young man did not sit down, but stretching out his arms in the direction of the first car he shouted so loudly that Tomyski heard:

"Forgive me. Will you forgive me?"

With discreet respect the Germans allowed him to stand and shout. When the car started up one of the Gestapo supported the Englishman who swayed. Kindly they helped him to be seated. All this lasted perhaps a minute. The cars were leaving. Only then Joseph noticed and heard two village women with milk cans who stopped alongside him. They were looking at Sophie Nussen's prominent profile and one said to the other:

"They're Jew women. How did they ever find them? And that civilian, the young one, the one that was threatening them so in German, must have turned them in."

"What's for them today, is for us tomorrow," said the second. "Only the bare earth will remain of this Poland."

"What's for us tomorrow is for them the third day," replied the first.

These words were the sole epitaph that honored the death of three women who sat in a German car on a beautiful summer morning.

1948

Zofia Kossak

(1890—1968)

Zofia Kossak-Szczucka was born in 1890; she spent her youth in Skowrodki in Volhynia, on an estate leased by her father (after he left the military service in the Austrian Army). In her novel *The Blaze* (1922), she described the tragic years 1917–1919. In 1922 she settled with her father in Silesia, receiving a literary prize for her novel *The Unknown Country* in 1932.

Zofia Kossak continues the great Polish tradition of the historical novel with a series of books on various subjects, e.g., *Beatum Scelus* (1924), *The Golden Freedom* (1928), *The Holy Fools* (1929), *The Field of Legnica* (1930). Her novel, *Blessed Are the Meek* (about St. Francis of Assisi), received world-wide recognition and was a Book-of-the-Month-Club choice.

In her historical novels, Zofia Kossak gives a vivid account of men's struggle for power; but she is also concerned with their normal predicament. Her saints, warriors and common people come to life against the background of a superbly drawn tapestry that stretches from Europe to the Middle East and Asia.

In such novels as *The Golden Freedom,* Kossak explores politics, patriotism and religious problems while she portrays the exuberance of eighteenth-century Polish life. Her treatment of history is metaphorical. She does not draw social conclusions in her narratives, but she stresses the evolutionary values of human existence. The old and the new are linked imperceptibly by a subtle use of rhetoric and the skill with which she humanizes the anonymous reality of history. Zofia Kossak depicts the religious movements of the sixteenth and the seventeenth centuries, their origins, development and results; but she is primarily interested in the impact those movements had on the minds of the contemporaries. Her historical novels thus turn into psychological studies of the human personality, and the defeated protagonists are often portrayed as the true victors. This method of psychological analysis enables the author to combine religious problems with political ones, and the private lives of her heroes with the story of Poland's statehood.

Her most important works are *The Holy Fools, The Crusaders, From the Depths* (published in 1946 and based on her experiences in the Auschwitz concentration camp) and *The Covenant* (1957).

In 1944 Zofia Kossak escaped to England, and in 1957 she returned to Poland.

The Covenant

Ab-Ram did not sleep at all that night. He felt troubled to the depths of his soul; he was profoundly anxious, overwhelmed with grief. Grief for himself, or for his tribe? He did not know. One moment he was angry with his fellow tribesmen for demanding a sign from God; the next he reminded himself that at one time he had been like them. They wanted a sign. Only the Lord could give them that. Would He not be angry at such a request? What sign would completely convince them? For the hundredth time he regretted that the Lord had called him, an unlearned man, to His service, instead of Nergal-Sar, or Melchizedek. They would both have known what to do. But Nergal-Sar had departed almost unknown, and Melchizedek also had died some years since. Both these guides and masters had vanished, as though removed by the Lord's hand so that he, Ab-Ram, should carve his own way. Now, like a hungry man seeking scraps of bread in the larder, he recalled all the details of his conversation with Melchizedek concerning people who thirsted for a visible sign. The priest-king had not been indignant, as Ab-Ram was; he had admitted that this demand was proper to human beings. He had mentioned the Egyptian rite of circumcision as a sign and seal that might satisfy the human desire for something visibly testifying that they belonged to God. At that time Ab-Ram had rejected the idea out of hand. But now his anger and grief for his fellow-tribesmen drove him to consider the question in a different light. They wanted a sign: let them have it! A painful, hard and ineradicable sign! Let them suffer! He writhed inwardly at the thought that he would have to begin with himself. He rejected the idea, and sought further. But the conversation with the royal sage, on the rooftop in that stone city, obstinately returned to his memory. "Do according to your measure," Melchizedek had said. The people needed to be given a sign according to their measure. No one dressed a child in the robes of a grown man, for in them it would get entangled, and would perish. Would not that sign be fitted to his people's childish minds? Melchizedek had said that the seal of circumcision testified that the one so sealed was ready to shed his blood for his Lord. Not as men offer children to the gods, but sacrificing his own true body, his own blood, his own pain. This gift would be made to the Lord and be accepted as an acceptable sacrifice. Now Ab-Ram wiped out of his mind the anger he had felt for his tribe since his discovery of the teraphim, and lost the loathing with which he had regarded the idea of circumcision. In fact he was coming to think that the greater the loathing and fear, the more valuable the offering. Had he not again and again regretted in his soul that, blessed as he was by the Lord, he had nothing with which he could show his gratitude?

These thoughts began to possess him so completely that he looked impatiently for the dawn. The answer for which the people were waiting, and even his own hesitations, were overshadowed by the realization that he could show the Lord his own gratitude and devotion. It was part of his nature to act at once on every decision he made, and so, shutting himself away in his tent, he set to work. He mutilated himself painfully and clumsily, he could hardly restrain a groan; but he achieved his purpose. Weak and sick, he lay down on the couch. Despite the almost unbearable pain he had a feeling of satisfaction. Now he had truly offered the Lord his own blood, not that of heifers, bulls, or sheep. He lay quietly all that day, defending himself as well as he could from the anxious women, who were alarmed by his sudden illness. He refused food, though they brought him the tastiest of morsels; but he greedily drank water, and demanded only to be left in peace. In the evening he grew feverish. Half asleep, he was visited by visions. The tent seemed to be an ark borne on the waters and falling downward with the waves. In his half-conscious meditations, groaning with pain every time he moved, Ab-Ram felt ashamed of the anger he had displayed towards his own tribe only yesterday. The Hebrew shepherds were only a small part of the great human throng which was crying out for God, and thundering the questions: "Whither go we? What to? Whose are we?" But Ab-Ram, who by the special dispensation of God had come to know the truth, and could have given an answer to this question, had been silent for years, making no attempt to share with others the treasure he possessed.

"But how can I speak?" he asked himself anxiously. He recalled the knowledge and wisdom of the priests, unequalled in all the world; their knowledge of the secrets of the stars and the earth, the several stages of the temple at Ur, each filled with tablets containing all manner of sciences and knowledge. Against that power, which even kings did not dare to affront, was he, a simple, illiterate man, skilled only in the rearing of cattle and sheep, to set himself? The comparison seemed amusing, and he could not help thinking of himself as ludicrous. And he was so dismayed that he again lost strength. But once more, as soon as he closed his eyes, through his feverish brain poured waves which were not the waves of the sea but the generations of the sons of earth, seeking God.

He reached out for a cup of water tinged with wine, which Sarai had set by his head, and the visions vanished. He grew sober. What was it he was thinking of attempting to achieve? Alas! You are driving your flocks to a too distant pasturage, shepherd! You think to measure yourself with kings, to quarrel with the priests of Marduk; and so far to have not even subjected your own tribe to the Lord! You will do much, and very much, if you convince your own people. Think only of them. Give them a sign—the same sign which you have carved in your own body. From your own tribe you will create a fortress and sanctuary of the Lord.

The entrance flap was lifted. Eliezer slipped in quietly, and stared at the sick man with eyes expressive of his anxiety. He was surprised and delighted when his master gave him a friendly, though miserable smile.

"It is good that you have come, Eliezer," Ab-Ram whispered painfully, moistening his parched lips with his tongue. "Tell the men of the tribe that in a day or two, when I am well again, in the name of the Lord Most High I will give them the sign which they have demanded. Let them wait in peace, untroubled. Bring me some water . . ."

"Live forever, my lord! I have brought water. The people will rejoice when I tell them what you have said. They were smitten with fear that your god had struck you down, in anger at what they had done."

When the servant had departed, the sick man renewed the broken thread of his meditations. Henceforth his tribe would have no other god and no other faith than that of the Lord Most High. To him, Ab-Ram, it fell to be chief and priest in one, as Melchizedek had been to his people. And one who takes on priesthood must change his name, renouncing his ancestral origin. Of the generations of man one said: "the son of Terah, the son of Nahor, the son of Haran." With the priest it was not so. The father of the priest was the god whose name was included in his new name, Sep-Sin . . . Awen-El . . . Nergal-Sar. . . . And so he, Ab-Ram, should do; but the Lord had not revealed His Name to His servant. The unutterable Name of the Lord was not to be given shape in the mouth of a mortal. As he considered this problem, the name which Melchizedek had persistently repeated years ago suggested itself: "Ab-Raham." And now the name which had once terrified him seemed to have some connection with the innumerable generations of people who were passing in a feverish vision before his eyes. He decided to adopt the name of Ab-Raham.

But was he alone to change his name? In taking on the priestly office, would he not draw his wife after him? He felt strongly impelled to do something in recognition of his faithful comrade, Sarai. Nor, indeed, only for her. The words Lot had said when he and Ab-Raham had been riding on the one camel came vividly to his mind. O, memory, infallible steward! Like a miser you seize on everything, even things seemingly of no import; you conceal them in your secret places, to bring them out at the suitable moment and to set them before the eyes. When Lot had remarked that the law underestimated women,

Ab-Ram had not thought much of the words, he had dismissed them
with silence. But now they seemed to him so just, so valuable, that
he thirsted not only to distinguish his wife, but in his wife to honor
Woman.

Night came on, and with it the fever returned. The pictures were
again confused; they erased the bond between dream and reality.
Now he seemed audacious, mad, arrogant in his own eyes. His mind
swarmed with great intentions, he had decided to be a priest of the
tribe, he wanted to change his own name and Sarai's; but what certainty had he that the Lord required all this? Hitherto he had only
listened and waited. The Lord had spoken to him when it was His
will to speak. But now the servant wanted to compel the Creator.

And, humbled, afflicted, Ab-Ram also, like the shepherds whom he
had recently despised for this same weakness, began to implore the
Lord for a sign.

"Many years have passed since Thou last spakest to me," he said.
"That does not disturb me, for Thou art Eternal, and a thousand ages
in Thy sight are like an evening gone. It is not for me, but for my tribe
that I am anxious. So work, that they may know Thy glory. Make a
covenant with me and with all the tribe, that they may descry Thee
whom they see not and may know Thee whom they know not. I put
my trust in Thee. So work, that others also may trust in Thee. Without
Thee there is neither light nor peace. Be our Goel, our King and
Guardian. We will be Thy servants. I have never asked Thee anything
before, O Lord. . . . Now I will ask, and will not cease asking. . . . Thou
knowest the hearts of men, and knowest that I do not ask for myself,
since nothing will diminish my faith. But my people want a sign. Give
them a sign!"

The pulse in his temples drummed like a hammer, the pain from
his self-inflicted wound pierced through his body, the tent, like an
ark rose, floated, swayed. . . . Ab-Ram had the feeling that, just as once
he had been caught up in the air, so again he could see himself below
himself; and he thought he heard a voice:

"I will make a covenant with thee and thy people . . ."

Then everything was confused, was mingled into a single roar that
engulfed his memory, his consciousness, his thought.

*   *   *

Only on the fourth day did Ab-Ram emerge from his tent, well,
though still weak. He at once summoned the men of the tribe and
declared to them:

"The Lord Most High, the True God, has promised to make a
covenant with the tribe of Hebrews. Before he does so they must
openly renounce all other gods, and must throw all tablets and amulets

into the fire, if any possess them, since the Lord will not come where another reigns."

They listened in gloomy silence, taken aback, for they had not anticipated that they would have to renounce the old gods. Of their own choice they had been taken in the snare. If they refused, they would affront the God of Ab-Ram; but if they obeyed they would draw down upon themselves the anger of vengeful demons. Woe! Woe!

Inexorably stern, Ab-Ram stood in the center of the ring, naming one after another all the gods known to the tribe. He asked whether they rejected them in their own name, and in that of their descendants. They assented with trembling, looking about them fearfully. They renounced the god Ea, the god En-Lil, the god Anu, the god Enu, the favorite god of their fathers, Nannar-Sin, the goddess Damkina, the goddess Ishtar, the goddess Zirbanit. They renounced the spirits called Anunnaki, Ekimmu, Utukki and many others. They renounced the demons of the air, the earth and the water. They renounced the evil Labartu, Ilu, Galu and Rabisu. As with trembling they pronounced the words of apostasy, they stealthily thrust into the fire their amulets bearing the image of the demon named. Things that hitherto had been as a saving shield, now, after the renunciation, would become a menacing weapon of the affronted spirit. They spoke and acted hurriedly, hoping that the demon would not notice their words and actions in the general confusion.

When all the men had sworn that they would have no other gods but the god of Ab-Ram, when the tablets, images and amulets were cracking and turning to ash in the fire, Ab-Ram began to make preparations to conclude the covenant with the Lord. In his simplicity he behaved as ancient custom directed. So from the flocks and herds he chose a heifer, a goat and a ram, all without spot or blemish; and he also took a turtle-dove and a young pigeon. After slaughtering the animals he divided them in the middle, not removing their skins or their hooves, but he did not divide the birds. In the center of the valley he cleared a narrow track of grass some ten paces long, and no wider than one pace, and he set the divided bodies of the animals on either side of the track, each half against its other half, so that if put together they would be as though whole. He did not divide the birds, but set them one on each side of the track, their beaks towards each other. In this labor he was assisted by Eliezer, Sur, Yahiel, Mosa, Aser and several others. The rest of the men surrounded them in a ring, watching the preparations anxiously. They knew that He whose Name might not be pronounced or even known would reveal Himself to their eyes and, in accordance with custom, would pass between the divided carcasses. His steps would be followed by Ab-Ram in the name of the tribe and thenceforth nothing could violate the covenant thus concluded. The God of Ab-Ram and the Hebrew tribe would become one, just as the halves of the heifer, goat and sheep had been one. One blood in their veins, one heart, lungs, kidneys, liver. No one had ever heard of any of the gods concluding such a covenant with a man before, so the Hebrews rejoiced, even though they were also terribly afraid.

The preparations occupied all the morning till noonday. And the day was burning hot, windless. The path of the Covenant had been made in the middle of the valley, for all to see, far from the shade of the oak grove; and the people sitting about it and waiting for the Coming of the Lord were faint with the heat. Only Ishmael shouted merrily, amused by the whole affair, and Sur had difficulty in restraining the lad from running along the sacred path between the divided animals. Though still very weak, Ab-Ram took a branch and drove off the flies gathering about the carcasses. Seeing this, Eliezer took a second branch, and the two men silently beat on each side. The dead animals had to be defended from more than flies. The scent of meat attracted the vultures, and they began to circle high above in the sky, gradually dropping lower and lower. Ishmael asked for permission to shoot at them with his bow, and sent arrows flying though the air; Aser and Sur picked up spears and drove off the more persistent of the birds. The time passed slowly, it almost seemed to stand still; the sun roasted them with fire; but no one came. The women brought their men food in platters. They ate but little, drank their fill of water, and again waited. Leaning heavily on his stick, Ab-Ram gazed up at the sky grey with heat; he gazed eastward to the mountains beyond which was the city of Uru-Salem; westward, to where the Great Sea roared; southward to the land of Negeb, dry and burnt; northward to where the city of Harran stood below the snow-covered mountains. He did not know from which direction the Lord would come; his limbs ached intolerably, his head swam with weariness. He swayed on his feet, but he would not sit down. The Lord might come unexpectedly, and he wanted to be ready. Worse than all the weariness and the heat was the fear that the Lord might not come at all. That He had been offended by the impertinent request. Even as Ab-Ram's own people had been astonished, and with reason, for covenants were concluded only between equal and equal, king and king, warrior and warrior, shepherd and shepherd, never between god and man. What frenzy had taken possession of him when he had made such a demand?

The heat streaming from the heavens did not lessen, the air was still sultry. From time to time a sudden afternoon breeze sprang up, sent columns of dust whirling, then dropped again, intensifying the sultriness and bringing no refreshment. The carcasses of the heifer, goat and sheep began to swell and turn black with the heat. Exhausted by the waiting, the people relieved one another at their posts; some went away, others kept watch. Only Ab-Ram endured the vigil, standing and turning his head in all directions like a crane. He felt an unbearable pressure on his heart. His reason cried: "No one will come. Deceive not yourself and others." An unknown secret voice replied: "Have confidence! No one will come if you doubt. With your faith you will compel the Lord." So he strengthened himself in the faith that was departing from him. Realizing that the weariness of his will would overcome his desire, he yielded himself entirely into the hand of the Lord. He ceased to think of what the disappointed people would say. Calm, still empty of all impatience, he stood in the perfect obedience.

But now dusk crept over the sky. Now the sky began to be lit up by lightnings closer than those of the everyday. Alarmed by the oncoming evening, the vultures flew off; the buzzing of the flies died away. Eliezer thrust his unnecessary spear into the ground. Parts of the carcasses had a bluish hue; the jackals began to steal out of the undergrowth. Even the men who had been keeping watch dozed off; only Ab-Ram kept guard. He watched, resting on his staff.

He watched, resting on his staff, even when a thunder-clap broke so overwhelming and close that the earth trembled, and the sleepers started to their feet. They stood for a moment, then fell to the ground again, stricken with dread. For with their own eyes they saw a great and glowing, fiery ball fall from the sky; amid a deafening thunder it rested momentarily on the point of Eliezer's spear, then fell still lower and rolled between the divided animals. Passing a little beyond them, it disappeared.

The roar of thunder was still rumbling about the earth, shaking the trees, terrifying the hearts smitten with dismay. Only Ab-Ram had no fear. As though in a dream he followed in the track of the flaming ball, strode along the path, smelling the scent of scorched hair. His heart was beating like a hammer. The Lord had come down. He had not abandoned His servant. He had made an everlasting covenant with the tribe of Hebrews.

The others were still lying face downward on the ground, not daring to raise their heads. Forgetting his weariness, the chief called on them to rise. They had seen the Lord pass, dread and terrible. Henceforth they were confederates of God himself. The Lord would keep faith with them, if they kept faith with Him. So long as they did not violate the covenant not one hair would fall from their heads. And now they would receive a token, the seal that they belonged to the Lord and that no one but God had any right to them. By the light of a torch he laid himself bare before them and showed them what the sign would be. They listened in amazement, yet ready to obey, assenting to all. The God of Ab-Ram had proved himself a mightly God. Their knees were still trembling with the terror they had experienced. It would be good to be under such protection. If the token which Ab-Ram demanded of them secured them against demons, it was worth a little pain.

Then their chief announced his own change of name. They accepted even this incomprehensible news more easily than they would have done at normal times, when their tongues wagged swiftly and their brains worked clearly. On such a day as today they would not have been astonished to see Ab-Ram rising in the air, or taking fire into his hands. The heaven and the earth were filled with mysteries and menaces, and they were as helpless as lost children.

So they accepted without protest the command to call their chief henceforth not Ab-Ram, nor Ab-Ram son of Terah, but Ab-Raham. Ab-Ram son of Terah, their chief, their goel, their judge, whom they had known as long as they could remember, had vanished without trace. Instead there was Ab-Raham, the servant and priest of the Lord Most High. His wife also was to receive a new name. Instead of Sarai, henceforth she was to be called "Sarah," which means "princess," "eminent," "lady."

Next morning Ab-Ram began the circumcision of all the men of the tribe, from the oldest to the little children. He summoned them in turn, by name according to their age and rank. Those who were first called suffered no little from the operation. But as their chief grew more practised, those who came later suffered much less. They all bore the suffering with dignity, regarding the mark as an honorable distinction and guarantee of divine protection in the future.

Ab-Raham felt very happy. As he shed the freely given blood of his tribal brothers—the blood which is the essence of life, is life itself, is the sacred possession of God—he was sanctifying them to the Lord, he was confirming the covenant made between him and God. The joy of that day was marred for him only by Ishmael, who was unwilling to submit to the rite. Unmoved by the example of his youthful companions in the camp, who obediently though anxiously waited at their fathers' sides, he fled and hid in the bushes. When at last he was tracked down he struggled and tore himself away, and bit the hands of Sur and Eliezer, who were taking him back. When reduced to helplessness he screamed vociferously. He had to be held still by four men. The sweat beaded Ab-Raham's face, his hands trembled. In his anxiety to spare his only son he added to the boy's pain. Hagar ran like a mad woman round the tent in which the token of the Covenant was being made in the flesh; she cursed Ab-Raham and all his designs, she howled like a wild beast. When the bawling lad was released he took refuge in his mother's arms, and their mingled weeping and their upbraiding of his father were heard for a long time after. The men gathering for the rite behaved as though they had not noticed anything of all this, in order not to bring shame on Ab-Raham, who was already deeply afflicted by his son's conduct.

Meanwhile the women prepared a banquet. Ab-Raham ordered that wine was to be issued abundantly, and as much olive oil as was desired, to anoint the wounds. Myrrh was added to the wine, for it had the property of drugging pain. But the majority of the revellers preferred to drink the wine without the addition of the bitter herb. Some of them had to endure much more pain when a leopard had torn their shoulder or they had been kicked and trampled by a stampeding herd.

His trouble with Ishmael forgotten, Ab-Raham sat intent and cheerful among the banqueters. Let the armed potentates raise gilded temples to their gods in Babylon, Nyneveh, and Egypt. Some new conqueror would destroy them or set new gods up in them. The One God, the True God, the Creator of heaven and earth has founded His indestructible habitation here, in Ab-Raham's people.

He looked back over the past days, the road traversed since that morning when some unknown power had lifted him into the air. Suddenly dazzled with light, he realized that all that had happened during these past years had been significant, had led to the end planned by God. Even his own weakness and faults and aimless wanderings and apparent immobility. Every day had brought nearer the time of maturity, thoughts had bored their way into his mind like beetles into a tree. And he realized that all the people he had met in the course of his life had helped in this task: both Nergal-Sar, who had been the first to point to the anticipated Truth, and the Babylonian Hammurabi, who had played such a large part with his attempt to enyoke the Hebrew tribe; both Sep-Sin, who had been afraid of the burden of the Truth, but who when the Lord had seized hold of him had valiantly given his life for it, and the well-remembered priest and king Melchizedek to whom Ab-Raham really owed this day. All of them—friends, kinsmen, enemies, even people with whom he had only momentary acquaintance. Knowingly, or not, they had all brought a handful of clay to the edifice planned. His own fellow-tribesmen, whom he had regarded as unwise children, had been of great assistance. They had forced him to act, had violated his will, by demanding that he should show them the Lord. Of a truth, without them he would have gone on quietly dozing, forgetting his unfulfilled obligation.

Bela, Mosa's wife, lamented over her husband's pain, but the shepherd laughed merrily. The wine he had drunk made him expansive and so he told her the reason for his satisfaction.

"I have kept an amulet with an image of the demon of fire Girru. Ab-Ram, son of Terah, whom we now call Ab-Raham, evidently forgot and did not mention that demon at all. I swiftly slipped the amulet into my bosom and here it is!"

Mosa fell asleep happy, for it is pleasant to feel secured on all sides.

From *The Covenant*, Part Three, "Son of the Promise,"
Chapter Two, Roy Publishers, New York

Joseph Wittlin

(1896–1976)

Born in 1896 in Eastern Galicia, educated at the universities of Lwow and Vienna, he saw military service in the Austro-Hungarian Army during World War I. After the war he worked for some time as a secondary school teacher in Lwow. In 1922 he became literary director of the Municipal Theater in Lodz and co-founder and professor of its Dramatic School. Settling in Warsaw in 1924 he devoted himself to manifold literary pursuits. The outbreak of World War II overtook him in France. After the collapse of that country he managed to escape to the United States and since 1941 has been living in New York.

A poet, novelist and essayist, he published his first collection of poems, *Hymns*, in 1920. Though showing traces of the influence of Kasprowicz, Wittlin gave expression to his sensitiveness and sympathy for human suffering in an original and forceful manner. A regular contributor to all major Polish literary journals, he is the author of two volumes of studies and essays, *War, Peace and the Soul of the Poet* (1925) and *Stages* (1933), and of an old Babylonian novel, *Gilgamesz*. Active also as translator, he translated over twenty novels, and plays and selected works of such poets as Dehmel, Rilke, Stephen Vincent Benet and Langston Hughes. Wittlin's outstanding achievement in this field is his masterful rendering of Homer's *Odyssey*, for which he was awarded the Polish Pen Club's prize in 1935.

Also, in 1935, Wittlin's major work of fiction, *Salt of the Earth*, made its appearance. Translated into thirteen languages it has been universally acclaimed. The English translation (New York 1941) won for the author a rare distinction, the awards of the American Institute of Arts and Letters and of the National Institute of Arts and Letters (1943). *Salt of the Earth*, conceived as the first part of an intended trilogy, is a modern epic of a "patient foot soldier," a simple Hutzul of Eastern Galicia, drafted into the Austro-Hungarian Army at the beginning of World War I. Bewildered and puzzled by the strange events around him, the hero's experiences assume a universal significance. The objective narrative is informed with a discreet lyricism and humor. Wittlin's love of humanity and understanding for the simple man have in this war novel found most eloquent expression couched in language that is clear, concise and economical, simultaneously suffused with genuine poetic radiance. In light of the excellence of the novel it is truly regrettable that the manuscript of the further two parts has been lost in the French debacle. The novelist is working on a reconstruction of the lost parts.

Two Selections from *Salt of the Earth*

1. PROLOGUE

Everybody rose. The old rococo armchairs breathed with relief, suddenly freed from the pressure of the dignitaries' frames. Below, in front of the portals, stomped the iron-shoed boots of the palace guard. The soldiers of the 99th Moravian infantry regiment had the age-honored privilege of guarding these holy places.

"*Gewehr heraaaaus!*" the picket shrieked like a locomotive whistle, paying last honors to the victims of a train wreck. The guard presented arms.

A bald, tall dandy, sporting a cold smile under his small black moustache, cleared his throat. Today he had a most important task to perform. Already in his childhood he had liked history. Very much. With an arrogant look he once more sized up the ministers who froze in anticipation. Their pompous faces, ordinarily rather sour and down-cast, bore testimony to rapidly advancing sclerosis. The worn-out pistons laboriously pumped blue blood into the hearts of those gentle-men. It was generally known for whom those hearts were beating. History itself will testify to whom they had pledged their "last drop" of blood. Especially, when nobody demanded it. Meanwhile, it struggled with its own degeneracy.

The courteous dandy's glance rested in turn on the silver wig of Maria Theresa, whose eyes stared from a huge portrait; large and shamelessly masculine eyes they were, surveying the bald heads and the beards gathered around the table. Above the wig, over the gilt frame, big jewels embedded in St. Stephen's crown burned with a red, green, violet light, and a cross stood aslant on the top of the crown. That crown glittered in the glow of the setting sun, dripped richly with color, but the eyes of the empress glowed more brightly. She never suffered from sclerosis.

A carriage rumbled to a stop before the gate. A dry thud of rifle butts set down against the soldiers' feet. A dry coughing down below.

The magnificent portals were thrown open. Two slim officers of the guard placed themselves motionless on both sides of the entrance, like two statues from the vestibule of the court theater. The mysterious ceremony suddenly walled in two live bodies into the dead stillness, as though into the empty niches of cold marble. That stillness swal-lowed the broken, glassy clink of spurs.

The gentlemen's faces soon assumed an air of festivity. The short, stout Chief of the General Staff drew together his bushy brows. His greying head, his hair cropped short, inclined lightly toward his left breast, on which before long would sprout the highest crosses and stars. The bald dandy, Minister of Foreign Affairs, impatiently shifted his weight from one foot to the other. His tight leather patent shoes which he had to wear so often in the course of his duty, gave him corns. One had to know how to impress embassies. He alone in that gathering used perfume. To be sure, very discreetly. He used to buy his perfume in Paris. He distrusted the native brands.

Suddenly two old men in generals' uniforms, their chests adorned with sashes colored like scrambled eggs, ushered in a third old man in a light blue tunic. He was bent and leaned on a cane with a silver knob. All three wore sidewhiskers and resembled each other like three postage stamps. A life they lived in common for many years, the boredom and pleasures they shared—lent them the same appearance. And were it not for the Golden Fleece under the third button on the chest of the stooping figure, a stranger to this house would be unable to tell which of those three old men was by the Grace of God the Emperor of Austria, the Apostolic King of Hungary, King of Bohemia, Dalmatia, Croatia and Slavonia, King of Galicia and Lodomeria, King of Illyria, Archduke of Upper and Lower Austria, Grand Duke of Transylvania, Duke of Lorraine, Carinthia, Carniola, Bukovina, Upper Silesia, Lower Silesia, Count of Habsburg and Tyrol, Margrave of Moravia, King of Jerusalem, etc., etc., and which were his aides-de-camp: Count Paar and Baron Bolfras.

The Ministers and Generals lowered their heads. Only one, in this instance the third bewhiskered double of His Majesty, stood erect. He had a right to this. On his chest, indeed much younger than the Emperor's, he also wore the Golden Fleece. After all he was the grandson of the victor of Aspern, Archduke Charles.

The armchair in which the Emperor sat down was of red velvet and stood right under the portrait of Maria Theresa. It seemed for a while that the Empress' eyes were seeking over the head of Francis Joseph the bushy brows of little Baron Conrad, Chief of Staff, to remind him that the highest reward for an officer of the Imperial and Royal army was, had been and would be, her Order, the Order of Maria Theresa. Conrad knew why he was getting it. He knew Heinrich Kleist's *Prince von Homburg* almost by heart.

At this moment dusk began to diffuse and to distend the contours of the old portraits. The portraits grew, grew, grew until they were fused into one grey mass with the wallpaper and woodwork of the resplendent hall. With a last gleam of the black, sleek armor Prince Eugene of Savoy sank into the dusk from which a moment ago protruded the golden baton and the signet ring on his finger. The crinoline of Maria Theresa swelled like a gigantic, globe-like water-filled pillow. You might say: In a moment the old mother of the Habsburgs would step out of the gilt frame and with her fleshy elbows would push these sclerotics aside, and would sit down familiarly by the withered scion of her exuberant blood. She would put her bare, plump arm around the little old man, and would breathe vigor into the parched bloodlessness and would roar lusty laughter.

But the lights of St. Stephen's crown were already extinguished, and the fire went out of her eyes.

The butler entered. He switched on the electric light in the crystal chandeliers. But not all the bulbs, for His Imperial Majesty cannot bear strong light. With a trembling hand he puts on his glasses. After a while he takes them off and polishes them with his handkerchief for a long time. Now the patience of the bald Count Berchtold, Minister of Foreign Affairs, has been exhausted. He pulls out certain papers from his briefcase and looks at the Monarch sharply though officiously. His Parisian perfume pleasantly tickles the nostrils of his closest neighbor, His Excellency Krobatin, the Joint Minister of War. This fragrance in the dusk brings back recollections of youth. How wonderfully the Magyar girls kiss!

The Emperor stopped polishing his glasses. The starched faces of the highest state dignitaries became animated. No trace of sclerosis.

The Emperor speaks. In a toneless voice he expresses thanks for something. What dear Count Berchtold had spoken about yesterday has saddened him greatly. If he is not mistaken, that is, if his memory does not fail him: Belgrade?—With joy he takes cognizance of the great embitterment of his dear peoples which demand . . . demand . . .

The Emperor cannot recall what his dear peoples demand.

Therefore they began explaining it to him. Something which the Emperor evidently, despite everything, did not wish to understand at any cost. At first they reasoned with him like a mother with her child until they lost self-control and began to gesticulate. When at last he understood, they started bargaining with him. The Emperor objected for a long time, resisted, hesitated, coughed, recalled the murdered Empress Elizabeth. Once he even rose, stood up under his own power, and struck his cane with the silver knob on the table so that the live statues of the Guards shook and the eyes of Maria Theresa sparkled.

Archduke Frederic, the grandson of the one of Aspern, rose abruptly. He approached His Majesty, bent over the pink ear stuffed with tufts of grey cotton, and for a long time poured into this ear some heavy words. In this inclined posture met the two Golden Fleeces on the breasts of the Habsburgs and for a few moments they swayed in harmony. Then the Emperor yielded. He surrendered to the will of his dear peoples.

He had only one wish: According to tradition let them stick oak leaves in their shakos and let them sing. At this moment Archduke

Frederic interrupts the Monarch again and observes aloud that in the twentieth century the troops in the field do not wear shakos but ordinary light caps. The Emperor excuses himself. It is a long time since he has attended maneuvers. There flicker before his eyes the old heads of veterans of Novarra, Mortara, Solferino, the pandours, Radetzky . . . Shamefacedly he turns to the Minister of War, like a pupil to his teacher: perhaps His Excellency would be kind enough to remind me how many troops I have?

"Thirty-eight peacetime divisions, without counting the *Landwehr* and the *Honveds*."

"Thank you, I have thirty-eight divisions!"

Thirty-eight divisions! Francis Joseph relishes in his imagination each single division, takes delight in the size and multifarious color of this figure, sworn to him for life and death. In his mind he recreates the last parades which he attended, the last fictitious battles when the enemy could be identified by a red band on the soldiers' caps. At that time he himself mounted on a horse commanded one of the fighting armies, and his adversary was no one else but Francis Ferdinand, heir apparent to the throne, murdered only four weeks ago. Here his memory does not fail him; this one does not forget! The former wrath stirred in the old man at this recollection. For a moment he once again felt his old dislike of the fictitious adversary of the maneuvers, whose real death he and the entire Imperial and Royal armies are to avenge. The blood rushed to the old man's head at the thought that even after his death this stubborn rival disturbs his peace; he who for so many years had in vain awaited the Emperor's natural death. Something triumphed in the old man: and after all I survived him! But even this quiet solitary triumph was marred by grief for his unforgotten only son Rudolf who did not get a chance either. *"Mir bleibt nichts erspart!"*

An unpleasant silence fell upon the hall. The sweetish odor of Berchtold's perfume rose like frankincense over the bodies of the murdered men. Adieu Parisian perfumes! The road is closed: the Triple Alliance—the Triple Entente! Count Berchtold knew this well, he knew what the new course of history spelled. It spelled being restricted to domestic products. But in that ghostly silence even the jovial Krobatin no longer smelled his perfume. Neither had he ever smelled gunpowder, but he was always Minister of War.

The Emperor mused. His blue eyes became clouded under his glasses. His clean-shaven chin fell into the gold braided collar, the cotton-like whiskers protruding from it. The gleaming cross on St. Stephen's crown inclined even more and threatened to fall upon the old man's head. He continued to be silent, lost in the gloomy catacombs of his recollections of the dead. The atmosphere over the round table thickened more and more. The old armchairs squeaked. The sclerosis in the palladins' veins advanced one step. At length the impatience of the Crown Council transcended the bounds of etiquette. Then Generals began to whisper: "It is high time!" "He must sign!" Krobatin could no longer endure without a cigarette. Then Count Berchtold nudged Count Paar. The latter placed before the Emperor a long sheet. The other of the doubles held a pen with a new, unused nib, in accordance with court ceremonial. Everybody's eyes turned to the withered, delicate hand of the Emperor. Finally he woke from his reverie and adjusted his glasses. Everyone breathed with relief.

For a few minutes the Monarch with a cold glance scanned the black, stiff rows of letters. He scrutinized severely each word, each comma. But after reading the first sentences his eyelids reddened and his eyes began to smart. His glasses became steamed. Lately reading fatigued the old man greatly, particularly by artificial light. Thus he lifted his eyes from the sheet and seeing the impatience of the Crown Council guided the pen with a trembling hand toward the black jaws of the inkwell. His hand returned with the pen, dipped in the poisonous liquid, and quivering it landed on the paper like a flyer who sensed solid ground under his feet. Presently the left hand came to its aid and held fast the paper. The Emperor was affixing his signature for which the Ministers had been waiting so long. After writing the word "Francis," however, the pen ran out of its liquid breath, the ink was drained. For the second time the Emperor reached over to the inkwell and with the trembling pen lightly scratched the thumb of his left hand. A tiny drop of blood oozed from his finger. It was red. No one noticed this scratch and the Emperor quickly wiped his finger and in one strong stroke added: "Joseph." The ink was blue.

Count Berchtold took the document. On the following day it was translated into all the languages of the monarchy. It was printed and posted on all the corners of cities, towns and villages, and began with the words: "To my peoples . . ." The town criers read the manuscript to the illiterate.

The Emperor rose, helped by his aides-de-camp. While on duty he never shook anyone's hand. This time, however, he gave his hand to the Prime Minister. On the threshold he turned back once more and said to nobody in particular:

"If I am not mistaken . . . blood will flow."

Then he left. Archduke Frederic treated Bilinski, the Minister of Finance, to a Havana cigar. Below stamped the iron-shoed boots of the infantrymen from the 99th regiment.

The dry thud of riflebutts set down to the soldiers' feet. In the nearby barracks retreat was sounded. Nine o'clock.

The soldiers in all the monarchy go to bed at nine o'clock.

2. THE LAST NIGHT

Peter was returning home. The village lay three kilometers behind the station. Along the road stretched out wet meadows, strewn
with buttercups in the spring. At this time of the year the meadows
were mown, and large hay ricks stood in a motionless battle formation,
like an enchanted army. At a certain moment it seemed to Peter that
the hay ricks were moving forward. But the illusion soon vanished. As
far as the eye could reach there was no living soul. That is, if the grass-
hoppers, so loudly and indefatigably piercing the night, have no
souls. The earth, violated somewhere far away by shrapnels, groaned at
regular intervals. The night was cool. The moon had not yet ventured out of its lair, which it kept behind the hill, behind Czernielica,
but it already began shedding silvery powder over the village of
Topory. The stars twinkled at him invitingly, but they were very small
and faint, like the flames of small kerosene lamps. The moon had plenty
of time. It was plotting something that night.

The village sent out to Peter its strongest smells: of over-ripe onions
and parsley. And when he reached the first huts, the timeless odor of
the peasant rooms drifted in his direction with the tranquility of village existence: the smoke of burnt wood, cheese, whey, chicken manure
and poverty—all mingled together. The black, unglazed pots, and
sundry kitchen utensils sat on the stakes of the fences, like helmets on
the heads of crusaders. In many huts lights were burning as numerous
draftees had to leave for Hungary tomorrow. Now their bundles and
boxes were being packed, and victuals prepared for their journey.
Only in the hut of Hrycio Lotocki it was dark. He slept peacefully; he
was over sixty years old, and the emperor had not summoned him to
war. Lotocki's dog rushed out of his shed at the sound of Peter's steps
and, clanging his chain, barked long at the passer-by, as if he were a
thief. Wakened by the baying, other dogs stirred, but did not keep their
bond of solidarity with Lotocki's sheep dog very long. One after
another they retired to their lairs.

But Bas recognized Peter's steps from afar, and joyfully leaped at
him. He was waiting before the house together with Magda, who had
learned in the village about Peter's departure having been advanced.
She decided to spend this night with him. They entered the room.

Peter lighted the lamp. The air was stuffy. Magda opened the
windows. Instantly night butterflies, moths and colored beetles
swooped inside. Many of them perished noiselessly in the tempting
flame, like the soldiers who that night were falling from the fire of the
cannon on the Drina, on the Sambre, and on the Meuse, because at the
moment the retreat of the Austro-Hungarian armies from Kragujevac
in Serbia had begun, and from the north the 4th and 5th Russian

armies were just beginning to advance, and from the north-east the 3rd and the 8th, converging on the line of Przemysl-Lwow. By the shaking of the long unwashed window-panes in the house of Peter Niewiadomski the armies fighting in Galicia announced their increased activity.

Peter sat down on the bed without removing his cap. He was very tired and hungry. Magda cleaned out the ashes left over in the hearth from before the war, cut some wood and kindled the oven fire. Thoughtfully she had brought some milk, bread and potatoes. They were silent for a long while. The live fire on the stove slowly began to reach them. Magda spoke first:

"Are you going?"

Although for the past four years Magda had been for Peter what civilized people call a mistress, she did not dare to address him by the familiar form of "thou"; only during the moments of their greatest intimacy did she allow herself this. When those moments passed she was separated from Peter once more by a barrier erected by her respect for him and his age; he was seventeen years her senior. He always addressed her as "thou"; she only on duty—in the service of Venus. Outside that service she existed only as a humble orphan who had no right to forget her inferiority.

"I am going," he replied.

And again they were silent. Only during supper, which they ate together for the last time, Peter said:

"Take care of Bas, don't let the Russians take him away. Everyone is eager to get a dog."

And he stroked Bas, squeezed his snout with both hands so forcefully that the dog whined.

Magda was hurt. He always cared more about the dog than about her. She remained silent, however, for even orphans have a sense of honor. After supper Peter came out in front of the house, lit his pipe.

He sat on the threshold and gazed at the stars. One of the stars broke away from its flock, crossed the entire horizon and vanished in the river Prut. Peter grew pensive. He heard that stars fell down when someone was about to die. He laughed out loud: were the stars to fall for each man who kicks the bucket in the war, they would have to fall constantly and as thickly as hail, and soon not one would remain in the sky.

He did not know that there were more flaming and extinguished worlds than soldiers of his Imperial and Royal Majesty.

Having smoked his pipe, he rose heavily and went into the garden. All the trees bloomed fantastically black in the milky gleam of the hidden moon. Neither of the two apple trees bore fruit that year, and the plums were still small and green. Nevertheless he picked one and put it into his pocket. Then he went around the house and probably for the one hundredth time decided that it was a pity to lose such a house. It could be repaired.

Under the thatch hung the bare cobs of corn. They were drying for seed. In the dusk they looked like sleeping bats suspended by their claws.

Peter went back to Magda and their night of love began.

The girl had washed the dishes and the pots and had fed the remnants of the supper to Bas. The sated dog ran outside but he soon returned discontented: evidently he could not find a comfortable sleeping place. He began therefore to make himself comfortable under the bed. A cricket sang, hidden in the crevice between the hearth and the floor. Magda knelt before the image of the Blessed Mother, closed her eyes and prayed long in a fervent whisper. Then she untied her apron string, shed her apron, took off her skirt, undid her two thin tresses and pleated them into one thick one. Then she put out the lamp and lay at Peter's side.

At that moment Bas moved uneasily, reminding them of his presence. Peter was ashamed of Bas. This living witness was embarrassing. He had to be removed. Peter jumped off his bed, opened the door and attempted to coax Bas at least into the hallway. But the dog refused to obey. He was stubborn: He did not want to leave his master voluntarily on that last night. Humiliated, Peter used force and with a stick, yes, with a stick, he chased his only love outside. The exiled love howled painfully.

Peter had never loved Magda; he only "lived" with her. But was he capable of love at all? Who knows whether love is not a luxury which only privileged souls can afford. How, for example, did his love for Bas manifest itself? Was it the boundless trust of the beaten man for the beaten animal, a fellowship of a dog's lot on this earth, which they both walked with lowered heads, or was it something else besides? And perhaps love is concealed at the bottom of the dull, mutual submissiveness? Because Peter too yielded to Bas often, despite reason, and the irrational submission to a weaker being is at times regarded as love. Probably only in really serious situations, for instance when the dog was threatened with danger, Peter imposed his will on him. Otherwise, he rarely displayed his superiority. What does a Hutzul mountaineer know about a dog? Peter attributed great intelligence to Bas. It seemed to him that the old dog saw everything, felt and understood every human gesture. And that is why he was ashamed of Bas whenever Magda remained for the night. Often because of Bas's presence, there was no intimacy between Peter and Magda. The dog could not bear anybody touching his master; he seemed to be jealous. He threw himself on the foreign body, trying to tear it

away from Peter. But even when Bas behaved quietly, Peter did not
feel he was free to do as he liked. This time, however, the excitement
prevailed, and it was heightened by the events of the day and the
hazy foreboding that this was his last night with Magda. He did not
want to give it up, and he could not do it in Bas's presence. So he
chased him out.

The trouble with the dog cooled his desire, constrained his ardors.
It seemed silly to return to love-making, interrupted by the stubborn-
ness of the beast. Moreover, at the back of his mind, like a captured
insect, sat the war, oppressing him with the thought of the following
day. He had to rouse his blood anew, to kindle the fires, to exclude
reason, to overcome his fears. At last Venus triumphed.

No, Peter never loved Magda. He enjoyed her body the way one
drinks vodka, or takes a bath necessary for one's health. Only this was
not an addiction. Peter had no addictions. Magda's body, thin, small,
firm, was always cool. Even in the moments of the most ardent ec-
stacies it did not perspire. It gave Peter a gentle, servile passiveness.
Therefore Peter came to like it. In the orphan's arms he experienced
both a sense of relief enjoyed by every man, and a dulling of consciousness and strength. Eventually, Magda's body was the only field
on which he felt victor. It is difficult for masculine self-love to do
without this. Peter conquered Magda without resistance, but not without effort, and only the barrenness of his seed spoiled his short-lived
pleasure. It robbed this union of the two bodies of deeper meaning,
and stripped it of dignity, for it brought no results. But it also protected him from debauchery. Besides, Magda's sensuality was kept in
check by still other restraints: her faith and Peter's age. A younger
man, perhaps, would have succeeded to bring Magda's body to ex-
cesses, and her soul to lose the sense of sin. "Living" with Peter, she
never forgot that she was sinning, therefore she at least tried to sin
with moderation. And therefore, probably, she prayed so fervently
before she went to his bed. As if she wanted to win forgiveness in
advance.

Nor did Peter get intoxicated with Magda; he always controlled
his instincts. He fulfilled an unconscious duty, as it were, handed down
to him by his unknown Polish father.*

The nights with Magda gave him a temporary enjoyment of life,
not found anywhere else. The orphan's body was thus for him both
café and opera, and a distant sea voyage—everything that music,
sports, noble delights of the mind are for other people. It contained
no surprises however; it was common—like the daily bread. Peter
found in it rest, a softness, and for several seconds he would be trans-

---

* His name *Niewiadomski* means "of unknown origin."

ported beyond the confines of his own life. Woman, vodka and religion—these were the three delights, protecting the soul of the ignorant Hutzul mountaineer from despair and hell on earth.

However, Peter never took Magda with him into his dreams. The orphan stopped at the threshold of his dream and of his waking existence, just as she did not dare to approach him with a "thou," during the day. Peter was lonely in his dream, although her arms enveloped him. Sometimes he was visited there by his mother, sometimes even by his bad sister, Parashka—never by Magda. But she dreamed of him often. That night she was completely united with him. She first dreamed of him as of a little child sucking her breast, then the child suddenly grew....

The window panes shook, the earth trembled rhythmically, as if torn by a spasm of love. Dull, dark, distant explosions amid the night's stillness were not terrible: On the contrary, they were even exciting. All through the night the cricket played for them, that Mozart of peasant hearths. Only the whining of the exiled Bas filled the night with disquiet and rankled some unhealed wounds.

Decidedly, the moon was up to something that night. It did not show up, although it was supposed to be over the Topory village a long time ago. Only about midnight did it roll out majestically from behind Czernielica, and with cold silver light flooded the night and the sleeping lovers. Peter and Magda floated out of the darkness like two silver phantoms. Peter snored. The window panes tinkled like silver.

At that moment death, having deserted the battlegrounds, tore across the halls and chambers of the Vatican. In vain did the Swiss guards defend all entrances with their halberds. Death cheated their vigilance, and invaded the bed on which the old man Melchior Joseph Sarto was lying. The Cardinals and the Monsignors already recited the psalms of penitence. One of the domestic prelates of His Holiness held forth the cross to the lips of the dying man. The death of Pope Pius X took place at 1:20 A.M. The Cardinal Chamberlain della Volte confirmed this personally. After which the Cardinals and the Monsignors began to read the office, the *officium defunctorum*. Death, having fulfilled its task, returned to the battlefields. The so-called battle of Lorraine had just begun. Peter Niewadomski snored.

The stars were already growing pale, the night was breathing its last when Magda awoke, with loud weeping. She had had a terrible dream. She dreamed of Peter. He was lying in the yard of Ivan Bury. He was lying stark naked, and in his belly he had a huge, hideous wound. The sow in farrow belonging to old Maryna Prokipczuk, was dipping its snout in the wound and lapping up the blood, so loud, so loud.

Magda's sobs wakened Peter. Otherwise the world was wholly

still. The cannonade ceased before day-break, you would say, in order that it might draw breath. The window panes no longer shook. Only the cricket continued to sing in the crevice between the hearth and the floor. Peter was frightened by the sudden stillness of the earth and that sobbing of Magda.

"What ails you?" he asked. And only now seeming to perceive all the misery of the orphan, and all his misery, and all the misery of the species to which he belonged, he added, tenderly embracing the weeping girl: "My poor child."

Magda, her whole body shivering, from cold, from fear or perhaps from the love that welled up in her, stammered through her tears:

"If you wished it . . . if you wished it—I would love you unto death . . ."

And she told him her dream. Peter laughed, but between him and Magda there was now the word: death. She cried some more, sighed, and at last Peter calmed her. And for the last time in his life he fell asleep in the thin arms of the orphan, Magdalena Mudryk.

Translated by ADAM GILLON
and LUDWIK KRZYZANOWSKI

Jan Parandowski

(1895–1978)

Jan Parandowski is considered a foremost scholar and the most distinguished aesthete of contemporary Polish prose writers. He was born in Lwow in 1895. After studying philosophy and philology he became a university professor, novelist and essayist, noted for his brilliant style. Parandowski does not distinguish between historical and current times, and his prime domain is the ancient world, particularly ancient Greece and Rome.

His literary career started with the publication of a biographical novel about Oscar Wilde, *King of Life* (1921). But it was a collection of ancient legends, *Mythology*, and a group of love stories, entitled *Eros on Olympus* (1924) that drew critical attention to his work. Later, his historical sports novel *The Olympic Discus* (1933) won a bronze medal at the 1936 Olympics. The book that followed, *The Sky in Flames* (1936), reflected the religious doubts of his youth.

Parandowski is one of Poland's outstanding translators; he rendered Homer's *Odyssey* into prose and also translated such authors as Conrad, Julius Caesar, Chekhov, the Greek writer Longos, Montherlant, H. G. Wells. He has also published three volumes of short stories, essays, sketches, autobiographical notes and many short items that defy classification, e.g., a dialogue between Caesar and Cicero. These books appeared under the titles: *Three Signs of the Zodiac, Mediterranean Hour* and *The Sun Dial*.

His *Alchemy of Words* (1950) is a remarkable study of a writer's task and profession, abundantly illustrated with historical and literary material.

Since 1933 Parandowski has been the President of the Polish section of the P.E.N. Club.

An Ordinary Day

When we found ourselves in Sweden after the war, the people we met there and who soon became our friends, people of peace and untroubled prosperity, questioned us about our war experiences. But they could not imagine what these had been like. They wanted to know what made up our day—in detail, hour by hour, just any ordinary day. Some added: the day of a writer. We selected out of our crowded memories a day which stood out from the others because of a few memorable details, and related it in four voices—our two and our older children's. Piotrus was then scarcely two years old, and everything had happened outside his consciousness, preoccupied ex-

clusively with the charms of the Swedish land and his childhood
affairs. I shall now repeat that narration as a page from my diary:

I rose at six o'clock. It was still dark. The moon was shining. It
was a full moon; I could do without light. I went to the kitchen and
put the water on to boil. Then I took the bread from the pantry—
there was more than half a loaf. Before slicing it, I estimated whether
there was enough. The slices would have to be thinner than usual.
I sliced this gray, crumbling, rationed bread. Then I spread the slices
with the rationed beet marmalade. The two slices set apart for my
daughter's lunch at schol, I covered with thin layers of butter and
then topped them with the marmalade. We called these sandwiches
"double-deckers." My daughter had longer lessons and a longer way
to go. She had to go to Union Square while my son returned home
after a few hours and his school was close by at Mianowski Street.

As I did every morning, while waiting for the children to wake
up, I reached for the *Psalter* as for a faithful and strong arm on which
to lean. Man suffered, feared and prayed, certain that God would hear
him through these verses invested with the incomparable charm of
Kochanowski's language and poetry. This spirit of a thousand years
ago spoke of a loneliness as great as an empty cathedral in which the
stained glass windows have gone to sleep and even the eternal lamp
has muffled its flame like a flower in the night and only the fervent
whisper of contrition smites the hollow, dark dome. And the edge of
the seared page was always bright with hope. One gathered this
particle of light into oneself and set out into the stony desert of the
day.

There had never been a greater solitude. The world was snatched
from us. All the voices of the lands and seas had been stilled. Even
our own country had departed. The sight of the map was painful. It
hung in my son's little room and every day as I came to wake him
up, my first glance was for the map. The large green area of our
plains with the yellow and brown patches of our tablelands and
mountains and the bluish cloud of sea. The whole edged with a red
border as with an artery of purple blood.

My son slept, not yet aware of my presence. The moon shone
upon the map like a lantern. In a whisper that did not part my lips I
repeated the litany of rivers and cities. Those I knew flashed some
sign—a church spire, a town hall, the water's current under bending
willows—the unknown names groped for a form in my imagination;
at times the very charm of their names clothed them with fantasy
like creeping vines covering a wall. Walt Whitman had sung a hymn
of happiness and rapture with the thousand names of his native land,
but to our lips Poland rose like a sponge saturated with vinegar and
gall raised on the steel head of the enemy's lance.

My son opened his eyes and as if divining my thoughts began to move his sleep-laden eyes over the map which he knew by heart, having lived with it constantly. Embracing him for "good morning," I then turned to my daughter. She slept in my room, which had been my wife's room before the war. Now bookshelves were there and under the balcony stood the piano as before. These changes had been made when we sublet half our apartment. We slept in what had been the children's room, with a balcony overlooking the yard.

Breakfast would be ready when the milk was delivered. There was a knock at the door. It was the milkman who, by hidden paths in the pale dawn or twilight, carried away from the Germans what they had not yet stolen from us—milk, bread, meat. His head was bandaged. He had fled from the Germans, fallen into a ditch and cut his head on a stone. "But I didn't spill the milk, not a single drop of it!" he choked with laughter.

The whole house was in motion: my wife took over the command from me and immediately everything became bright and gay, as if the sun had risen. The children ran to the bathroom and dressed hurriedly, but they became pensive and reticent at breakfast. Every slice of bread, almost every crumb was of great value. Wanting to please me, they praised the coffee which I had prepared myself. My son collected his notebooks and books. My daughter still had some time; she was leaving later.

I accompanied my son to school. We went by Dantyszek Street along the edge of the square. The moon was still shining. Everything was silver and quiet. A sparrow peeked out of a crevice in the wall on the corner of Krzycki Street and pulled in his head again. Day was dawning as I returned; there were people on the streets which had been almost empty. On the steps, I met my daughter's classmates, who were going to school with her. School! Not the beautiful Slowacki High School which she was to have entered in September 1939. The Germans were quartered there now.

We always felt uneasy when the door closed behind our daughter and as we listened to her running down the stairs. We accompanied her in our thoughts and our hearts trembled as she jumped into the streetcar. Most frequently it was the same car and the same jovial conductor who greeted the group of girls with a joke. He never asked for their tickets, just as he never asked the other passengers. "Who wishes to pay his fare?" he asked gaily and was answered with suppressed laughter. Until finally, his provocative joke caught the ear of some German or Volksdeutscher and the conductor was taken directly from the streetcar and sent to Auschwitz.

Having been left alone, we each went to our occupations: my wife busied herself about the house and I returned to my desk. This was my wife's desk, an old-fashioned piece of furniture which recalled my childhood and was overlaid with family history and amusing adventures. My own desk, a large and heavy mahogany piece, bought to celebrate my first book, *Rousseau*, in the eighth class at the Gymnasium, remained where it had stood before, in my study now occupied by our tenants who had been expelled from Poznan. There also stood the large mahogany cabinet filled with albums, illustrated works on the history of art and yearbooks of periodicals.

I took my typewriter in order to finish a chapter of *Rome* which I wanted to take that same day to Director Piatek. I had a formal contract for this book. Signed a year ago, it did not bear a "war" date. We had put down a fictional date—April 1939. For under occupational law, it would have been a criminal offense to sign a contract since a Polish writer did not have the right to practice his profession. I worked on the book with great pleasure. It was my escape from inactivity in the midst of distress and worry. I delivered every chapter in two copies as soon as it was typed and received my monthly advance of 300 zlotys. How I needed the money that day!

The chapter I was typing dealt with the Comitium, curia, rostrums and Cicero. I could see distinctly every stone, every unevenness of the ground between the ruins and fragments of the Forum. I, myself, stood where Cicero had stood and looked at what he might have seen in the full brightness of the untouched buildings of the Senate, the Emilius Basilica, the temples of the Castors and Vesta up to the slope of the Palatine Hill where his house stood. And nearby, I could see the leaves of the old fig tree, *ficus Ruminalis*, move in the light breeze.

No force can exert its power over this, over our thoughts and dreams. Never was Rome closer or more familiar. I could see everything more plainly and more clearly in my mind's eyes than if I were gazing with my real eyes. But at times this closeness was painful. I had lost all sense of reality and when I looked out of the window, I could not at first understand how this strange street with its marching and yelling units of German soldiers had come there.

"Nonsense," my wife remonstrated, "the same things are certainly going on in Rome and if the Krauts are not there yet then you can be sure that the Fascists are yelling and marching in the same way."

True, we could have been there now, like many others. A year ago all our friends tried to persuade us to leave. We even received letters from abroad, secretly of course, and we yielded to these sensible persuasions, promised to leave and then finally decided to remain in Poland. I remember the day and the moment when we rejected the temptation. I remember the day and the moment and it was strange, the unexpected sense of relief, almost of joy that we were not going, that fate had resolved our decision in the proper manner.

I remember the day and the moment . . . sitting on the balcony in the May sun, I was reading *Dawn* through tears. Like *Forefathers' Eve* and *The Book of the Polish Pilgrims,* this was one of those family treasures which—and who does not remember this?—we had placed in a souvenir chest after 1918. How eager we had been, how certain that they would henceforth be relics and that it would not be fitting to display them on these ordinary days which were ours at last. We wanted to sample these ordinary days as quickly and as fully as possible and to be like all other nations. Sooner than could have been foreseen even in the blackest prognostication, we received a calendar in which all the dates were red . . . an old Polish calendar, tattered, torn by bullets and like a scapulary saturated with sweat. There was no other choice than a life of struggle, or thoughts which were a hidden form of struggle. This form, too, had its victims, its defeats, its triumphs. One threw pieces of one's soul into the fire.

It is difficult to return to my interrupted work from these reminiscences and thoughts. I sat motionless at the silent typewriter. But there was my wife setting out for the market. We would go together.

Narutowicz Square was now a large market place. We no longer remembered how and when this had happened. The sun had freed itself from the clouded and foggy sky and brightened this square of color and movement. It was gayer than usual. The center of merriment was a girl, well known here, tall, good-looking, wearing high boots with a red heart painted on each bootleg, who had been selling radishes, recommending them in a powerful voice "big as roses," and who today had the prettiest stall piled with fruits and vegetables. A German, in civilian clothes, asked her something, drawn by her beauty and, not sensing anything wrong, began to ask how to say this and that in Polish. As if answering him, the girl with steadfast earnestness pronounced the most vulgar words, which he then repeated. He was finally brought to his sense by the laughter which could no longer be suppressed. He realized that he was being made a fool of, and, infuriated, hurled an oath and left.

Another person appeared, a forty-year-old man in a brown overcoat and hat of the same color. He was carrying a brief case and looked into it from time to time. He examined the stalls as if wanting to count all the bunches of the soup greens, stooped over the baskets and stuck his nose into every booth.

"I know that chap," the old herb vendor said, "comes from Volhynia —from Lutsk. I don't recall his name, but he must have another now so as not to be recognized. But he can't change his face. I'd know him at the end of the earth."

In another corner of the market a young man was calling people to his table. He was turning a bottle in his hands and calling out incessantly:

"As much as I've been thrown out, I'm honest. Everyone will find what is written for him."

He dropped clean pieces of paper into the bottle and, after turning it, took out the same card with a horoscope printed on it. People bought. Everyone wanted his fortune told. Some read Nostradamus or Blake, others were satisfied with a scrap of paper taken out of an empty liquor bottle.

"Isn't it the beginning of the end?" asked a stranger who was passing me. "These Germans are selling weapons."

And he pointed to two German soldiers standing at the corner booth. I was standing on the opposite side, on Akademicka Street, on steps from which I had a view of the whole market. But I was noticed too; one of the Germans nudged the other and whispered something to him. The other turned, looked in my direction and momentarily both entered the crowd and disappeared.

"You've frightened the Germans," laughed Irene, my wife, who had observed the whole scene.

And that is the way it remained in our minds. The laughing commentary at home was: "That was the day dad frightened the Germans who were selling weapons."

We were returning home in a playful mood. Jaksa Bykowski was sitting on a bench in the yard and greeted me joyfully.

"Oh, it's so good to see you smiling. You are always so sad. You mustn't be sad. We cannot be sad."

And he told us about the chauffeur who lived in our housing co-operative in the corner house of Dantyszek Street. He was in Auschwitz and from the very first hour he had told himself that he must survive, that he must be of good cheer and feed on hope. This was more nutritious than bread. He did survive. A few days ago he had returned—serene and composed. Poland stands on such people.

It was ten o'clock. I went to the pantry, took a handful of coffee beans, ground them up and made some coffee. This constituted the only and the least expensive luxury in our poor household. This coffee had been sent to me from the "world," from Portugal, from Spain. The Madrid firm of "Miranda" had particularly impressed itself upon my memory for the high quality of its coffee and its charming name that roared with the sounds of Shakespeare's *Tempest*. Affected by the first parcel, I took Shakespeare off the shelf and read the enchanting drama which, like everything else in those times, was momentarily cloaked in poignant metaphors. Caliban became the counterpart of Hitler. Cheered by the coffee, I quickly completed my chapter of *Rome*, which was intended for Director Piatek that day—and just in time. A quarter of an hour later, I might have been incapable of doing it. The mailman—a rare visitor these days—brought a letter which upset us. From the Bruhl Palace. Some German office, I do not remember which, summoned me as the vice-president of the "Book Council" to submit the financial report of that institution. The very fact that a German office had directed a letter to my address was dangerous. I knew that a certain German scholar, Grundmann, a former student of Zygmunt Lempicki, officiated in the Bruhl Palace. He held an important post now. I had never heard of him before the war but he knew me. Recently, someone had told me that when some flustered writer had gone to register there, Grundmann was furious. He shouted, "This sort of fellows come here. But where is Nalkowska, Parandowski?" Our friends wondered then whether we should not leave Warsaw.

I took the letter with me when I went to Director Piatek.

So rarely did we venture beyond our district that walking along Marszalkowska and Wilcza streets, we stopped in front of every shop and almost every house. We even entered the halls of buildings and looked in at the yards. Our hearts trembled with emotion. Never had this city been so dear to us. The old-fashioned houses, recalling Prus, were as beautiful in our eyes as noble historical architecture. And they were alive with the pulse of our own blood. Hundreds of homes were concealed behind these gray façades, thousands of rooms and kitchens with the same everyday occupations amidst the same troubles, fears and hopes. We were grateful to these walls that they had withstood the September fire, that they had not crumbled under the bombs; we were grateful to them that they existed, that with their cornices and balconies they would remain until the day of triumph and joy.

In normal times one knows one's city superficially. Riding a streetcar one reads a paper, or in a taxi one does not have time to notice anything aside from the pedestrian who hesitates, not knowing whether he will manage to cross to the other side. One knows a few houses where friends live; the rest is a conglomeration, a crowd, a row of buildings. It simply does not exist in our consciousness. But now everything was distinct, attracted our attention and moved us. A cracked windowpane sealed with paper tape, a pot with a violet shrub which still had a few buds, a large jar with syrup—cherry or cornel? Someone had placed a card in the window advertising home-made dinners. Someone else repaired runs in stockings.

Never had the common things been so unusual; never could they have laid claim to the pathos which they now contained. We were ready to weep for a dead stranger whose obituary hung on the gate with the stamp of German censorship. Died a natural death at the age of 72 after long and painful suffering. Received the last unction. How

does Tacitus say it? *Bella est res sua morte mori.* It seems to me that
this sentence refers to Nero's time . . .

Director Piatek lived at 1 Wilcza Street, on the corner of Ujazdowskie Avenue. On the opposite corner stood the house with the
"haunted" apartment on the second floor. For years no one had wanted
to rent it. But fear had fled or lurked, waiting for peaceful times.
Someone was living there now, maybe a German, because the whole
Avenue was a German district. We did not enter from the Avenue
but through the yard from Wilcza Street. Piatek was home, of course,
"officiating." Sierzputowski was sitting in the adjoining room. There
was something touching in the operation of this semblance of a large
firm. Nothing was done here for the present day, everything for an
undefined but infallible tomorrow. Piatek signed contracts with
authors, as he did with me, collected manuscripts, paid out advances.
And I, too, received mine.

I showed him the letter concerning the Book Council. Piatek did
not treat it seriously.

"This actually concerns me. I was the treasurer. Leave it with me
and don't answer anything."

"That didn't even enter my head. But isn't it possible that this
may lead somewhere else?"

"I don't think so. It's a sign of that fragment of zeal that German
officials show in order to save themselves from the army. You have
no idea how many similar papers I have received as the director of
Atlas Publishers. They were followed by dead silence."

On our way back, we stopped at Gajewski's. This was a tradition
with us. We always bought cakes on the day of my advance payment.
Irene took a long time choosing the sweets, thinking of an equal distribution for our whole little group.

When we got out of the streetcar at Filtrowa Street, Irene went
home and I went to the drugstore, I don't remember for what. There,
I met Irzykowski. Smiling a bit shyly and a bit maliciously, he explained that he had bought some nitroglycerine.

"It may be necessary to blow oneself up," he joked.

He walked with me to the corner of Zimorowicz Street. He himself
lived a little further on at the corner of Raszynska Street. He said that
he was reading my *King of Life.*

"This is the picture of our literary life," I thought, "two writers
and they meet like strangers or like acquaintances in a shop." Entering our hall, I startled two Jewish children who soon grew calm
because they knew me. They were under the care of our cooperative
and now they had left the cellar where they slept, carrying their dinner
pails.

Their appearance wrung one's heart. Swaddled in unbelievable rags, like tatters of their mother's dress, covered with the filth of cellars and holes, they carried the cruel, incredible tale of the ghetto, of that walled-in settlement of misery and despair over which the Germans had strung up a sign: *Seuchengebiet.* Their words, always few, revealed a view, dimmed as if by clouds stitched with lightning, of a world shorn of all human rights.

One could see similar children covered with wounds and boils, dying in the streets from hunger; one could see houses transformed into human swarms, dozens and scores living in one room, the ceaseless hunt for bread, for a mouthful of warm food; one could see the horrible parody of law and authority wearing the uniform with a blue star; one could hear the hollow rhythm of hours, minutes, seconds measuring the footsteps of death. No one yet understood; no one yet knew anything; everyone could still hope . . .

"And our brother," she said emphatically and nudged the boy standing at her side with her elbow, "smaller than him. There were five of us. But the others are older and they go to work."

She fell silent. Her wide-open black eyes stared straight ahead. A child's eyes! These eyes were not translucent, trusting, joyful, with a marvelous calm like the eyes of children who gaze upon the day flowing under their swift feet as if it were a stream, new and unexpected, and still carrying in the corner of their irises the sparks of a vision of a different world from which they had come, a world of marvelous mysteries. No, these eyes contained sadness—terrifying, as deep as an inexorable chasm.

I hear Irene's voice from the second floor. She must have dropped in on Renata Wylezynska, our administrator. She had pleasant news for us. A stranger had come to her about an hour ago (maybe she did not want to mention his name) and this is what he told her: "We have found out that Parandowski is beginning to sell his books. Please tell him that he should not give up his library. There'll always be some money for him." And he left one thousand zlotys. Throughout the whole occupation, I received similar unexpected help, sometimes quite considerable as compared with the straitened circumstances of life. And I do not even know whom I should thank for this.

My son had returned home and was manipulating his constructor —the last gift before the war. My daughter would return for dinner. Irene was finishing the preparations, saying that we were having *un plat luxueux* for our second course: potato pancakes fried in lard which we named thus in memory of a young French poet. The war had caught him in Poland. He was destitute and he often visited us and shared our modest fare. When once a little diffidently, I began to explain potato pancakes to him he called out entranced, *"Mais c'est un plat luxueux."* He was no longer with us; the Germans had deported

him and to this day Kasprowicz's "Book of the Poor" was lying on my
desk. We had been reading it together, translating it word for word.

My daughter ran in laughing, still exhilarated from school and the
friends who had walked home with her. She was hungry; we were
all hungry; the soup and *plat luxueux* disappeared in a trice, garnished
with the stories of our and their adventures. The letter from Bruhl
Palace was an additional gay event. Finally, Irene placed the cakes on
the table and I went to make the tea. With what absorption, I might
even say piety, the children took the portions of cake assigned to them!

"Dad, must you always be so sad?" my daughter rebuked me.

No, my dear child, this was not sorrow but meditation. I was thinking of our uncommon life and where this happiness, this desire for
laughter comes from. A few years hence, if God permits us to live
that long, we shall no longer understand how we could frolic and
laugh in such times.

We cleared the table; my wife and daughter remained in the
kitchen to wash the dishes. Later, they would do German lessons
together. My son returned to his game and I retired for a nap.

I had a strange dream. I was walking along a straight, white road
which stopped at the city walls. I couldn't recognize the town. It was
neither Warsaw, nor Paris, nor Rome but each of these cities had
given it something. At a distance I recognized churches, buildings,
columns. As I approached, the city began to fade in a fog, different
from all earthly fogs. It did not obliterate the contours but seemed to
enclose the city in an impenetrable ring. I felt that the fog was
mystery itself. Some unknown force had sealed its streets, houses,
gardens. I woke up with the pervading sensation of fear that must be
felt by a person lost in the night.

I did not say a word about it because Irene would take it for a bad
omen. Shortly, I myself forgot about it. Mrs. Morawska had arrived
with her daughter Magda and, always in good spirits, told us amusing
anecdotes and jokes. Suddenly, Mrs. Wylezynska came in. She did not
want to sit down, saying that she was in a hurry and that she must
visit a few others in the house. She had received a warning that the
Gestapo might visit the house that night. No one knew for whom
but she would advise me to sleep elsewhere. We immediately relayed
the information to our tenant because of her son and husband. We
decided to go to Aniela Zagorska. Our children would remain under
the care of Miss Stasia.

It was late when we ran out of the house, perhaps three quarters
of an hour short of the curfew hour. We found a rickshaw and asked
him to hurry. The young man only smiled—he knew, of course he
knew, every Pole was a trusted friend. Aniela Zagorska was very
happy to see us because we had not met for such a long time. Maria

Godlewska, who lived with her, busied herself with the tea. Unexpectedly, Waclaw Sieroszewski, who lived in the same house, dropped in.

"Oh, Jan, Jan," he said in a plaintive voice, "when will this end? When will this bloody rabble go to the devil?"

He fell silent and stared into the cup which Mrs. Godlewska had set in front of him. Suddenly, he pushed it away and began to speak in a strange, agonizing whisper:

"Misfortune is galloping along the uncounted roads of our land. I see lips sealed with lime, eyes strained in mortal fear; I see hands bound with wire, freshly dug holes . . ."

He raised his hand and opened and shut his small fist as if grasping something in the air, and without finishing his words, he dropped his hand to the edge of the table. His eyes had reddened and welled with tears. We sat quietly, holding our breath. No one dared break into his painful solitude. He woke up with a naive, helpless smile and as if embarrassed by the purple passage with which he had astonished and moved us, he again became his usual, homely self. He began to tell us that he was now writing his memoirs.

"And if I can't remember something, my wife tells me." And as if he were suddenly seized by a longing for her, he said good-by and ran upstairs.

"You are more surprised than I am," Aniela Zagorska said, "you never see him now while I see him every day. The old man has moments as if he were launching upon a new and unknown creative period. If Conrad had lived longer . . ."

And now our talk was only about Conrad. Miss Zagorska was translating *The Arrow of Gold;* she read us a few excerpts and we discussed separate sentences and phrases. Finally, she spread out on the table photographs of her visits with Conrad, of his stay in Zakopane at the beginning of the First World War, and told us a number of interesting things. I began to scold her for not having written down her reminiscences.

"But I don't know how to write."

"Certainly better than Jessie."

I had but recently read those very inferior memoirs of Conrad's wife and I spoke of them with irritation. With her innate sweetness, Zagorska defended Jessie. We had completely forgotten the war, the occupation and the Germans. It was very late when she led us into the adjacent room and made our bed.

The following morning, I woke up as usual at six, but I did not get up because I did want to wake Irene. Lying in bed, I listened to the street sounds. Gornoslaska spoke in a different voice than Filtrowa.

It was less noisy. I could hear the infrequent footsteps outside the window and the blinds of neighboring stores being raised.

I could remain in bed no longer. Noiselessly, I slid out of bed and walked up to the window. The curtains were not drawn; we had not turned on the light at night. I picked up from the table the cigarette Miss Zagorska had given me the day before, an English cigarette. Its taste and smell brought back memories of London and that troublesome afternoon dream seemed elucidated. I found in it the familiar streets of Chelsea and Globe Place.

One year before the war, I was a guest of the owners of that building which is now the seat of the P.E.N. Federation's International Secretariat. My room was on the second floor. We assembled on the ground floor for the meetings of the Executive Committee. They were held in a strange octagonal room which several centuries earlier had served as a chapel for the Huguenots expelled from France. It had a glass ceiling wreathed with the branches of the fig tree whose roots were in the ecllar of the house. It was November. The large, broad leaves dropped to the table or on the faces of the members of the conference. This caused quite a lot of amusement. Ensnared in these memories with the smell of an English cigarette, I did not at once notice what was happening outside the window. A crowd of teen-age boys, wearing brown uniforms with swastikas on the shoulders, had suddenly burst into wild yells and raced up the steps in the direction of Ujazdowskie Avenue. I walked away from the window.

The telephone rang as Aniela Zagorska was preparing breakfast. Mrs. Wylezynska said that the night had passed peacefully despite our expectations. The alert had proved unfounded, everything was in order at home. Immediately after breakfast, we made ready to return home. Saying good-by, Aniela Zagorska asked when we would meet again. "We shall try to make it soon. Or perhaps as unexpectedly as this time."

Walking along Piekna Street, we looked in at the yard of the house where Berent had lived not so long ago. How many houses were there now which re-echoed with memories of friends—dead, vanished or deported from the country during the days of conflagration! From where we were standing, we could see the house on the corner of Chopin Street, now occupied, together with everything that belonged to our friends, by the *Oberbürgermeister* of Warsaw. We quickly turned toward the Three Crosses' Square in order to leave this German district.

On the square, we hesitate, undecided whether to go in the direction of Nowy Swiat or to follow Hoza Street toward Marzalkowska Street. Suddenly, I noticed an unusual commotion at the head of Hoza Street: people were running from that direction and rushed into doorways, shops and St. Alexander's Church. There was no doubt: a roundup. Two trucks drove up and blocked off Hoza Street. Instinctively, we retreated toward Ksiazeca Street to the building with the memorial tablet in honor of Pope Pius XI who had lived here during his years as Papal Nuncio.

"The same kind are waiting at the corner of Marszalkowska," said a man in a brown coat who had joined us. He was very pale and breathing heavily. "I escaped. This is the third time. How long will I have to run this way? I am thirty years old, could be in the army, and all I do is hide and run. But it must end now. I'll join the army in the forest."

And he disappeared as he had arrived, a specter of our cruel life, one of the voices in which our common misfortune confided, voices unknown but never strange. We gazed after him for a while. We could see the brown coat among the pedestrians. We then walked toward Nowy Swiat, alert to every movement, every voice in the crowd. We moved through the streets of our own city, through the capital of our own country, with the fear that one feels in a jungle. Every green uniform noticed at a distance could conceal a beast.

We trembled at the thought of our daughter. Who could tell us whether she too had not fallen into the trap on her way to school? That thought paralyzed us for a moment; we stopped, incapable of making another step. Finally, we took courage and boarded a streetcar. We rushed home from the last car stop. Unbounded joy! Our children were home! They were shackled by their concern for us and preferred not to go to school until we had returned.

Our Swedish friends listened attentively to us. They asked for explanations concerning persons, streets and, if one can call them that, economic conditions. They simply could not take it all in. They were most disturbed by the question of whether this nightmare was truly a normal day in our lives under the German occupation? "There were worse—much worse," we answered, without going into the details which exceeded their imagination. Through the weeks, we had been preparing them for the nightmare of camps, gas chambers, street executions, prisons and torture, for the ghetto uprising and the destruction of Warsaw. Did they understand? Could they imagine it? I doubt it. And it upsets me that there are so many nations, so many hundreds of millions of people in this world for whom the tragedy of our native land, that horrible cycle of 2,000 days, remains inconceivable and simply cannot be encompassed by mind, imagination or heart, let alone memory. . . .

Translated by CHRISTINA CEKALSKA

Juliusz Kaden-Bandrowski

(1885–1944)

Juliusz Bandrowski (also known as Kaden, from his mother's name) was born at Rzeszow in Austrian Poland, the son of a successful physician. He was educated in Lwów, Cracow and later in Brussels, where he specialized in music. During World War I he fought with the legionaries of Pilsudski, and after the latter's coup of 1926 became the chief spokesman of that group and of "official literature." He celebrated the legion in a collection of impressions, sketches and stories, entitled *Pilsudski's Men* (1915).

Bandrowski began his writing career with the novels *Niezgula* (1911) and *Dust* (1913), based on the life of Polish students in Belgium. His collection of short stories, *Professions* (1911), was praised for its originality of treatment and style. He is known as a Realist-Impressionist with a visionary quality, which is novel in Polish literature of the time. One of the most mature examples of his style is the *Black Wings* cycle of three novels: *Leonora* (1928), *Tadeusz* (1929) and *Mateusz Bigda* (1933). While these books present a realistic and authentic picture of working life in the great Dabrowa coal basin, they are also steeped in an atmosphere of eery vision.

City of My Mother (1925)—from which we introduce several excerpts below—is considered his finest work from the artistic point of view, despite its relative simplicity and occasional sentimentality.

Two Selections from *The City of My Mother*

1. Student Kastalski*

It happened right after our return from the country.

"As of tomorrow you will always have to get up at the same hour, for the next dozen years—to be in school by eight," our Father said to us at bedtime. "Hard as it is, I've got to educate you."

We did get up at the same hour, at seven o'clock in the morning. There was no more talk about anything else.

For breakfast we had hot milk with fresh rolls and then "the whole house" marched off to school.

"Nothing else can be done," Father said to our Mother who buttoned our coats up our necks, and planted a grave, "official" kiss on everyone's forehead.

---

* Titles supplied by the translators.

When we left our gateway Father indicated with his cane the large, black clock on the townhall tower. The heart of the golden minute stood near eight, while the hour hand was almost on the hour.

"You should always leave at the same hour. You mustn't be late." Having said this, our Father turned down Bracka street.

"The whole house" went to school since I was to take the examination to the first grade of elementary school.

I was afraid to write the letter "f", for I never knew where to put the line across it, and I was afraid to write the figure eight, for the upper circle would turn into a tiny, ill-shaped whip. Otherwise, everything was fine: a clean, new sponge was suspended from my new slate—the slate-pencil rattled bravely in its case.

What happened next I don't know. I only remember that two of us, a certain Kastalski and myself, took the examination.

I was short, and Kastalski towered over me. We stood at the blackboard together. My parents were sitting on the first bench. Father's keys jingled in his pocket, and Mother rustled with her silks.

Much farther back, almost on the last bench sat a sort of a janitor and his wife. Later they proved to be Kastalski's parents. Until then I had never imagined that parents could *generally* be so poor.

The giant Kastalski and myself were taking the exam, or rather he was taking it, while I was being used as an assistant. It began with the ladder.

The teacher told Kastalski to draw a ladder on the large school blackboard. I don't know whether Kastalski was scared or what. In the very corner of the blackboard he smeared on something senseless. It was simply a doodle.

"Well, what about you?" asked the teacher.

Having bowed elegantly, I promptly drew two long parallel lines, then I began to draw the rungs from the bottom, as though I were about to climb, to ascend them, as though my heart too would run upwards. One rung, and another, and yet another—there was no mistake about it. I glanced at Kastalski involuntarily. He was standing open-mouthed, in his high boots, his be-patched jacket and reaching his hands out for the chalk. I had not a moment to lose—I didn't give him the chalk. I went on drawing the rungs of the ladder higher and higher, while Kastalski was swallowing hard.

Then they asked questions in arithmetic—to count up to twenty. Kastalski could count only to fourteen. Beyond this figure he confused everything. His mother had thrown off her kerchief from her shoulders, and rising from the bench, whispered loudly, "Fifteen!"

The teacher observed that prompting was not permitted. Who knows, perhaps I'm mistaken, but it seems to me that even my father turned around and cast a resentful glance at the woman in the kerchief. The teacher turned to me with the words, "Well, lad, and you?" I began to count, again as if climbing upwards, as if my heart ascended high on those figures—up to twenty, thirty, forty. I don't know why, but from thirty on I no longer counted for the teacher's benefit, but aimed at Kastalski, who was blushing and seemed to swell up with each figure I spoke.

When I drew breath at the figure eighty-one Kastalski's head sank on his chest. Then came addition and subtraction—up to twenty. Kastalski was first. He would first swallow each question audibly. When it was swallowed it would drown in him so that he could not remember what it was he was supposed to answer. At first I was waiting quietly. But when the teacher busy with Kastalski would look at me, I no longer waited for his direction. Looking at Kastalski's thin neck and seeing that he was swallowing the question, I would answer at once. My parents and the teacher nodded their heads approvingly, and I looked sharply at Kastalski's face, as if cutting it with a penknife; I knew that he didn't know it! And then I proceeded to say what *I* knew! And I would smile even before Kastalski raised his embattled head. Now I would no longer let him open his mouth, for I knew it all!

I know it beforehand, for myself and for him—the stupid fellow. I know so fast, so loud that the teacher is looking only at me. I know so well that even when Kastalski begins to answer I tear his words from his mouth! My answers are so good, so fast, loud, neat and excellent that they make Kastalski cover his eyes with the sleeve of his jacket. His father keeps putting his cap from one hand to the other. The teacher strokes my head lightly and says to my father, "Why, of course."

Suddenly Kastalski bursts into tears.

Such things should not happen in school.

I am looking for you now, my dear Kastalski, for I want to tell you what a great injustice this had been! No one was right there, before the blackboard on which I had drawn the ladder, no one except your mother when she whispered tearfully, "Fifteen."

I want to tell you that we all cheated our country that day, for we should have helped you and not fatten me up on your misfortune. I don't know whether you are alive, and whether you remember that ruddy boy in the blue sailor's suit, who had torn words from your mouth, looking at the teacher with a miserable, flattering glance. This boy, my dear Kastalski—is me. . . . I want you to know that your wrong had not done me much good, for I have not accomplished anything great.

2. THE TEACHER

There are two kinds of teachers in school: the good ones and the bad ones. One usually does not remember the good ones, for they cause no trouble to the pupils. They can work smoothly under wise guidance and only later, after many years, we detect in our adult lives the traces of their cherished labor. That labor is at the bottom of all our knowledge, and in more difficult moments of our lives it shines through like gold through sand.

The bad instructors one always remembers. Our lives point out their faults to us. Sometimes we suffer painfully because of them, in turn condemning the memory of the bad instructor to the heaviest penalty a man can mete out to another man—that is the punishment of contemptuous ridicule.

Besides good and bad teachers there are still others, the indifferent ones. They build a wall of indifference between themselves and the students, and coldness and resentment grow on both sides. Sometimes it happens that for no apparent reason the instructor wants to extend his loving arms to us across this wall. But then it is already too late for understanding.

The school ought to be the only place in the world in which nothing is ever too late.

That is what happened with our teacher of Greek, Mr. Gorzkowski. One day he reached to us from across the grey wall of his indifference and extended his friendly arms. We replied with a roar of deadly laughter, for which Gorzkowski cursed us and himself—and from his teacher's desk he cursed our common work.

It happened thus: we knew a little about the other teachers—not much, but we did know something. Something human, ordinary, personal. Our science teacher was afraid of skeletons; the German teacher was a drunk; the Latin instructor was always escorted to school by his two little daughters; the religious instructor was a domestic Papal prelate; the physics teacher never succeeded in his experiments; the history teacher fought the Papacy; the mathematics teacher was a peasant's son, and the principal walked about in felt slippers.

About Gorzkowski—nothing. He didn't even change his suits in the summer, always came in the same shiny trousers, the same long coat, the same black tie. He couldn't remember our faces, always resorting to his class list. He was always the same, always looked at us in the same manner, with half-closed eyes, when he crammed Greek tenses into our heads, or took Homer apart, or when Xenophon began to show "the fresh horse's droppings on the fifth parasang." Even

Gorzkowski's notebook was the same, identically filled with his shriveled grades.

In springtime and in the summer one could still endure his classes, but in late fall or in the winter we went crazy.

He was so dull that it wasn't worthwhile to play tricks.

Thus we stewed over the wonderful shield of Achilles, delivering ourselves of such prodigious yawns that we practically wrenched our jaws out of their joints.

The spell of boredom which Gorzkowski managed to cast over us was so overpowering, in a sense so perfect, that it invaded the classroom even before his arrival.

Who does not know the extraordinary splendor of that short moment between the bell and the teacher's arrival. This is just the time when pens, stamps and books are best traded. Nothing happens, however, before Gorzkowski makes his appearance. The students look at the hazy, misty window pans and doze.

The door opens; we rise without even looking at him. Why should we—he doesn't change, he is always the same, walks the same way, always takes the same number of steps from the door to his desk. Today—although he is dressed as usual and takes the same number of steps, he does not sit down. He remains standing. We are waiting until his customary, lifeless "Sit down" would fall. But the "Sit down" does not come. Gorzkowski looks at the misty windows, and his turgid, prescribed look wanders among the benches. He begins with Baranski, the honor student, continues on to the average ones, surveys all the rowdies who are sitting way back in the room. Then he looks around at the walls.

Suddenly he threw his arms forward in a light gesture, as if he were about to catch a butterfly, laughed to himself in a quiet, subdued tone and spoke slowly into the drowsy stillness of the classroom: "We have a son."

Nobody said anything. At the first moment we simply failed to understand what he meant. Will anyone have to translate "we have a son" into Greek, or was it a title for a composition, or the beginning of a series of new exceptions? Gorzkowski let his hands fall and, stretching his long neck out of his loose collar, repeated timidly: "We have a son." The class as a whole still did not respond. Only the old rowdy from the back of the room who didn't care anyway asked, "It means you have a son, sir?" "Yes," Gorzkowski replied, carefully placing his black notebook on his desk. "We have a son as of today, five o'clock in the morning."

"That one will know Greek for sure," the eldest of the rowdies thundered into the silence. The words "that one will know Greek for sure," served as a signal to all the class. Without sitting, continuing to stand in our benches, we began asking Gorzkowski at random about "everything." Could the teacher's son speak from the very beginning? Did he have a full head of hair; did he have six fingers on his hand; does he know how to conjugate "paideuo," and what was the first word he spoke?

"How does he speak? How, how?" the whole class roared.

Gorzkowski spread out his thin, yellow hands, as though he were catching a butterfly again. We fell silent at once. He gazed into the wall, frowned, raised his grey bushy eyebrows, recalling with tremendous effort something which had to be repeated faithfully.

"How does he speak? Of course, he does not speak Greek, or any other language. He says "ou, ou, ou." Looking at the wall, he began to croak softly, piously, imitating the whimper of a baby. The class burst into spontaneous roar. We pounded our benches with joy, we stamped our feet, and our books fell from the desks and flew through the air. Someone went to the blackboard and scribbled hastily: "Long live the teacher's son, Paidee!"

Even Baranski laughed and shouted with the rest of us. The rowdies hit one another over their heads, the dust and the yelling filled the room. The tallest of the rowdies, Faliszewski, suddenly stood on a bench and on behalf of the whole class shouted at the top of his voice:

"Sir, we ask that your son also become a teacher!" Then something terrible happened, something nobody expected. Gorzkowski snatched his notebook from his desk, threw it to the ground, and screamed: "Shut up!"

Still gazing at the wall, as if not at us, but at the school walls, he shouted as if something was breaking in his chest: "He'd rather be a plain laborer on the road . . . he'd rather break stones with his hands . . ."

We wanted to ignore it, and one of the rowdies even yelled, "Long live the stone-breaker!" when the door was opened and in strode the principal himself, wearing his soft, felt slippers.

Translated by ADAM GILLON
and LUDWIK KRZYZANOWSKI

Witold Gombrowicz

(1904–1969)

Witold Gombrowicz was born in the Kielce County in 1904. His first collection of stories appeared under the title *Bakakaj* in 1937. The novel *Ferdydurke* (from which we present one chapter) was published in 1938, and it was the predecessor of the modern anti-novel fiction, causing a critical storm from the first.

Gombrowicz now lives in Argentina, and his writings often appear in the Paris magazine *Kultura* (Culture). His other important books are *Transatlantic* (1953), *Fragments from a Journal*. He has also written several dramas, of which the best known is *Iwona, The Princess of Burgundy*.

Gombrowicz's works are often experimental in nature; the absence of conventional novelistic plot, his wry, often sardonic humor, his vision of an illogical, distorted world—these have made him one of the most controversial of modern Polish writers.

Philifor Honeycombed with Childishness

The prince of synthetists, recognized as the greatest synthetist of all times, was the higher synthetist Dr. Philifor, who came from the south of Annam, and was Professor of Synthetisiology in the University of Leyden. He worked according to the pathetic spirit of higher synthesis, generally using the method of adding infinity, though sometimes, when occasion arose, he adopted that of multiplying by infinity. He was a well built, rather corpulent man, with a shaggy beard and the face of a bespectacled prophet. By virtue of Newton's principle of action and equal and· opposite reaction, an intellectual phenomenon of such magnitude could not fail to provoke a counter-phenomenon in the bosom of nature; hence the birth at Colombo of an eminent analyst who, after obtaining his doctor's degree and the title of professor of higher analysis at Columbia University, climbed rapidly to the top of the academic tree. He was a dry, slightly built, beardless man, with the face of a bespectacled sceptic, and his sole interior driving force was to pursue and humiliate the distinguished Philifor.

He worked analytically, and his specialty was breaking down individuals into their constituent parts, with the aid of calculation, and more particularly flicks of the finger. With the aid of the latter he was able to invite a nose to enjoy an independent existence of its own and make it move spontaneously this way and that, to the great terror of its owner. When he was bored he used frequently to practice this art on the tram. In response to his deepest vocation he set out in pursuit of Philifor, and in a town somewhere in Spain succeeded in procuring for himself the title of Anti-Philifor, of which he was very proud. Philifor, having discovered that he was being pursued, immediately set out on the heels of his pursuer, and the mutual pursuit of the two men of learning went on for a long time—without result, however, because each was prevented by pride from admitting that he was the pursued as well as the pursuer. Consequently, when Philifor was at Bremen, for instance, Anti-Philifor would hurry there from The Hague, refusing, or perhaps being unable, to take into account the fact that at that very moment Philifor for reasons identical with his own was taking his seat in the Bremen–The Hague express. The collision between the two—a disaster on the scale of the greatest railway accidents—finally took place by pure chance in the first-class restaurant of the Hotel Bristol in Warsaw. Professor Philifor, accompanied by Mrs. Philifor, was carefully consulting the indicator when Anti-Philifor, who had just got off the train, entered breathlessly, arm-in-arm with his analytical traveling companion, Fiora Gente of Messina. We who were present, that is to say, Dr. Theophilus Poklewski, Dr. Theodore Roklewski, and myself, realizing the gravity of the situation, immediately started taking notes.

Anti-Philifor advanced silently and gazed into the eyes of Professor Philifor, who rose to his feet. Each tried to impose the force of his personality on the other. The analyst's eyes traveled coldly from his opponent's feet upwards; those of the stoutly resisting synthetist worked in the opposite direction, from the head downwards. As the outcome of this struggle was a draw, with no advantage accruing to either side, the two contestants resorted to a verbal duel. The doctor and master of analysis said:

"Gnocchi!"

"Gnocchi!" the synthetisiologist retorted.

"Gnocchi, gnocchi, or a mixture of eggs, flour and water," said Anti-Philifor, and Philifor capped this with:

"Gnocchi means the higher essence, the supreme spirit of gnocchi, the thing-in-itself."

His eyes flashed fire, he wagged his beard, it was obvious that he had won. The professor of higher analysis recoiled a few paces, seized with impotent rage, but a dreadful idea suddenly flashed into his mind. A sickly and puny man in comparison with Philifor, he decided to attack Mrs. Philifor, who was the apple of her worthy professor-husband's eye. The incident, according to the eye-witnesses' report, then developed as follows:

1. Professor Philifor's wife, a stout and majestic woman, was seated, silently absorbed in her thoughts.

2. Professor Anti-Philifor, armed with his cerebral gear, placed himself in front of her, and started undressing her with his eyes, from foot to head. Mrs. Philifor trembled with cold and shame. Professor Philifor silently covered her with her traveling rug, casting a look of infinite contempt at the insolent Professor Anti-Philifor, but nevertheless betraying some slight traces of anxiety.

3. Professor Anti-Philifor then calmly said: "Ear, ear," and laughed sardonically. At these words the woman's ear appeared in all its nakedness and became indecent, and Professor Philifor ordered her to conceal it beneath her hat. This was not of much use, however, for Anti-Philifor muttered, as if to himself, the words "two nostrils," thus laying bare in shameful and analytical fashion the nostrils of the professor's highly respectable wife. This aggravated the situation, for there was no way of concealing her nostrils.

4. Professor Philifor threatened to call the police; the tide of battle seemed to be turning distinctly in his opponent's favor. The master of analysis said with intense mental concentration: "Fingers, the five fingers of each hand." Mrs. Philifor's resistance, unfortunately, was insufficient to conceal a reality which disclosed itself to the eyes of those present in all its stark nakedness, i.e., the five fingers of each of her two hands. There they were, five on each side. Mrs. Philifor, utterly profaned, gathered her last strength to try to put on her gloves, but an incredible thing happened. Professor Anti-Philifor fired at her point-blank an analysis of her urine. With a loud guffaw, he exclaimed victoriously: "H_2O, C_4, TPS, some leucocytes, and albumen!" Everyone rose, Professor Anti-Philifor withdrew with his mistress, who giggled in a vulgar manner, while Professor Philifor, aided by the undersigned, hurriedly took his wife to the hospital. (*Signed*) T. Poklewski, T. Roklewski, Anton Swistak, eye-witnesses.

Next morning Roklewski, Poklewski, and I myself joined the Professor at Mrs. Philifor's bedside. Her disintegration, set in train by Anti-Philifor's analytic tooth, was proceeding apace, and she was progressively losing her physiological contexture. From time to time she said with a hollow groan: "My leg, my eye, my leg, my ear, my finger, my head, my leg," as if she were bidding farewell to the various parts of her body, which were already moving independently of her. Her personality was in its death-throes. We racked our brains for some way of saving her, but could think of nothing. After further consultations, in which Assistant Professor S. Lopatkin took part—he arrived by the seven-forty plane from Moscow—we were confirmed in our conclusion that the situation called for the application of the most extreme methods of scientific synthetism. But none existed. Philifor thereupon concentrated his mental faculties to such good purpose that we all recoiled a step. He said:

"I've got it! A slap in the face! Only a well-aimed slap in the face can restore my wife's honor and synthesize the scattered elements on a higher level."

It was no easy task to find the world-famous analyst in the big city; not until nightfall did we succeed in tracking him down to a first-class bar, where he was soberly engaged in drinking. He was emptying bottle after bottle, and the more he drank, the more sober he became; and the same applied to his analytical mistress; the truth of the matter was that both found sobriety more intoxicating than alcohol. When we walked in, the waiters, who had turned as white as their napkins, had timidly taken refuge behind the bar, and the two lovers were silently devoting themselves to an interminable orgy of keeping cool and collected. We drew up a plan of action. Professor Philifor would first of all feint in the direction of the left cheek and then strike out in earnest at the right, while we witnesses, i.e., Poklewski, Roklewski, and myself, all three holders of doctor's degrees in the University of Warsaw, accompanied by Assistant Professor S. Lopatkin, would proceed forthwith to the drawing up of our report. It was a simple and straightforward plan, calling for no very complicated action, but the professor raised his arm, only to let it drop to his side again. We witnesses were left in a state of stupefaction. The slap in the face did not take place. I repeat, the slap in the face did not take place. All that took place was two little roses and a rough illustration of two doves.

With satanic insight Anti-Philifor had foreseen Philifor's move. The temperate Bacchus had had two little roses tattooed on each cheek, as well as something resembling two doves. Anti-Philifor's cheeks and Philifor's planned blow were thus deprived of meaning; slapping roses and doves would be as idle as casually slapping a piece of painted paper. Thinking it out of the question that our learned and universally respected educator of youth should expose himself to ridicule by striking a piece of painted paper because of his wife's illness, we succeeded in persuading him to abandon a course of action which he might subsequently regret.

"Vile dog!" the professor growled. "Vile, vile, vile dog!"

"You are an amorphous collection of disparate parts," the analyst replied, in a burst of analytic pride. "You are an amorphous collection of disparate parts, and so am I. Kick me in the stomach, if you like; it won't be I whom you kick, but my stomach, and that's all. You wished to provoke my face by slapping it? Well, you can provoke my cheek, but not me. I do not exist! I simply do not exist!"

"I'll provoke your face! As sure as God's in His heaven, I'll provoke your face!"

"My cheeks are impervious to provocation," Anti-Philifor replied with a sneer.

Fiora Gente, who was sitting by his side, burst out laughing. The cosmic doctor of double analysis leered sensually at his mistress and walked out. Fiora Gente, however, remained. She was perched on a high stool and looked at us with the relaxed eyes of a completely analyzed parrot. A little later, at 8:40 P.M. to be precise, we, that is to say Professor Philifor, the two doctors, Assistant Professor Lopatkin and myself, held a conference. Assistant Professor Lopatkin as usual wielded the fountain-pen. The conference proceeded as follows:

The three doctors of law: "In view of what has occurred, we see no possibility of settling this quarrel in an honorable manner, and we therefore advise the respected professor to ignore the insult to which he has been subjected, because it came from an individual incapable of giving satisfaction."

Professor Philifor: "I propose to ignore it, but my wife is dying."

Assistant Professor Lopatkin: "There is no way of saving your wife."

Professor Philifor: "Don't say that! Oh, don't say that! A slap in the face is the only hope! But there is no slap in the face, there is no cheek! There is no method of divine synthesis! There is no God! But yes! yes! There are faces! There are slaps! There is a God! Honor! Synthesis!"

Myself: "I observe that the professor is being illogical. Either there are faces, or there are not."

Philifor: "Gentlemen, you forget that I still have my two cheeks. His cheeks do not exist, but mine do. We can still achieve our aim with my two cheeks, which are intact. Gentlemen, what I mean is this: I cannot slap his face, but he can slap mine! It will come to the same thing. A face will have been slapped and synthesis achieved!"

"But how shall we get him to slap the professor's face?"

"How shall we get him to slap the professor's face?"

"How shall we get him to slap the professor?"

"Gentlemen," the brilliant thinker composedly replied, "he has cheeks, but so do I. There is an analogy here, and I shall therefore be acting less logically than analogically; that will be much more effective, because nature is governed by the law of analogy. If he is the king of analysis, I am the king of synthesis. If he has cheeks, so have I. If I have a wife, he has a mistress. If he has analyzed my wife, I shall synthesize his mistress, and in that fashion I shall get from him the slap that he refuses me."

Without further delay he beckoned to Fiora Gente. We were left speechless with amazement. She approached, moving all the parts of her body, ogling me with one eye and the professor with the other, smiling with all her teeth at Stephen Lopatkin, projecting her front towards Roklewski and her behind towards Poklewski. The impression she made was such that the assistant professor muttered:

"Are you really proposing to attack those fifty separate parts with your higher synthesis?"

The universal synthetisiologist, however, possessed the virtue of never losing hope. He invited Fiora Gente to sit at the small table, offered her a Cinzano, and by way of preamble, to test the ground, said to her sympathetically:

"Soul, soul."

She did not reply.

"I!" said the professor impetuously and inquisitorially, desiring to awaken her annihilated ego.

"You? Oh, all right! Five zlotys!"

"Unity!" Philifor exclaimed violently. "Higher unity! Equality in unity!"

"Boy or old man, it's all the same to me," she said with the most complete indifference.

We gazed in discouragement at this infernal analyst of the night, whom Anti-Philifor had brought up in his own image, and perhaps trained for himself since earliest childhood.

The father of the synthetic sciences refused, however, to be discouraged. A phase of intense effort and struggle ensued. He read to her the first two cantos of the *Divina Commedia,* for which she charged him ten zlotys. He made an inspired speech on the higher love which unifies and encompasses everything, and that cost him eleven zlotys. For agreeing to allow him to read to her two superb novels by two well-known women novelists about regeneration by love she asked a hundred and fifty zlotys, and refused to consider a farthing less; and finally, when he got to the point of appealing to her dignity, she insisted on fifty zlotys.

"Fancies have to be paid for, grandpa," she said. "For fancies there's no fixed rate."

Opening and shutting her self-satisfied owl's eyes, she remained entirely untouched by the experience. Her charges kept piling up, and Anti-Philifor, wandering round the town, shook with interior laughter at all these desperate endeavors.

In the course of the subsequent conference, in which Assistant Professor Lopatkin and the three professors took part, the eminent seeker after truth summed up his defeat:

"It has cost me several hundred zlotys already and I really do not see the slightest possibility of any synthesis," he said. "In vain I had recourse to the supreme unities such as humanity; she turns everything into money and hands back the change. Meanwhile my wife is steadily losing what remains of her homogeneity. Her leg has already got to the point of walking round the room on its own. When she gets drowsy, she tries to hold it with her hands, but her hands refuse to obey her. It is the most shattering, appalling anarchy."

Dr. T. Poklewski, M.D.: "And meanwhile Anti-Philifor is spreading the story that the professor is a vicious and depraved old gentleman."

Assistant Professor Lopatkin: "But might we not after all be able to catch her with the aid of money? I do not yet see clearly the idea for which I am groping in my mind, but things like that happen in nature. Let me explain. I had a woman patient who suffered from shyness. It was impossible to inject boldness into her, because she was incapable of assimilating it. But I succeeded in injecting into her such an enormous dose of shyness that she could not tolerate it. Finding shyness intolerable, she took courage, and became very bold indeed. The best method is to cure the disease by the disease itself. There must be some way of synthesizing her by means of money, but I confess that I do not . . ."

Professor Philifor: "Money . . . money . . . but money always adds up to a definite sum, a definite amount, which has nothing in common with unity in the true sense of the word. The only sum of money that is indivisible is a farthing, and nobody is impressed by a farthing . . . But gentlemen, suppose . . . suppose we offered her such a huge sum that she was thunderstruck by it!"

We were left open-mouthed in astonishment. Philifor rose to his feet, his black beard trembling. He was now in one of those hypermanic states which invariably affect genius at seven-year intervals. He sold two houses and a villa in the neighborhood of Warsaw, and changed the 850,000 zlotys thus realized into one-zloty pieces. Poklewski looked at him in amazement. A simple country doctor, he had never had any understanding of genius, and that was why he failed to understand it now. The philosopher was now sure of himself, however, and sent Anti-Philifor an ironic invitation. The latter sent a sarcastic reply and turned up punctually at nine-thirty in a private room at the Alcazar restaurant, where the decisive test was to take place. The two scholars did not shake hands. The master of analysis laughed, and his laughter was dry and malicious.

"Carry on, sir," he said. "Carry on! My woman friend is obviously less liable to composition than is your wife to decomposition. On that my mind is at rest."

But he too entered progressively into a more and more hypermanic state. Dr. Poklewski's fountain-pen was poised and Assistant Professor Lopatkin held the paper at the ready.

Professor Philifor set about things as follows. First of all he laid on the table one zloty. Fiora Gente did not budge. He put down a second zloty; nothing happened. He put down a third; again nothing happened. But when he put down the fourth, she said:

"Oh! Four zlotys!"

At the fifth she yawned, and at the sixth she remarked with an air of indifference:

"What's up, grandpa? Have you gone crackers again?"

Not until after the ninety-seventh zloty did we observe the first symptoms of surprise. At the 115th her eyes, which had been wandering from Dr. Poklewski to Assistant Professor Lopatkin and myself, started tending to synthesize somewhat on the money.

At 100,000 zlotys Philifor was gasping painfully for breath. Anti-Philifor was beginning to show signs of alarm, and the hitherto heterogeneous courtesan acquired a certain concentration. She gazed fascinated at the pile, which, to tell the truth was ceasing to be a pile, and tried to count, but she had lost her head for reckoning. The sum had ceased to be a sum, had turned into something impossible to grasp in its entirety, something so tremendous, so inconceivable, that the mind boggled at it, as it does when it considers the dimensions of space. The patient let out a hollow groan. The analyst tried to dash to her assistance, but the two doctors restrained him. In vain he whispered to her to divide the total into hundreds, or five hundreds, but the total refused to yield to this treatment. When the triumphant high priest of synthesis had spent all he had and crowned the pile, or rather the mountain, the Mount Sinai, of money with the last single and indivisible zloty, it was as if some divinity had taken possession of the courtesan. She rose to her feet, showing every symptom of synthesis —tears, sighs, smiles, thoughtfulness—and said:

"Gentlemen, myself. My higher self!"

Philifor uttered a cry of triumph, and with a frantic yell Anti-Philifor broke loose from the two doctors' hold, dashed at Philifor, and struck him in the face.

This synthetic lightning flash snatched from the analytic entrails dispelled the shadows. The assistant professor and the doctors heartily congratulated the gravely dishonored professor. His sworn enemy writhed and gesticulated in a frenzy against the wall, but no amount of frenzy could now deprive the victorious march of honor of its momentum, and the whole affair, which had hitherto been not very honorable, was now firmly set on an honorable course.

Professor G. L. Philifor of Leyden appointed as his seconds Dr. Lopatkin and myself; Professor P. T. Momsen, known by his honorary title of Anti-Philifor, chose the two doctors present. Philifor's seconds honorably challenged Anti-Philifor's seconds, and these in turn challenged Philifor's. Each of these honorable steps created more and more synthesis, and the professor of Columbia University writhed as if he were standing on hot coals, while the sage of Leyden stroked his beard and smiled. At the municipal hospital Mrs. Philifor started regaining her unity; in a barely audible whisper she asked for a glass of milk, and hope revived in the doctors' breasts. Honor had made its appearance among the clouds and was smiling down upon mankind. The duel was fixed for Tuesday at 7 A.M.

It was agreed that the fountain-pen should be entrusted to Dr. Roklewski, and the pistols to Assistant Professor Lopatkin; and that Dr. Poklewski should hold the paper and I the overcoats. The tireless advocate of the cause of synthesis refused to be affected by doubt, dismay or fear. I recall his saying to me on the eve of the duel: "Young man, I know that I am just as likely to be left on the field of honor as he, but, whatever happens, my spirit will survive and be victorious, for death is essentially synthetic. If he dies, his end will be a tribute paid to synthesis; if he kills me, he will do so synthetically. Hence in any event victory will be mine!" In this state of exaltation, desiring to celebrate more worthily his moment of glory, he invited the womenfolk—his wife and Fiora Gente—to attend in the capacity of simple spectators. I was filled with grim forebodings, I feared . . . what did I fear? I did not know myself. All night I lay a prey to grim anxiety, and not until I reached the appointed duelling ground did I tumble to the reason, which was symmetry; for the situation was symmetrical; hence its strength, but hence also its weakness.

For every move of Philifor led to a similar move by Anti-Philifor, and the initiative was Philifor's. If Philifor raised his hat, Anti-Philifor must do the same. If Philifor fired, so must he. Moreover, the whole of the action was confined to an imaginary straight line drawn between the two duellists; and this line was the axis of the whole situation. But suppose Anti-Philifor departed from it? Suppose he treacherously wandered from the straight path, basely evaded the iron laws of symmetry and analogy? What vileness, what intellectual depravity might not be hatching in his brain? I was plunged in these thoughts when Professor Philifor raised his arm, aimed at his opponent's heart, fired, and missed. The analyst likewise raised his arm and aimed at his opponent's heart. It seemed almost inevitable that if the former fired synthetically at the heart, the latter must do the same, there seemed to be no possible alternative; no alternative seemed intellectually conceivable. But the analyst made a surpreme effort, uttered a savage yell, deflected the barrel of his pistol from the axis of the situation and fired. Where would the bullet strike? Where? Mrs. Philifor, accompanied by Fiora Gente, was standing a little to one side, and it struck her little finger. It was a master-shot; the finger was cut clean off and dropped to the ground. Mrs. Philifor in astonishment put her hand to her mouth. For a moment we seconds lost all control of ourselves and let out a cry of admiration.

This was too much for the professor of higher synthesis, and something dreadful happened. Fascinated by his opponent's precision of aim, virtuosity and symmetry, and annoyed at our cry of admiration at his marksmanship, he too diverged from the axis, fired, hit Fiora Gente's little finger, and let forth a short, derisive, guttural laugh.

Then the analyst fired again, severing Mrs. Philifor's other little finger and causing her to put her other hand to her mouth. Again we exclaimed with admiration. A fraction of a second later the synthetist fired, and with infallible aim deprived Fiora Gente of her other little finger from a distance of six or seven yards. She put her hand to her mouth, and we could not refrain from another exclamation of admiration. And so events took their course. The firing continued, incessant, angry, and as magnificent as magnificence itself; and fingers, ears, noses, and teeth fell like the leaves of a tree in a high wind. We seconds were left with no time to express our admiration at the accuracy of the hail of fire that ensued. The two ladies were soon deprived of all their extremities and natural protuberances; if they did not fall dead it was simply because of lack of time, and I also suspect that they felt greatly flattered at being the target of such consummate marksmanship. With his last round the master from Leyden holed the upper part of Fiora Gente's right lung. Once more we exclaimed with admiration, then silence fell. Life passed from the two women's bodies, they collapsed to the ground, and the two marksmen looked at each other.

And then? They went on looking at each other, without knowing why. And then? And then? They had both run out of ammunition. The dead bodies lay on the ground. There was no more to be done. It was nearly ten o'clock. Strictly speaking, the analyst had won, but what difference did that make? None whatever. If the synthetist had won, it would have made no difference either. Philifor picked up a stone, threw it at a sparrow, and missed; the sparrow flew away. The sun was getting very hot. Anti-Philifor threw a lump of earth at a tree-trunk, and hit it. Philifor threw a stone at a hen which passed across his line of sight; he hit it, and it went and hid behind a bush. The two men of learning then abandoned their positions and went their separate ways.

At dusk Anti-Philifor was at Jeziorno and Philifor at Wawer. The former was shooting rabbits from under the shadow of a windmill; the latter, when he came upon a gas-lamp in an isolated spot, fired at it from fifty paces.

Thus they wandered about the world, firing at what they could with what they could. They sang popular songs and broke windows when they felt like it; and they also enjoyed spitting from balconies at the hats of passers-by. Philifor actually became so skilled that he was able to spit from the roadway at people on first-floor balconies; and Anti-Philifor could put out candles by throwing matchboxes at the flame. Things that they enjoyed even more were shooting frogs with small-calibre rifles and sparrows with bow and arrow; and sometimes they would stand on bridges and throw grass and paper into the stream below. But their greatest pleasure of all was buying a red balloon and chasing it across the country, waiting for the thrilling moment when it burst noisily as if struck by an invisible bullet.

And when someone from the academic world recalled their glorious past, their intellectual jousts, analysis, synthesis, and the fame that had now vanished for ever, they would answer rather dreamily:

"Oh, yes, I remember the duel . . . the shooting was excellent!"

"But professor," I once exclaimed, simultaneously with Roklewski, who had meanwhile married and settled down in Krucza Street, "you talk like a child!"

And the puerile old man replied:

"Young man, everything is honeycombed with childishness."

From *Ferdydurke*, Chapter V, Harcourt, Brace & World, Inc.
Translated by ERIC MOSBACHER

Jerzy Andrzejewski

(1909–   )

Born in 1909, Andrzejewski started his literary career in 1936 and was awarded the Young Writers' Prize of the Polish Academy of Literature in 1938 for his novel *Harmony of the Heart*. Because of the theme of this novel, the hero of which is a Catholic priest, it is not surprising that Andrzejewski should have been labeled a "Catholic" writer and acclaimed as a Polish Mauriac or Bernanos. During the German occupation he was regarded as a moral authority in matters of the non-written patriotic code to be followed with regard to the Germans. The novel *Ashes and Diamonds*, published in 1948, indicated Andrzejewski's departure from his previous attitude and a veering, though not without reservations, towards the new line of Socialist Realism with its condemnation of the war-time émigré-directed Polish Underground Army. Though not entirely satisfactory from the Socialist Realist view point—the early adherents of Communism in Poland are not depicted as blameless heroes and the members of the Home Army are presented, at worst, as tragically misguided—the novel was awarded a state prize. In its successful film version it was also shown in this country to high critical acclaim.

Andrzejewski's trip to the Soviet Union in 1951 resulted in a book, *About Soviet Man*, in which he stated that: ". . . It is necessary to choose liberty—either the one offered by Truman or that given by socialism." Any middle road must inevitably lead to "imperialist servitude."

The three allegories *The Slipper, The Great Lament of a Paper Head* (written in 1953) and the *Golden Fox* (1954) attest to the significant role Andrzejewski played in the cultural and political "thaw" which preceded the so-called October Revolution of 1956. It was in that year that the three brilliant allegories were published under the joint title *The Golden Fox*. His disaffection with the Party was manifested when in 1957 he resigned his membership in protest against censorship. Significant for his development in his short novel, *Darkness Covers the Earth* (1957), published in an English translation as *The Inquisitors* in the United States (1960). Though dealing with the Inquisition, the novel is an allegory of the period of Stalinist repression in Poland, and is indicative of the Polish intellectuals' frame of mind in their enforced Communist environment.

Several of Andrzejewski's works have been translated into French, English, German, Czech, Swedish, Bulgarian, Serbian, Hebrew, Persian and Japanese. A rather unsympathetic psychological portrait of Andrzejewski as "Alpha, the Moralist" is presented by Czeslaw Milosz in his well known study of *The Captive Mind*.

The story which follows is taken from the collection *Night* (1946) based on the experience of the German occupation of Poland during World War II.

The Trial

It happened during the first days of October 1939.

The forest ranger of Rudawica gave the same replies to all of the questions. The arms found by the Germans near his house were left the day before by the Polish soldiers from the division routed in the vicinity of Zamosc. Accustomed to many years of solitary life he was caught too suddenly by the whole thing to invent a plausible lie on the spur of the moment. He confessed truthfully: he himself had buried all the rifles, the revolvers and the box of ammunition—without anyone's help. That is precisely what the Germans from the panzer unit refused to believe.

They had two officers, both under thirty. They were sitting at the table without having removed their raincoats and steel helmets. Their battle attire alone gave the impression that the hastily called court-martial would end immediately. Peter was standing on the opposite side of the table between two hefty soldiers. Kaczynski, the shopkeeper from Rudawica, pale and frightened, served as interpreter with his poor German.

The elder of the two officers, a lieutenant, conducted the interrogation. His tanned sportsman's face, of harsh regular features, expressed coldness and contempt. The other officer, with light blond hair and the appearance of a Prussian Junker, was leaning his head back against the wall, indifferently looking out the window. The small windowpanes revealed a checkered landscape; the brown mud of the yard, a wooden fence, a rusty patch of the sky cut across by the crane of the well, two blackish appletrees, and beyond them a pine forest steeped in the misty blue of an October afternoon.

Peter saw nothing of this. From the beginning of the hearing he gazed stubbornly at the floor. In the place where he was standing there were traces of the mud brought in by the retreating Polish soldiers the night before. The dried clods had partly sunk into the rough boards of the floor.

There were five of them. They were all thin, dirty and unshaven; their faces were dark with fatigue, their boots torn, their coats bespattered with mud and soaked through. They stayed briefly. They fell upon the remnants of brown bread and old lard ravenously like men who had not eaten for many days. This was all the food Peter had. During the month of September the poor household of the forest ranger was completely cleaned out by crowds of fleeing civilians.

That night resembled the present night. From afar through the stillness of the forest came the hollow rumble of artillery. It was the surrounded division of General Kleeberg, the last of the routed and defeated Polish army, making its last stand. The Germans had not yet reached the Rudawica forests. Although the soldiers could hardly stand on their feet, they did not want to spend the night at the ranger's house. Their weariness and fear of being taken prisoner heightened their anxiety. Every now and then one of them would jump up and come to the window or look out into the yard, listening for the rumble of tanks from the nearby highway. They were gone before it grew dark. Actually not one of them thought of returning home. They intended to retreat further south to the Carpathians in order to get to the Hungarian border across the German positions. But they had no more strength to carry the arms that they had salvaged. Each retaining two revolvers, they left the rifles and the box of ammunition in the hall. Peter asked what he was to do, and they advised him to bury the things. They were hoping to return here shortly. Peter agreed.

Night fell when he started digging. He selected what seemed to him the best place, at the back of the yard by the fence behind the well. He brought out an old chest from the attic, lined it with hay and carefully placed the arms inside. He worked in complete darkness, by the dim light of a lantern covered by an old rag. The digging was hard. The clayey ground was heavy from the recent rains. Besides, the chest was quite tall so that he had to dig a hole of at least three feet deep. This took several hours. When he awoke at dawn the German Panzer units were rumbling along the highway. He got up and throwing the sheepskin on his shirt went into the yard to check whether he had evenly and thoroughly covered up the hole. It seemed to him that this was so and this reassured him. But despite his fatigue he did not go back to sleep. He spent the whole morning loafing around the house. The enemy tanks rumbled on ceaselessly from the forest. The air shook with the roar of cars and motorcycles. A chilling dread came from that unseen might which like a flood of iron and steel seemed to trample the earth and life with immensity. The day was as the one before—wet and rainy. At times there rose gusts of a keen autumn wind.

At noon Charles Walicki came from Rudawica. He wanted to warn Peter of the Germans' arrival. He also brought a quarter loaf of bread, a few eggs and a piece of butter. Peter took him to the yard and showed him the spot where he had dug the hole. He wanted someone else, besides himself, to know about the hidden arms. Charles stayed only a short while. He was in a hurry to get back home, not wishing to alarm his mother by prolonged absence. The Germans' arrival had frightened her. Thus, Peter was left alone once more. He waited. Only in the late afternoon a number of storm troopers rode up to the ranger's house on their motorcycles. From their vehement shouts and menacing faces Peter guessed that they were asking about arms and Polish soldiers. He denied everything. He was not worried about his security.

Meantime, the soldiers with drawn revolvers scattered around the house and began to search in every corner. Some of them came up to the barn. Others looked in the yard. Peter saw through the window how one of them—a young, tall fellow—evidently bored with inactivity, wandered to the back of the yard. However, even when the man stopped exactly on the spot in which the chest was buried he felt no anxiety. Suddenly the soldier stopped and began to tap the earth gingerly with his heel. "Heinrich!" he shouted without turning. Another soldier came running to him. Soon there were several of them.

From that moment on—he was not aware how long it could have taken—Peter fell into a state of numbness. While he appeared calm on the surface, inwardly he reacted as though he were dreaming a dream that could not be interrupted. He penetrated into a deep darkness that was drawing him into its bottomless void, like a dark mirror reflecting the motion of tormenting shadows.

At a certain moment the lieutenant asked Kaczynski the same question for the second time. The unfamiliar, sharp and raucous sounds intensified Peter's sensation of being in a dream. But he did not dare to lift his eyes. He feared to find hostile judges in the officers sitting behind the table, to find the well-known shopkeeper in Kaczynski, and his own house in the darkness of his room. Meanwhile, it became more and more difficult for Kaczynski to control his trembling. He stood with a lowered head, a fat and stocky man, constantly rubbing his sweaty hands that had turned red from cold. Only when the lieutenant repeated his last question again did he stop rubbing his hands. A minute later he bent down sideways to Peter and stammered to him rapidly.

Peter understood nothing. Yet he did not raise his head. A cold paralyzed his feet and hands. He felt an emptiness in his chest. "Now I shall wake!" he thought. He was jolted by the fear that this would have to happen immediately so that he might bury the arms that the soldiers had piled under the wall in the hall.

Suddenly he heard the muffled whisper of Kaczynski. "Mr. Ranger!"

The shopkeeper was standing so close that Peter's lowered eyes saw his shoes. They were old, clumsy and mud-bespattered gaiters. A soiled lace from his drawers stuck out from under the trousers, equally torn and muddy. Looking at the formless shoes, Peter asked, dreaming it was his own voice:

"What's the matter?"

Kaczynski swallowed, moving his neck.

"He says he's asking you for the last time."

"The last time?" Peter repeated.

"He wants to know who helped you."

A more severe cold swept over Peter. He gritted his teeth to stop his shaking.

"No one helped me," he said at last, surprised at the clarity and the loudness of his own voice. "No one was here."

The silence which fell after his words seemed to him very long. At length Kaczynski began his stammering translation. Peter listened carefully to those awkward and hesitant sounds. When they ceased he heard the quiet voice of the lieutenant. And suddenly a violent blow to his jaw from below threw his head backward. Before he could understand what happened, he received a second, even stronger blow in his face. He reeled, dazed by pain. Trying to keep his balance he instinctively grasped the chair standing beside the table. It fell. Then, losing the only point of support, he collapsed heavily against the wall. The blows rained on him but he did not defend himself. He did not even try to shield his face with his arm. He thought, however, that what he was experiencing could not be a dream. But the pain obliterated this thought, and it hardly reached his consciousness. Everything in him turned to torture. Even his voice froze in his throat, as if he had lost it. And this seemed the most terrible thing. It was only when he was kicked in his abdomen that an inarticulate howl broke out from behind his clenched teeth. He coiled up. Then a soldier who towered over him, caught him by his arms like a manikin and propping him up against the wall began to kick him in the groin repeatedly at close range. Peter howled. Suddenly he choked and grew still. He was seized with convulsions.

"Halt!" the lieutenant nodded calmly.

When the soldier stepped back, Peter sank to the floor. Pressed into a corner of the room, his knees drawn up under his bowed head, he vomited on himself. At a certain moment he felt that he was being lifted from the floor and sat on a stool. Then they threw some cold water in his face. He came to somewhat. The pain still lingered in him, but in comparison with what it had been a minute ago, it seemed almost a relief. It was quiet in the room. A fly was buzzing on the window pane. The Junker looking out the window was whistling through his teeth. The tanks were rattling on the highway. More closely, a motorcycle was growling.

The hunched Peter, holding his belly with both hands, almost stopped breathing, fearing to unleash the pain again with a careless motion. Suddenly he felt a warm moisture on his face. When he raised his hand mechanically, he felt that his fingers were sticky with thick blood. It was flowing from his nose, and further below he touched his cut lips and bruised gums. He straightened his body. At first he saw everything through a ruddy, flowing mist. "My forehead must be injured," he thought indifferently. He wiped his eyes with his palm. Now he could see a little better.

Grey dusk began to fall on the room. The silhouettes of the two officers were outlined very clearly against the window and the forest, whose greyish-blue image appeared to reach the very house. Their immobility and their eyes turned to Peter from under the steel helmets, but, passing him by indifferently as though he were an object without importance, made them look like two stone statues. Slightly closer, he noticed Kaczynski, his grey, rough-hewn face and eyes under reddened lids, almost unseeing from fright. Behind him he felt the presence of the soldiers. Instinctively he cringed.

Suddenly the officers exchanged a few brief words. Although he did not want to do it, he looked at them. The pain froze in him at once. He only felt an icy cold within his head. He could neither move nor cry out. He no longer belonged to himself. And feeling more dead than alive for a moment, he now fell into the horror of the last conscious second its almost inhuman loneliness, that penetrated beyond death, into silence and darkness. No sooner had he shaken himself out of this dread, than he understood that he was lost and there was no escape for him. Then suddenly a thought broke through the frozen tension of terror, the thought that were he to find the hand of a friendly man now he would be saved. It was not death that seemed terrible but the loneliness before it. The fear grew in him. He heard how its dark and noiseless voice went round and round in his head ever more rapidly and violently. He ceased to feel the pounding of his heart. He existed only in the cry which raged under his skull. He was sweating profusely. "I shall go mad," he thought. Seized with a panic he could no longer bear, he jumped from the stool.

The two soldiers caught his arms simultaneously. He tried to wrench himself free. Again the blows fell upon him. But he felt no pain. Choking with the blood that filled his throat and his eyes, he went on wrestling with the soldiers, gaining strength from his fear. Finally he succeeded in pushing one of the soldiers away and pulling the other towards the table.

The blond Junker stopped looking out the window, and the lieutenant who was sitting closer slowly reached for his revolver.

Peter fell down on the table, striking it with his head. He tried to get up. His blood blinded him. And before the soldier could tear away his fingers clutching the edge of the table, he stammered out: "I'll tell you, I'll tell you!"

Kaczynski had not had the time to translate when the lieutenant gave a sign to the soldier to fall back. Peter remained alone. Clutching the table with both hands, his forehead leaning on the edge, he sank to his knees. And although he immediately realized his humiliation, he had no strength to rise. Everything became indifferent and unimportant to him. Only one importunate thought rang stubbornly in his mind.

Meanwhile, the lieutenant, gazing with his motionless eyes at Peter, was playing with his revolver. Suddenly he said a few words to Kaczynski. The latter stood, hunched and blinking his protruding eyes. The sound of the revolver thrown from one hand into the other could be heard distinctly in the room. The fly kept buzzing steadily at the window. At last Kaczynski bent over the kneeling man.

"Who?" he asked in a whisper.

Peter seemed not to have heard. He did not move.

"Mr. Ranger!" the shopkeeper said, "He's asking for the name."

The voice reached Peter from a very great distance. He felt that he was losing consciousness. But at the same time he realized that he must at once gather all his strength, to say the needed name. He raised his head. The German's face, shaded by the helmet, could scarcely be seen in the dusk. Only the eyes amid this shadow were visible: very bright, almost transparent eyes.

Peter closed his eyes. The salty taste of blood made him nauseous. Finally a sharp dazzling idea tore itself from the bottom of the soundless darkness. He breathed deeply and through the blood running from his parted lips he whispered:

"Walitzki!"

"Walitzki?" the lieutenant bent over him.

And he looked at the shopkeeper.

"Who is he?"

Kaczynski drew back and wrenching his fingers started mumbling incoherently. The officer rose and motioned him with his finger. The shopkeeper came closer.

"Walitzki?" the lieutenant repeated.

Kaczynski was silent. The German raised his dark brows and looked at him for a while. Suddenly he straightened his arm and across the table hit the standing man in the face. Kaczynski gave a short cry, and covered his head with his arms. He stood thus for a minute, breathing heavily, his mouth wide-open. At last, he spoke haltingly.

Charles Walitzki was a teacher in Rudawica, a kilometer from here. He was the ranger's friend. He lived with his half-paralyzed mother by the schoolhouse.

"Genug!" the lieutenant snapped and looked at his companion with satisfaction.

The latter nodded, stretched his arms lazily, and rose. Kaczynski looked at one then at the other, blinking his red eyelids.

"Raus, raus!" the lieutenant shouted and pushed him toward the door.

After a while Peter remained in the room with only one soldier. It was the same man who had kicked him in the stomach so ferociously a minute before. Now this German lifted him from the floor and sat him on the stool. He looked at him for a moment. Then he went to the hall and drew some water from the pail. Peter took the cup mechanically. As he drank greedily, the soldier looked at him with a feeling of pity mixed with contempt. He said something to Peter, waited a moment, and repeated his words. Seeing, however, that Peter could not understand him, he shrugged his shoulders, brought another stool to the window, and sat down, lighting a cigarette.

The dusk grew thicker and darker. The forest, still bluish, now turned into a formless mist, like a motionless cloud growing out of a greyish-gold earth; and over it an unseen wind blew other steel-like and brown clouds. The two solitary apple-trees framed this landscape with their black supple branches. In the stillness, the raucous voices of the German soldiers sounded like mysterious outcries. And from the depths of the dusk, the rumble of the tanks and motorized columns came as if the night was heralding its darkness with an awesome growl.

Peter almost felt good. Only the cold bothered him. He huddled to contain the cold within himself. Again it seemed to him that it was all a dream. And, as it happens in dreams, he began to worry lest he be late for the meeting with Charles. When Charles was leaving for Rudawica he promised he would try to come in again before nightfall, if he could. He came at this time almost daily.

The shortest way from the Ranger's house to Rudawica runs through the forest. Peter crosses the potato-field behind the house, and hastens along the familiar path. He meets Charles mid-way. Charles is hatless as usual, in a heavy, grey jacket and well-worn trousers. They return to the house by a somewhat longer route, for Peter wants to take a look at the nursery of young spruce. The forest is filled with blue light, in which the brown trunks of slender pines, cut off from the ground and the roots, sway softly with the wind. When it is quiet the pine branches rustle, causing the illusion that the rustling comes from the clouds. Charles goes first. He is whistling a rhythmic, joyous melody, in which Peter immediately recognizes the first bars of *Eine kleine Nachtmusik*.

Charles looks at him.

"Would you like me to put on a record for you? I like it very much."

He stoops over the record album and by the light of the dying candle finds the record he wants. The fire is crackling in the stove. The small orchestra begins to proclaim its joy. Peter listens with closed eyes. When he open them, he sees Charles' profile in front of him, his low forehead and above it, dark, thick hair. The loneliness of his own life suddenly seems less painful than usual. He thinks that upon his return home he will be alone in an empty house, but he thinks at the same time that he will see his friend again tomorrow. Waiting—does it not soothe one's solitude?

"It's Mozart," Charles explains, when the serenade comes to an end. "Did you like it?"

"Sure," Peter replies.

Then, late in the evening, Charles accompanies Peter back to his house. They go through the forest. A March rain is falling. The earth steams with fresh moisture. The whiff of the wind from the meadows behind Rudawica is mild and warm. High above the cloudy sky, as if belonging to another, more perfect sky, a few timid stars gleam through.

"Look," says Charles, "soon it will be spring."

"It looks that way," Peter assents.

He shivered with cold. He opened his eyes. The room, like the outside, was steeped in blue light. This gave the impression that nothing was separating its interior from the dusk. The glowing cigarette lit up the soldier's face from time to time, absent, immobile in a fixed stare.

Peter moved. The soldier started and turned towards him quickly. After a minute he stood up and came to the prisoner. They looked at each other in silence.

"Zigaretten?" the German asked.

Peter nodded. When the soldier offered him a pack he took one cigarette. The moment he bore it to his mouth he felt how swollen and sore his lips were. But he took the light from the soldier's cigarette and inhaled the smoke. He immediately began choking and coughing. The slightest movement sent a pang of pain through his head and chest. At last the attack ceased but he was afraid to straighten up lest the pain surge up again. The cigarette which had fallen out of his hand lay on the floor, still glowing. The soldier squashed it with his boot. He kept looking at Peter. Finally he said slowly and deliberately:

"Die . . . you want not? No . . . pity . . ."

Peter remained motionless. To die? This word, spoken in a bad and funny accent, seemed empty and meaningless.

"My life isn't at all interesting," says Peter.

Charles is looking at him.

"What do you know about it?"

"Well, who is to know?"

Charles is silent. Only after a while does he speak up with slow reflection:

"We don't always know what is important in our lives."

Peter rises suddenly and stops at the open window.

"But, really, there isn't anything important in my life. I'm not important, that's all."

He gazes into the night. An August star rolls across the sky like a fiery streak. Fog near the forests spreads so evenly as if it were shallow, whitish water. Peter sits on the window sill.

"To be sure, I was liked by many people. But I am not indispensable to any woman or man. Nobody needs me. I can exist or not exist, it's all the same."

He keeps looking at the yard. At a certain moment he hears Charles rising. Now he paces in the room.

"A bat has flown by," Peter observes.

Charles stops.

"I think," he says with the previous deliberation, "that indeed it is important to be indispensable to some person. But perhaps it is even more important if another man is indispensable."

Peter leans out and passes his hand over the rough sun-flowers growing under the window.

"I would be afraid of this."

Charles looks at him with astonishment.

"Why?" he repeats.

Peter husks the unripe, soft seeds and throws them through the window, into the green thicket.

"I don't know," he says at last. "But I would be afraid."

Suddenly from the direction of the forest the rumble of an engine reached Peter's ears. At the same time he heard his own voice, pronouncing Charles' name. Before he opened his eyes he understood that the Germans were going to Rudawica to get Charles. The room was murky, and night stood beyond the window. He wanted to get up, to run, and to recant his accusation. But he had no strength. Only his consciousness worked in him ever more intensely and more clearly.

Suddenly, brakes screeched violently, and a car pulled to a stop before the Ranger's house.

The soldier guarding Peter straightened up. Outside somebody shouted out loudly. Peter immediately recognized the lieutenant's voice. Simultaneously the hall was invaded by the stomping of heavy boots. The door was thrown open by a kick and enormous shadows filled the room. A large carbide lantern, swaying in a soldier's hand, brightened the dusk with a yellow gleam.

A flame swept through Peter's chest as he huddled on his stool. His heart froze in him for a moment. Someone grabbed him by his arms, pulled him and forced him to stand. He lifted his head.

Scarcely a step from himself he saw Charles, surrounded by several

huge soldiers. He seemed small and frail among them. He was wearing his usual grey jacket. He was pale but calm. When their eyes met,
Peter trembled. He understood at once that Charles knew everything.
But he found no hatred or condemnation in his eyes. Overcome, he
lowered his head. He kept on his feet with the last remnant of his
strength. His whole face was smeared with blood, his sunken eyes were
cavernous.

"I was scared . . ." he whispered through his swollen lips.

The soldier next to him struck his back with his rifle butt.

"Maul halten!" he shouted.

Quick steps were heard in the hall. The soldiers jumped to attention
at once.

The tall lieutenant was the first to enter, and following him came
the blond Junker, his hands in the pockets of his raincoat. The younger
stopped on the threshold, and the other cast a brief glance at the group
of men as he was standing in the middle of the room. When he saw
Charles he leaped toward him with clenched fists and broke into
savage shouting. Hitherto cool, collected and contemptuous, the German turned into a totally different man in the twinkling of an eye.

Charles' pallor deepened, but he didn't take his eyes off the
frenzied officer even for a moment. He gazed at him calmly, with an
intensity which only Peter noticed. And his friend's calm was im-
parted to him. He straightened his body.

"I lied," he said aloud. "He had nothing to do with it. Only me."

The lieutenant had not noticed who dared interrupt him and was
speechless at the first moment. Realizing that it was Peter, he sank
into him his eyes, white from rage.

"Was?"

Peter took a deep breath.

"I lied," he repeated. "He's innocent."

"Raus!" the lieutenant screamed.

Meanwhile, Kaczynski drew closer to him and stammering began
to explain something.

"Raus!" the lieutenant howled.

And he hit him without looking. The shopkeeper groaned and
reeled towards the wall. The officer suddenly grew calm, stepped back
and turned to his companion.

Staggering, Peter made a motion as if to go towards them. Charles
stopped him with his eyes.

"Leave it," he said in his quiet and even voice. "It's no use." And
he added more softly:

"It's all finished . . ."

Peter hunched his body and almost soundlessly whispered his

friend's name. But Charles heard him. His lips quivered and his eyes
darkened. But he controlled himself immediately.

"Hold on!" he said dryly.

The soldier at his side pushed his arm.

"Shut up!"

At this moment the lieutenant standing at the door turned around
and with a short gesture pointed at Peter and Charles.

"Shoot 'em!"

He went out without looking back, and the young Junker followed
behind.

A commotion began in the room. One of the soldiers pushed Peter
toward the door, another lifted the lantern high, and its light illumined
the dark hall. Peter, bending his head at the threshold from habit,
crossed it first and was at once enveloped by the cold air of the
October night.

Darkness lay over the earth. When he raised his eyes he saw turbulent clouds hanging low, and above them, in the very distant depths
he could see another sky, calm, frozen almost, and starry. A certain
memory passed through his mind, but he could not grasp it. He looked
back. Behind him Charles was also looking at the sky.

"Charles!" he whispered again.

The soldiers were talking, apparently discussing which of them was
to carry out the execution. Suddenly Peter felt Charles' hand on his
arm. He was shaken by such pain as he had not known until now. His
hand trembled.

"Don't be afraid," Charles whispered, leaning towards him.

Peter had no time to reply, for he was pushed in the back with a
rifle butt. Mechanically wiping the blood off his face with his palm,
he obediently moved forward. The lantern lit up the way with a narrow
streak. But he stumbled on the stones several times. They were being
led to the back of the yard. Although he was not looking over his
shoulder, Peter knew that Charles was walking behind him.

"Remember," he suddenly heard his muffled voice, "even this can
mean hope . . ."

The darkness was still. Among the sounds of stomping iron-shod
boots, Peter could distinguish his own steps, and behind him every
step Charles made. Suddenly someone behind him began to whistle
loudly. Peter stopped instinctively. He was certain he recognized the
lieutenant's voice.

"Schnell, schnell!" one of the soldiers prodded him on. He stumbled
again, but before he moved on, he managed to turn back and to cast
a glance at Charles. He was also listening.

The high-pitched whistle penetrated the night with the first bars
of Mozart's gentle serenade. Peter lifted his head. Thick clouds were

whirling above, but higher, like a pale light in the darkness, still shone a few stars, distant and solitary. "Hope" he thought mechanically, but without the certainty that he had a right to it.

They finally reached the end of the yard, near the fence. Beside them loomed the black hole, in which the arms had been buried. The rustle of the forest flowed here in a dark wave.

"Halt!" one of the soldiers yelled.

They stopped. Another soldier, broad-shouldered and helmeted, took out his revolver and came up behind Charles. The latter straightened himself, and raised his head. In the darkness he now seemed taller. The shot rang out, brief and hollow. Charles staggered and with his hands pressed to his body fell on his face into the darkness.

Before the soldier approached him in turn, Peter managed to look at the sky once more. A single, dying star still burned amid the dark and silent abyss. "Hope" he thought with despair.

From *Night: Tales,*
translated by ADAM GILLON *and* LUDWIK KRZYZANOWSKI

Adolf Rudnicki
(1912-   )

Adolf Rudnicki has been called the "Jeremiah of the Warsaw ghetto." Born in 1912 in Zabno, he has made a name for himself as the chronicler of Jewish life in Warsaw and the small provincial towns.

In his first novel, *The Rats* (1931), the theme is the desperate grayness of everyday life. The author relates in detail the inner experiences of a man whose spirituality is broken down by the mysterious content of quotidian drabness. In the self-analysis of an average youth in an average little town Rudnicki detects a tragic and poignant aspect. His hero is the downtrodden "little man," the individual who lacks destiny and who is continually thwarted by life. In the ambiguous father-son relationship one can find the echoes of Dostoyevsky and Kafka, but Rudnicki does not lack originality. Although his style and his organization of narrative elements are not perfect, his novels and stories have great power.

In *The Soldiers* (1933) he gave an account of his own military service, which stirred a great deal of controversy at the time; he continued his psychological investigation in *The Unloved One* (1937).

His other works are: *Summer* (1938), which describes life in a Polish artists' colony; collections of short stories *Shakespeare* (1948), *The Flight from Yasnaya Polyana* (1949), *The Dead and the Living Sea* (1952)—selections from previously published work; short stories "Pure Current," "Blue Leaves" (1956) and two volumes of stories: *The Cow* (1960) and *The Fiancé of Beata* (1961).

"The Great Stefan Konecki," which appears below, is from *Ascent to Heaven*, a collection of stories published in English (Roy Publishers, New York, 1951). The book reflects Rudnicki's preoccupation with the fate of Polish Jews and, more generally, with the suffering of the population under the German yoke. But, as in his first novel, he is concerned also with the portrayal of psychological nuances, the metamorphosis of the human soul under the stress of mental and physical suffering.

The Great Stefan Konecki

My initiation into history, as unforgettable as love is good, came in the winter of 1939–40. It was in Lwow; the city looked like an oriental bazaar; at every step were refugees in fantastic attire, yet no one took any notice of it, any more than they listened to stories of the recently ended September campaign. The streets swarmed with people every one of whom formed the most interesting part of someone else's biography, but whose own biographies were of no interest to anyone, for world history seemed to be the only thing deserving of attention. During that winter these refugees, dressed in peasants' sheepskins or town raincoats, shod in legboots or canvas tennis shoes, according to the extent of their cash, ingenuity, or credit available across the frontiers, huddled on the edges of chairs in the smoke-filled "Rome" and "George" cafés and asked one another: "What's the latest?"

When it grew dark the streets were deserted, but the rooms of the houses were as crowded as Russian baths, and littered with improvised beds and mattresses. And then the refugees huddled round wireless sets to listen to the voice of history. And they heard that on the western front the day had passed quietly on the whole, with increased patrol activity on both sides; we had taken three prisoners, our own losses amounted to one killed. "Nothing happening!" the refugees said to one another miserably. Next morning they would start up from improvised beds, run in their improvised attire to the cafés, into the streets, and wonder what was going to happen next, what they ought to do next. "Are you planning to get into Hungary?" "Into Rumania?" "To Vilno?" "Have you a way?" "A reliable guide?" "Does he want payment in advance?" "In dollars?" "Or zlotys?" "Is there any way of getting beyond Vilno?" "Are there any assistance committees functioning there?" "Or perhaps you're thinking of going back home?" Not everybody contemplated long journeys; there were some who thought of their September wanderings simply as a rather strenuous walk, after which they would return home, brush the dust off their trousers, have a good cry on some beloved breast, and then life—a little changed of course—would go on. They did not expect it to be changed very much.

In December 1939 the war flung me into the streets of Lwow in a state of mind such as makes even the most thick-skinned realize how difficult life is without a mother. I had only just shaved off a beard of three months' growth. My soldier companions had called me "old boy," though I was not yet thirty. My boots were in holes, I had no overcoat, I had no idea which way to go: right or left. With a faint feeling of hope I buttonholed some timid creature and asked for Stefan Konecki, the chairman of the local branch of the Polish Writers' Association. Konecki had been the uncrowned king of Lwow writers for years, so I thought I could not do better than go and see him.

When I entered the two small rooms of the branch office in Ossolinski Street I realized that I was not the first to have had this idea. That modest little office was crowded with writers, famous, not so famous, and unknown. All wanted help, and all looked exactly as I did. I had never met Konecki before, so he questioned me closely; he took pains to ensure that no one should join his center without good reason. I had only just broken into literature, my name was not widely known, and quite possibly he heard it now for the first time. When his secretary, a youngster named Walega, whom I knew slightly, certified that I belonged to the Warsaw center Konecki proceeded to assess my requirements. I had nothing but myself.

Having got so far, he thought it necessary to tell me that there was no difference between the Germans from whom I had fled and the Russians among whom I had arrived. I stared at him: this was something new, something I was not prepared to listen to. I hated that sort of talk, I had no ears for "objectivity." I was fresh from my military adventures, I had taken part in battle, I had seen with my own eyes that it is not a matter of indifference whether one kills or is killed. Pain and hunger cure a man of objectivity, I had not come across it anywhere during the fighting! My wounds were too fresh for me to listen quietly: I walked out. I was called back, and my name was added to the list of beggars on whose behalf Konecki pestered the more affluent citizens of Lwow. In the name of fidelity "to her who has not yet perished"[1] he demanded that we exalted spirits should be taken into their homes and treated in the manner that was our due. He did not beg, he demanded and threatened; for "Poland is watching, is listening, and will recompense the faithful and punish the unfaithful."

The ranks of the refugees thinned out. Those who did not wish to live under the Soviet regime went off to Vilno, to Rumania, to Germany. Yet the great majority of people remained where they were, inquisitively watching these newcomers from the East, about whom such contradictory reports were spread. For some time both sides eyed each other like boxers in a ring, without admitting the fact. At first the Soviet authorities had no objection to Stefan Konecki—the life-chairman, as everybody thought, of the Writers' Association—organizing help for his fellow writers. But as time passed the authorities began to take a more direct interest in the writers' fate. An "Organizational Committee" was set up, called "Komorg" for short, and assigned Count Ɓ's mansion on Copernicus Street. For some time the count continued to stalk among us writers on his long legs. One day he buttonholed a well-known author and told him wheezily: "I am infinitely delighted to have writers as my guests. I'd been told that when the Bolsheviks came they would stable horses in my house."

The writers flocked into the "Komorg"; the mansion grew crowded, the office in Ossolinski Street was deserted. No one ever went to see Stefan Konecki now. The people of the left did not trouble to, for the "Komorg" was their headquarters. Nor did those not of the left, for

---

[1] The first line of the Polish national anthem: "Poland has not yet perished."

in that tragic and fuelless winter they too preferred the fine, warm, mansion. They stayed there for days on end, playing chess, but not writing; they were "waiting for the development of events."

The winter of 1940 was rich in snowfalls, the snow dazzled. From the mansion windows the members of the "Komorg" could see Konecki passing on his way to his office in Ossolinski Street every morning, about 10 o'clock. He never even glanced at our mansion, which had made his center and himself redundant. He was left to himself.

All his life Konecki had been a member of the right. During the last few years before the war the National Democrats had raised hell for Jews in the streets of Lwow, but they had always shown great respect for him, they had applauded him tumultuously after his Thursday speeches in the Municipal Club. That was not to be wondered at, since he always fulminated against the reds and the pinks. In their articles to Warsaw papers the reds and pinks openly called him a fascist, yet they did so quite nicely: remember, this was before the war, when the meaning of words was still concealed; and besides, in Poland the ideological conflicts are milder than elsewhere, for the ideas themselves are imported.

As a writer Konecki had always been concerned not with life but with death. At first this was simply the expression of a neurosis and that peculiar fascination which death has for the young. But later, in everything he wrote one sensed a man continually starting out of bed at night, continually trying to break through the lid of a coffin. He never probed deeper into life, he never chopped it finer and finer like meat for a Vienna steak. He had no interest in life as such, so he could not be any friend of the Bolsheviks, who do not include death among the objects of their enthusiasm.

There is nothing sadder than a life which the general current has left behind, especially that of an old man, whose fate it is to see values exalted which he has always depreciated, and sanctities glorified which he has always hated. It was a bitter experience for the old lion. I think I was the only writer who ever dropped in at Ossolinski Street; and when the authorities closed down his office on the ground that two writers' associations were not necessary, I still went to see him at his flat in Lenartowicz Street.

O yes! I was not having too bad a time now, life was comparatively civilized, and I was slowly forgetting the battlefields, the September roads; I was beginning to develop "objectivity" again. When I arrived in Lwow in the December I had been like dough flung into a very hot oven: burnt outside, but raw inside. In the new warmth and well-being my soul gradually recovered its former color: I went as white as bone, and as I whitened I readily listened to the old reactionary. Naturally, nothing pleased him; but I am one of those people who find

grumbling as harmonious and soothing as music. A marvelous thing,
is grumbling! There is no government so stupid as the one that tries
to suppress grumbling. "Can I still talk to you?" old Konecki would
ask, and when I smiled he would whisper: "He's a genius, I tell you; a
strategic genius! And what's more, he knows *them*. This Mannheimer
was a tsarist officer himself once; remember that name!" The sounds of
Red Army men singing floated up from the street. Konecki lectured
me: "Buffalo Bill, I tell you! An elephant on clay feet! A giant with
too small a heart! One really strong blow will be sufficient."

As was becoming to a man enamoured of death, Konecki had a
luxurious flat. He occupied three rooms, which according to the housing regulations was far too much for one person, especially a person
on such bad terms with the authorities. After the Ossolinski Street
office was closed down Konecki suggested that I should occupy one
of his rooms, for he was afraid of having some stranger billeted on
him. Naturally I agreed, for my objectivity was now demanding a
luxurious flat. But, as of course you will guess, in my beautiful abode
my soul turned red again, like wine in autumn; for we appreciate the
rapid current of life most of all when we are plunged into the mire.

At four A.M., under the sky of early dawn, I stood in the street,
feeling tired and sick of adventure, like someone sick of the sea as
soon as he dabbles his toe in its icy waters. It was June 1941. Late in
the afternoon of the previous day I had gone out into Lyczakowska
Street, known in those early days of the German-Russian war as "Let's
get back" street, for it seethed with fleeing people. Their restless hands
clung onto the cars which drove past in their hundreds; but the
crowds numbered tens of thousands. Those in the cars did not cut off
the hands clinging to the sides, to the back; shouting and accelerating
were sufficient. Yet by a miracle I climbed into one of these cars. However, at the village of Winniki, four miles outside Lwow, our driver, a
man named Isaac Teitelbaum, declared that he would not go on any
further; he must return to the oil works for "gas." But with us was also a
Russian chief engineer of some factory, together with his family, and
he would not hear of return. However, in a car it is the driver who has
the last word. Teitelbaum was adamant; he had a wife in Lwow, and
he wanted to go back for her.

When we arrived at the oil works after six hours of terrible traveling it was already in flames. None the less the military seized us—us,
mark you!—on the charge that we had set it on fire. The Russians
managed to clear themselves, but I was the only non-Russian, and all
the mountain of suspicion suddenly crumbled down on me. No one
said a word in my defense; in fact the chief engineer declared he had
never seen me before. "What? But at Winniki? Don't you remember
Winniki?" I shouted in the desperate tones of a man who knows what

awaits him. I presented the lieutenant in charge with document after document; he did not even glance at them, his eyes and ears were fixed on me. I revealed to him the secret of my origin. He was quite unmoved. Then he ordered me to hand over the sack I had across my shoulders. Out of it he fished a change of underwear, foot-rags, socks, a loaf of bread, a packet of sugar; and finally he came to my bottle of Cinzano. He pulled out the cork and sniffed at it. What all my documents had failed to achieve, that one sniff did: the bottle contained cold tea. A fifth columnist setting fire to oil-tanks and refreshing himself with cold tea! He set me free. But the chief engineer would not hear of taking me with him to the East. He drove me to the city and flung me out in Potocki Street at four in the morning.

The night was just drawing to its close. The sky looked like an archipelago of a thousand islands sprinkled with blue dye. I returned to my room in Lenartowicz Street; I returned to Konecki, to whom I had said goodbye only the previous day. Stefan Konecki . . . I thought; what a fine record he has for the time now coming; the old chairman had remained adamant, irreconcilable, to the end. He had never even visited the "Komorg" in Copernicus Street. For him the greatest tragedy of the past year had been the thirty-line note he had published in the local *Red Standard* after the Bolsheviks had arrived. It had been the most futile, the most trivial of notes, expressing his joy that the bombs had stopped falling. I had never imagined that anyone could suffer so much over thirty lines. He had asked me again and again if I thought Poland would forgive him . . . Yes, he had a fine record . . . and a fine name. Except that its suffix was completely artificial, a useless, arbitrary appendix. For his name was really Kon, plain Kon. A fine name for the time that was coming!

2

Exactly a week after the opening of hostilities the Germans entered Lwow, and the city, hitherto a town of plenty, was turned into a wilderness. In this last city of Europe, as the Nazis called it, they came up against a phenomenon they had not encountered elsewhere: here there were no private shops. Elsewhere, shopkeepers had hidden away the greater part of their stock until the situation cleared, and so they were still able to sell oddments. In Lwow the only shopkeeper, the Government, had withdrawn to the East. The Germans at once took over, and sent westward Russian tea and Russian leather, soap and flour, furniture and cattle. The German pharmaceutical industry was regarded as the finest in the world, yet the German officers hunted around for anti-typhus serum manufactured here, on the spot, or in Russia; they had no confidence in the German serums marked *Ober-*

kommando Wehrmacht, they had no confidence in anything German except bullets. The trucks which brought in their troops did not return empty. Goebbels wrote: "We know what the English will say: the German army flung itself like locusts on a prosperous city and stripped it." With Joseph to put it across, the old trick once more deluded and astonished the world.

Hunger reigned. When the crowded and colorful city grew as quiet as some off-the-map suburb—quiet and starved—the Germans brought out their star turn: Jew-baiting. A year later an article entitled *Das Verbrechen von Stalingrad* appeared in the German *Völkischer Beobachter.* Was the crime of Stalingrad that the Russians preferred to turn their city into a heap of ruins rather than surrender it to the enemy? No. The crime was that the Jews had been evacuated out of Stalingrad, and so *das grossdeutsche Heer* did not know where to begin.

The shops were closed down for good. The bakeries baked their last reserves of flour, but the people waited patiently in the queues; horror, which did not alleviate their hunger, at least taught them patience. Columns of men and women had been seen, being driven along in the direction of Pelczynska Street, and none of them had returned. The massacres in Brygidki prison and in Lacki Street were known to all. No bread was being issued to anybody, but at least non-Jews were allowed to queue, they were not deprived of all hope, they were even promised ten dekagrammes of meat per person. The butchers' shops were always closed, but someone or other frequently changed the notices on the doors. The first to be posted read: "For Aryans, 10 dekagrammes of meat without bone; for Jews, 5 dekagrammes without bone." The second read: "Aryans: 10 dekagrammes without bone; Jews, 5 dekagrammes" (no mention of bone). The meat did not arrive, but a third notice was pinned up: "Aryans, 10 dekagrammes without bone; Jews will not be issued meat." The shops remained closed, but the great star act was performed with a continual change of glorious detail. The enemy fed the imagination.

Before long the Germans were displaying all their ingenuity: monetary imposts and murder, the threat of the ghetto, temporary suspension of the threat at the cost of a new impost, more murder, further deportations to camps only too well known as places of torture. The nation melted before my eyes. The nation was perishing, wriggling like a worm under a spade-edge.

When political prisoners were taken out of their cells and packed into lorries, they had to lie down on the floor; then the lorry was covered with a tarpaulin and black militia were posted at the corners. One day I saw one of these lorries halt outside a church. Two of the militia-men got down from it; was it that they felt a need for prayer before proceeding to the execution? The weather was still fine, the street was dozing in the last sluggish warmth, like a fluffy, golden cat. Suddenly the tarpaulin began to heave with the movement of the living bodies beneath it. The passers-by caught their breath.

Other prisoners were also driven in lorries along these same streets, but not under tarpaulins. There were the Jews. Visible to all, old men with thin, bluish necks, like those of plucked cocks, sat terribly calm. They smiled as if to reassure not themselves but their friends compelled to clean the streets: "Don't think about us, don't grieve over our bitter lot, dear ones, our dear, only ones!"

The secret death hidden beneath a tarpaulin was human by comparison with the open, cynical death exhibited for all the world to see. And that was a difference of some importance.

The Jews were hunted down, they were murdered. With eyes blinded by tears I looked on at the extermination which was passing me by. My soul as full of song as the "Songs of Songs," and as full of pain as the *Book of Job*, I walked unscathed; for I had a face which had brought down on my father the bitter reproach that he had not given his little Benjamin one *human* feature. At prayers my father's friends, devout like himself, had turned their eyes away from me in repugnance. It's a sin, they had said, to look at *such a monstrosity*. That was in long past days. Now those who knew stared at me closely: "Possibly the eyes give you away, but that may be because we know . . ." Only the palms and the knees betray you, so the experts told me. I had a face fairer than the fair, hair more flaxen than corn. My face was tinted with the hues of meadows and lakes, I harmonized with the Polish street like a willow with the Polish road. With my flaxen head and pickpocket's eyes I could go about the city as freely as others. The "undertakers"—the black-uniformed Ukrainian militia—frequently checked documents. My documents also certified that I was Polish. I always regard myself as a Pole first and foremost, the rest is my own involved affair. That Poland regards me otherwise is unfortunately her own involved affair.

The nation was perishing. If I suffered less than others physically, not being condemned to resort to a thousand desperate subterfuges daily, morally I suffered even more, just because I was not exterminated physically. After the merciless winter, which for us was mitigated by hope, the weather began to turn warm. The water no longer burst the pipes, the earth returned to life, went as brown as the hair of a dachshund. As I walked home of an evening I was enveloped in the breath of a sky ever clear, of air scented with freedom, which more than all else is security. I grew more and more conscious of my heart. More and more often I fell into a deep musing.

For the first time since the early days of the war I longed for

Warsaw, and for a few people whom I had barely remembered
hitherto, but whom I now longed to see again as keenly as an old
man longs to revisit his birthplace. They were not relations, for I had
no family, but now casual acquaintances seemed to be friends: longing
always changes the proportions. They were living in the Warsaw
Jewish district. I all but whined after them, I desired to be with
them for good or evil. I did not hanker after any "better situation," I was disgusted with my "better situation." I knew all about the
hunger, about typhus, about graves as deep as lakes. I imagined I
knew everything, and yet I longed to be there. The nation's sufferings
did not terrify me, on the contrary, they fascinated me; I wanted to
drink the cup that was my portion as soon as possible. And besides,
any fate seemed better than this pining in loneliness in Lenartowicz
Street. Lwow, wonderful, crowded Lwow, had become a wilderness.
All who could had gone, had fled. Here I no longer had one friendly
soul; there were days when I had no one to talk to.

I was the incarnation of longing, all anxiety, when a reply came to
one of my many letters. The go-between, a trusted person, stared at me
fixedly.

"But are you nicked?" he asked.

I knew at once that he was referring to circumcision.

"Yes."

"But with your appearance . . ."

"I want to be with them . . ."

Stefan Konecki was also invited to go, and perhaps the invitation
was chiefly for him. An old friend, Dr. Braun, wrote that if Konecki
happened to be left to his own devices and had no other possibility, he
could come to Warsaw, where "a few people still remember who he is."

My joy was smothered by bitterness. It no longer had—I am speaking of the joy—that purity, which something has when we feel that
we are the only favored ones. Moreover, I thought of Konecki as quite
unworthy of anyone's solicitude. He had not deserved it.

He was still getting along quite well. Now Walega, his former
secretary, a youngster with a head on his shoulders, was staying in
the flat with him. Other connections were also proving useful; he had
a hide-out in readiness and personally he did not suffer very much.

I passed on the Warsaw invitation to him. He replied:

"At such a time as this only a madman would return to the denomination of Moses."

On Sundays the "denomination of Moses" were driven into the
streets to clear away the snow. With crowbars in their hands they
stood outside the houses which until recently had been their homes,
and broke up the ice. As they had no shovels they collected the fragments of icy snow with their hands and piled them up at the edge of
the sidewalk. They were not allowed to wear anything made of fur

or wool, so they wore heaps of rags. They were walking ragbags, they were filth itself, the street was soiled where they stood. The enemy was a great believer in cleanliness, so he made them the filthiest of creatures. Wearing distinctive armbands, hung around with tin discs, they reminded one of penned horses. Not long before my talk with Konecki about going to Warsaw I had seen one such little group standing some distance from a church. Through the open door came the sound of a choir accompanied by an organ. The service ended; the men and women poured out, refreshed, scented, alien—as though they were foreigners from overseas, they were so different. Two thousand years ago Someone had died for them. And indeed, as one observed two such dissimilar destinies, one might for a moment think that He was still continually dying in order to save them. . . Yes, it would be madness to admit one's Jewish affinity.

I studied Konecki from the aspect of his affinity. Fifty years old, tall, bowed, with shoulders like rolls of bread, milky-white hair as thick as a boy's, he had an irascible face with angular lines—a face which in past days had been feared by many—and fleshy, unpleasant lips. Various explanations could be found for the characteristic quality of his face, but his swarthy complexion betrayed him.

"Someone told me of a certain incident today," Konecki said, "A woman with three little children went along to see the Social Welfare Committee at the Jewish Community office. 'We can't do anything for you,' the clerk told her. 'Then what am I to do?' she asked. 'Throw yourself out of a fourth-floor window,' was the answer. In all the world is there any other people with 'social welfare' like that? Is there anywhere else where a clerk would dare to talk like that to a mother with children? Why, that nation is sick. . ."

He was always telling me similar stories. "Why don't the Jews revolt?" "Why don't they fight?" "Why don't they go off into the forest?" "Why do they work?" "Why do the Germans say: *Die Juden sind die billigsten und willigsten Arbeiter?*" (The Jews are the cheapest and most willing of workers). He asked the questions asked by all who have stony hearts and cold eyes.

"A sick nation?" I replied. "I know that. Literature has known the term 'times of contempt' for the past decade. We, of the denomination of Moses as you put it, have known those times for two thousand years. I go and call on Goldberg: 'Look here,' Goldberg says to me: 'Look here! What's all this that everybody's talking about? Baths of death? Only our sick minds could put those two words together like that. Soap made from human beings? How women burn worse and men better while children often come out of the gas-chambers alive? A guillotine which uses a stone instead of a knife-edge? Look here, who is it that's spreading such yarns? It's hyenas who come here from Warsaw to wheedle our last ear rings, our last stones or bracelets out

of us. Those same hyenas tell us there's a bridge over Chlodna Street.
Look here, I know Warsaw, and I know Chlodna Street; since when has
a river started flowing along it? we're a *sick nation* . . . All the world
says we exaggerate, we get hysterical, and apparently the world is
right. The Germans are always telling us so. What is the point of all
this beastly gossip? Aren't things bad enough for us already?" Later
on, as we went out, Goldberg caught me by the sleeve: 'Don't ask me
what I think. Don't ask a defenseless man his opinion; a defenseless
man clings to anything that holds out the least shadow of hope. You
saw my mother sitting paralyzed in her armchair; they shoot such
people on the spot, or throw them out of the window. How often can
I manage to carry her down to the cellar? My oldest boy is twelve, he
thinks an armband's fun, like a scooter or a new cap. One day he went
along to the Skorkowskis; they have a son just his age, and the two
boys are chums. He wanted to swap his Guatemala stamp. They took
his stamp away, tore his raincoat and knocked him about into the
bargain. For days he went around as though poisoned, he wouldn't
eat, he demanded justice. 'Daddy, make them give me back my Guatemala.' What do I care about Guatemala? I was shivering with fear
that they might take the boy away, for they're already rounding up
lads his age. My younger son is crying all the time. 'They're shooting
again, daddy.' What am I to do? Wherever you look, it's nothing but
hatred for us. If only they thought a little, if only anyone wanted to
think a little. . . And you say: *a sick nation*."

I paused for a moment, then added:

"This is not the first time I've known you say that, I well remember
the famous article you wrote in 1922, in which you listed all our
virtues: our hypersensitiveness, our invariable readiness to serve the
strong and the rich, our dislike of Poland and the Poles, our restless-
ness, our keenness to share in any filth, our arrogance, our lack of
moderation and balance, our failure to realize what is permissible and
what not, our lack of good breeding, our inability to recognize and
keep to our place. You always took our very existence as a personal
insult, because someone somewhere stung you over us . . . *A sick
nation!* Even today, when every hour lays bare the source of our
sickness, you go on accusing us whose one crime is our weakness. The
world oppresses the defenseless, and it hates those it oppresses. The
only time you ever used the word Jew was in that article. For in literature, the literature of the sublime to which you attach so much importance, you turned your back on all that is contained in the word 'Jew';
at all costs you wanted to be like *them*. In order to find a place for
yourself in their narrow little stream you closed your eyes to a great
sea. You were so anxious not to violate the spirit of their language
that you completely assimilated their style. You must have known what
the result would be of all this pseudonymous writing, your efforts to

be more Polish than the Poles. Now listen: You knew all the difficult, filthy, painful content of the word 'Jew,' and you should have burst their sacred bonds, your writing should have been clamant with your suffering, you should have vomited up your never-ending pain, you should have thrust aside their greasy fleshpots and set your own of bitterness in their place. They would have pulled faces, but in the end they'd have reached out for that cup. You should have told about us, about us above all else, and asked yourself time and again whether what you were writing about was really your subject or theirs, whether you had any right to deal with such subjects. And in fact you never said anything of real value about the things which are theirs! You should have been ruthless to yourself, ransoming your life with speech, not with silence. You would have gained as a writer, and possibly we would all have gained as human beings. Our nearest, our dearest might have died differently. Not in the mud, not spat upon, not despised. . . ."

"Gloves . . ." he said. For a moment I thought I had not heard aright. But then he repeated quite clearly: "Gloves . . . Have you noticed that Aryans always wear gloves? It's by such details that people recognize you. You must never forget your gloves. . . ." But then he added: "I shall be going into the country in a few days. Thank Dr. Braun for me. How young you are! As for me, I haven't the strength. I never did feel that I had the strength to carry that cross, that inhuman cross. . . . You can see for yourself. . . ."

3

I had a good journey and reached Warsaw without incident. As I waited to pass through into the ghetto I examined its walls; they made a gloomy impression. I passed through. I had every intention of remaining, but my stay behind the walls did not last long. After three days I came out, and friends helped me to get a room in Chlodna Street, on the Aryan side, quite close to the bridge. For a wooden bridge spanned the width of Chlodna Street, linking the little with the big ghetto. The roadway of the street was Aryan, the sidewalks were not. People passed on foot across the bridge from one ghetto to the other. The children of the Aryan quarter gazed enviously at the beings whom day after day fate exalted so high in the air.

During the first six months of 1942 the bridge over Chlodna Street was the busiest spot in Warsaw; one's head reeled with gazing at that continual influx of people. It was said that four hundred thousand souls were living behind the walls, but this was only an estimate: no one ever knew the exact figures. In the winter of 1941–42 not a week passed without the Germans adding hundreds and thousands of people to the burden of the Warsaw Jewish Community;

they rounded them up in the provinces, loaded them into lorries just as they were, and flung them behind the walls. The Jewish Communal Council accommodated these newcomers in so-called "trans-shipment centers," where famine and typhus reduced their number by 30% per month. Thus the Council's burden was lightened, but not for long, as the places of the dead were quickly taken by new deportees from the provinces. The people on "this side" raised their eyes to the bridge constructed by Schmied and Muntzermann Ltd. and asked: "How many are there really behind those walls?"

From my window I could survey a large part of the Jewish district. Every day I gazed over "all the land of Gilead unto Dan, and all Naphtali, and the land of Ephraim, and Manasseh, and all the land of Judah, unto the utmost sea." Over all the land which had been promised to Abraham, Isaac, and Jacob. . . .

When the wide-open pincers of the front reached the Channel on one side, and the Volga on the other; when, after the winter disasters the Hitlerite armies again began to achieve such successes as to make even the most optimistic abandon hope of a speedy end, and to contemplate a long period of war between continents, in the torrid summer of 1942 the Germans set to work to exterminate the largest Jewish community in Europe.

The soldiers who arrived under the walls were the personification of ugliness, one would have said they had been specially chosen. In black coats with green collars, black hats of dumpling shape, or discarded helmets that slipped over their eyes, equipped with ancient rifles every one of which was different, and not one of which was of any use against an armed opponent, hunchbacked and pockmarked, small and dumpy or tall and bowed, they all had faces at which the soul shivered. They were said to be Ukrainians, they were also said to be Latvians; for long afterward the very sight of these troops made me tremble with revulsion.

In just under a week all the inhabitants of the little ghetto were driven across the bridge to the larger area. The steep flights of steps sucked in crowds loaded with bundles and suitcases, packed with the very essence of their homes, for the homes themselves had gone. They did not halt on the farther side of the bridge, but were driven deeper and deeper into the big ghetto, while the streets left behind shrank like a severed limb. During that summer the Germans deported over three hundred thousand people from the ghetto. People who had grown like trees, were sorted out like tin figures. One day I saw an incredible sight; there was no one on the bridge. No one was left in the little ghetto: it was a town without people, as in the fairy-tale.

As sector after sector was cleared of Jews, gendarmes with dogs and accompanied by two or three civilians took over. The civilians were experts in the task of listing and valuing the booty. When they had finished their work it was possible for Aryans to buy a Jewish flat for three to five thousand zlotys, with the right to drill floors and walls in search of the legendary gold. And over the remains still warm, through the blood still wet, life began to put forth young shoots. Here and there curtains appeared in windows; a new confectioner's shop was opened in a half empty house, a solicitor's plate was fixed in the gateway, life gradually revived. During the summer and autumn of 1942, at the cost of one part of Warsaw the Germans presented the other part with a royal spectacle. A task which our backward minds might estimate to take a hundred years was achieved in a few weeks. One day when I awoke I did not recognize the street: the bridge was gone. From "all the land of Judah unto the utmost sea" the Germans began to remove the landmarks.

Yet there were a number who escaped the extermination, and whose very existence was illegal and expensive. Money flowed in from the West for their support; they were like children, and others had to take care of them. Dr. Braun was one who escaped. The Treblinka crematorium in which the most outstanding of the nation were burnt had the effect of exalting him. He became one of the chief trustees of the money sent from the West for distribution. And he needed assistants. One day he sent for me and harnessed me wholly and completely into the service of the Jewish misery, without equal anywhere else in the world. From time to time I had to travel to the provinces. And some fifteen months after I had left Lwow I found myself back there again—in Konecki's flat.

4

I did the work I had been sent to do; I felt all the satisfaction of a doctor grappling with an epidemic, who finds that the number of cases has fallen from 100 yesterday to only 95 today. Walega was one of our representatives; the money assigned to Lwow was sent to him, and from time to time he visited Warsaw; he had gone off on urgent business the previous day. Konecki's former secretary was a great help, his conduct was to be admired. This unassuming lad had the secret ambition to keep Konecki's flat unviolated, not selling any of the writer's belongings. As heavy as animals, as lush as duckweed on sunless ponds the carpets still lay in each room, each one of different colors, but all of the same magnificent quality. Tapestries protected the walls like bark. These rooms—rich in books and pictures —had been cultivated like gardens. So far the great conflagration of history had passed them by. Everything was still in its place except the owner, who was either dead or as good as dead, since he had been sent to a camp after all. Friends could not help him.

I was due to leave Lwow by train in a few hours; I was alone.

The November Sunday afternoon soon faded into dusk. I tried to switch on the electric light, but there was no current; I left the switches on. The dusk crept into the corners, gradually all the visible world was transformed into little specks. I lay on a couch as though at the bottom of a great bellglass. The right-hand wall remained distinct longest of all, like a hill emerging from a flood; on that side objects showed up white like the bones of unknown monsters. The Sunday twilight is an hour when time is obliterated, the dead blend with the living, endless cables stretch out into an eternity as familiar as the city of one's youth. That eternity was covered with the dusk like a table-cloth.

I do not know how long I had been letting my thoughts wander when I heard a knock. There was darkness everywhere: in the ante-room, in the hall, on the stairs. The form I let in could see me better than I him, for I was lit up by the last glimmer of daylight through the hall window. I clearly heard my own name uttered. Taking no notice of me, muttering something, the form slipped into the flat. It moved about with all the certainty of a resident, it did not mistake the bathroom door for that of the sitting room, as strangers usually did. Groping for an armchair, the newcomer sat down. I began to search for matches, but in my bewilderment I could not find them. The thatch of white hair, the height, but above all the voice, all indicated something that was quite incredible, yet not very surprising, for we were accustomed to impossibilities happening every day. I was sure that the visitor was none other than Stefan Konecki.

I hung around that armchair without asking a single question, though I felt that I was asking thousands. Time after time I was seized with doubt whether it was really Konecki, more than once his name was on the tip of my tongue, yet something restrained me. At last, in a whisper I suggested that he should lie down. I had the impression that he shook his head. Then in a single breath I got out perhaps twenty questions, not one of which was answered. I bent over the chair, I called to him: not a sound. The light had not yet come on, I could not find the matches, I preferred not to trouble the neighbors. In the long protracted silence I slowly settled down. I waited for the light.

5

Again and again during the past few months I had realized how unjust I had been to this man; I had realized that I had no right to say what I had said to him, that I myself was very much like him and not at all like the imaginary being I had tried to contrast with him. When I had passed into the ghetto fifteen months previously I had had every intention of remaining there. Yet after three days I had come out, I had fled; I had fled ignominiously. I had been unable to hold out for longer than three days. My meeting with the nation had ended in my complete defeat.

The very first person I had seen in the ghetto was a beggar. He was wearing a yellow eiderdown tied round him with hempen rope, his swollen legs protruded from beneath the eiderdown, he had a mug tied to his belly. He made for me as though advancing into empty space. There was no change in the expression of his staring eyes, but his voice rose from a mumble into a wail such as I had never heard before. The immensity of that misery stifled all my capacity for compassion, leaving only horror. When I looked about me I was astonished to note that this creature, whom I found so extraordinary, made no impression at all on anybody else; this tragic circus was full of similar performances. The people did not walk along the streets, they flowed in a crowd like that coming off a train or out of a cinema. Wailing, and solid crowds—these were the two plagues of the ghetto streets. Swarms of beggars chanted passages from the Scriptures, the Psalms, or the latest song-hits in heartrending voices; these were the professional beggars of pre-war days. During the typhus epidemic in the winter of 1941–42 all the poor people in the ghetto died off—but not the professional beggars, who are energetic and resourceful creatures. New poor flowed in from the provinces, dragged out of their homes with only what they were wearing. Condemned to beggary, they stood now along the walls, silent, or asking shame-facedly for alms which no one ever gave them. They, too, died off, to the scorn of the old, brave professionals.

On the third day of my stay in the ghetto, Dr. Braun invited me to a musical evening he had organized. The program was a potpourri of everything from the Psalms to the latest jazz. All through it the Jewish lot sounded the same note. But I could no longer listen to it!

I loathed sacrifice, I loathed the Prophets, I had no use for the Prophets, I did not want shrouds, all I wanted was calm, calm—the calm to be found in any of *their* poorest cobblers, but which is not to be found in any of us. The chariot of Elijah, the mantle of Elijah, the Wailing Wall filled me with repugnance. I just wanted a simple life, that very life which we were most denied. I did not want suffering, those walls were bursting with suffering, with such suffering as is not known by anyone else in the world. I did not want this life beyond all worldly estate, beyond all human capacity. I did not want a mission, I did not want Job; in every house within these walls there was more suffering than in all the Book of Job. In any section of these walled-in streets there was more pain than on the road to

Calvary. The pungent savor of suffering, misery and hopelessness had
been choking me for three days. I had had enough.

Then musicians came on to the platform and with them someone
looking like a penguin—the famous conductor Leon Madry. They
began to play Mozart's *Eine kleine Nachtmusik.*

Of the hundred people gathered in this small, ugly hall with bare
walls, the majority had probably had what we call a good education.
Mozart brought them back the taste of childhood, so dear to all men,
and the taste of their former life, sweet-scented like an apple in May.
Why is it that even men who are completely unmoved by anything
in life weep in the darkened cinema or over a fictitious character in
a novel? Is it not because art strips one of all the hard crust of
ambition, because it acts on man like a purge? Dr. Ignacy Fries, one
of the finest heart specialists in the country, was sitting next to me;
he took his head between his hands as though trying to twist it
right off. He half closed his eyes, and nodded his head in rhythm
with his own inward feelings; he wept. The tears trickled from
under his closed eyelids as though from the lip of a bottle. He was not
the only one weeping: the majority of the audience had their heads
buried in their hands in such a way that it left no doubt of their reactions. Now they wept over Mozart as lately they had wept over
Job. This silky, crystal Mozart, ringing with life, singing with life,
was altogether inconceivable, incompatible with the events of the
world outside. Dr. Ignacy Fries wept without stint.

The orchestra stopped playing, but it remained on the platform.
Dr. Braun came on and recited a poem about Mozart, an old poem of
Konecki's. Dr. Braun had disinterred it, and now he presented it as
proof of the culture of a member of his nation. Dr. Braun thought of
us in general terms, as a critic thinks of authors, as a young girl
thinks of men. For him we were simply Jews, he was not interested
in nuances. Three days earlier I would have thought of this poem
as bastard and alien, but now I accepted it without reservation as
my own. Dr. Braun could not have sealed my reconciliation with
Konecki more perfectly. Next day, I fled.

I had not been fair to Konecki; there were many things I had not
understood. I had not known that it was ever so: the Jews were a
nation with whom one could do anything. *Die ewigen Verlierer*—the
everlasting losers—as the Germans said. Wise Jews? Where were the
wise Jews? More and more I was coming to see that true wisdom is
to avoid getting into a hopeless situation. But our position has always
been hopeless. To be at the mercy of all other men's humor and ill-
humor: what a bitter fate! To have to meet the expenses of all human
history! To be the first to pay, and never cease to pay! But if one or

the other of us doesn't want to? But if one or another simply does not feel strong enough to meet that bill?

Stefan Konecki's famous 1922 article had been the outburst of a young man. I do not deserve unqualified confidence as a commentator on Konecki's pronouncements and conduct. He had adopted a pseudonym because he wanted others to forget, because he could not endure the harshness of his own inward essence; he did not feel strong enough, and besides, he was afraid of *them.* Like most men, he was afraid of want. What a profound joy I had sensed in him that day when he told me he was about to go into the country! "Trees! I shall be among trees!" Yet it was not a question of trees, but of experiencing a different fate. He did not wish to return to us, he did not desire our lot. Unlike me, he was old enough to know what it meant. History! We bleed to death in order to understand something that those before us understood perfectly.

Was Konecki the only one to fear that cross? How about myself? If I am to be honest, should I not confess that something similar had happened to me too? The never-drying sea of suffering in that Jewish district spread its fetid breath far over the city, even before the war. Whenever I had crossed Bielanska Street to plunge into the ghetto I had always felt my heart constrict. And when that day I had waited to pass inside the walls I had recalled that I was not trembling for the first time, that our Jewish cross had always terrified me. Me like others.

But was that entirely true? Did the great German star turn which brought millions to a horrible death smother all links with the nation in those who survived?

I distributed money to those who were in hiding, and I knew how they were feeling. One man said he would leave Poland, he would go to the other end of the world if necessary, but even at the end of the world he would not start using his Jewish name again or take up his Jewish nationality. Another said that after the war the very word "Jew" would be forbidden in his home together with all bad language. But I also came across men and women who looked forward to the end of this era of assumed Christian surnames. When the ghetto went up in flames and the Germans surpassed all bounds in their bestiality I was regularly calling on a certain shopkeeper who baked matzos and made me distribute them among his family. I knew another shopkeeper who put on the phylactery and prayer-shawl for prayers every morning. I knew a woman who had a casual, almost haphazard habit of lighting the Sabbath eve candles every Friday evening. There was one couple I knew for whom I simply had to get hold of a Mohel, because they insisted that their newly born son must be properly circumcised.

I understood nothing. I saw only one thing: those who had to be burnt, were burnt; those left alive continued in their former ways of life. Did I find this true only by observing others? As I studied my own feelings I realized that I, too, preferred those hiding wretches to the others. But why? Tell me, why?

One day I went into a stationer's to buy some Christmas cards. Two youngsters were sitting on a couple of chairs inside: She was eighteen, he was possibly twenty. One glance at them, and there was a flash of lightning: in all three pairs of eyes flashed the one thought: Hunted beings sensing other hunted beings. I bought my cards and went out on their heels. Only then could I see all their wretchedness. He was tall and thin, and walked with a limp; he was wearing canvas shoes and a wretched raincoat, his trousers were in rags. She was dressed just as poorly; her ragged coat seemed to be hanging over a post; her stockings had fallen down over her summer sandals. They wanted to buy some apples and passed from stall to stall, but they could not find any cheap enough. As I followed them I trembled: supposing one of the women stallkeepers, not through any ill will, but simply annoyed because they were handling her apples, let fly at them with her tongue; for after all they did look like . . . In my suddenly quickened love I realized that one is naturally restricted to one's own people, that it is from them first and foremost that a man draws his sustenance.

There was still no sound in the room, and the darkness was now so deep that the form began to fade into the dusk.

"Is it you?" I cried like a little child.

Once more I received no answer.

6

Konecki had left Lwow even before my own departure for the Warsaw ghetto. An Aryan land-owning friend had given him shelter on his estate. After three months the place grew dangerous, it was rumored that it was "to be smoked out," and the landowner took Konecki to Warsaw, where his family undertook to look after him. The bracing Warsaw air revived Konecki; he ran about the town without heeding the warnings. One day as he was turning a street corner he felt someone's eyes fixed on him. He had forgotten why certain people might stare at him, he had forgotten it so completely that he went back, intending to call on someone in a street he had already passed. Two ruffians fastened on him. The taller of them held out his hand, which Konecki confidently took, convinced the man was some old acquaintance he had failed to recognize. "We know each other," the ruffian muttered, "from the other side," he pointed in the direction of the ghetto. Only now did Konecki understand. He shouted that he hadn't any time for idle talk, he had turned back to look for someone; and he hurried away, leaving the two blackmailers standing. He would have escaped, but instead of hurrying off as fast as possible he began to check the house numbers, presumably to give his story verisimilitude. The blackmailers went up to him again. The tall man said angrily: "If you've got nothing to be afraid of come along to the police with us, and they'll examine you." "All right, all right!" "All right or not, come along. We haven't any time to waste. It doesn't make any difference to us, as they pay us by the head." Konecki seriously thought of trying to resist them. Then he changed his mind and was prepared to go to the police station, but the next moment he tried to bargain with them. They demanded ten thousand zlotys. The tall man said: "I can't do it any cheaper. I do my job and move on. When the Russians come you'll get it all back out of me. You've all got money for your business expenses. We haven't time to play about. Either you find the money or we go to the police." The other man was just as impatient. At last they pushed him into a gateway, stripped him of his coat and sweater, took his notecase with a thousand zlotys in it, and in all probability would have let him go.

They had just finished stripping him when a pock-marked secret agent who specialized in racial matters came down the stairs, together with a small, fair-haired girl. "What you have got," he said to the blackmailers, "you can keep; now I'll take charge of him." He struck Konecki again and again in the face, shouting: I'll go on smashing you till the end! My brother, this child's father, was murdered only today. And you're the murderers. You're paying money for our people to be murdered. You're the cause of it all! You provoked the war. You'll go to the Gestapo this very day. . . ."

Konecki spent the night in the police station, for prisoners were sent to the Gestapo only in batches. After the pock-marked man had gone another secret agent took Konecki out of the cell and asked whether there was anyone who would be prepared to buy him out. "Here's a telephone you can use, no one will listen, we're a decent lot. If you like you can write a note, we'll send it out, and you won't bring trouble on anyone, you needn't be afraid. That pock-marked fellow's a devil for his job, but I don't want to see anyone done in, we're all mortal." To his own surprise Konecki declared there was no one who could help him, though he had intended to say something quite different. "Well, I'm sorry for you," the agent said, "but in that case you'll have to be a 'result.' We have to supply the Gestapo with a certain number of heads, we have to show results. And we send them those who can't get bought out."

At Gestapo headquarters it came out that the Lwow department was wanting Konecki. So he was sent to Lwow. But *Obersturmführer* Wendlandt, who had been wanting him had long since left the city. His successor considered whether he should dispose of Konecki at once or send him to one of the camps outside the town (which was as good as death). He chose the second course. All these details of Konecki's fate had been told me by Dr. Braun, who had his own intelligence service.

The light came on and suddenly flooded the room. The man seated before me looked—my God!—as though taken out of his own tomb. An owl, a terrified owl! His eyes followed me about as a shot bird watches the hunter. His body was wrapped in a sack, as peasant women wrap themselves in a rug; he was wearing drawers; the big toe of one bare foot was scratching the other like a dog scratching himself; I could not tear my eyes away from that big toe. Under the shock of milky-white hair lurked a face inanimate and withered, but even darker than of old; that swarthiness could never be washed off, it was the true sign of the curse! And this figure was the great Stefan Konecki! And he stank. Stank like the inmates of the death camps, like so many other victims of those times. Before me I saw the uttermost depths of misery.

Now something Walega had told me before he left took on meaning. He had said that the prisoners in a camp outside Lwow had risen in revolt, knowing only too well what awaited them. In the struggle some had perished on the spot, others had been shot afterwards. Only a few escaped from the massacre, exactly how many was not known. When night fell they had flung off the dead bodies which had been their salvation and had crept away. They were naked. They knocked at cottage doors. No one opened to them; no peasant ever opened his door at night, unless he were threatened with a rifle; often even a rifle was insufficient. They stood outside the windows and called for help, for pity. Some rags were thrown out to them, and they pulled them around their bodies. When dawn came they separated, reckoning they had more chance if each went alone. One of the group reached Lwow, sought out Walega, and told him all the story. Walega did not wish to get me agitated before my journey, so he had done no more than hint at "an acquaintance of ours who took part in the revolt and probably had perished...."

But Konecki had not perished. After these adventures he had been drawn to his home as a wounded animal is drawn to its lair. And now he was sitting in his luxurious flat, with its carpets as lush as duckweed on sunless ponds, with its rooms cultivated as carefully as gardens. He huddled down, overtaken by the fate which he had dreaded all his life.

I stood in front of this human rag, I bent over him, I called first quietly, then louder, anxious to extract at least one word from this shattered creature. Stefan Konecki moved his lips, his jaws worked— all in vain; he could not say a word. After a while I noticed that his face, which was turned to the door, began to thaw out; something distantly akin to a smile blossomed over it. Now at last I heard the voice that I longed so much to hear—he started to sing. Stefan Konecki was crooning an old Jewish song, a Yiddish melody, recognizable as such even at the ends of the world; such songs were commonly sung in the death-camps. And as he began to sing I had a feeling that someone was at the door. I turned round. A Ukrainian militia-man was standing there.

"Jude!" he said to me, pointing to the great Stefan Konecki, the famous pseudonym of Polish literature during Poland's second independence.

"Jude!" he repeated, and laughed coarsely.

From *Ascent to Heaven,* Roy Publishers, New York, 1951.
Translated by H. C. STEVENS

Bruno Schulz

(1892–1942)

One of the most original Polish writers of this century, Bruno Schulz was born in Drohobycz in 1892. This modest art teacher at the Drohobycz secondary school startled the literary world with his collection of short stories, *The Cinnamon Shops* (1934) and *Sanatorium Under the Hourglass* (1937). These were followed by *Comet* (1938).

In 1963 a collection of short stories was published in England under the title *Cinnamon Shops*; it appeared in the U.S.A. as *The Street of Crocodiles*.

Although most of his stories portray life in Drohobycz, Schulz is a commentator on the contemporary world and its apparent contradictions. His is a distorted, Kafkaesque universe, in which the "father" hero of his novels, the author of the derisive "Treatise on Mannequins" heralds the ultimate catastrophe of mankind in the brave new world. Drohobycz, which was close to some newly discovered oil fields, was a confused place, where modern industrial civilization sprang up beside an almost obsolete patriarchal one. His heroes are ordinary men destroyed by the new world of mannequins. They are deprived of their final illusions and hopes, and they suffer defeat. They are irretrievably lost. But the mannequin-man cannot be happy either, for he is merely a mechanism of utmost precision, devoid of any spiritual life, and he cannot distinguish between a state of happiness and its opposite. And the progress of this mechanical man is bound to result in the end of the world.

This new world which he feared and abhorred so much proved destructive to Schulz himself. He was killed by the Nazis in a Galician ghetto—a prophetic enactment of the macabre and frightening world which he dreaded so much.

Cinnamon Shops

BIRDS

Those thoroughly dull yellowish winter days had come. The reddish earth was covered with a riddled, threadbare and inadequate mantle of snow. There was not enough for all the rooftops and black or rust-colored tiling and shingles to secrete the sooty expanse of garrets, black cathedrals, bristling with rib-like rafters and girders, the dark lungs of wintry gales. Each dawn uncovered new chimneys and vent-holes that sprang up during the night, magnified by nocturnal gusts —black pipes of the devil's organs. In the evening the chimney-sweeps could not scare off the crows which, like vivid black leaves, perched on the branches of trees near the church, took wing and fluttered about, finally to roost again, each in its proper place, on its proper branch. At dawn they flew away in great flocks—clouds of soot, flakes of smut, undulating and fantastic, staining with their glittering crowing the hazy yellow streaks of dawn. The days became hardened from cold and boredom, like last year's loaf of bread. They were cut into with dull knives, without appetite, with lazy drowsiness.

Father no longer left the house. He fired the stoves, studied the inscrutable essence of fire, sensed the salty, metallic flavor and smoky odor of winter flames, the cool caresses of salamanders, licking the shiny soot in the chimney's throat. During these days he passionately performed all the repairs in the upper regions of the room. He could be seen at all times of the day as he squatted on the topmost rung of the ladder and manipulated something near the ceiling, near the cornices of the tall windows, by the weights and chains of the hanging lamps. He used the ladder in the way painters do, like huge stilts, and felt good in this bird's-eye view, close to the painted heaven, the arabesque and birds on the ceiling. More and more he withdrew from the practical matters of life. When mother, filled with concern and worry because of his state, attempted to draw him into a conversation about business, about the settling of the latest note due, he heard her out with distraction, full of uneasiness, with a twitching in his vacant face. It also happened that he would interrupt her with a sudden imploring gesture of the hands in order to run to the corner of the room, place his ear to a crack in the floor and with raised index fingers of both hands expressing concentrated examination—listen. At that time we did not yet comprehend the sad background of these extravaganzas, the grievous complexes which were maturing in him.

Mother had no influence over him; on the other hand he paid great respect and attention to Adela. The cleaning of the room was for him a great and important ceremony which he never neglected to witness, following all of Adela's manipulations with a mixture of fear and a voluptuous shudder. He ascribed deeper, symbolic meaning to all her activities. When the girl with her young and bold movements pushed the long-handled brush across the floor it was almost beyond his endurance. Tears then flowed from his eyes, his face convulsed with laughter and his body shook with an orgiastic spasm. His sensitivity to tickling reached the heights of frenzy. It sufficed for Adela to move a finger as if to titillate him, and he would at once race in a panic through all the rooms, slamming doors behind, until finally in the last room he would tumble on the bed and writhe in convulsions of laughter under the influence of the very prospect, without being able to stop. Thanks to this, Adela had practically an unlimited reign over father.

It was then that we noticed in him, for the first time, a passionate interest in animals. At first this was the passion of both a hunter and artist; perhaps it went even deeper, a zoological sympathy of a creature for its kin, for different forms of life, experimentation in untested fields of existence. It was only in the later phase that the matter took on an uncanny, complicated, profoundly sinful and unnatural turn which it is better not to drag out into the light of day.

It began with the hatching of birds' eggs.

At great cost in effort and money father imported from Hamburg, Holland and from African zoological stations fertilized birds' eggs for which he used large Belgian hens as brooders. This was a most fascinating procedure for me—the hatching of the fledglings, true freaks in shape and color. It was impossible to recognize in these monsters with huge, fantastic beaks which opened wide immediately after birth to hiss ravenously with their gaping throats—in these lizards with weak, naked hunchback bodies—the future peacocks, pheasants, woodcocks and condors. Placed in baskets with cotton wool, this dragon's brood reared blind, film-covered heads on skinny necks, noiselessly quacking from mute throats. In a green apron like a gardener in a hothouse with cacti, my father paced the length of the shelves and out of nothingness wheedled these veiled eyes, pulsing with life, these indolent bellies accepting the outside world only in the form of food, this excrescence of life pushing gropingly towards the light. A few weeks later when the blind buds of life burst forth into the light, the room became filled with a colorful, flashing, chirping tumult of its new tenants. They perched on the valances of the curtains, the edges of cupboards, nested in the zinc branches and arabesques of the multi-branched hanging lamps.

When father studied the large ornithological compendium and looked through colored tables it seemed that feathery fantasies flew right out of them and filled the room with their bright flapping, splashes of purple, smears of sapphire, moss green and silver. During feeding time they created colorful wavy flower-beds on the floor, a live carpet of which with someone's careless entrance fell apart, scattered into mobile flowers, rising into the air to finally settle down in the upper regions of the room. One particular condor has remained in my memory, a huge bird with a naked neck, a wrinkled face covered with warts. This was a thin ascetic, a Buddhist lama, full of undaunted dignity in its entire behavior, governed by the rigid ceremonial of its great race. When he sat opposite father immobile in his monumental posture of immemorial Egyptian gods, with his eyes drawn by a whitish lid which moved over the pupil from the side, in order to close completely in the contemplation of his honorable solitude—his stony profile seemed to be my father's older brother. The same quality of flesh, the lined and wrinkled hard skin, the same dry and bony face, the same deep eye sockets. Even my father's hands, strong in the joints, with long, thin palms and convex nails, were analogous to the condor's claws. I could not shake off the impression, seeing him thus asleep, that I had before me a mummy, a wizened and hence smaller mummy of my father. I believe that my mother was also aware of this strange resemblance even though we never raised the subject. It is characteristic that the condor used a joint bedpan with my father.

Not content with hatching more and more new species of birds, my father arranged a birds' wedding in the attic. He sent out matchmakers, imprisoning in nooses and holes in the attic attractive, lonely fiancées and thus brought it about that the roof of our house, a large, double standing, shingled roof, became a real birds' hotel, a Noah's ark to which all types of winged beings from far-off places flocked. Even long after the liquidation of this birds' inn the world of birds maintained the tradition, and during their spring migrations entire clouds of cranes, pelicans, peacocks and other birds often swooped down on our roof.

After a short-lived splendor this affair, however, took a sad turn. It soon became evident that it was necessary for father to change his location to the two rooms in the attic which were used for storing junk. Already from early dawn could be heard the varied clamor of birds' voices coming from there. The wooden box-like rooms in the attic, aided by the acoustics of the roof's expanse, resounded from the rustling, crowing, quacking, and clucking. Thus we lost father from sight for a space of a few weeks. He seldom came down to the apartment, and then we noticed that he became thinner and shrunken. Sometimes, through forgetfulness, he would lunge out of the chair by the table and, flapping his arms as though they were wings, let out a prolonged crowing and his eyes became covered by a misty film. Then, embarrassed, he laughed together with us and attempted to turn the incident into a joke.

Once, during a period of general house-cleaning Adela appeared unexpectedly in father's bird kingdom. She stood at the door and wrung her hands in despair over the stench which rose in the air and the piles of manure lying on the floor, table and furniture. She quickly decided to open the window, after which with the aid of a long brush, she sent the entire mass of birds into flight. Up rose a hellish cloud of feathers, wings and screams in which Adela, resembling a mad maenad, hidden in her whirling, danced a dance of destruction. Together with the flock my father flapped his arms and in fright tried to rise in the air. Slowly the winged cloud thinned out until finally there remained on the battlefield only Adela—exhausted, winded—and my father with a worried and embarrassed expression, was ready to accept any capitulation.

A while later he came down the stairs from his domain—a broken man, a banished king who had lost his throne and kingdom.

The Mannequins

My father's ornithological show was the last outburst of color, the final and brilliant countermarch of fantasy which this incorrigible improviser, this master of originality conducted against the ramparts and trenches of the barren and empty winter. Today I understand the lonely heroism with which he declared war on that boundless element of boredom benumbing this city. Deprived of all support, without appreciation on our part, this strange man defended the lost cause of poetry. He was a wonderful mill into which poured the bran of empty hours so that the spices of the East in all their colors and aromas should blossom in its wheels. But accustomed to the amazing juggling of this metaphysical prestidigitator, we were prone to become acquainted with the value of his sovereign magic which rescued us from the lethargy of empty days and nights. Adela was not reproached for her thoughtless and stupid vandalism. On the contrary, we felt some sort of base pleasure, an ignoble satisfaction from the curbing of these exuberances which we greedily savored to satiety only to perfidiously evade responsibility for them afterward. In this betrayal there was perhaps secret homage to victorious Adela to whom we vaguely ascribed some sort of assignment and mission of strength of a higher order. Betrayed by everyone, father retreated without a struggle from the place of his former glory. Without crossing swords he surrendered to the empty room at the end of the hall and entrenched himself there with loneliness.

We forgot him.

Again we were enveloped on all sides by the mournful grayness of the city, blossoming in the windows in a dark tatter of dawn, a parasitic fungus of twilights extending into a downy fur of long wintry nights. The wallpaper of rooms, loosened blissfully in the former days and accessible to the colored flight of that winged crowd, now became closed within themselves, dourly enmeshed in the monotony of bitter monologues.

The lamps blackened and faded like old thistles and weeds now hung listlessly and sorrowfully, quietly tinkling their crystal pendants when someone groped his way across the half-darkened room. In vain Adela stuck colored candles into all the holders of these lamps, inept substitutes, pale reminders of the bright illumination which blossomed forth from their recent hanging gardens. Oh, where was that warbling budding, that hasty and fantastic maturing in the bouquets of those lamps from which, as from bursting enchanted pastries, flew the winged fantasies, shattering the air into decks of magic cards, showering them in a colored applause; falling in thick flakes of peacock azure, parrot green, metallic sheens; drawing lines and arabesques in the air, flashing traces of flight in a lavish and sparkling atmosphere? Even now hidden in the gray aura, were the echoes and possibilities of colorful flashes but no one stirred or twisted through the stuffy layers of air.

Those weeks became strangely sleepy.

Beds unmade all day long, stacked with bedding wrinkled and crumpled from heavy sleep, stood like deep ships ready to sail into the wet and complicated labyrinth of some black, starless Venice. At early dawn Adela brought us coffee. We dressed lazily in the cold rooms by candlelight reflected many times over in the black window-panes. These mornings were full of disorderly bustle, extensive searching in various drawers and cupboards. The whole house resounded with the flopping of Adela's slippers. The shop assistants lit the lanterns, took from mother the large store keys and went off into the thick, swirling darkness. Mother could not manage her toilet. The candles in the candlesticks began to die out. Adela vanished somewhere in the outlying rooms or in the attic where she hung clothes to dry. It was impossible to call to her. The freshly laid but hazy and dirty fire in the stove licked the cold, shiny layers of soot in the chimney's throat. The candles became extinguished, the room was plunged in darkness.

Only half-dressed, with our heads resting on the tablecloth amid the breakfast leftovers, we kept falling asleep. Lying with our faces on the furry belly of darkness, we floated away on its undulating breath into a starless void. We were awakened by Adela's vigorous cleaning. Mother could not manage her toilet. Before she finished combing, the assistants returned for dinner. The haze on the market place took on the color of golden smoke. In a moment these opaque honeys, these misty ambers could usher in the loveliest of afternoon colors. But the happy moment passed, the amalgam of dawn faded, the swollen ferment of day, almost attained, fell back into helpless grayness. We sat down at the table; the assistants chafed their redcold hands and suddenly the prose of their conversation introduced immediately the full day, gray and empty Tuesday, a day without tradition, amorphous. But when the platter of fish in vitreous aspic arrived at the table, two

large fish side by side, head to tail like figures of the zodiac, we
recognized in them the escutcheon of that day, the emblem of a nameless Tuesday in the calendar, and we quickly portioned them off between us, relieved that in it the day achieved its physiognomy.

The assistants consumed it with unction, with respect to the
calendarial ceremony. The aroma of pepper wafted through the room.
And when they mopped up the remains of the aspic with the bread,
contemplating the heraldry of the following days of the week, and
only the heads with their boiled eyes were left on the platter—we all
felt that the day was defeated by joint forces, and that the rest of the
day no longer mattered.

In effect, Adela, with the rest of the day at her disposal, did not
go in for pomp. Amid the clatter of pots and the splash of cold water,
she energetically liquidated those few hours remaining to twilight
which mother dozed away on the couch. In the meantime the dining
room was already being prepared for the evening scene. Polda and
Pauline, two seamstresses, made themselves comfortable here with
the requisites of their profession. Into the room they carried a silent
immobile woman, a lady of horsehair and cloth with a black knob instead of a head. But once placed in the corner between the door and
stove, this quiet lady became mistress of the situation. From where
she stood, motionless, she supervised in silence the work of the girls.
With full criticism and displeasure she accepted their efforts and
courting which they offered kneeling before her, measuring the parts
of the dress marked with white basting. With attention and patience
they served the silent idol which nothing could satisfy. This Moloch
was unrelenting as only female deities can be and always kept sending
them back to work anew, and they, spindle-shaped and slender like
the wooden spools from which they unwound thread, and as dexterous
as spools, manipulated with graceful movements over the pile of silk
and cloth. They snipped into the colorful mass, whirled the machine,
pressing the pedal with a cheap, patent-leathered foot and around
them rose the heap of remnants, vari-colored shreds and scraps like
spat-out shells and chaff around two fastidious and wasteful parrots.
The uneven jaws of the shears opened with a squeak like the beaks of
those colorful birds.

The girls trod carelessly over the variegated cuttings, wading unconsciously as though in the rubbish heap at some carnival, in the
junk pile of some large, unrealized masquerade. They shook themselves free of the scraps with nervous laughter, titillating the mirror
with their eyes. Their souls, the swift magic of their hands was not
in the irksome dresses which they found on the table but in these
hundreds of snippings, in the frivolous and giddy scraps with which
they could shower the whole town like a fantastically colored snow-

storm. Suddenly they were warm and opened the window so that in the impatience of their loneliness in the hunger for strange faces at least to get a look of some anonymous face pressed against the window. In front of the fluttering curtains they fanned their heated cheeks by the night cold, unveiled their inflamed bosoms full of hatred for themselves and rivalry, prepared to stand battle for that Pierrot which the cold night breezes might blow to the window. Oh, how little they demanded of reality. They had everything within themselves, they had a surplus of everything within themselves. Oh, they would have been satisfied with a Pierrot stuffed with sawdust; just one or two words for which they had long since waited, to be able to slip into their role prepared long ago, ready to come forth full of sweet and terrible bitterness, wildly stimulating like the pages of a romance swallowed at night along with tears shed on blushing cheeks.

During one of his evening meanderings over the flat whilst Adela was absent, my father came across this quiet nocturnal séance. With lamp in hand, he stood for a moment in the dark doorway of the neighboring room, enchanted by this feverish flushed scene, that idyl of powder, colored tissue and atropine for which the winter night, breathing amid the billowing curtains, served as a meaningful setting. Putting on his spectacles, he drew a few steps closer and circled the girls, illuminating them with the raised lamp in his hand. The draft from the open door billowed the curtains; the young ladies allowed themselves to be inspected, turning at the hips, shining with the enamel of their eyes, the polish of their squeaking shoes, the clasps of the garters showing under the dresses billowing from the wind. The scraps began to scurry across the floor like rats towards the opened door of the dark room, and my father carefully observed the racing creatures, whispering softly . . . "genus avium . . . if I am not mistaken . . . Scansores of pistacci . . . most worthy of attention."

This accidental meeting became the beginning of a whole series of séances during which my father managed to quickly enchant both young ladies by the charm of his strange personality. In reward for conversations replete with gallantry and wit which filled up their empty evenings, the girls allowed the enthusiastic researcher to study the structure of their lean and flimsy bodies. This took place in the course of the conversation which, because of its seriousness and purity, deprived the examination of the most risqué parts of any ambiguous pretense. Removing the stocking off Pauline's knee and with loving eyes studying the concise and noble construction of the joint, my father said, "How charming and how fortunate is the form of existence which you ladies have chosen. How beautiful and straight is the thesis which your life is allowed to reveal. But besides that with

what mastery, with what finesse you go about fulfilling your task.
If I were to cast aside respect for the Creator and should wish to
indulge in a criticism of creation; I should shout—less content, more
form! Oh, how this decrease of content would relieve the world.
More modesty in intentions, more moderation in claims—gentlemen
Demiurges, and the world would be better!" exclaimed my father
precisely when his palm bared Pauline's white thigh from the con-
fining stocking. At this moment Adela stood in the open dining room
door, carrying a tray with afternoon tea. This was the first meeting
of these two forces since the great encounter. All of us who attended
this meeting experienced a moment of great fear. It was most painful
to witness a new humiliation of a man who had already suffered so
much. My father rose from his knees very confused, wave after wave
colored his face ever darker with the influx of embarrassment. But
Adela was unexpectedly up to the situation. She approached father
with a smile and tweaked his nose. At this signal Polda and Pauline
happily clapped their hands, stamped their feet and, hanging on
father's both arms, danced round the table with him. Thus, thanks to
the good heart of these girls, the beginning of an unpleasant conflict
was dispelled in general gaiety.

This now was the start of many interesting and strange talks
which my father, inspired by the charm of that small and innocent
audience delivered during the following weeks of that early winter.

It is worth noting how, in coming into contact with this unusual person, all things somehow reverted to the root of their existence, restored their appearances to the metaphysical nucleus, somehow returned to their primeval idea so as to foreswear it at this point
and incline it towards those doubtful, risky and ambiguous regions
which we here briefly call regions of great heresy. Our heretic moved
amid things like a magnetizer, infecting and seducing them with his
perilous charm. Should I also name Pauline his victim? In those days
she became his pupil, a disciple of his theory, a model of his experiments.

Here, avoiding all bitterness, and with proper caution, I shall
attempt to relay those extreme heretical doctrines which at that
time enmeshed father for many months and dominated all his deeds.

A Treatise on Mannequins or the Second
Book of Genesis

"Demiurge," my father said, "did not possess a monopoly on creation
—creation is the privilege of all spirits. Matter has limitless fertility,
inexhaustible vital force and, simultaneously, a seductive power of

temptation which entices us to form. In the depths of matter indistinct smiles take shape, tensions arise, attempts at shapes take form. All of matter undulates with endless possibilities which pass through it in nauseating tremors. In awaiting the animating breath of the spirit it flows within itself unceasingly, it tempts with the thousands of sweet circles and softnesses which in its blind fancies it exacts from itself.

"Deprived of its own initiative, voluptuously susceptible, womanly plaint, it succumbs to all impulses—it constitutes a field barred to law, open to all types of charlatanism and dilettantism, a domain for all abuses and doubtful demiurgic manipulations. Matter is the most passive and defenseless thing in the cosmos. Anyone can knead it, shape it; it is obedient to all. All organization of matter is unstable and loose, easy to retrogress and dissolve. There is no evil in reducing life to other and new forms. Killing is not a sin. It is often a necessary violence against stubborn and ossified forms of existence which have ceased to be attractive. In the cause of an interesting and important experiment it can even be a service. This is the starting point for a new apology of sadism."

My father was inexhaustible in his glorification of that strange element which is matter. "There is no dead matter," he expounded, "death is only a phase behind which are hidden unknown forms of life. The scale of these forms is endless and the shadings and nuances infinite. Demiurge possessed important and interesting recipes for creation. Thanks to them a multitude of varieties were created replenishing themselves by main force. It is not known whether these formulas will ever be reconstructed. But this is unnecessary, since even if these classical methods of creation proved once and for all to be inaccessible, there remain certain illegal ones, a whole gamut of heretical and unlawful methods."

As my father proceeded from these general cosmogonic principles to the field of his narrower interests, his voice shrank to a penetrating whisper, the exposition became ever more difficult and involved and the results to which he led became lost in the more and more doubtful and risky regions. His gesticulation took on esoteric solemnity. He half shut one eye, placed two fingers to the forehead; the craftiness of his glances became simply uncanny; he bored into his listeners with this cunning, he seduced the most bashful, the most intimate reserves in them with the cynicism of his stare, and reached into the deepest, most evasive niches, pushed against the wall and tickled, scratched with an ironic finger until he unearthed a spark of understanding and laughter, laughter of admission and agreement with which in the end one capitulated.

The girls sat motionless, the lamp smoked, the fabric under the machine's needle slipped to the ground long ago and it rattled on empty, stitching the black starless cloth that unrolled from the cloth of the winter night outside the window.

"Too long have we lived under the terror of the matchless perfection of Demiurge," said my father, "too long have the achievements of his creation paralyzed our own creativeness. We do not want to compete with him. We do not have the ambition to emulate him. We want to be creators in our own, lower spheres, we desire creativeness for ourselves, we crave the joy of creation—we desire, in brief— demiurgism." I do not know in whose name my father proclaimed those postulates, what collective, what corporation, sect or order, lent its solidarity to the paths of his words. As to us, we were far from demiurgic temptations.

But meantime my father was solving the program of this second creation, a picture of this second genesis of beings which were to stand in overt opposition to the ruling epoch. "We are not concerned," he said, "with beings that possess long breathing, or creatures for the distant future. Our creatures will not be heroes of romances of many volumes. Their role will be short, succinct, their character without further plans. Often for one gesture, for one word we undertake the work of bringing them to life for that one moment. We frankly admit: we will not place emphasis on durability or good workmanship: our creatures will be as though provisional, made for only a single time. If they be people, we shall give them, for example, only one side of the face, one hand, one leg, specifically that which they will need in their role. It would be pedantry to show concern about the other leg which does not count. In the back they can be simply sewn of cloth or ticking. We will place our ambition in the proud device: an actor for every gesture. To the servicing of every word, every deed, we shall evoke another man. Such is our taste, perfected and complicated matters, we give precedence to shoddiness. It simply attracts us; we are fascinated by cheapness, shabbiness, tawdriness of material. Do you understand," my father asked, "the profound sense of this weakness, this passion for speckled tissue, for papier-mâché, for enamel paints, horsehair and sawdust? This is," he said with a painful smile, "our mystical consistence. Demiurge, that great master and artist, renders it invisible, orders it to disappear under the play-acting of life. We, on the contrary, love its clashing, its resistance, its clownish awkwardness. We like to see in every gesture, in every difficult undertaking its helplessness, its sweet bearishness."

The girls sat motionless with glassy eyes. Their faces were drawn and stupefied with listening, their cheeks painted with blushes, it was difficult to determine at the moment whether they belonged to the first or second generation of beings.

"In a word," concluded my father, "we want to create man for the second time in the image and likeness of a mannequin."

In order to keep our records straight, we must at this point describe a small and trifling incident which occurred at this point in the talk and to which we do not attach any weight. This incident, completely incomprehensible and senseless in this series of events, can perhaps only be explained as a certain type of partial automatism without antecedents and succession, as a certain type of malice toward the object transferred to the psychic sphere. We advise the reader to ignore it with the same nonchalance as we have. This is the course it took.

The moment my father uttered the word "mannequin," Adela glanced at her wrist-watch, after which she threw a knowing glance to Polda. Now she moved herself with the chair, a foot forward, picked up the hem of her dress, slid out her foot swathed in black silk and stretched it taut like a serpent's head.

Thus she sat during this entire scene, completely rigid with large, fluttery eyes, deepened by the azure of atropine, with Polda and Pauline on either side. All three stared at father wide-eyed. My father cleared his throat, fell silent, bowed and suddenly turned very red. In one moment the lines of his face, so recently vivacious and vibrant, became subdued, submissive features.

He, an inspired heretic, barely set free from the whirlwind of emotion, suddenly gave way, collapsed and retreated. Perhaps he was exchanged for someone else. This other sat stiffly very red, with downcast eyes. Miss Polda came up and leaned over him. Patting him lightly on the shoulder, she spoke in a soothing, encouraging tone: "Let Jacob be sensible. Let Jacob listen, don't be stubborn. . . . Now, please, Jacob, Jacob."

Adela's protruding slipper quivered lightly and sparkled like a serpent's tongue. My father rose slowly with downcast eyes, took a step forward like an automat and slid to his knees. The lamp hissed in the silence, knowing looks ran to and fro, in the thicket of the wallpaper flew the whispers of vicious tongues, zigzags of thoughts.

The following evening father took up his dark and complicated subject with renewed fluency. The lines of his wrinkles unfolded and folded with refined shrewdness. In each spiral there was hidden the missile of irony. But now and then inspiration broadened the circles of his wrinkles, which grew with a great whirling threat, flowing in silent volutes into the depth of the winter night.

"The panoptic figures, dear ladies," he began, "are the tormented parodies of mannequins, but even in that form beware of treating them lightly. Matter knows no jesting. It is always full of tragic seriousness. Who dares to think that matter can be jested with, that it can be treated as a joke, that the joke does not become embedded in it, that it does not corrode like fate, like destiny? Do you have an inkling of the pain, the mute suffering, unreleased, the torture of this dummy imprisoned in matter who does not know wherefore she is, why she must survive in this violently imposed form, being a parody? Can you conceive the might of expression, form, semblance, of this tyrannical willfulness with which he throws himself on this defenseless clod and dominates it as his own, tyrannical, imperious soul? You bestow upon some head made of hair and cloth the expression of anger and you leave it once and for all with that anger, with that convulsion, with that strain locked with blind anger for which there is no escape. The crowd laughs at parody, my ladies, over your own fate, seeing the misery of imprisoned matter, oppressed matter which does not know what it is or why it is, where this gesture leads, which has been given it once and for all.

"The crowd laughs. Do you understand the terrible, intoxicating sadism, the demiurgic cruelty of this laughter? For, after all, my ladies, it is necessary to cry over the fate of this miserable matter, this violated matter against which terrible crimes have been committed. From here stems, my ladies, the terrible sorrow of all clownish Golems, all clowns tragically contemplating their funny grimace.

"Here is the anarchist Luccheni, murderer of Empress Elizabeth, here is Draga, the demonic and ill-fated queen of Serbia, and here the clever youth, the family pride and hope who perished due to the unfortunate habit of onanism. Oh, irony of those names, those semblances.

"Is there indeed something of Queen Draga in this dummy, her replica, at least the farthest shadow of her being? This resemblance, this semblance, this name silences us and does not allow us to ask what is the unfortunate creation to its own self. This must, however, be someone, my ladies, someone anonymous, someone menacing, someone unhappy, someone who never in their dull life has heard about Queen Draga.

"Have you heard at night the frightening wail of those wax dummies locked in the market stalls, the mournful chorus of those torsos of wood and porcelain beating their fists against the wall of their prison?"

My father's face, agitated by the dread matters he conjured out of the darkness, became a whirlpool of wrinkles, a funnel reaching down into the depths, at the bottom of which there kindled the ominous eye of the prophet. His beard bristled strangely. The wisps and tufts of hair darting from the warts, the moles, and nostrils bristled at their roots. Thus he stood stiffly with feverish, eyes, trembling from inner emotion, like an automat which began and stopped at a dead point.

Adela rose from the chair and asked us to shut our eyes to that which would occur in a moment. Then she went up to father and with her hands on her hips, assuming a very decided appearance, spoke emphatically. . . .

The ladies sat stiffly, in a strange rigidness, with lowered eyes.

A Treatise on Mannequins (Conclusion)

One of the following evenings my father continued his dissertation with the following words:

"It is not about these embodied misunderstandings, not about the sad parodies, my ladies, the fruit of common and vulgar intemperance that I wanted to speak in my talking about mannequins. I had something else in mind."

Here my father began to build before our eyes a picture of that "generatio aequivoca" dreamed up by him, some sort of generation of semi-beings, some pseudo vegetation and pseudo fauna, the result of the fantastic fermentation of matter.

"These are creations similar in appearance to living beings, to vertebrae, crustacea, to the articulate, but this appearance is misleading. These were indeed amorphous beings without an inner structure, the offsprings of the imitative tendency of matter which, endowed with memory, repeats from habit a once accepted shape. The scale of morphology to which matter is subject is, on the whole, limited and a certain number of shapes repeat themselves continuously in various forms of existence.

"These beings—mobile, sensitive to stimuli, but, nevertheless, far from real life—could be obtained by placing certain complicated colloids in a solution of kitchen salt. After a few days these colloids become formed, organized in a certain thickening of substance recalling lower animal life.

"In creatures thus arising it is possible to confirm the respiratory process, metabolism, but their chemical analysis does not show even a trace of protein compounds or any carbon combination.

"Nevertheless these primitive forms are nothing in comparison with the wealth of shapes and magnificence of the pseudo flora and fauna which appear sometimes in certain specific surroundings. These surroundings are old flats, permeated with the emanations of many beings and happenings—consumed atmosphere, lavish in the specific ingredient of human dreams, rubbish heaps abundant in the humus of memories, longing, sterile boredom. In such soil this pseudo vegetation sprouts rapidly and superficial, as a parasite lavish and ephemeral, it hurries the brief generation which blossoms abruptly and beautifully only to wither soon and die.

"In these houses the wallpaper must already be thoroughly worn out and bored with the ceaseless travel through all the cadences of rhythm; nothing strange that they stray off to distant, hazardous realms. The pith of the furniture, its substance must already be slack, degenerated and subject to wicked temptations; then, like a beautiful rash, a fantastic invasion, a colorful bountiful mould will blossom forth on this ailing, worn-out and barren soil.

"Do you ladies know," my father said, "that in old houses there are rooms which are forgotten; not visited for months, they wither in their neglect among the old walls and, seemingly, they become locked within themselves, overgrown with brick, once and for all lost to our memory; and, likewise, they slowly lose their existence. The doors leading to them from some part of the backstairs can be overlooked by the household for so long that they become ingrown, merge into the wall which obliterates all trace of them in a fantastic drawing of cracks and fissures.

"Once," said my father, "in the early morning toward the end of winter, after many months of absence, I walked into such a half-forgotten place and I was amazed at the appearance of those rooms.

"From all the chinks in the floor, from all the cornices and frames thin stalks had shot forth and filled the gray air with a quivering leafy filigree of lace, an azure thicket of some hothouse, full of whispers, sparkling, stirring, a sort of false and blissful spring. Around the bed, under the many-branched chandelier, along the cupboards swayed groves of delicate trees, their luminous crowns shivering upward in a fountain of lacy leaves, showering even the painted heaven of the ceiling with its sprays of chlorophyll. In the quickened tempo of blossoming, white and pink flowers sprouted in this enormous greenery which budded before one's very eyes, soared from the center with a rosy flesh and overflowed the edges, losing its petals and falling apart in swift decay.

"I was happy," said my father, "with this unexpected blossoming which filled the air with a flickering rustle, a quiet murmur, spilling like colored confetti through the thin twigs of the branches.

"I saw how from the trembling of the air, from the fermentation of an over-rich aura, is emitted and materializes this rapid flowering, the maturing and disintegration of fantastic oleanders which filled the room with a rare, lazy snowstorm of large pink blossoming clusters.

"Before evening fell," concluded father, "there was not a trace of that superb flowering. The entire illusion, that mirage was only a mystification, an accident of strange simulations of matter which passed off for the appearance of life."

That day my father was strangely animated, his glances, cunning, ironic glances, sparkled with verve and humor. Later, turning serious abruptly, he again reviewed the endless scale of form and shadings which many-sided matter assumed. He was fascinated by the marginal forms, doubtful and problematic, such as the ectoplasm of somnambulists, pseudo matter, cataleptic emanation of the brain which in certain cases expanded from the lips of the sleeper over the entire table, filling the whole room as buoyant, rare membrane, an astral body, bordering between body and spirit.

"Who knows," he continued, "how many suffering, crippled fragmentary forms of life there are, like artificially botched-up lives of cupboards and tables hastily hammered with nails, crucified wood, the silent martyrs of the cruel ingeniousness of humans. The terrible transplantation of foreign and inimical races of wood, the binding of them into one unfortunate aggregate.

"How much old, wise suffering there is in corroded grain, in the veins and streaks of our old, trusty cupboards. Who can see smiles and glances in their old, planed features polished beyond recognition?"

As he said this, my father's face broadened with thoughtful wrinkles, became likened to that of the knots and grain of an old board from which all memories had been planed off. For a moment we thought that he would plunge into a state of numbness which befell him sometimes, but he awakened abruptly, collected himself and continued.

"Ancient, mystic tribes embalmed their dead. In the walls of their houses bodies, faces were framed and embedded—father stood in the salon, the stuffed and tanned wife of the deceased served as a rug under the table. I knew a certain captain who had in his cabin a lamp fashioned from the corpse of his murdered mistress by Malayan embalmers. On her head was an enormous pair of antlers.

"In the silence of the cabin this head, suspended from the ceiling between the branched antlers, slowly opened its eyelids, on the parted lips glistened bubbles of saliva which broke from soft whispers. Insects, turtles and huge crabs hung on the rafters as candelabras and decoration. They moved their legs unceasingly in this silence, walked and walked in place. . . ."

Suddenly my father's face assumed an expression of concern and sorrow when his thought, following some unknown association, turned to other examples.

"Should I remain silent," he said in a quieter voice, "that my brother turned into a coil of rubber hose as a result of a long and incurable illness, and my poor cousin carried him in a pillow humming to the unfortunate creature unending lullabies of winter nights? Can there be anything sadder than a man transformed into a hose? What

a disappointment to the parents. What a disorientation for their feelings. What a disintegration of all hopes connected with the promising
young man. But the true love of my poor cousin accompanied him
in this transformation."

"Oh, I cannot listen to this any longer," moaned Polda bending
forward in the chair. "Quieten him, Adela."

The girls rose; Adela went up to father and with an outstretched
finger made a gesture denoting tickling. Father became confused, fell
silent and with fear began to retreat backwards before Adela's
wagging finger. She continued to follow him, threatening him
menacingly with the finger and step by step drove him from the
room. Pauline yawned and stretched. Together with Polda, leaning
against each other's shoulders, they looked into each other's eyes with
a smile.

Kazimierz Brandys

(1916–   )

During the years immediately preceding the war, Kazimierz Brandys was a Law student at the Warsaw University. He first attracted public attention by publishing a courageous open letter protesting against the discrimination towards Jewish fellow-students. His first novel was *The Wooden Horse*, written during the occupation but published only after the war. The novel depicts the nightmare of the occupation through the eyes of a man who seeks escape from reality in psychic isolation. Brandys' subsequent works showed his main interest to be in the sphere of the current political and psychological problems. His second book was *The Unvanquished City*, a satirical novel, also on the subject of the German occupation of Poland, and it was awarded Warsaw's literary prize.

Working with two weeklies, *Kuznica* (The Forge) and *Nowa Kultura* (New Culture), Brandys began writing a series of novels called *Between the Wars: Samson, Antigone, Troy, an Open City*, and *Man Never Dies*. These novels were published between 1948 and 1951, and they established the author as one of the most forceful commentators on social and political questions of his age and also as a sensitive explorer of man's psychological complexity. During the years 1953–1954 Brandys wrote the novel *The Citizens* which was attacked by some Polish critics for lacking in "positive heroes" and shunning proletarian themes. His series of letters, collected under the title *The Letters to Mrs. Z*, won the literary prize of *New Culture*.

Some of Brandys' stories stirred discussion even abroad, e.g., "The Defence of the 'Grenada'" (1955, in an anthology, *The Broken Mirror*, New York, 1958), "The Mother of Kings" (1956), which was issued in the U.S.A. as "The Mother of Kroles," and in Great Britain as "Sons and Comrades." The former is an account of several enthusiastic young people whose faith in socialism is broken by what one Polish critic called "soulless routine and dogmatism." The latter is a moving tale about a worker's family. Brandys' collection of short stories appeared in a volume, *The Red Cap*, and four stories in a book, *Romanticism*, which was warmly praised by the critics.

How To Be Loved

The girl in the uniform has unfastened my safety belt. We are flying. It seems we can smoke now. I am tired, I won't talk. She smiled at me as she went away, and I thanked her with a smile. I mustn't speak—they will recognize my voice.

The take-off did not have much effect: the roar of the engines, a
few shakes and then I did not look down below. The wing hides my
view, that's good. For the moment I am quite happy with no view; a
landscape as if shaken from a box, ant-like cars, that's all right, but I
can do without it. I feel somewhat strange in this aircraft, really it
was madness—what did I do it for?—I did not have to go away; on
the other hand I could have gone by train. Silence, rustling of newspapers, the aircraft wing lit up by the sun. Nobody saw me off.

Have I forgotten my cigarettes? No, here they are. I do hope my
daughter will await me in Paris. A man sitting next to me has produced a lighter. A flat cigarette lighter in a large, masculine hand—
a smile. I nod. Quite a good approach, but no new acquaintances.
I did not break away from the earth in order to have adventures in the
air. The distance—a bit of comfort—a glass of Madeira on the balcony
of "Cafe de la Paix"—museums, lonely walks along the Seine. How
much will a glass of Madeira be? Also the prison cell of Marie-
Antoinette, that's a must and van Dyck.

And if she arrives late at the airport?

As soon as we land I must buy a map of Paris. Two weeks is
slightly too short—but still. A pity it came so late.

It was owing to me: my first holiday after seventy weeks. Seventy
times: Felicity—seventy dinners—seventy times my own voice. In a
week's time one million people will hear of my departure. Felicity took
off in a silver, four-engined aircraft—flowers—goodbyes on the airport—Tom alone. I can just imagine how he'll talk about it.

They thought of that old friend only last week specially so that
he could take my place. He will suddenly call at our home the day
after I left. A type of a permanently unlucky man—they will play
chess with Tom. Not a bad idea—this muttering over a chessboard
mixed with sentimental comments about me. And I far away. Quite
a good idea. Then a postcard of the Eiffel Tower will arrive. *"A
beautiful city—*I shall write—*but there is no place like home."* Patita-
tam—rififi. . . .

In the footnote I will naturally remind him not to smoke too much.
I must be popular among the wives. One *million* will await my return.
The return of my good old low, slightly hoarse voice. What a laugh!

We hit some bumps. I can feel my heart.

When I took the forms for my passport, after I said a few words
I could hear the whispers in the queue. Somebody asked me:—How
is Tom?—and whether the chestnuts did him any good. Last Thursday
he complained of arthritis, so I told him to keep chestnuts in his
pockets. An argument on superstitions ended in a marital kiss. Well.
There were a large number of letters. Apparently chestnuts really do
help.

The man next to me is talking to the girl in uniform. To that *stewardess*. He speaks Polish, but with a foreign accent. Grey temples —sunburnt face—about fifty. It's hot, there is a reflection of the sun from the wing. Only fifteen minutes of flight. I hope my pocket mirror did not get broken. No, still in one piece. What do I look like? Face— oval. These forms make no sense. I used to have red hair. Wide eyes with a surprised expression and a milk-white complexion. Now I paint my eyebrows and eyelashes and bleach my hair. Red-haired, milk-white Ophelia—that was all right before the war. I wondered how to fill in these forms: red hair or blonde? I put "reddish blonde."

No peculiar characteristics: my father was an army captain. What lies! At home they were afraid I should be a midget. Perhaps they had their reasons, apparently grandfather drank. Somehow I managed to grow, I was very thin with sharp knees and elbows. Let's say: medium height. The aircraft lurched and dropped suddenly.

Yes, I could have been a fascinating Ophelia or St. Joan—something afflicted and frail—in the theatre they said I had an inner light. Perhaps I had that light but I also had bad luck. One cannot count on anything and at the same time expect everything. The date and place of birth—two things one cannot lose. But has one anything in common with them?

I sat over these forms for most of the night. Some questions still haunt me. The marital status. I wrote: a widow. Then I crossed it out. I suppose it's: spinster.

Before the take-off the two Brazilians sitting on the opposite side by the right wing made a simultaneous sign of the cross in identical gestures: with the tips of their fingers joined they touched the forehead, chest and lips—quickly, sadly. Somehow that did not cheer me up.

Quite a lot of foreign newspapers. Behind me a conversation in French. You can always recognize the Poles: there is something loose-skinned and worn out in their appearance. The stewardess, a head taller than I, watchful, silent with a smile stuck to her face. I should say her lips are too widely parted, some like them that way. Those born during the war and after are of much better quality. If she went through what I did, her complexion would be less peach-like. The fact is I did not have to live through anything; circumstances helped me not once but a hundred times—

What is the time? In fifteen minutes I will be heard down below. They will listen to my voice from a tape recorded a week ago. Felicity has collected her passport—the pains of travel fever (—*I did not go away for years, I suppose you want to get rid of me?*)—Tom pacifying his wife, most endearing.

—seventieth time—it will be eighteen months in September since they offered me the job. A peculiar feeling, it's as if I walked to the chair across the Sahara desert. Forty years of walking barefoot on hot sand behind the army, after forty years I say: all right, I shall be pleased to. Life smiled at me, but I did not smile back. In moments like this it is better to sit quietly, with a serious expression on one's face. A bomb? A cyclone? Paralysis? Everything is possible. I am ready. It's not my first engagement which I am accepting. And since I am accepting, I realize its consequences.

—I, sitting in the chair (last year's black coat, knitted gloves, a handbag with a broken lock) and sitting opposite, behind a desk a dark handsome man with spectacles who congratulates me. He says:— The tone, your particular tone,—and I bend to hear better. This tone I got from drinking too much vodka. I always worried about getting hoarse.—Your tape recording is excellent, a human voice at last.

—my tape?—I did not understand at first: what sort of tape? He asked me whether I wanted to hear it, pressed something and said:— Could I have the trial one.—A small light appeared above, whispers, followed by something like mewing and suddenly somebody sighed: —*I wanted rest in my old age, but here I have to start all over again. Darling.*—He has offered me a cigarette, I smoke and listen, he smiles, my hands shake. I cannot say I like it. It embarrassed me, this voice, I don't talk like that in real life, I don't use such expressions, I don't have anybody to say it to. And, anyway, what does it mean "to start all over again." I could never say it like that. I listen, drop cigarette ash, my own hoarse voice above me. Somebody interrupts me, I complain of something up there, above, apparently I don't understand something—then dinner. I lay the table. The noise of soup poured into the plates. My husband is eating.—How do you like it?— It's not bad.

—my tape, I'd like to listen to it, I don't remember everything I said in my life—maybe it's not important, but it's the tone which interests me—the tone which changes with one's attitude. I used to believe that something will answer. Nothing ever answered. I myself had to answer. I started to speak. But not with my own voice any more. Those words, for which one waits, sometimes have to be said in one's own voice:—Please do not worry—I spoke to him with a voice of a ventriloquist—I will not leave you.—I felt that he did not even need these words, he shuddered. It was I who needed them. Under the hood, surrounded by the noise of the rainfall I offered him my new tone. Here you are. I tuned myself to a new situation in a second. It's just that afterwards one is not exactly that oneself any more—that particular oneself of the second before. He asked me if I believed in his escape.—Nothing will happen to you.—I would not utter such words a second before. And the result: thirteen years of obsession.

I admire myself. To get through a wanted man, carry him in a cab through the old, narrow streets full of Germans, to encounter on every corner posters with his face and a reward for any information leading to his arrest, yet at the same time to tell him with absolute certainty:—It's not far now, soon you will be safe—it's not a bad beginning for a play script. In real life it's less amusing—rain, wet stockings, slow trot of the horse's hooves and my growing hatred towards that horse. From these moments my skin has retained a camouflage-grey color, which I could never wash away.

My neighbor here with the cigarette lighter has a much more hygienic appearance—he smells of something rarely used. I like men of about fifty with steel-grey, innocent eyes and greying temples—physical training, electric massage, orange juice, porridge.

I bet he was a pilot during the war—my father was murdered behind barbed wires by the greenish creatures with shining steel heads and small eyes—those people who spent those years in the air or at sea are much better preserved and know less of life.

Is he married? He is not wearing a ring but I can feel a woman around him. In the morning: good morning, darling—in the evening: goodnight, darling—I'd go out of my mind.

I am jealous of that girl in uniform, he smiled at her again. Behind me a conversation in Polish about the standard of living. Apparently the peasants ride their own motorbikes. I am not sure if that is a good thing.

Peasants on motorbikes, I in an aeroplane flying to Paris. My country? Yes, perhaps. I don't know. I have not thought about it. Can one in my place talk of love to one's country? Surely, it's enough that I have not stirred out for so many years. Everything which hits us we call life, it's only afterwards that we realize it's our country. I did not choose it.

No. Nobody. Not even him. I had no idea what it was all about. I only saw when he slapped Peters' face—at that moment I was serving coffee at the next table. Next day they came to me and said:— You have to get him through to a safe place, a price has been put on his head.—A cab and darkness.

—after thirteen years I heard a scream in the courtyard—I ran from the bathroom—I slipped—the window! A window and darkness.

Enough, I should not think about it, it's no good to me. A glass of water or juice—a "Mepavlon" tablet.

I spill the tablets. My neighbor bends down to pick them up.
—*Merci.*

Naturally, now he thinks I am French. Why did I say "merci" and not "thank you." Instant consequences:
—*Vous-vous sentez mal, madame?*

Luckily I understood:
—*Non. Merci. Pas du tout.*

What a wealth of expression. Rififi. . . . He did not recognize my Polish handbag, that means he was only in Poland for a short time.

All this time my beating heart. I was not made to be carried up in the air. Down below there is some sort of grassland and puddles. From the height of two kilometers the earth looks less serious than if you walk on it.

A road among the trees, houses, a village.

I believe that in villages like this one, the peasants murder their wives with axes and then hang themselves on trees. From this height it would never be noticed.

I always had a feeling that nobody sees us, but I did not realize it was to this extent. Perhaps the faithful should not look at the earth from the bird's eye view? There is something sinful in it and my heart reacts to it badly. I always felt worst in situations in which I cannot even count on the fact that I shall be considered. I can't stand it. Excuse me: I have my own considerations, let them also take me into account. I don't want to be a grain of dust. A human being has his own natural greatness and the right to be seen.

—then, in that first year of war, when I transported him through the rain and darkness, then I understood what it means. I was filled with fright. Not of what could happen to us, but that whatever happened to us would be of no importance at all. A very unpleasant feeling. I prefer to be accused. When they tried me after the war, I felt innocent, but at least my case was considered. The trade union tribunal sentenced me unjustly, but I had that certainty that I, myself, was being taken into consideration—whether justly or not is a different matter. Anyway, they saw me as a being, whose past they were considering. And that is not the worst even when the verdict is unjust. Not to feel anybody's eyes on me—that is the worst.

I bet this man never lived through such moments. He looks to me like someone, who if he ever risked his life, always did so in connection with leadership; such men always inform their chiefs first before a leap in the darkness.

The stewardess is serving breakfast, perhaps I shall not have to jump out? What if I had to? I jump out and drop on a peasant murdering his wife with an axe. Theoretically it is quite possible. He would take me for an angel who descended to warn him and he would drop on his knees with a cry. But it does not happen like this. Even though the technical progress moves on, in the sphere of providence we are very backward. The peasant would kill his wife and I would drop a kilometer away breaking my neck. Is that meant to be progress? A complete lack of inter-relations. Logic? Perhaps this man believes in it, I don't.

—the earth, plants, animals, something uncertain and uneasy, something which moves by itself, devours, runs about, grows—I am afraid of birds in a room—nature gets tangled up in one's hair, it is blind, dumb and always frightened, one can only talk to a human being, appease him, deceive his evil, to which he has never reconciled himself.

I think a glass of brandy would do me good.

He has taken out from the pocket of his coat a tiny wireless set, bound in ivory colored plastic. I have not seen one like that. He is sitting by the window now fiddling with it.

A double snoring: the Brazilians.

What is he doing it for—is it not enough that we are flying in the air? He wants to be accompanied by music. What hands, how carefully looked after. But the wireless set won't cooperate. It just won't play.

The thin stewardess is coming towards me with a tray. Brandy and sandwiches, at last! I can feel the warmth inside me. A cigarette. Tiriraram-ti-rififil . . . I feel fine now, my heart in the right place, four engines work so that I can fly—spinster? widow? married?—and this good old trash which I voice every Thursday—my God, how wonderful, I couldn't care less, there will be no back corrections.

I could not foresee all the events, but I fulfilled all my duties. I was saving him. Then they tried me. That does not mean anything: they passed a sentence for what happened to me—but I deserve a medal for what I did. This man sitting next to me would not understand much of it.

—that is something one has to live through, my dear, just imagine a thin actress with red hair, who was supposed to play Ophelia in the provinces, and whom they found during rehearsals to be *fascinating* —yes, the first great part in my life, in few days' time the first night with the ominous date: September 3, 1939. Unfortunately, the last rehearsal was interrupted by an air raid, Polonius ran away—he came back with the Germans—and a month later I was serving vodka in the "Artists' Bar." An interesting place. Polonius was not stabbed there with a sword, but very ordinarily had his face slapped. The next day they found his body with the brains shot out—the body of a traitor.

—it did not matter to me whether *he* killed him—I did not care about Peters and I would undertake to transport *him* in any circumstances. He killed—he did not kill, anything could have happened. I never asked him about it, such questions are all right on a large stage—anyway I had neither the reason nor time to ponder over it. It sufficed that it was him. He never paid any attention to me during the rehearsals, but then I felt my chance: he wouldn't tell me to go away and become a nun. I would wait for him in a cab, they would dye him, he would have black hair, the nuns gave a safe address, the posters on the corners promised high rewards. The cab moved, I touched his hand. He was pale and his eyes were closed. From under the hood I guessed my way: the Theatre, City Walls, the Tower. . . . I did not know the price which I was going to pay, I only knew that nuns meant bad luck.

The stewardess takes away the tray—the wireless set suddenly starts playing. The sound of buzzing is interrupted by a crackling noise, followed by a distant music.

My neighbor is satisfied, he smiles—I smile back. After all, what does it matter to me? Why think about the past? I lived through it, that's enough. The past is bad for the nerves, they should find some tablets for unwanted memories. The sweet memories—who on earth thought of that one?

—what did I say? washing?

—I think it's something about some washing which I was supposed to do before going away. . . .

I feel rather odd. This man caught my voice from last week. My whisper fished out from the air. Of course, it's the last program repeated for the holidays. Felicity is afraid of air travel, Tom is getting angry:

—*. . . So many years*—

crackling, the sound is bad:

—*you have not seen your daughter*—

I think I missed something, it's awful—

—*. . . and now you are hiding behind my pants?*—

A guaranteed laugh from one million of listeners on the ground. I cannot hear anything again, only rustling and crackling. And suddenly my whisper:

—*How will you manage without me?*—

it's better now, I can recognize the accents:

—*. . . and who will queue for meat? and your herb tea?*—Crackling noises.

The station is lost in overwhelming crackling together with me. With a pity, I like my voice so much.

I have tears in my eyes. I am deeply touched. I have never realized I could reach that high. That my voice flies with me in the air. I don't talk like that, that's true, but on earth they love me for those words. I speak them in the name of one million subscribers. They would never accept my real script. I don't blame them. I don't like it myself. My truth should never be transmitted. Nothing makes me different from a tree or a dog except memories, but much more is asked of me. I prefer my Thursday script.

Something about pants again. Not in the best of tastes—but what can one do—after such remarks there are always heaps of letters. I can just see a parcel with pants: *"Dear Felicity, The Women's League from Piotrkow sends you a pair of pants for your husband. Have a good time on your trip and come back and best regards for your daughter."*

Pants, ham, medicine—revelations, sins, despair, cries for help—hand-embroidered tablecloths and abuses of betrayed wives—all this for my disposal. My voice attracts life.

Women write to me: "Our Mother"—I have a letter from a would-be-suicide case, who decided to live because I exist. I feel a bit unhinged, but who could foresee it? Nobody knew until after shifting the program one hour they received five thousand protesting letters. From all over the country. Only then they realized that people were listening to us from all over the country. Unbelievable! Thursday dinners at Mr. & Mrs. Konopka, a provincial program for elderly couples became a top popular program. That made a noise.

What a fool that man was, who wrote—what was it called now?—A sociological essay. Yes, an essay on "From King Stanislaus to Felicity." In it he tried to prove that my dinners will also make history. What a moron. And yet, I was rather pleased.

Now they cannot end, they will last forever. Every Thursday I shall serve soup to one million people. They listen to me in hospitals. I receive letters from the patients, nurses, doctors. My voice has even cured somebody.

Everything is possible. I don't wonder at it—but I am amazed that they require so little. When I say to Tom: *Do eat that piece of meat, darling, the one nearer the bone*—I feel their gratitude and I know that I shall receive many letters. I am capable of much more in real life, but they only know that piece of meat and sacrifice, this spoonful of soup and the certainty that I shan't eat so that he will eat well, that I never betrayed him and if I ever loved anybody else I renounced them quietly. He, his hard work, his pants and troubles, our honesty and our adult children. The soup, the meat, and a bone with a piece of simple life—few grumbles and anecdotes, the warmth of a home—that's what they love to listen to.

I don't laugh at them, perhaps they are right. I laugh at myself. At the first rehearsal Tom was slightly put out:—I considered you innocent, but I felt hopeless in that atmosphere.—Oh, so was I. Only I was the accused. If one is so weak one should not sit in a trade union tribunal. Here you are, this large piece is for you, the meat is dearer again, I have nothing against you.

—*I beg your pardon?*

Ah, he has seen "Przekroj" showing from the pocket of my coat. Very well, let him know whom he has to contend with. Smile—smile.

—*But of course.*

I lend him the paper. I hope he will give it back to me, because if I don't have "Przekroj" in my coat pocket, *my daughter* won't recognize me.

—*Do you smoke?*

—*Thank you.*

We smoke his cigarettes. The first steps of getting acquainted are over—what now? He seems to ponder before every sentence as if he was sending me a telegram.

—*We should be in Berlin in an hour's time. We are on schedule.*

—*Really? I did not expect it.*

—*Yes. Extremely good atmospheric conditions.*

His teeth are very white. When he turns his head to me, a dazzle: everything about him seems to shine. This smooth cap on his head. Hair does not grow like that on true Poles.

—*I suppose you don't live in Poland?*

—*No, I live in the U.S.A. I have visited Poland for the first time in thirty years.*

—*That's certainly a long time.*

—*It certainly is. The changes there are enormous. It's not really the same place any more.*

—*You have summed it up admirably.*

I feel his pleasant glance—the blueness of an empty condensed milk tin—and I smile mysteriously. I can be subtle.

—*I came to Warsaw for a convention of bacteriologists. That's my profession.*

—*Oh yes, I see.*

—*Yes. I am doing research in vaccines.*

—*And now you are going back to the U.S.A.?*

—*Not really. At the moment I am going to Brussels. I have been asked to give several lectures. From there I am going back to New York.*

All this is extremely interesting, what a pity I have nothing to say about vaccinations. I suppose it must be very pleasant to fly from a convention in Warsaw to Brussels irrespective of what it's all about. I can well imagine him how he talks to a hundred fellows like him, with that voice of his devoid of doubt.

—*I have discovered that in Poland there are a number of well-known people specializing in vaccines. I am very surprised.*

—*Really? That's very interesting.*

—*Yes. After my lecture in the Academy of Sciences we had a*

*very high level discussion. They certainly know a lot about the newest
discoveries in serology.*

—*Well, well, that certainly is extraordinary.*

I rather like him, I never slept with a man who gave me a complete
sense of security—in some stages in my life they could only be police-
men—and that is why perhaps I immediately recognize this strange
kind of masculinity. Divorced?

—*It seems to me that Poles do not take advantage of their new
chances. Don't you think so?*

—*Yes, perhaps you are right. But—*

—*I understand. I think the Partition of Poland still has an effect
on Polish psychology.*

—*That's exactly what I wanted to say.*

The aircraft wing seems to be asphalt-grey and still. In a moment
he'll ask me about the war.

—*Yes. I was in Poland during the war.*

Silence. He looks at me for a long time.

—*I used to be in the R.A.F. I find it difficult to imagine your
suffering. These tortures.*

—*Oh well, that was a long time ago.*

—*Quite. You have a different attitude towards it. I respect women
who lived through those times and kept their place.*

And kept their place? That's very nicely said. I say:

—*Really, everything then used to be much simpler than now.*

Blueness and steel. A condensed-milk tin. He is deep in thought
now and silent. And I with this cliché on my lips. Simpler? These
sentiments are expressed by various pseudo-intellectuals to the foreigners in "Bristol." Simpler. Perhaps I should tell him about it? Yes,
I survived it. I seem to remember. That sweating rope-dancer,
that's me.

—in my dreams I used to fall on the concrete below, and during the
day I went round to fortune tellers to find out what would happen to
him, madness or death? and how long would I last? From the time of
the arrest I lost contacts, people who entrusted him to me ceased to
exist, transformed during the executions on the City Walls into a
bloody mess, well mixed with earth. If I ever had mentioned it to
him—I don't know, he felt lost anyway—I think he would have
given himself up to the Germans. I never said anything about it. Not
to anyone. I wanted him all to myself. And I am not quite sure if he
would have given himself up.

—damn it, where, how, to whom was I supposed to go? I could
only trust myself one hundred percent, any other person would share
the news with somebody else from sheer fright and—no, no, I was in

a trap, I fell into it, my head was swimming, I ran about like mad—
oh, you idiot, you wanted a prince, well now you have him!

—he regarded me as the cause of his misfortunes. I understand it
now, that it was unavoidable, but then?—Is it my fault—I shouted—
that you hit Peters in the face when you were drunk? Is it my fault that
he was a volksdeutch and that they found him shot dead the next
morning? And the fact that I agreed to help you, perhaps that's my
fault?—Those shouts were really unnecessary. A human being simply
won't comprehend what nerves are, and will claim his lost sense of
honor from the tortured and the mad. Whom was he to blame? Fate?
But I was his fate. Only I, for five years. He could not get out into the
streets. The posters on the corners were washed out by the rains, but
his face—they would recognize him instantly—he was Oswald, Gustav,
Fortun. Alcest . . . I brought him meals to that tiny room with a
kitchen which I found by a miracle, when he could not stay with
the nuns any longer. A ceiling at an angle and a sofa—true. I bought
him the sofa. It stood somewhat away from the walls, fifteen—twenty
centimeteres.

—*Perhaps you will tell me about your squadron?*

—there is a saying somewhere to the effect that a man chooses a
woman so that his failures can have a face and eyes. He did not even
choose me. I fell on him like a ginger cat from a roof. That is why he
had more right to revenge himself on me, it is so simple really, I was
his only audience for five years. I was stupid, I understand nothing—
. . . something about Canada, he is talking to me about Canada, he was
trained there, he volunteered . . . —I did not understand that for five
years I was his walking misfortune because in those years which he
cursed, he only saw me. Isn't that enough?

—*I don't know Canada. Is it a rocky country?*

I shut my eyes and listen about Canada.

What sort of animals are there—kangaroos?

Ottawa in winter.

A maple leaf.

The night-flying exercises. He was a navigator.

Fasten the safety belts. We are going down.

Berlin.

2

No, no satisfaction whatsoever. I thought I should feel something,
but I feel nothing at all. Glass. A waiting room with armchairs,
"Lufthansa" posters and a voice in the loudspeaker speaking in
German. I was waiting for a shiver: nothing. A nondescript smell—
rubber? oilcloth? paint? We were sitting in the armchairs, people pass

us by. Germans, of course. And nothing. Doors labelled "Herren"—doors labelled "Damen." I entered and locked the door. Glossy paint, whiteness and bareness and a calm noise of water. Balls of disinfectant. What is the name of their river? Spree? Here I am by the Spree in a modern toilet on the passenger airport, on my way to Paris. And not a trace of feeling pleased. I did not get out with a purpose of revenge, but not to feel anything at all? I just don't understand it. In those few minutes I tried to force myself to remember: "Remember, darling—I thought to myself—what they did to you? Well, look about you now, look what you can afford to do now. Go on, feel something, be merry, jump for joy!" I remember my father's death in a concentration camp and my mother's illness, followed by her death from insanity not much later, and my friend, a Jewess who was pushed naked into a gas chamber, gassed and burnt. I feel nothing. At last I took out a pocket mirror and I begin to laugh. At myself. I laughed with my teeth and gums, my cheeks and my forehead but my eyes were earnest and dead as they looked back at me. I always looked well after my teeth and my skin, on the whole I don't look too bad. I spared myself, yes, well, no doubt I managed to survive those years—I don't know whether in my own place, but I survived. But there is something about my eyes. I don't have the look of a winner. I attach great importance to hygiene, even in the worst possible days I had to have a bath and brush my teeth with a sharp, hard toothbrush, I went to a dentist regularly every three months, I thinned my eyebrows, I did not drink during my periods and I am of the opinion that all this has a meaning even greater than most people think. But a quarter of an hour ago, behind this door labelled "Damen" I felt that I had been completely defeated. If it is impossible to give a wild triumphal cry, it means defeat. I don't know, perhaps it is not just myself, perhaps everybody including that man sitting next to me—why should I care? I am furious, because for the first time I feel a ghastly lack of satisfaction from the fact that I exist, this empty nothingness full of holes which I have inside me, this earnest indifference. Surely it's quite clear: I lost. But who won over me?

A kangaroo again. As soon as it starts swaying there is a tiny kangaroo jumping inside me. Probably also from vodka, although the cardiogram did not show anything.

Just a minute, when was it I started to drink? Yes, in the "Artists' Bar." Then I had to drink with him, now I like to do it on my own from time to time. It makes more sense. Then one can feel one's being in three dimensions as it were. After a glass of vodka I feel like a sculpture. Something smooth with intersecting shapes, with which I fuse completely. Oh yes, in such moments I feel like a monument—and then I fall quickly asleep. I have never drunk in order to sleep with *somebody*—in spite of the fact that I have had quite a number of men.

Perhaps too many? Maybe. Well, I don't know. They went away, I never reproached them, I waited, the next one appeared. Should I have refused? What—my body? For what reason? They used to say—I need you—and it certainly was the truth. If a human being is needed by anybody at all, it is mainly when a man needs a woman in bed. To consider other cases in detail is much less important—no one ever knows for how long a man needs a woman and that is their common risk. He does not know it himself. One cannot hold it against him that he is upset when after five or twenty nights he finds out that he already has had all she could give him. It's very unpleasant for him too. It matters a lot the way in which this is announced. Some cannot hide their discontent. And that is unpleasant. One should know how to behave in a situation in which nobody is to blame. When the passion goes—one should force oneself to a smile of gratitude—or invent an emotional conflict. In the last resort, recall the memories of the past. This I value greatly. Nature is brutal, only idiots don't understand this. Apart from desires a man has skills and this obliges him to a definite conduct. In each of us there is a bit of an artist—nobody in any situation has a right to behave like nature: suddenly freeze or suddenly evaporate. And I think that such expressions as "his passions were cooled" or "anger boiled inside him" are out of place. A man should behave on a higher level than nature, from which after all we don't expect much.

This man has dozed off. Perhaps he is dreaming of the Battle of Britain? He took part and distinguished himself in it. To people like him everything proves all right, even the results of their own behavior. He wanted to fight the Germans—now he has a medal for courage. He decided to destroy bacteria—and he discovered a vaccine. A wonderful man, who always knows how to behave. Causes—results, decisions—conclusions. A well-bred fellow, who never found himself between a sofa and a wall. In a space covered with a mattress. In a hole in which a man could only fit in flat as a pancake. I wonder, how would he behave then?

—during the night arrests when they took all men from the house —*Wo ist ihr Mann?*—All that time I was wondering if his foot was showing behind the suitcase.—*Mein Mann ist weg.* His foot! This second one was Latvian. They looked at me with their beady eyes walking around the room:—Spirit?—In the window between the panes stood two bottles of vodka. They drank one. The Latvian went out. The one who stayed told me what he wanted. Afterwards the Latvian came back and he went out. I was moaning. They were in a hurry and I was crying with pain. When the black Marias left, I was afraid to move. Then—suddenly—a moment of courage, through tightly clenched teeth I whispered that everything was over. Yes, I think that at that moment I was wonderful and terrible. . . .

—I moved the sofa. I tried to bring him round. He really fainted. At any rate I was grateful to him for that. We drank the second bottle of vodka all through the night. We swore, mumbled, raving mad, happy, unconscious with relief, not looking at each other's eyes. And we slept through the whole day until dusk—frankly, there was nothing to wake up to.

Well, how would this man behave, how? A kangaroo. It's becoming more and more bumpy, air pockets probably. The aircraft wing is now darker and has lost its shine; I cannot see the earth—a mist? It's stuffy, silent and solemn. Nobody talks.

I would prefer him to wake up. I wish he would talk to me. I like his metallic voice—a voice of a steady man. I survived those times in my own place. The fact that I accepted a part in "Stadttheater" at *that time* gave me a great deal of satisfaction. I decided to do it. Only towards the end, that is true, after they shut the "Artists' Bar," after three months of looking for a job and a work permit. I wanted to have good papers. A certificate with an official seal so that I could hang it on the door. On *his* door. After that night I had to be safe—I swore that to myself. I am not certain whether there exist great men, but there exist moments when a human being is great. I was great then. At the time when I was saving him. When I took that part, when I was telling him that I've got a job with the Red Cross and later, when I sang in the "Street Melodies" my teeth chattering with fright in case they caught me on my way back home—during the night through the City Walls and shaved my head. I could afford to stick myself somewhere. That is why after the war, when I made statements in front of that green table and when they asked me if I knew of the consequences of my behavior, I answered:—Consequences! But naturally. If they would only think of me like that.

That made it worse for me. Three years without work permit. Well, after those five years I could stand another three. They even killed some women for war crimes. That's very unpleasant. I cannot bear situations in which a man murders a woman neither from jealousy nor love, but from conviction.

On the whole the trial paid off. Everything was worth it because of one sentence, one word, to be exact, which he spoke. He said that in those years we were *married*. He testified as a witness in my case. I was grateful to him that he came after all. He did not look at me but he said it. Married. I grew hot. I so very much wanted him to use that particular word. I think there were tears in my eyes.

—I sat smiling at a wall above his shoulder listening to his testimony. In that moment I neither wished him death nor disgrace. I was certain he would come back to me. He had to live with other women in those first years after the war, he couldn't do anything else. But then I knew that he would come back. We were married. I am a widow. *Une veuve. Eine Witwe.*

—he knew I had a right to him—I gave him a hundred times more than any woman could give a man, more than pleasure and fidelity—great things indeed; almost any woman is capable of that. I gave him my head—my own head which I laid by the side of his photographed face on the police notices with a reward, doubled after a month. Serving coffee in the "Artists' Bar" I was listening to the gossip of his death: *he fell from the window* when he saw some Germans who accidentally pulled up in a black Maria in front of the house in which he was hiding. In front of the house in which he was hiding! Oh, how I listened to that.—Afterwards I was telling him:—What's new? The fact that you are dead. You fell from a window—do you hear?—from the window to the pavement. Some people even know from the best sources that you have been buried near the Tower—you understand?—they buried you!—And we drank in silence to this death of his, so that he would sleep in the morning.

I know too much. If I was to become a wife of this man who sits next to me today, I would have to feel a slight contempt for him. For the fact that he knows that much less. To feel contempt and jealousy of everything which he perceives. . . . Everything which he thinks natural, rational and verified. And of those moments in which he'll say:—we are only human, and at other times:—this is really below the level. And most of all to be contemptuous and jealous of this condensed certainty of his, that he will know how to *behave* in any situation.

It's quite idiotic. Yes, I like his mouth, his profile with his eyes closed and his thick hair like some minister's, who never tasted any debauchery. But my husband was a man who tasted everything.

I held his head in my hands—if only I did not go to the bathroom —oh, this woman howling on the balcony!—so he wanted to have me near him that day, he knew what he asked of me and he knew I would not refuse.

The thin stewardess is coming towards us with a smile stuck to her face—a mare with a perm walking between the put-boxes towards the arena—what has happened?

We are flying into darkness. The aircraft behaves like a frightened fish—chasing? running away? The air has humps, we go into them—a jump-up—jump-down, we trample a herd of raving camels.

A paper bag? No, thank you. But if I was to wake this man?

My heart jumps—a huge, strong kangaroo. A kangaroo, camels, a fish running away: nature revenging itself.

Fasten the safety belts? Thank you very much.

After all I've been through, was it not enough? My feet are getting cold. I am afraid. Of what? A crash. I told Tom: it's best to stay at home. All because of that impulsive idiot in Paris. True, I have her letter in my handbag. . . .

—*Dear Felicity*—jump up!

—*I listen to your words every week*—here we go again!

—*as a girl I had a name like you and*—

My God!

—*I feel as if I was your daughter. I want to invite you to Paris*— a hump! up we go again—*my children speak Polish*—down, further down! into an abyss—*and Jean will be very happy to have you. I shall send you a ticket, please come!*

This Jean is a French engineer, she met him in Germany in a labor camp. Wanda, nee Konopka—oh yes, she mentioned the Warsaw Rising. A year of my life for a glass of brandy.

Everybody is staring at the door of the pilots' cabin as if it were a cinematic screen.

Around us a yellow-grey cottonwool—one cannot see anything.

Behind me an elderly passenger in a boater says something very loudly to the stewardess in French, who cannot understand him. They are both blushing, somebody intervenes, I don't know what's going on.

What's going on? Why did I go away? Lately my life has become clear and simple, I have started to forget my past—only here, in this aeroplane everything comes back to me. Perhaps this is the end? In one minute? In one second?

I shall go mad. My neighbor is awake.

—*Could you ask the stewardess for a glass of brandy, I beg you.*

I thank him with my eyes—I drink in small gulps.

It's almost dark, this terrible dense cottonwool became even denser. Another request for checking the safety belts. Silence, the aircraft stumbles in the air. A "Mepavlon" tablet . . .

—*have seen several thunderstorms over the Channel. On the whole they are worse than this. I remember one night flight in June nineteen* . . .

—I knew from the beginning—an eye was winking at me all the time. All the time some shameless signs—a dip, my heart, I don't think I'll survive—it's gone . . . These signs mentioned something. Something in connection with me . . . I sweat and go cold . . . —I am positive that existence is sin, for some time I felt that something is rubbing against me, announcing this horrible conclusion . . . all right, I'll take this paper bag—this cynical, filthy conclusion! To be quite honest—I was certain. Falling down?! No, another gust . . . Of the fact that I shall have a terrifying, very stupid end. And the first hint

—that's the end, I am dying—were the uncomprehensible words in the part. . . . ah, that's a bit better—in the part of Ophelia. The wing! The wing is dropping off! Oh, I am worn out . . . Yes, twenty years ago, I said to the King in the fourth act. *"Well, God 'ild you. They say the owl was a baker's daughter. Lord* . . . A lightning flash! I can see a wet expanse of the wing . . . Just a moment, how did it go: *"Lord, we know what we are, but know not what we may be. God be at your table."*

It's not so bumpy now. I did not understand those words, especially about the owl—they were dark, I was afraid of them.

It's very nice of him to let me hold his hand, he is a true gentleman.

—Darling—said the producer—they will explain themselves to you on the thirtieth performance.

On the thirtieth? We never had the first one. I think I remember only these words from the whole script—and even today I still don't understand them.

—if only I had not been in the bathroom at that time—God—I was too late—darkness, lights in the windows, a hysterical scream from a woman on the balcony—I was holding his head, begging him not to die. What did he feel then? What did he feel? I was wiping the sweat off his forehead, he was saying something but I couldn't hear it—pink bubbles were forming round his mouth. No, that's enough, that's the end. . . .

Nobody talks, except those Poles behind my back, who say that this is quite normal, not very pleasant because it's bumpy, but the meteorological office has issued a storm warning. Normal? Here I am tied with a belt to the stomach of a winged, metal fish tossed by whirling winds, two kilometers above the earth! In murky brown darkness. And this is supposed to be normal? Thank you very much.

—*Are you feeling better?*

—*Much better, thank you. I am very sorry to . . .*

—*Don't mention it.*

He is looking at me, probably with surprise, because I held his hand. Well, so I did, so what? That sort of thing can happen to him once in a lifetime.

—*More brandy?*

—*Thank you.*

Refreshed, polite, energetic. Dear Sir! The stewardess gives me a cool look from under the eyelashes. Too bad, my dear, not everybody has your training. If your mother is listening to the radio, she will hear my voice in four weeks' time. I shall talk about this storm. I shall pay you off for that extra brandy—with a slightly hoarse voice of an aging woman very much like your mother. One day, my dear, when you will stay at home for the night, she'll ask you if perhaps it was with you that Felicity went to Paris. And she will describe this storm with all the details, using my expressions.

Oh, it's starting again. I grow stiff, I am falling, I am dead. A hand, where is his hand!

—*Take a deep breath, it helps.*

Breathe in—breathe out. Breathe out—deep breath in. Several times. He looks at me with interest. Perhaps I was thinking aloud? I can just imagine. What a script! This raving carp and inside it my voice, my prayer into the past. They would listen, I am quite sure. Thank goodness one can think without any witnesses.

—*Have you a family in Paris?*

—*A daughter. She has married a Frenchman. An engineer. She is going to wait for me at the airport.*

I must be mad. What am I saying it for?

A grain of "Ondasil." The flight is becoming more smooth.

—*It's been a long separation, no doubt?*

—*Fifteen years.*

—*I should think—you must be—*

—*Oh, I am very excited. I find it difficult to get accustomed to the idea.*

—*I hope you don't think me indiscreet. Are you going to stay with your daughter in Paris?*

—*Oh no. I've left my husband in Warsaw. I am rather worried if he will manage without me. And my son. He is studying aerodynamics. They only let me go for a fortnight.*

Voilà.

I often make up my own text, which upsets the authors. Still, I like my additions best. At that time, for example, when Tom demanded that I should sack the girl who comes to clean. It came out that she has an illegitimate child. *How did he say it?—I am not a puritan, hm . . . but a woman who has no respect for herself, hm . . .* —I think that according to the text I was supposed to answer:—*All right, if you think so, I shall have a word with her tomorrow*—and something about the morality of modern times. But as soon as he came up with it, I started to laugh—*Really, my dear, who do you think you are? Perhaps she loved him? Not all men are like you. If she is taking care of the child we had better help her!*—and I bang one plate against another, to make it appear as if I was clearing the table. He was stunned. After a while he muttered:—*Well, you'd better do as you think best. . . .*—It came out very naturally and in the following week a girl in the post office smiled at me:—You were quite right about your charwoman.—Well! How many letters came? five hundred? six hundred? About that. Most of them from abandoned mothers in villages.

I feel I could laugh: I reach the peasant minds.

I am a sister to the lonely and a wife to the widowed.

I cheer up the melancholy and the blind.

A team from a State Factory of Electric Bulbs has sent me a souvenir album and named the factory nursery after me.

I have models of gliders and ships, figures from rock salt and coal. The queues in shops disappear on hearing my voice, the civil servants become sentimental on the sound of my words.

If I ever write a diary I shall give it a title "From Ophelia to Felicity, or how to be loved."

The wind shines again. The indistinct beige lines seen from under the white wisps, that's the earth. I am feeling fine after my third glass of brandy.

—*And you? I suppose you have a charming wife, children?*

I smile and then I meet his eyes. I stop smiling.

—*I lost my son last year. He committed suicide.*

I grow quite numb. I feel awful. Why did I ask him about it?

—*It was a question—of a woman. . . . There were also some other reasons which I don't understand.*

We fly for a moment in silence, a sun shines behind the window, below one can see straight lines of intersecting roads, his hand is warm—and it occurs to me, a sad and mad thought, that in spite of everything I could have been his wife.

We are to land in Brussels in fifteen minutes.

3

Patitam—ti—rififi. . . . Funny how this tune is haunting me. Before the take-off on the radio: "Rififi"—on the airport in Brussells: "Rififi." A sharp vibrating tone, which goes right through me. Sometimes a musical background is indispensable. One would behave quite differently if they only played an accompaniment more often. Reality hasn't enough melody in it and perhaps that is why people suffer for it, prostitute and make swines of themselves. They say there is harmony in nature. So far, I haven't noticed it. Harmony? Nature, that's something shameless and unaccountable. That storm was horrible. Storms may be beautiful in symphonies or novels. Only artists are haunted by a feeling of shame for nature. They want to repair its muddled madness which drives a human being to despair. I think that's a really deep remark. Tariram-ti-rififi! . . .

They played that record when I said goodby to him. In a cocktail bar in the Brussels airport. We drank another three glasses of brandy sitting on those high stools by a shining, snake-like bar—the barmaid put on that record and I felt pathetic. He, with a raincoat over his arm in a stiff black hat which went very well with his hair—and I, with a romantic past written all over my face, sentimental, wise Madame X without illusions. In a piercing moan of "Rififi" I was bringing to my lips a small glass of honey-bronze liquid with a meaning smile when he said that he would remember me and that he liked my voice. My voice—naturally. Multicolored bottles blurred in front of my eyes, I listened, looking at this shining altar with a barmaid making graceful movements with a cocktail shaker and I thought: "Dear Sir" . . . He said he was haunted by memories all during the flight and he felt grateful to me for being able to talk about it.—I was also haunted by memories—I said. And I thanked him for his help during the storm. When the record stopped, the barmaid started to play it again. I touched his hand:—I wish you every success in your convention. Many, many miraculous vaccines, isn't that so? —He laughed:—I don't know. There are many people more clever and younger. Nobody has told me that I shall be the successful one.

—I am quite certain—I said—that you will be very successful.— And I gave him a look of a gracious sorceress, the look which brings luck. Patitiri-tirififi! . . . tirififi! God be at your table.

Once again I am flying alone. My blood well mixed with six glasses of brandy, the flight is majestic and calm, I spread myself in my seat, raising my eyebrows with a slight surprise. Good, very good indeed.

—*My dear*—I said in the last program but one—*our life is not a bad one because we can be honest. That's the most important thing. I believe that human nature is a good one, only one must be careful. You look after me—I look after you. One has to live in such a way that your neighbors will respect you. How do you like this joint with beets?*

A rustling of papers and bits of conversation can be heard again. The Brazilians, who became ashen during the storm have returned in their milk-chocolate coloring. In their thin brown hands they are holding illustrated papers with pictures of white buildings, looking like mushrooms on the background of red bricks.

I don't know any of these people, their thoughts, their landscapes. The Poles behind my back are saying that the French only wash once a week. We look at each other with an indifferent, glassy stare, none of us care about the others. They say in the West people don't stare at one another, they are more discreet. But I am going to stare at them, I can afford to, because I am an actress.

—actors are a walking denial of discretion—their faces are masks imitating real human features in an exaggerated way. I can recognize

them instantly through that indecent clarity of theirs—the bastards,
they seriously pretend to be people—I adore them. For that appearance of theirs of scientists, countesses, ministers, courtesans, monks
—always a bit too scientific, too ministerial, too much like a typical
courtesan—I love their aping irresponsibility on the world's account,
which they mimick, ogling and slightly despising it. And the fact that
they will never do anything serious, which counts in practice—no
dictatorships, no wars, no new inventions or new taxes, yes, that's
what I love them for best. . . .

—when was it really?—that I stopped loving him? I don't know.
Perhaps I never did. One of two things: either I never stopped—or I
never started loving him. What is this that other women call love?
That's something which nobody knows. We all know our feelings and
call them by their approved names: goodness—love—hate—evil. And
what if it was only by imagination, my nerves, my fright? If he had
stayed with me after the war I am not sure if it would not have ended
very quickly. But he didn't wait. Not a lay longer. I shall never forgive
him for being so cruel. To leave without a word after those years—
how could he do it? He went away, came back after several months
with a woman. He drank. Then another woman. He drank more and
more—he got swollen with vodka. In those years I saw all his parts.
All were bad—non-existent. He was puffed up and empty. I could
feel he did not want to act. I wished him defeat, bad luck, humiliations. I was giddy—giddy with hate. For him, for those women. I
sent him cursing letters. I lived in a rage, like a lunatic, I used to get
drunk and spit in the mirror cursing myself for this cat-like fury, for
this love. Love! I know what to think of it—I had a complete training from the beginning to the end. One raving thought on one raving
subject, hallucinations on a sacrificial pyre. I created everything myself, his presence was no longer necessary, I didn't see him for months
on end, and he played less and less. They said he could not remember
his script, he was afraid of longer parts. Every night they carried him
out from a pub. He shouted:—I have killed Peters!—Apparently, after
a few drinks he mumbled it to anybody who was drinking with him.
He had on him that German poster with the photograph, I don't know
how he managed to get it after the war. He used to show it round,
spread it on the bar, he boasted that the Germans were giving a
reward for catching him and he described how he killed Peters. In
some places they would not let him in any more. I was waiting. I
lived on curiosity: what would become of him?

—perhaps all this happened because of me? perhaps he paid for
that night, for that hole between the sofa and the wall? I always had
a stronger head. In those years when I had to drink with him, he was
already unconscious and fell on the bed while I could still hold semi-

conscious monologues on future, with a prattling whisper drum hope
into him—that he would get out, that we should start a theatre and
that we should become famous.—Do you think—I used to whisper—
that when the war ends we won't make up for all this villainy, this
poverty? I shall tear out happiness from their throats! Do you hear?
There must be a reward and punishment, otherwise the world will
die. I used to get excited, I had in me the strength of a devil, I spoke,
I drank, I spoke, I swore, hissing with triumph and passion in that
gloomy cage with dirty walls and a sloping ceiling, in that three-floor
shack, where nobody was ever to know of his existence. Yes, I was
powerful and I had a head like a two-litre container. Six glasses of
brandy means nothing to me. Want to get me drunk—me? Just try.

For example, now I can see this man with his smooth, silver
temples taking a cool shower in a hotel in Brussels—how he washes
away my look, my indiscreet glance—out of his brown, well exercised
body with a soft smelling, rarely used skin—

—"Two glasses of brandy too much"—he thinks rubbing his chest
with a soft, rough towel and thinking with an unpleasant feeling that
he confessed something about himself to a slightly suspicious looking
woman, living in his old, unsteady country—she certainly did not tell
him the truth about her life.

My dear sir. We know what we are, but we should keep it to ourselves. One should not go too deeply into the outcome of one's life—
it's better to pretend that it makes sense. One should make the
prescribed gestures for the benefit of the world and forget that one
is a bastard. I am telling you, I am fully trained and my contention
is that there are three principles which one should adhere to, in order
to achieve happiness.

First of all: never let go of yourself. A person who never lets himself go, makes others listen to him.

Secondly: create advantageous situations for other people, that
is, such situations in which they appear better than they thought they
were.

Thirdly: never try to achieve complete satisfaction in any field
of activity, especially in an erotic one. Insufficiency is the best state
to be in.

That's almost all I've got to say—I cannot foresee the rest.

I could do with a short sleep. My eyes are heavy, my mouth is
dry. What is this country over which we are flying? Flat, yellow fields,
a river with grey banks. Schelde? It doesn't matter. To sleep.

—too many stormy scenes in my life, fresh, never described—
that's fatal, human life should be an imitation and not a new creation,
there must be models, patterns, inherited motives and examples, on
this our existence depends, to fill one's time like a frieze with known

scenes and live, live like the good Lord commanded us, amen—amen
—amen.

—I am not a standard. In the moments in which I recognize my-
self in other people, I see it as their ugliness. The standard with which
I compare life is always greater than I. I despise everybody in whom
I discover my own evil, even though I forgive it in myself.

—I forgive, I forget, I seem to think it's annulled because I know
of it.

—but that which I discover in myself I automatically hold against
others—and I begin to judge them by that, with which I am unable
to cope. I am disgusted with those Brazilians because they were
afraid of the storm, and with those Poles sitting behind me—because
of their complexes when they are with foreigners, and all others here
in this aeroplane for their dumb zest for life at any price, at the price
of lives of those remaining. I am exactly the same as they. Exactly the
same—that is why they seem to me much worse.

These are not Christian feelings, but it is love. I could not exist
without them. Only a very exceptional love depends on something
greater than that.

Ophelia—Polonius—Hamlet. I—Peters—he. Gestapo—Peters—he
and I. He hit a traitor's face—the next day they found a blood-stained
body—thirteen years pass—again a blood-stained body. Nobody was
guilty. And I—always I, going about in deadly horror, in darkness, in
dread ...

I used to cook them dinner from sawdust, which spilled from a
sofa—both were made of plastic with flat painted eyes, I fed them
with a spoon, dressed them and told them fantastic tales—Mr. and
Mrs. Plastic—I made them green capes from an old overcoat, they
loved me, nobody loved me as much as they had, since, Mr. Plastic
and Mrs. Plastic, if it wasn't for them I would die from boredom and
fright.

No, I am not asleep. To break away from earth is nothing—let me
break away from myself.

What is this stewardess thinking about? About landing in Paris
or about the first time she parted her knees?

I shall buy myself a new suspender belt in Paris, black, transparent, the best quality. Only for my own pleasure. I shall stand in it
in front of the mirror—I have to make it up for those years.

—*in those years.* When in a café he asked me if I could come back
to him. No, I think I said it first. I asked ... like in those years?—
and he only repeated:—In those years. I am paying for them now.
—I did not understand him. Several years without keeping in touch
is a long time in matters like these. I waited for eight years, and if to
add five years of war that would make thirteen. Thirteen years of

waiting. What for? For those five days? for that last night? for . . .

—I could not understand *how* he had changed, what key would fit him. I looked into his eyes, I tried to turn him inside out and kept asking him stupidly why they spoke of him so badly. I had an empty space and I kept stumbling against it. He was silent and then began to explain, that all *that* did not pay.—All that?—I asked—what all that?—Those years in which you hid me—he made a wry face— do you understand? I should have gone and let them execute me.— I shouted with anger:—To whom are you saying it? To me? You have no right! Even now I wake up howling every night that they have come to arrest you!

—what does he want of me—I thought—now, when I am able to exist at last. Why did he drag me to this filthy café, full of black-marketeers? I was biting my lips, upset, because I couldn't understand anything:—What do you mean, you are unable to live? Surely, you've got everything the way you want it. I am not in your way, am I?

—he started beating about the bush—he spoke quietly and in-distinctly, I still could not understand him. Something about a woman with whom he broke off. I did not want to listen then about the war: —You know, we are both the unknown soldiers of this war, not a bad joke, eh?—He laughed and suddenly was silent. He looked at me. And then, in that instant I realized that he was waiting for my voice of those past years. I sat there, not moving, from surprise and pity and perhaps disappointment.—Stop drinking, do you hear me! You've got to stop.

—I looked without compassion at his bloated, too heroic face with softly curved mouth. In a month's time it would be clear that I would not care for him any more, I was certain of that—almost certain. But after a while I started to speak with my old, hissing— my war-years voice:—We shall be together. You will act. You can act all your parts. It isn't true that the war finished you. With me you will become yourself again—I said accentuating every word and I could feel my eyes becoming green,—but you have to listen to me. Do you understand?

—he asked me if I did not think it was too late and even then it did not occur to me to shut my mouth.—For what, you idiot? too late for what? Do you think you must sleep with me? I am not a moron.— I looked at him with a magical gaze of those years:—You will stop drinking, do you hear? I shall put you in a home. Do you hear? You will be lost for three months, only I shall know where you are. You poor thing, I can see I have to take care of you, you cannot live alone. Don't worry, I'll take care of everything. Everything—do you hear? —except drink.

—and then I was stunned: he said he stopped drinking last year.

Suddenly he pulled out his wallet and took out those letters—they fell
on the table.—Do you see?—he looked at me with spite—well, have
a look, read them. I took them, I began to read them. They were about
him and about me—about the price paid to the Gestapo for his life.
I felt tired: letters, more letters . . . —Do you see—he repeated—
they don't believe us. They don't believe that there was another way
in which I could save myself. I don't care what they think of us. I
showed them to you because you should know that it didn't pay even
in this instance. If I did not let you take me into that cab they would
regard me today as a hero.—I hissed through tight lips:—Tear it up,
throw away this dirt.—People in the café began to look at us.

—as we were going out he stopped and smiled at me asking if I
heard, what they said about Peters' death? No, I did not know.—
Apparently the Germans killed him—he smiled—because it transpired
—he kept on smiling as if hit with something—that he was a French
spy.—He looked at me sharply and I think I answered that one never
knows who one really is, or something to that effect, and that he
should not have hit him in the face.—I always was of the opinion that
it wasn't necessary to hit him—I said it literally, revenging myself
with this tactless remark for those eight years. My poisonous calmness
has returned, again I started to plot. And two days later as I was un-
packing my things out in his flat I had no idea that this was the conclusion.

Conclusion! Only that part which I did not want to give up has
ended, that part which I created for myself. It seems to me that one
should not take away half of my life—I have honestly acquired the
possession of it. But as it dropped off of its own accord, something else
has begun. Background—yes, I had a feeling I was becoming a part
of a background, a part of that, which up till now was going on behind my back, deep down, into which I never looked, in which I never
took part. Very interesting. This new, broadened, background life
appeared to be much more like happiness than the first one. I felt
like a worn-out bow. I did not need to strain or bow, something
loosened up in me, yes, I suppose I could take a rest. Step out, step
back towards my own background, look from some distance at my
own trodden place—that's very important. After his death—

—we came back drunk, for five days we drank every night, and it
was I who urged him—so that everybody would see us together in
that pub—and it was I who opened the window saying it was stuffy
in the room—do not put the light on—he said—the moths will fly in.
I filled the bath tub—noise of the running water deafened everything,
I stood naked when there was a cry in the courtyard, this woman
screaming on the balcony. The window was wide open, in the darkness I slipped, but around me all the windows were lit up. Why did

he do it? why did he want me to be there when it happened? why did he leave the sofa standing away from the wall?

—after his death, when I started to play small parts in the "Fairies Theatre" I understood at last that I was not doing too badly. *That* became a bad, mistaken, pointless play, as it were, in which I played a part of a tragic comedienne and now I moved behind the scenery. Three, four, five glasses of vodka a day was quite enough for me in those days. Family? love? a man? It is quite possible to do without these things, only one must have the inner depth.

And a pleasant voice—that's a must!

I went there calm, to record my tape. I wasn't surprised. It's just that they heard my tone. They asked me to take part in a competition for *Felicity's voice*, because somebody said that as a witch in the "Land of Dreams" I had an interesting, hoarse voice. And only while I was sitting in the manager's office, when they told me of their decision, only then did I feel inside me this burnt-out desert through which I had walked for years. Very well—I could be Felicity.

I do not rebel, I do not accuse. Never have I had any grounds to accuse the world. Everything that we encounter—from the earth, from the air, from the fire and from the people—I consider as something natural, with which one should only bargain wisely. And to allow oneself to be indifferent towards matters which are unknown.

The aircraft wing looks now like a knife shining in the sun. Like a huge blade cutting my life into two uneven parts. The owl was a baker's daughter? I would like to find a producer who could explain to me what it really means, my thirtieth performance has not come up yet. But do we know for certain who we are?

What we become is usually preceded by an instant offer. At that time, they asked me to get him through—and the result—I, of those years. The next engagement was less risky, I had no reason to refuse. And as a result—I, Felicity Konopka, am flying to meet my daughter in Paris.

But really, is it so very important? We know what we are—we cannot guess what we shall be a year from now—we forget what we used to be. My true fate really depends not on what will become of me, but *what* will I become—and I think it will never be played to the very end, because it is impossible to listen back to all my tapes, to judge myself as an achievement.

The elderly gentleman in a boater who spoke French to the stewardess, has sat in the empty place next to me.

—*Vous permettez, madame?*

—*S'il vous plaît, monsieur. Naturellement.*

Healthy, red face with a trim moustache, about sixty, slightly like Tom. He is looking at me. This does not worry me at all.

Down below light, wispy clouds. A white steam over warm, opal earth. We are flying lower down. We are changing the direction of flight—the view seems to be at an angle to the wing.

I sit up straight, smiling. I know that those Poles recognized me before and will again listen to the conversation with my neighbor.

—*Oh, oui, Varsovie est une ville très interessante.*

Frankly, he is very pleasant and looks respectable. Cigarette? Cork-tipped, of course.

—*Oui, c'est vrai, la reconstruction de la capitale est miraculeuse.*

We are swimming. We are moving through huge shiny streaks of powdered light. In a moment I shall see Paris below.

Have I lost my handbag? No, it's in its place. Compact? The mirror did not break. A touch of powder, a spot of lipstick. I must admit I don't look too bad in spite of the long flight. A tablet, just in case. A copy of "Przekroj" is showing in my coat pocket; I shall send a postcard to Tom from the airport: *Darling, the journey was marvelous. . . .* he will read my words in the program in two weeks' time. So that they will know that I have remembered them.

A luggage ticket—handbag—gloves . . .

Have I everything? Yes, that's all.

Fasten the safety belts? All right.

Translated by MAGDALENA CZAJKOWSKA

Jerzy Zawieyski

(1902–1969)

Jerzy Zawieyski was born in 1902 in a village near Lodz. He completed his secondary education in Lodz and later studied philosophy and history of art at Warsaw, Wilno and Paris universities. For a time he was an actor. In the thirties he travelled extensively in Europe and Africa. He made his literary debut with a novel in 1932 (*Where Are You Friend?*).

Zawieyski came into prominence as an outstanding Catholic writer after World War II. His plays were produced in many Polish cities, but he was forced into total silence in 1950, resuming publication in 1956, on Gomulka's accession to power. In recognition of his high moral integrity manifested during the years of Stalinist repression, he was chosen president of the Club of Catholic Intelligentsia, vice-president of the Association of Polish Writers and in 1957 was elected deputy to the Sejm and member of the Council of State.

Zawieyski is the author of twenty-five plays, four novels, two collections of short stories, several volumes of essays, journals and poetic prose. Though his novels (particularly *Hubert's Night,* 1946), his essays (e.g., *Trials of Fire and Time,* 1958) or poetic prose (*Lyrical Notebook,* 1956) are not to be disregarded, his prime contribution to modern Polish literature has been through his plays and short stories.

His dramatic writings are characterized by a great variety of style and subject matter. Whatever the setting or period, Zawieyski's plays deal with one essential theme: man and his often hopeless, but never pointless, struggle for integrity and freedom from tyranny, political, social or religious. He has been labelled as a "Catholic" writer, but he avoids subservience to dogma, writing from the purely human point of view, only occasionally limiting himself by the choice of a religious subject. His recent plays have been marked by ultra-modern and experimental techniques. Three have been translated into English (*Crossroads of Love, Socrates* and *Jacob's Rescue*).

What has been said of the plays applies also to Zawieyski's short stories which are an important part of his writing. He invariably chooses subjects that are deeply moving and charged with moral significance, and develops them with great psychological insight. His settings are historical or biblical but usually he writes of most recent history, e.g., "Requiem for Both of Them" (set in the Warsaw Ghetto); "Meeting with Emanuel" (about the Warsaw Rising of 1944); "Cry in the Void" (a moving story about the extermination of the inmates of a mental institution by the Nazis); "True End of the Great War" (shows the lasting effects of war on the survivors); "Antigone's Brother" (about a Stalinist political trial).

Zawieyski's stories have been made into successful films, and his latest collection has been very well received both by the critics and the public.

Cry in the Void

Before this story begins . . .

The events described here by Renata W., a doctor at the Mental Hospital in our town, took place in June 1942. As part of their theory of racial purity, the Germans treated mental ailments as incurable, and they had therefore decided to solve this problem in the simplest possible manner, by exterminating those who suffered from these illnesses.

Such was the fate of our Hospital too.

Renata W. did not want to desert the patients and made up her mind to go to her death with them.

She died on the 8th of June 1942, together with the patients, who were transported by the Germans to goods wagons and then gassed with the mixture known as "Zyklon B."

Such are the bare facts.

But Renata's story reaches above and beyond the bare facts. She set it down in a stock-book on thirty pages which became both a document of her resolution and a testimony to it.

Renata W. describes happenings which, as it were, conspired to shake her resolution. Like, for instance, the unfortunate business with Narcyz, the former dancer, a schizophrenic tormented by depressive hallucinations which urged him to take his own life.

But that is not the important thing in this story. The most important point is Renata's attitude, her firm, consistent "no" hurled like a cry into the void of the world.

In conclusion, we have to add that our Mental Hospital now bears the names of Renata and Karol. This happened at the instigation of Doctor Adam Skrzyniarz, the director-in-chief of the Hospital, who holds the position to this day. The Hospital is now a temporary place of residence for the patients, thanks to modern drugs and advances in methods of treatment.

That is all. Now let Renata tell her story.

The First Day

Today there were still sixty-two patients—forty-two women and twenty men.

For the last three days it has been raining, and the wet chestnut trees outside the window have been rustling incessantly, loudest of all in the evenings and at night. The garden on the other side has also been rustling, but not in the same way as the trees.

So—sixty-two patients, and a week ago there were still a hundred and seventy. First of all, we managed to send the men away in groups of half a dozen or a dozen. If they had families, they were sent to their families; if not, Skalski took them to the forest to join his partisans. It was easier with the women, because nearly all of them were cured and so they went to work as maids or help on farms. We managed to get ninety men and twelve women out. The rest, these sixty-two, are chronic cases, mostly schizophrenia. Now they wander semi-conscious about the empty building, but they do understand that there is some threat hanging over them. Before this decision came through, there were German civilian and military doctors coming here in groups. Thus we knew only too well what was coming. For the hospital in B. and the hospital in M. had both been liquidated. This was an operation covering the whole country, with the purpose of exterminating the mentally sick. It was during the period of these visits that we got the men out wherever we could, and then the women. The hospital has been occupied for three days now. Lists were made of the patients, at this late stage!—and the doctors were relieved of their duties. They went, not without resistance, but nonetheless they went.

I stayed behind alone.

The rain is pouring down, the cold gale is battling through the chestnut trees and banging on the window. The light has been cut off, but I have a supply of candles.

Perhaps it will be tomorrow? Or in the night? The patients think they are going to be moved to another town or into the country. They thronged around me when the doctors were leaving—after the big scene with me—and shrieked and wept and implored me to stay with them. If I stayed—if I stayed, they stammered and sobbed, nothing would happen to them. So would I stay? Really?

I reassured them that I would. I had no home, I had no one, just like them. I had already decided earlier that I was going to stay, I explained patiently.

The same day I spoke to Narcyz, the former dancer.

"From tomorrow, Narcyz, serve drippings and margarine for breakfast as well as marmalade for the bread. You must kill the hens too, how many are there? Thirty? Well then, ten each day. From tomorrow too, serve afternoon tea. And, Narcyz, in the garden after each afternoon tea, you can perform your party turns under the apple tree, you know, the fight with the cocks. The patients like it and always laugh and shout with delight. Will you remember what I'm saying, Narcyz? We can't go on with treatment any more, because the pharmacy is sealed off, and anyway, there are no doctors now. If it's fine tomorrow, bring the patients out into the garden, open the windows, and air the wards. Appoint some cleaners, because the cleaners have gone too. Sweep up, clean out and scrub the toilets. There are only the two of us here now and we are responsible for the patients. I'm asking you to help me, Narcyz."

I glanced at Narcyz. He was staring at the windows, which were streaming with rain, for it was still coming down in sheets.

"Repeat what I just said, Narcyz," I said after a while, breaking the silence.

Narcyz withdrew his gaze from the windows and hung his head, as though he felt guilty about something. He looked about twenty years old, though in fact he was over forty.

So he neither wanted to look nor to say anything. But did he understand?

Suddenly, with one bound, he gained the table, blew out the candle and rushed out shouting that he would not allow the hens to be killed nor anyone to go near the hen-house.

He had understood, however, at least about the hens and the hen-houses.

With difficulty I found the matches to light the candle again. There was no one in the street. In the distance I could hear train whistles. All was quiet in the building itself. Would it be tonight?

But tonight the telephone rang. It was gloomy. In the trees the birds were calling, probably happy that the rain had gone off and that the wind had dropped.

"I can't sleep . . . I just can't get to sleep," Doctor Skrzyniarz called into the receiver at the other end, "once again I ask you, I ask you, more than that, I beg you not to go through with it—it's crazy, and you're not one of those people who usually get up to crazy tricks, so listen, Renata, don't torture me, don't torture us, you can leave right now while they're asleep. Renata, Renata, think of your husband, think of Karol who wouldn't have allowed . . . Do you hear me? Say something, say something, you must hear me asking you, you must be able to hear my despair! Despair, Renata . . ."

I spoke—very softly as though in my sleep. Skrzyniarz's word buzzed sharply and with a whistle in the receiver, interspersed with the sound of his breathing, and it was all hasty and ridden with fear. I could not shake off my sleep and did not feel like summoning up my voice to say some of the things which had come so easily to me that morning.

I sat down by the table on which the telephone stood, and closed my eyes to bring back my sleep. After a while it came back. Again the same tunnel through which I was walking swiftly along the rails, afraid that a train might approach from the opposite direction. I could hear familiar footsteps, still in the distance . . . and then again a few of those terrible words whistled in my ear: "You're making us into beasts for the slaughter, Renata, and we're only human, it's just that we don't want to die, that's all, and you're making us into beasts for the slaughter! Renata . . . Renata . . ." The steps had receded again, but they were there, they were there somewhere. I heard Skrzyniarz's groan in the receiver. Could he have been weeping? Karol was going away again—I knew right away that it was Karol who was coming to meet me, and I could not hear anything now. The receiver had gone dead too. I called for a long time: Hello! Hello! Adam!

I got into bed frozen and only now really wide awake. The birds in the trees were singing in chorus. I pulled the quilt over my head so as to drown the noise of the birds and shut out the light of dawn.

Once again, everything that had happened since that morning had to pass through my mind for the hundredth time. It must have been Skrzyniarz and the other two, Zielewicz and Peterek, who had sent that major, a man like some character from an edifying novel about a noble enemy. The German major was still a young man, about Karol's age, and his name was Hugo von Schwengruben. The moment he came in, he made it known that we would probably understand one another better in French than in German. *N'est-ce pas, madame?* I nodded my head and offered him the armchair. He sat down on the edge of it, spent a long time taking his glove off and fixed me with a piercing gaze. I strained myself to the utmost to understand what he was saying. A barrier was set up between us by the foreign language, which was not always clear and demanded hard work in instantly searching one's memory for the forgotten meanings of the words. Schwengruben said that he had come in secret and in his private capacity (*à titre personnel*) and that the authorities did not know of his visit. But he had heard about my decision from some military doctors he knew and from Doctor Skrzyniarz, was shaken (*bouleversé*) and full of admiration (*plein d'admiration*), but nonetheless he felt duty-bound to prevail on me to alter my decision, because, after all, I was sentencing myself to death with the patients, and my death would not benefit anyone, it would be fruitless (*stérile*), incomprehensible and pointless (*inutile*). Then I lost the thread of the conversation through falling into a day dream over the word "envisager," and before I managed to decipher it, the stream of French speech had turned into a dark barrier again and it was impossible to penetrate to its inner depth. I looked at Schwengruben, at his narrow mouth which curled up a little at the left—"*Croyez moi, madame, croyez . . . croyez . . .*"—he was saying insistently, softly but firmly. Again the incomprehensible words flowed out, devoid of meaning, isolated, useless so far as I was concerned. Nevertheless,

whether as a result of the change of subject, or because I had accustomed myself to Schwengruben's speech, I later understood what
he had been saying. And he had been saying that he had known me
by sight for some time, because, just like me, he liked to sit in the
afternoon in the little Café Helena, but he was not surprised that I
did not recognize him because he always went there in civilian
clothes, and anyhow, for a beautiful woman like me he could not
really hold any attraction, and he was not surprised that I had never
so much as glanced at him. Only one woman really loved him, and
that was his sister, who—wasn't it amazing?—liked to wear white
dresses, white hats, white shoes, everything white, just like me, which,
with her dark complexion and dark hair, looked very becoming.
"Vous me rappellez ma soeur, madame, me soeur Lotha, and so you
remind me of the one woman who loves me, who really loves me."

To stop Schwengruben going on like this, I asked firmly:

"Is it you who's going to seize the hospital and take the patients
out to their deaths?"

"No, not me, it'll be Colonel Miller, or General Schneider. The
Colonel might carry out this dirty work personally (*cette sale affaire
. . . personnellement*), because he's interested in you—he knows all
about it, and when he found out, he didn't have you removed by
force or persuasion, because this was an interesting case (*un cas
intéressant*), but whenever he talked about it, he would burst into a
long, loud laugh, as only he can, he would laugh, I'm sorry to say, as
though it were a ridiculous thing to do, coming to a decision like that.
He's capable of anything, but, you know *madame, vous me rappelez
me soeur, Lotha,* I can't get over it, oh, I'm sorry, what am I to say
to you? A strange man, in enemy uniform, has come to ask you to do
something, in the knowledge that he is exposing himself to ridicule,
so please try to understand all the same—it's my sister Lotha whom
I'd like to try and save. That's all. *C'est tout.*"

Now Schwengruben's mouth closed, compressed by the narrow
lips. His nimble, watchful eyes had taken on an attentive and impatient look. Schwengruben was waiting.

"*J'ai déjà réfléchi,*" I said after a while, and to prevent him starting
all over again, I stood up and gave him my hand to say goodbye.

"*Adieu, monsieur, adieu,*" came into my mind rather than "au
revoir," which would have been a lie, or at least a false hope for him
that I might change my mind.

Schwengruben started to go, but he stopped at the door, as though
he still had something to say.

"*Adieu*"—with this word I closed his mouth, and he went out.

Immediately Skrzyniarz and our two doctors rushed in. They were
packed up, all ready for leaving and impatient at every moment
which might cut off their way to freedom, to life. They knew every-

thing that might happen from the accounts of what had been done to the hospitals in M. and B. So one could not really blame them for being afraid and glancing at their watches every few minutes, so as to be out of the hospital by twelve noon, as they had been instructed. It was now approaching twelve o'clock. They did not speak this time or try to dissuade me, as they had done yesterday, but they shrieked, clutched at their heads, and one of them, the youngest, Doctor Peterek, was even weeping.

Then the patients crowded into the room, and there began a real bedlam of shouting and wailing.

Through the windows which were streaming with rain, I saw the doctors getting into the car. Skrzyniarz was the only one staying behind in the town, because he had a house and family here—the others were going off in different directions.

It struck twelve o'clock, but by this time the car had driven off noisily, leaving behind it a trail of blue vapor.

Right away lunch was served. To keep up an appearance of normality, I told Pelcia as usual to set the table neatly, spread a clean cloth and put flowers on the table. Pelcia is replacing Irene, the charwoman, who, like the rest of the charwomen, left the hospital yesterday. At the second course—cauliflower and potatoes—Pelcia had an attack of her peculiar and very perseverant way of saying (it was really a stammer, and not a speech habit) the word "miluk." I sent her off to the ward and cleared the tables myself. Then I went to bed, for it was still raining incessantly and I had no work to do, at least not for the moment, and anyway, before you can get down to work, you have to collect your thoughts. But first rest, until something else comes along or those lorries drive up, the death trucks. Let them drive up soon, today if they want, or this evening or in the night, as long as it is not right now. Now sleep, sleep, to the rhythm of the rain and the wind.

When I awoke from my dreamless sleep, darkness had fallen and it was still raining, so I lit a candle and at once felt a surge of energy. I summoned Narcyz ...

THE SECOND DAY

The next day, from early morning, there were signs of a storm. In the afternoon, darkness came down, it began to thunder and the gale broke, but the storm did not last all that long and passed over somewhere to the side. Suddenly it was fine again. At last the sun came out and day was day, and not night any more.

I went down to the garden, as had long been my custom, to collect the underground newspaper left there every morning by Skalski's people at a pre-arranged place where our garden bordered on the Bishop's. The way to it led past the summer house, now over-grown with weeds, where in September 1939 Karol had died. Every day I pass by there with the same words: "Why did you have to do it, why did you have to run out . . . after that madman?" We were in the shelter while the bombs were falling, the patients were quiet and calm, and no one could have foreseen that a dazed catatonic would suddenly leap up and rush out into the garden shrieking. Karol ran out after him; it was day, but in a flash the day became night, and then there was that whistle and a dull thud. That was the last bomb which fell on our town. Throughout that day, in the smoke and dust, we searched for the scattered remains of Karol. What we managed to gather up lies in a grave on the other side, between the two elms which Karol had liked so much.

So today I was once again taking this walk to the place where Karol had died, probably for the last time, and it was certainly not for the news sheet hidden in the wall that I went there, but in order to see the heap of rubble, set out in some geometrical figure whose base was the one standing wall of the former one-story building.

Gladioli and climbing-plants now grew on the rubble. Someone must have been there not long ago, perhaps even a moment before, for where else could the scattered eggshells have come from? They had not been there yesterday. I gathered the shells together and pressed them into a gap between the bricks, although I was not wor-ried about tidiness—not now that even today, perhaps in a moment . . . for everything was possible now, and all we could do now was to wait.

In the wall, under the brick, was the "consignment," wrapped in stout cardboard, but already soaked through by the rain.

In the administration office, where there always used to be plenty of movement and noise, there now reigns solitude and silence—a really lifeless place. Narcyz should have been there; he has always lent us a helping hand as long as he did not fall into his depressive hallucinations, which forced him to seek ways of committing suicide. But Narcyz was not there.

I slowly unwrapped the saturated package from Skalski.

At the top of the package there was a letter, it must have been a letter, written on a piece of paper in blue ink, which had smudged with the rain, making the writing illegible. Skalski rarely ever wrote, and if he ever wanted to ask us for something or pass some news on to us, he would use his liaison people.

This time Skalski had written, knowing that access to the Hospital was impossible because of the German sentries who would not let anyone in. But how was I to decipher this letter? He was the only one not to protest when he heard of my decision, and while the others, including Skrzyniarz, accused me of deliberately trying to ruin them by working on their consciences, or of piling crime upon crime, or of making myself the laughing-stock of the Germans, who, like Miller, sneered at the stupidity and histrionics of the Poles—he alone remained silent. Among the patients, his only interest was in the men who were capable of working for the partisans. He was not unduly worried about the others, and as for the criminal action of the Germans against our Hospital, he simply stated that he had no comment to make, but that he had informed his superiors and was waiting for orders. He was waiting for orders—he emphasized several times.

I put the letter down to dry out in the hope that it might be possible to decipher it later, because it certainly contained news, important news, but for heaven's sake, Skalski could not be worried about the same thing as Skrzyniarz expected, or the German major, that wry-mouthed Hugo von Schwengruben.

"I can't desert the patients," I said aloud in the empty room, and these banal words echoed round the walls.

I took to reading the bulletin "War and Freedom," but the newsprint had smudged too, the sheets were stuck together and in places it was difficult to separate them. From a superficial glance, one learned that the Allies were continuing the struggle, with heavy losses, and that the human casualties were great, especially on the North African front. There was also an item about the Yugoslav partisans and the German crimes in the occupied states. In our country there were street executions, executions in prison, mass deportations, investigations and torture. A description of the escape of a group of prisoners from the camp at Dachau ended on a page which was stuck to another, and I could not get them apart. So I left off at this item about the escape of the prisoners who were trying to save their lives—for the simple reason that you must save life, you must, Karol, but why did you have to do it? . . . why did you have to run . . . after that madman? Oh, if I speak like this, it is only because I myself do not know the answer. If only you had stumbled, if only someone's hand had held you back or if I had called you to come back, that split second might have been enough to make you realize that you should not run out, because it was a matter of life and death, and the man's life was not really worth calling a life at all. But this split second did not come, and, Karol, I can't understand it, and I talk about it in the same way as Skrzyniarz is now talking of me. But despite this, I do not accuse you, and I too will not desert them, even though I have more than a split second to think and make up my mind.

I left Skalski's letter on the table, straightened it out, smoothed it at the edges, and weighted it down at the top with a heavy inkstand and at the bottom with a brass ashtray. It could stay there to dry out, but meanwhile I had to go to take a look at the patients, I said to myself as I made my mind up, but I began to feel more and more uneasy, I was afraid of something, and yet fear under these circumstances, when I was ready for anything . . . how could it be?

As I was coming out of the office to go over to the wards by the internal corridors, I could hear thunder. It went dark, the clouds piled up thicker and thicker and, dark grey in color, hung low over the earth; some of them had white crests. Now I understood why I felt so afraid and uneasy. A storm was approaching, and I had been afraid of storms since I was a child. I had always been scared to death and used to look for other people to avoid being alone.

Now darkness was descending from the clouds, and day had ceased to be day, so I had to look for people, even if only Narcyz, who had disappeared since yesterday and should be either in the administration office or in my study, on the corridors, somewhere about.

The women in Ward 1, the oldest, and all cases of dementia, were dozing, except for two of them, who were walking up and down with careful precision along the same stretch of floor by the table. They appeared not to notice me, or else they did not want to notice me, but, to make up for this, a group of patients thronged around me in the next ward and, clapping their hands, expressed their joy at the fact that "you've come, doctor, but you haven't brought any medicine, you've just come ordinary like . . . to have a chat." None of the women had seen Narcyz, but, yes, one of them had seen him, perhaps an hour ago, but it had been in a dream, he had the features of the Gypsy and was eating fire. A delicate blonde, called Liliana by her fellow patients, was dressing a doll, for which she had made a "water" costume, all of green rags. Liliana suddenly asked, "Why are you afraid, doctor?" "I'm not afraid at all, Liliana, I'm just looking for Narcyz. I'm not afraid of anything, why, whatever should I be afraid of? And in any case, the storm will soon pass over, you mark my words." I was annoyed with Liliana for noticing that I was afraid of the storm—I had not been able to conceal my fear—and immediately the women began to press me to stay with them and not go away. I promised to come back once I had found Narcyz, who must be about somewhere, probably in the men's wing.

But he was not there either. The whole wing was neat and tidy, the wards were swept, and the patients washed and dressed. Clearly Narcyz was behind all this. But no one had seen him, and meanwhile the thunder became more and more frequent, with flashes of lightning preceding it, and the thunderbolts struck somewhere nearby, perhaps even in the garden.

In the last ward, I was suddenly confronted with the small, delicate, clean and white-headed figure of Ignacy Kocys, with his innocent eyes and innocent smile. Kocys, once a bookkeeper, had suddenly throttled his wife with his shapely hands while they were having dinner, because he had been so bidden by the powerful demon Zenobii-Ki. In this way he was to regain his freedom in order to carry out the mission which the demon had destined for him. He had been here for three years now, and was always pleasant and quiet, positively happy in fact, because he was working on a book about the struggle of the angels with the demons on seven levels of abstraction, a work supported by statistics, tables, sketch maps of the battlefields and geometrical patterns.

I could not pass Kocys by and go on, because further on there was nothing but a door leading out into the yard, and there was no one out there. Besides, a sudden gale got up, and I had to take refuge somewhere. I stayed with Kocys, tired and with all my energy sapped and my face and neck perspiring. I knew the story about Kocys' book and his demon was going to come, and usually when he started on it, I would ask him the firm, simple questions: "How old are you? What day is it today? What is your name?" At this, Kocys would break off his narrative, think for a long time, in search of a reply, and eventually he would go away discouraged, as though taking offense.

This time I decided not to interrupt Kocys, at least not before the storm was over, and this frenzy of roars and flashes had exhausted itself. Kocys was not affected by it at all, as though there were nothing happening out there and all this were in the normal run of things.

Today Kocys spoke differently, so I felt a certain disappointment and even surprise, and uneasiness too, an uneasiness quite different from my uneasy feelings about the storm, and there was no need for me to interrupt him with questions about his name, the day or his age.

"I knew you'd come to have a chat with me, doctor, I knew even yesterday, when the others left—and you probably noticed, doctor, that they left very hastily, as if they were running away. Please don't think, doctor, that I'm going to go on the same way as I often do— I mean, manifestation of megalomania and all that, or, to put it more simply, madness caused by a mission which one has been called upon to carry out. If it offends you, doctor, I may not speak of Zenobii-Ki and won't mention his name once. If you would just wipe off that drop of sweat which has stopped above your left eyebrow on the left-hand side, doctor, on the left-hand side of me, yes, that's right—then I would be free to say immediately that it won't be as you imagine it—please don't be angry and wrinkle your brow like that—I tell you it'll be completely different, which doesn't mean to say there's a possibility of any of us emerging unscathed from the verdict of extermination."

The lightning flashed across Kocys' face, but he did not bat an eyelid and withstood the blinding light. I caught hold of his hand, because the thunder had a thunderbolt in it, which struck somewhere nearby with a sharp whistle. The next flash of lightning lasted longer, but I did not see it this time, because I had my eyes closed and was asking Kocys to speak.

And so he spoke on and on—and kept stopping to ask me whether I understood and was listening. "But of course I'm listening, Mr. Kocys, and I understand."

"You can give it a different name, you know, doctor, for instance by using the abstract word 'element' instead of the name Zenobii-Ki, but whatever you use, it's all the same, because it's not the name that's important, but the wreaking of destruction, the contrary nature of contradiction, or the breaking up of order into absolute chaos and abracadabra. And it's not as though all this is anything new, for he has always been there and came upon the scene at the time when he created the first town after the killing of Abel. But let's leave the history of his crimes aside—everyone knows where they came from and how they went arm in arm with the ripening of humanity. Ripening to what? We'd better not say anything about that, no, we'd better not say anything because I see fear in your eyes again, doctor, and after all, it's only lightning, there aren't any thunderbolts. Please keep calm, look, it's dying down now, it's dying down, till the next flash of lightning comes and the next thunderbolt. It's dying down, so we can tell one another that we are above the wiles of this 'element,' above its wiles because we know them and know what they can lead to.

"But now I'm going to say something more important, something connected with your profession, only first I must ask you to rest comfortably on the pillows—the storm will soon pass over. Well then, this something more important concerns his dominion within us, I mean, the 'element's' or, oh I'm sorry, Zenobii-Ki's. I'm looking at you rather uneasily because anything might happen, one flash is enough, an ostensibly innocent thought, and it could happen, as it did with me when I was able to throttle someone over dinner—which is clearly only a rough, tactless comparison, with you it may be different, of course, but are you sure it'll last and you won't listen to Skrzyniarz or that sentimental Major Schwengruben?

"Oh, don't rub your hands like that, don't crack your fingers, because things are probable, and they are called 'human,' that is, woven from sins and contradictions and also from blind forces which toss us about like the storm does the orchard. But it's possible that this time a miracle will happen, because miracles do happen, it's possible, I say, that you will hold out and go to your death with those who were unwilling to fall into line and have gone forth from themselves, each with his own protest, with his own 'no.' And so we must die, not for our Country, not for ideals, nor for a leader or a cause, but for our

'no,' which you yourself know well, doctor, both know it and understand it, although you don't know where the source of this 'no' is and
what is its origin, nor can you do anything to remedy it apart from
holding out your hand with some liquid or powder which is supposed to induce sleep. But these are vain endeavors, for sleep does
not bring oblivion, so for us there's nothing else but death, disintegration or gas, it's all the same—oh, now didn't I say so? . . . the
storm's over, and now the sun will come out, and the air will be
clean and fragrant. Well, doctor, thank you for this—how shall I
put it?—this farewell talk. Adieu!"

Kocys stood up and came to the door with me. In control of myself again, but dogged by unpleasant feelings over my fears of the
storm and also ashamed because I really should have made some
reply to Kocys' arguments, I went out into the garden to compose
myself and get a breath of air.

In the avenue leading to the farm buildings, I met Narcyz, who
was breaking the shell of an egg against a tree and swallowing the
contents. Round about there were lots of pieces of eggshell, just
as there had been among the rubble at the place where Karol died.
Narcyz immediately announced joyfully that the hens were in a
safe place, but that he was not going to say where, because they
did not live to be killed en masse; people could die en masse, as
we were all going to, but the hens had done no one any harm and
he was surprised that such a thought had occurred to me . . . I
interrupted him to say that I was not worried about the hens,
he could do what he wanted with them, as long as he just cleared
up the pieces of eggshell, because, in spite of the circumstances,
we had to keep things neat and tidy.

Suddenly there were several patients around us, and then, while
I was walking around the garden with them, more came—some
from the women's wing too, led by Liliana clutching her doll to
her bosom.

But later, when I got back to my room and took my white dress,
white hat and white shoes out of the wardrobe . . . but I must not
hurry, for the last moments of life are always long, and inexhaustible, so I must not hurry, and perhaps I might make it, perhaps I
have a little time left yet.

II

To avoid missing anything or jumping over a link in the story,
I must go back to a pleasant and completely chance occurrence—
the walk around the garden, among the flowerbeds, along the
avenue of acacias and then over the paths of the orchard. The

women clung to my arms, each of them wanted to walk arm in arm with me on a proper walk, just as on an outing, and Wieliczkowa justly arranged that they should change two by two and that she herself would direct this interchange to avoid anyone being offended. As for the men, they could walk at a distance, as was proper, because one can talk and smile at a distance.

But for the sudden, fearful stammer of Pelcia, who was trying to indicate that lunch was ready, the walk would have gone on for a long time, because no one was in a hurry to get anything done and it was very pleasant to relax in the bracing air after the storm, and no one would have thought of interrupting it.

Wieliczkowa arranged that I should first have lunch with the women, and then—with the men. Excited and chattering, the women bore me off to their wing, and they were reluctant to let me go when the time came for me to go over to the men's wing. Wieliczkowa's authority won the day, and so, seen off by a crowd of women, I made my way to the men's quarters.

After lunch, I was hurrying through the garden and over the courtyard when suddenly two German officers appeared from round the corner with three armed soldiers behind them. The question "Is this it?" shot through my mind, but the officers stopped and saluted as they made way for me on the narrow pavement. I slowed down, so that they would not think I had been alarmed by their sudden appearance, but I was sure they were watching where I was going— and so, to conceal the fact that I was going to my quarters, I turned to the right, into the administration block. I had left the letter there in the office, and it would certainly have dried out by now. It had been a slip on my part to leave it on the table like that, because the Germans might have intercepted it, if they had gone into the office.

When I got to the office, I found Narcyz and Kocys already there, but the worst was yet to come—for there was no sign of the letter. Narcyz told me he had passed the Germans on the steps, but had noticed the letter before this and at the last minute had torn it up, and chewed it and stuffed the newspaper into the stove. Then Kocys had come—he knew German and thought he might be useful, but the Germans had only come up to the door and then gone away again—so everything was all right, after all.

I could not find out from Narcyz what had been in the letter. Had he read it? Had the writing been legible once the paper dried out? But Narcyz—as usual—at once hung his head and would not answer the questions. Kocys declared that there would yet come to pass more than one unforeseen event, because no one could be sure of anything, and anyhow, news from the outside world or from beyond the walls of our prison did not matter to any of us now.

I rushed out with the words: "You're wrong, Kocys, you're very wrong," but by the time I was out in the courtyard I regretted saying these words, I was sorry I had lost my temper, and the whole business of Skalski's letter seemed mysterious to me. A large part of this was my own fault, but it had looked like a storm when I was opening the letter and I had been unable to control my fear and uneasiness, thence my thoughtlessness in leaving it on the table and again my unnecessary snapping at Kocys, who had actually been telling the truth.

When I got back to my room, I opened the window a little. It was still fine, the sun was blazing, which perhaps heralded another storm, the blossoming chestnut trees swayed gently in the wind and I could touch their leaves by stretching out my hand.

So the fine weather had come back and it was going to be nice. I suddenly thought of dressing up and going into the town, which was scarcely a kilometer away, and having coffee in the Café Helena. I knew that the idea of leaving the Hospital was senseless, but nonetheless I opened the wardrobe and took out my white dress, white hat and white shoes. I spread out on the sofa a costume, which was also white, and set about deciding which of them to wear. I decided on the dress, and scarcely had I got it on when Pelcia came in with a plate full of raspberries collected in the garden. Pelcia looked at me attentively, but suspiciously, took the costume into her hand, stammered something as she shook it, and then rushed out weeping. I did my hair, put lipstick on, put my hat on and, standing in front of the mirror, told myself that this was the last time I would be dressing up like this—but that I would not be betraying the patients even if I did go out, because I would certainly come back, the German sentries would not prevent me, and I would be able to see the town again—the bridge over the river, the market place, the castle ruins, all the places which Karol had liked so much and which had made him decide to work here as opposed to elsewhere.

Suddenly I heard a buzz of voices, steps coming along the corridors, a bustle, and laughs and shrieks, and before I had time to see what was going on, the door was pushed wide open. The patients thronged outside in a huge crowd, but once at the door they stopped and fell silent. They were excited and were breathing quickly, presumably because they had been running, and now, transferring their gaze from me to the dresses spread out behind me, the shoes, hat and other articles, they stood and looked on. I asked calmly what had happened and why they had come, whether it was perhaps that the Germans had frightened them. Why had they come, I asked again

and again. I was standing in the middle of the room, but when I took
a step in the direction of the table to clear up my scattered things,
the patients too moved a step towards me, and so they advanced
as I retreated, silent and with their mouths firmly closed or else
half-open. Again I asked them to tell me what they had come for,
and met with nothing but silence maintained as though by agreement. So I laughed at them cheerfully and suggested that they should
sit down wherever they could find room, because since they had
come so unexpectedly, they might as well be my guests and take a
look at how I lived, but they might also break the silence and say
something, after all, they were not deaf and dumb. But this had
no effect. They were now so near that I only had to stretch out my
arm in order to touch them. But they were different now. Now the
lunatics, paranoiacs, schizophrenics and epileptics had assembled
here, each living in his own darkness, all stricken with mental disintegration at the hands of dark powers which urged them to kill me
and crush me against this wall where I was cowering. The threat
of violent death was but a step away from me, and I saw before
me hands bent on strangling me and tearing me to pieces—and it
would not be the Germans who would kill me, but the patients,
for that was why they had come here. With a sudden movement of
my hand, I tore off the hat, and in a flash someone's hand had
snatched it away and it was flying in tatters all over the room.

At this moment, which I really thought was my last, salvation
came in the person of Narcyz, who was running up the stairs, announcing happily that in a few minutes under the apple tree there
would be a performance such as the world had never seen before,
and that afterwards there would be raspberries for all. Narcyz at
once saw the danger I was in and began to push the patients aside,
saying that "everything was ready for the performance, and the doctor
was just going to dress up and come down to see the performance
with everyone else." I walked down the stairs slowly with the
patients, who were now laughing at the prospect of the spectacle
with the cocks and fire-eating.

Unable to stand the patients' coarse laughter and their constant
clapping, bravos and encores, I left the garden before Narcyz's
performance was over.

III

One mistake had led to another. Had it not been for my idea
of going out to town and for Pelcia's sounding the alarm by telling
the others that I was running away, then the patients would not have
come bursting into my room. My subsequent conversation with

Narcyz was another link in this chain of mistakes, and this might have found confirmation in Kocys' argument that, in everything human, there are dark, hostile and malevolent forces at work.

Narcyz turned up a few hours after his performance and I tried to tell him all about this, but it was difficult to get through to him in spite of my efforts to create a friendly atmosphere.

I told Narcyz that he had saved my life, that I was counting on him and that in him I had real protection and friendship. I suggested that he should stay and have tea with me, but he merely put his hands to his head and fell into his usual silence. I stroked my hand over his hair, and while I was doing this, he gripped it firmly and sobbed that he too had no one but me, which I must have realized for a long time now, because everything he did was for me. . . . He began to kiss my hands, and when I resisted his importunity, he deftly seized me round the waist and whispered.

"I'll come to you tonight . . . wait for me . . . I'll come . . . Yes? Yes?" he kept asking impatiently.

I nodded my head so he would release me from his embrace. He started to leave hastily, but came back from the door and took a crumpled letter from his pocket. It was from Skrzyniarz and had been handed to him for me by one of the bribed guards.

Thus I lost Narcyz, a real help and the only man, I thought, with whom I could be safe and whom I could trust. Now I had to work out some strategy of defense against him. I would have to run away and hide so he could not find me.

To resume the order of events and not anticipate later facts, I must return to the moment when the telephone rang.

This time I lifted the receiver eagerly. It was Schwengruben, and I was relieved and happy to hear his voice at this moment, after the scene with Narcyz. Schwengruben had rung up to tell me that he had had a violent quarrel with General Schneider over the fate of the Hospital, as a result of which he had been ordered to the front. He was leaving immediately, tonight in fact, but before he went he felt he must again ask me to come out of my voluntary imprisonment and do the same as the doctors, while there was still time.

I listened eagerly to Schwengruben's words, which were meaningless for me and unable to bring about any change, but which were the last words I would hear from the outside world. I was about to say that I would leave immediately if the Germans altered their decision and did not exterminate the patients, when Schwengruben suddenly stopped speaking, there was a grating noise in the receiver and the phone went dead. It did not ring again right up to the end. The other telephones in the administration block had been out of action for some time, so I was now deprived of this means of contact with the world outside too.

It had gone dark already, and now was the time for me to start thinking about dodging Narcyz and looking for a place where he would not be able to find me. I went into the corridor with a candle, searched every floor and in the end found a well concealed room, once intended as a medical library or record room, which had not been used for some time.

Only now, in this safe hiding-place, was I able to relax, and I decided to put off reading Skrzyniarz's letter till later. I had a good look at my new surroundings; everything was thick with dust and cobwebs and sticky with dirt. I lit the candle to read Skrzyniarz's letter, which I hardly expected to contain anything new.

I was not mistaken. Skrzyniarz again harped on my decision to stay with the patients and set out his various arguments. This time he wrote calmly and dryly, as though considering the problem from a detached position and in terms of theory. Having exhausted his objective arguments, he appealed to my common sense and justice, and to many other qualities of my character and intellect, he appealed time and time again—and not only in his own name. Towards the end, however, there was a different tone; Skrzyniarz begged me to let them hear something from me and not go away without a last word to them, because I must have given a lot of thought to the matter and perhaps (at last he admitted it!), perhaps I was right after all.

All right, all right, I decided, if I had time, if they did not come for us tonight, I would leave some message behind me, perhaps I ought to do at least that to prevent their being tormented by their consciences, so I had to find some words which would reach them when all this was over.

I hastily looked for some paper to write Skrzyniarz, but could not find any. I took the Stock Book for 1938 down from the shelf; only half of it had been used, and there were many empty pages left. The book opened in Karol's writing with a laconic description of the kind of articles set down in it; and it would close in my writing and become a chronicle, or rather a personal catalogue of the events leading up to our extermination. While I was sitting over the blank page, deciding what words to use for opening the story of the Hospital's last days, I heard Narcyz's familiar footsteps on the concrete path; his walk was light and quick. He came into the building and ran up the stairs. It was getting near midnight.

I knew that Narcyz would go straight along the first-floor corridor to my room, knock, open the door, look around for me and then try the bedroom, the bathroom and the kitchen. What would he do then?

What would he think? After a while I heard Narcyz's steps on the floor above, then a knock and the sound of him struggling with a door. But which corridor was the sound of his running feet coming from? Again there was the sound of feet drumming down the stairs on a lower floor, and then a cry "Renata! Renata!" rang out. There was uneasiness in Narcyz's cry, perhaps even a certain pleading tone, but it was now impossible to call out and betray my hiding-place. I sat in the darkness, over the Stock Book, with my hands resting on the white paper, on which I had not yet written a single word of the story of these last days. Now, good heavens! Narcyz was above me, one floor above, in the administration director's empty flat. His steps were hasty and faltering, as though he were walking between odd pieces of furniture, hemmed in by a motionless landscape of armchairs. Something fell on the floor. Was it hurled deliberately, or dropped by accident? A silence descended over the building. Seconds passed, then minutes, and I counted them up, trying to guess what Narcyz was doing now. It was a relief when I could hear his steps again on the stairs, and then on the corridors and all over the empty, lifeless building. Suddenly I heard the cry again—"Renata! Renata!" But this time it was a heart-rending shriek hurled into the solitude, into the void of the world!

"Narcyz," I said in a whisper, "Narcyz, I can't tell you I'm here, I can't call you or calm you, because I'm not a doctor any more who knows the methods of restoring your balance. Madness has affected me too. I'm afraid and I'm running away from you."

Narcyz was now running all over the building from top to bottom, along the corridors and through the empty wards, and kept shrieking my name in a fearful voice—"Re-na-ta! Re-na-ta!" In the end he burst into tears and wept like a child, sobbing and groaning softly. As he walked along the concrete path over the yard, his step was slow and heavy, staggering and rhythmless, and then at last everything was silent and enveloped in the solitude and darkness of the night.

So Narcyz went away, and I was now free and safe, but also very unhappy and lonely. Would Narcyz understand that I had to run away from him?

I waited a long time in case he came back, but no sound disturbed the nocturnal silence. The empty building, dark and desolate, was like a place through which the demon of destruction, that Zenobii-Ki from Kocys' fictions, had passed on his evil errands.

I took the Stock Book and went back to my room, now sure that there was no further danger. I decided to reply to Skrzyniarz's letter the following day, as long as the night passed without incident and the next day did not bring new surprises.

THE THIRD AND FOURTH DAYS

I was awakened by the voices of Germans outside in the corridor holding an animated conversation. Then they knocked at my door. I quickly dressed and went in the direction they showed me. In the garden, on the bench by the log under the apple tree, lay Narcyz with his wrists cut. He was dead.

I asked the soldiers to dig a pit, selected a suitable place and also found some wood to make a coffin. It took about two hours altogether. While I was waiting for the soldiers to finish making the coffin, I stood over Narcyz for a moment and noticed the edge of a piece of paper sticking out of his pocket. It was a letter from Skalski, informing us that an evacuation operation was being organized for the rest of the patients, but that it would take a few days to arrange it. I was to await further instructions and news.

After we had buried Narcyz in the pit, I went back to my room. Now I was completely free to fill up the blank pages of the Stock Book. I wrote all that day and late into the night, and the following day till noon. I began with the words "Today there were still sixty-two patients . . ." and have now reached the point where Narcyz died.

Now is the time to reply to Skrzyniarz, because what I have written so far is merely a chronicle of events since the doctors left the Hospital. An hour ago a large number of Germans drove up, and they are waiting all over the courtyard now and roaming round the garden. They are waiting for someone or something, and I am waiting too. It appears that Skalski's operation will be in vain, because apparently today is the day . . . the 8th of June . . . I am as old as Karol was when he died, that is, thirty-six and two months. The sound of the soldiers' steps reminds me of that dream in which I was walking in my sleep through a long tunnel to meet Karol. And again, sometimes the steps make me start and listen in case Narcyz is coming.

So you see, Adam, that we had a sort of crime here, and that, though I did not commit it with my own hands, I was nonetheless responsible for Narcyz's death. He would have taken his own life in any case some time; he had made more than one attempt before this. But before, it was his delusions which caused it, whereas this time . . .

You may all have a peaceful conscience, if you read the story of these last days carefully. You must collect the bits and pieces together and join them up so as to convince yourselves afterwards . . .

Translated by R. M. MONTGOMERY

Marek Hlasko

(1934–1969)

One of the most controversial young writers of today's Poland, Marek Hlasko was born in Warsaw in 1934. A former bell-hop and taxi driver who had to work for a living since the age of thirteen, he received little formal education. He began his literary career as an editor of *Frankly Speaking*, a student weekly transformed into a national paper in 1955. His first stories appeared in this magazine, and in 1956 a collection of his short stories appeared under the title *A First Step Into the Clouds*, which won phenomenal success. (One of these stories is presented here). His renowned short novel, *The Eighth Day of the Week*, was published in the November 1956 issue of the magazine *Creative Writing*, but it never appeared in book form in Poland.

In 1958 Hlasko received the Publishers' Prize for the volume *A First Step into the Clouds*, the first such award since the war, which, along with the stories themselves, made the young writer the center of a great controversy. Hlasko was attacked by the Polish and Soviet Communist press for his unorthodox brand of Socialist Realism, and later by intolerant Catholics and literary conservatives who were offended by his violent language and themes. In some provincial towns his books were burned on bonfires.

In 1958 Hlasko defected to the West; since then he has been living in West Europe and Israel. His novel, *The Graveyard*, is a bitter indictment of Stalinism. It was published by the Polish émigré monthly, *Kultura*, in Paris, which also printed Hlasko's *Fools Believe in the Dawn* (which was filmed but refused publication in book form in Poland), under the title *Next Stop Paradise*.

Hlasko is a Naturalist writer who does not engage in ideological polemic with Communism (except in *The Graveyard*). His main purpose seems to expose social evil. His early stories still bear the characteristics of the official literary doctrine of social realism, but he has progressed from it toward a sentimental or Romantic Naturalism. He often uses the grotesque and the ironic in his descriptions of the banality and vulgarity of men's lives. His typical motif is that of great love soiled and destroyed by the shabbiness of the surrounding setting and the deliberate or unintentional malice directed at the lovers. Another frequent theme is his expression of disgust at the corruption of the times.

Hlasko now lives in Munich with his wife, the well-known actress, Sonia Ziemann, who played the feminine lead in the film version of his *Eighth Day of the Week*.

A First Step into the Clouds

On Saturday the city's downtown section looks the same as on any
day of the week. There are merely more drunkards in taverns and
bars, in buses and doorways—the stale smell of alcohol floats everywhere. On Saturday the city loses its industrious face; on Saturday
it assumes the mug of a booze hound. On the other hand, there are
no people downtown on Saturday who like to observe life: to stand
in doorways, to roam the streets, to sit for hours on a park bench, and
all this simply to be able to recall twenty years hence that on such
a day one had seen a more or less strange occurrence. Along with
messengers who, still during occupation moved about in their red
caps, with sandmen who sold sand in the streets, or whisky tenors
who sang in courtyards—objective spectators of life have now become extinct in the city.

Spectators may be encountered only in the outskirts. Suburban
life has always been and continues to be, more compressed; on every
Saturday when the weather is fine people take their chairs out in
front of their houses, turn them around and, straddling them, observe life. The perseverance of these observers at times bears the
stamp of brilliant lunacy; they sometimes sit thus all their life and
see nothing save the face of the observer opposite. Then they die with
a profound grudge against the world, a conviction of its dreariness
and boredom, for it will but rarely occur to them that one might get
up and go around the corner. When they grow old these observers
of life become uneasy. They fidget, they look at their watches—it
is one of the absurd habits of the old: they wish to nurse time. There
comes a moment when their avidity for life and sensation become
stronger than in youngsters of twenty. They talk much and think
much, their feelings are at once wild and dull. Then they expire
quickly and calmly. Dying they try to make everybody believe they
had lived expansively. The impotent boast of their success with
women, the cowards of their heroism, the cretins of the wisdom of
their lives.

Mr. Gienek, a house painter by trade, had been living forty years
in the Marymont district of Warsaw and, for as many years, had been
observing its life. On that Saturday, Mr. Gienek was also sitting in
the small garden in front of his house and vacantly gazing at the
street. From time to time he spat and licked his parched lips: the
waning day was a scorching and tormenting one. Mr. Gienek was
irritated: nothing exciting had happened that day: no one had broken
a hand, no one had beaten up another, and Mr. Gienek was sucked

by a feeling of emptiness and boredom. He kicked a dog that had got in his way and yawning drearily, gazed at the street. It was empty, the infrequently passing motorcars raised clouds of hot dust. When he had lost all hope of seeing a bit of life he felt someone nudge him. He raised drowsy eyes and saw his neighbor, Maliszewski.

"Come along," said Maliszewski.

"Where to?"

"It ain't far."

"What for?"

"Wanna see somethin'?" said Maliszewski.

He was a small man with a benevolent face and crafty eyes. Despite a seeming heaviness, his movements were quick and agile like a young cat's.

"What's it all about?" asked Mr. Gienek; he yawned, he was frazzled with the heat.

"A kid," said Maliszewski.

"What of it?"

"Good show," said Maliszewski. "He is with a broad. You get it?"

"You bet," said Mr. Gienek. He got up; hope surged in him. He asked with animation, "Good-looker?"

"She is both pretty and she's young," said Maliszewski. "I'm tellin' you, fine work goin' on there." Suddenly he became impatient: "Comin' or not?" he asked.

"It's no use," said Gienek. "Before we get there, they will be finished. I am telling you, it's no use."

"They are not in their fifties like you," said Maliszewski. "They can go on playing like that for a long time. When I was young I could play like that for hours, that's a fact. We'll get my brother-in-law on the way and skip up there, eh? He is back from work already and will come with us like a shot. Oh, look there he's coming already."

And so it was. A young stoutish man was coming along the street. His shirt sleeves were rolled up, a blade of grass was between his teeth. His eyes were drowsy and mocking, the lids drooping heavily.

"Heniek," called out Maliszewski, "come 'ere a moment!"

Heniek approached them and leaned on the fence. His forehead was damp with sweat.

"Hi," he said. "How's tricks, Mr. Gienek?"

"Heniek," said Maliszewski. "Come with us."

"It's hot," said Heniek; he licked his lips and sighed: "No breath of air. In such heat even a saint couldn't make it stand up. Where d'you want to go?"

"I was among the garden plots," said Maliszewski, "I saw a boy and a girl."

"A chippy?" asked Heniek. He spat out the blade of grass, picked a new one and bit on it with his strong teeth.

"The hell you say," said Maliszewski. "I'm tellin' you: young and good lookin'."

"Well, we might go," said Heniek. "You know me: I like to look at life. If the girl's ugly," he turned to Maliszewski, "you will stand us a drink to-day."

They set off, walking rapidly between the garden plots. People came here after work to tend their potatoes, tomatoes and carrots. Now, however, it was empty: the suffocating, drowsy day had fagged everyone; people stayed home.

"It's damn close," Heniek. I can't do a thing on a day like that. My head is splitting all the time."

"Those kids they're hot too, I imagine," said Gienek.

"You bet," said Maliszewski. "We'll cool them off, eh, Heniek?"

"Last year," said Heniek, "a fellow used to come here, too, with a girl. They came here all the summer."

"Well, and what?"

"Nothing. I suppose they had no home."

"Did they marry?" asked Mr. Gienek with an effort; he was dreaming of a glass of cold, bitterish beer.

"I don't know. Maybe they did. She was a good-looker, too."

"A blonde?" asked Gienek again though he did not give a damn. He continued to have a sense of oppressive emptiness and distaste.

"A brunette," said Heniek, "I remember as if it was to-day. The fellow was blond. I couldn't understand why such a classy doll would go with a jerk like that."

"I don't know," grunted Mr. Gienek. He spat out thick saliva. He was angry with Heniek: he had reminded him that he himself had an ugly and rather stupid wife. He said: "A chippy, no doubt."

"Maybe? . . . Quiet now," said Maliszewski. He walked ahead and they followed him slowly trying not to make any noise. It was dusk already, the sun had set, bluish shadows lay on the grass. Presently Maliszewski turned his head and called out softly: "Come on!"

They continued a few steps on tiptoe and saw the boy with the girl. They lay close together. The girl had rested her head on the boy's shoulder and snuggled her whole body close to him. They lay tired out with love-making and the heat; they were both young and good-looking: the one dark, the other light-haired. The girl's dress was raised: she had long deeply tanned legs.

"She's pretty," said Heniek. "Very pretty."

"I told you so," said Maliszewski in a whisper.

They stood without speaking: Mr. Gienek again licked his lips and with a shiver of sudden aversion thought about his wife. Maliszewski

smiled stupidly. Heniek's heavy eyelids drooped still lower and he
shuffled from one foot to the other. Suddenly he asked with irritation:

"We gonna do anything?"

"You do it," said Maliszewski. "Do somethin' that'll make'em split
their sides with laughing so they won't ever get over it. You are the
one to do it, Heniek."

"The best thing's to frighten them, Heniek," said Mr. Gienek. He
snapped his fingers and repeated: "She's a real beauty. I haven't seen
such a babe in a dog's age. Just a kid, too. They shouldn't be doing it."
Suddenly he became impatient and said to Heniek: "Do something, or
if you won't, I will drop a bomb on 'em!"

"Hold on," said Heniek, "I'd better do it."

He stood looking for a moment at the girl's bronzed thighs and
torment was painted on his face. Then he walked out from behind the
tree and stopped in front of the young couple. Blinking his eyes, he
said:

"Playing papa and mama? Hope it is appetizing!"

Maliszewski and Mr. Gienek burst out laughing. The boy jumped
to his feet and stuttered:

"What do you want?"

"Nothing," Heniek said very slowly. He stood in front of the boy
and teetered on his feet. He was still chewing the grass blade and
spat green saliva. Then he said: "Watch your step, sonny. That's what
I came to tell you. Always watch your step."

Maliszewski stepped from behind the tree and stopped next to
Heniek.

"A cute baby," he said looking at her with his dark-grey eyes. "I
wouldn't mind getting acquainted with such a one myself. Let's get
acquainted, lady."

"Idiot," said the girl. She stood up behind the boy; she was red
and upset; Mr. Gienek saw how her slim back was trembling and
again thought with aversion about his ugly, fat and shapeless wife.

"Say you, chippy" said Maliszewski, his eyes became bloodshot
with rage. He spoke quickly, as though suffocating: "You are nothing
but a common whore, you understand? I have a daughter older'n you,
you little tramp."

"Go away," said the boy, looking into his eyes pleadingly. "I beg
you to go away from here. We haven't done anything to you. I really
beg you."

"Whom are you begging, Johnny?" said the girl. "That old fool?"

"Shut your girl's mug," said Heniek, "or I will do it. And don't
you try clowning either. I'm tellin' you, shut her mug."

"It's you that's got a mug," said the girl. She looked at him with scorn. She was almost fainting with nervousness but tried to laugh derisively. "Swine," she said and burst out crying.

"Say, you," said Heniek and tugged at her arm. "Who are you abusing? You come here to get laid and have the brass to talk?"

The boy tore himself away: he slapped Heniek's face once and again. It happened so quickly that Heniek had only time to blink his eyes. But in the next moment he grabbed the boy by his hair and smashed his face against his own knee, then he punched him on the mouth with his fist and threw him on the ground.

"That enough, smart guy?" he asked. "If it ain't I can let you have more. And at reduced rates, too. There's a very fine cemetery here." And he fired a string of the filthiest oaths. He closed his eyes but continued to see the girl's long, brown legs.

"Come, Johnny," said the girl. She wiped blood from the boy's face. She said to them: "We'll have a reckoning yet." And when they had gone a few paces, she shouted hysterically: "You're old rags, not men!"

They were returning home. And they were walking among the garden plots.

"It's sultry," said Heniek. "It'll probably rain." He sighed and said: "She was real pretty, that girl. Why did you tell her she's a whore? You don't know her. How could you tell?"

"But it wasn't me said she was that kind," said Maliszewski. "It's you said it."

"Me?"

"Yes, you."

"You're talkin' like a fool, I don't know her from Adam."

"I know her," said Maliszewski. "That is not the first time I seen them. They are very much in love."

"And what'll happen now?" asked Mr. Gienek.

"I don't know what will happen now. But I know they go out together. And I know that they did it for the first time today."

"How d'you know?" asked Mr. Gienek lazily.

"I heard'im ask her. He was scared and she was scared. Heard'em talk it over. They were scared there'd be a baby, that's what they said. But I think they were more scared of one another."

"Everyone is scared the first time," said Maliszewski. "But why did you fix him?"

"Well, you yourself wanted it."

"I didn't know it would come out like that. He spoke to her in such a funny way...."

"How?"

"I don't remember."

"It is getting cloudy," said Mr. Gienek.

"That is just what he said, something about clouds," said Maliszewski. "A poem. I'm tellin' you, they're in love."

"They won't make love any more," said Mr. Gienek. "They'll have had enough to last them for always. After what's happened they won't be able to look at one another. Too bad that it all came out like that."

"I know," said Maliszewski. "It's come back to me. That's how he spoke to her, that when he's . . . you know what . . . it'll be their first step into the clouds. That's what he was saying only it rhymed. And all she said was: 'I'm afraid.' And she cried."

"Maybe she was afraid of the pain?"

"I don't think so," said Maliszewski. "I don't think she was afraid of the pain. That comes later. Life, other people, gossip. But the first time it's really like being in the clouds. People in love can't see anything."

"We, too?" asked Heniek.

"They won't care for one another any more," said Mr. Gienek. "I myself know that if anything like that happened to me, I'd no longer care for the girl."

He suddenly became sad; boredom again sucked him. They had left the area of the garden plots and were again walking down the street.

"No," said Heniek, "they won't be in love any more. Something like that happened once to me. And I fell out of love with that girl afterwards."

"It's happened to each one of us sometime or other," said Maliszewski. "But why did you smash him in the jaw?"

"He hit me first," said Heniek. "Going to have that beer now?"

"We can go. I guess that girl won't come here again."

"I don't think so," said Gienek. "And why did you call her what you did?"

"Someone had at one time called my girl that, too," said Maliszewski. "And by God, I don't know to this day why."

"And you didn't fall in love after that?"

"No," said Maliszewski. He was silent a while and then said with sudden anger: "Leave me alone, damn you! I don't believe in love. I don't trust my woman either. I don't trust anyone."

"A stupid business," said Heniek. He looked at the sky and said: "It's getting cloudy. What was that he said to her there?"

"I think, a step into the rain or something like that," said Maliszewski in a tired voice. "Let's go have that beer. . . . Either about rain, or about a storm . . . I don't remember. I don't remember anything. I don't want to remember anything. If I hadn't remembered all this row wouldn't 'a happened."

"It is going to rain tomorrow," said Heniek.

"It always rains on Sunday," said Mr. Gienek. He frowned: he thought once more about his odious wife, about the boy, about tomorrow, about the pretty girl, her long brown legs, her breast, her fresh red mouth, her sun-tanned strong shoulders and frightened green eyes, and he mumbled again, for he had to say something: "It always rains on a Sunday."

Tadeusz Rozewicz
(1921–   )

Tadeusz Rozewicz was born in Warsaw in 1921. He began publishing his poems in 1939. During World War II, he taught Polish in a high school run by the Underground, and later fought with the Home Army. After the war he wrote prodigiously: Twelve volumes of his poems and stories have appeared since 1947. He received the State Prize for his volume of poetry, *The Plains* (from which excerpts appear here), and the first prize at the International Literary Contests held in Warsaw.

Many of Rozewicz's writings have aroused controversy both among Communist and Catholic readers. The former objected to his obsession with war and concentration camps and his refusal to accept their dogma without reservations; the latter accused him of cynicism and immorality. Both parties have overstated their cases, for Rozewicz does have something important to say as a creative writer. His poetry as well as his prose reflect a true understanding of human suffering, and his realism, warped as it is by party propaganda, is a significant contribution to contemporary Polish literature.

His short stories and poems have been widely translated; he also writes plays.

In the Most Beautiful City of the World

A weak bulb shone in the room. Stale rolls and an open tin box lay on the table. Ludwik was reading an old Polish newspaper. What a good thing he had wrapped the slippers in it. Now he had something to do in his free moments. In the morning he had been walking around the streets, gazing at shop windows.

Yesterday morning there had been packing. Suits, pants, four best shirts, handkerchiefs. Dictionary. Then the flight. At the airport a casual gesture of a French customs officer. Lights in the darkness. He felt that the life he had brought with him was grey. But he couldn't say so to his colleague who was sedulously entering in a little notebook his impressions of the day. His colleague wore striped socks and the moment he had arrived kept saying "it was time they went home."

Ludwik folded the newspaper carefully and put it away in the bedside table.

"What did you do in town?" he asked.

"I drank a glass of wine and I've been on the boulevard. Huge selection of women's shoes. I would like to buy a pair with stiletto heels. . . ."

"And how was the Casino de Paris?"

"Phoney."

"Tell us, old boy, you are smacking your lips!"

"Pagodas, altars and naked whores."

"And what were they doing?"

"Flourishing their behinds."

"But how?"

"Various ways. Listen, we've got to tell them to bring us cocoa in the morning instead of coffee."

"Forget it." Ludwik got up from the bed and went to the table. "*Mesyer* was grumbling today that you can't keep jam in the cupboard."

"He's a homo."

"Tell me all about this Casino de Paris."

"Castles, Chinese lanterns, ostrich feathers, gondolas . . . terrible. I tell you, it was indescribably phony. And the whole town is like that, I tell you. Phony. And what did you do today?"

"I've been to a museum."

"Look, is this shirt very creased?"

"Listen friend, it's a week since you've washed your feet."

"I'll wash them in the lavatory."

"Apparently you can order a bath here."

"I haven't come here to have a bath." Samuel smoothed his hair. "I'll have a bath when I get home."

There was a knock on the door. Samuel moved his stockinged feet uneasily. Ludwik said, "Come in."

A thin woman in a black pullover entered the room. Samuel sat up on the bed.

"Hello there," she said. "Imagine, they are in Paris! It's unbelievable! They've come. What are you doing here?" She kissed Ludwik on the cheek.

"We've been to the Louvre. Sit down. I'll repeat to you what your husband had said."

"What did he say?"

"Gerwazy said you mustn't run around too much."

"Yes, and what else did he say?"

"He said you must remember about meals and not run around. . . . He's coming in June."

"He said so in his letter. . . . What have you got to eat?"

"Rolls . . ."

"I've got bananas. I'll leave them here for you."

"Listen," said Samuel, "you've paid for the bananas and we can't sponge on you."

"Fool."

"All right: fool, but money doesn't drop down from the sky for you."

"The Master has asked me to pay his compliments to the Arc de Triomphe."

"You should eat the cheeses. Apparently they've got over two hundred varieties."

"I'm no expert on cheeses."

"I am sorry I didn't bring any dried sausage," said Samuel sliding his feet into brown shoes. "Shall we go out?"

"Let's!"

"Into town?" Ludwik shrugged his shoulders.

"Get a move on," cried M. "Do you want to lie in bed . . . here . . . here!"

They left the little hotel. Cars passed by. There were women inside. There were men. Dogs. All of them well groomed and beautiful.

A fat type in glasses was sitting in the famous Existentialists' café. He was ugly and pockmarked.

Ludwik said to Samuel:

"I say, that's probably Sartre."

"He wouldn't be sitting alone."

"Why?"

M. ordered three coffees.

"They don't come here," she said casually. "But you can meet various Germans, Austrians and Poles. That buffoon G. also hangs around here."

"Wait," said Samuel, "I'll hide behind you: a friend from Krakow is coming this way."

"It's too late!" M. laughed.

The acquaintance from Krakow was standing at their table with hands uplifted staring and smiling at Samuel.

"Don't you recognize me?"

Samuel looked uncertain though he tried to smile.

"Yes, yes indeed," he muttered. But the Krakow acquaintance was still standing with his hands up exclaiming:

"What are you doing here?"

M. gave Ludwik a sardonic smile.

Samuel was preparing an answer. He even said something incoherent.

M. stretched her hand towards the "acquaintance," but sideways, as if she wanted to wave at him. He was still standing, as if spellbound, with his hands on Samuel's shoulders. Only after a while did he sit down on a chair.

"Tell me what are you doing here? That's how it is"—he now turned to the others—"two mountains will not meet, but two people. . . ."

"That's exactly how it is," said M. and laughed loudly. "Listen Ludwik, here you must eat bananas, oranges and cheeses. That's the cheapest stuff. Two hundred varieties of cheese. Shall I order?"

"Perhaps," Ludwik said unenthusiastically, "but really it's a waste of money."

"God, what a lot of nonsense you talk." Her bright eyes now looked young.

A few moments later the waiter brought cheeses on a little plate. There were slices of several varieties. One white but green inside as if stuffed with mould, another yellow, hard and smelly. Ludwik said: "Walus' feet."

"What did you say," M. was biting a cheese with very white sharp little teeth. There was something of a rodent in her.

"It stinks like Walus' feet," Ludwik said solemnly.

The stranger, or rather the acquaintance, was almost sitting on Samuel's knees. He gazed at his face, saying something in a whisper, almost a twitter. Samuel spoke only now and again. His words were calm, measured out with precision:

"That's life for you."

"Samuel is an oaf," M. whispered rather loudly to Ludwik and smiled at Samuel who nodded his head in agreement.

"I won't stuff myself with that stinking cheese," said Ludwik. "Not for my palate. Am I to smell and kiss Walus' foot?"

"Why do you keep on about this Walus?"

"That was in the forest. Stupid Walus was in the Home Army and his feet stank just like that."

"You and your taste! Showing off like a schoolboy."

"I'm not showing off. I'm not eating and that's that."

"Then I'll eat it myself," M. said cheerfully, "It will do for my supper."

Ludwik took out a cigarette and lit it. A warm streak of smoke sailed up to his eye. He blinked and his eyelid moistened. He put the cigarette aside and sighed. Actually, he couldn't smoke properly and did not inhale.

The café was nearly empty. The people at the next table were speaking German.

"Let's go somewhere," said M.

Samuel and his acquaintance were locked in a prolonged handshake. At last the "acquaintance" left.

"Let's go," M. said again.

Samuel sat silent with a cup of cold coffee in front of him.

"That pockmarked chap in the corner with the newspaper isn't Sartre. It's Dziuba from Lodz. I've just recognized him."

"Do let's go," said M.

Samuel smiled and cried.

"Coming!"

❀   ❀   ❀

Ludwik watched M. She walked a slender figure in a black jacket and black trousers. She moved across waves of light. Sharp, swift.

Pink lights and sky-blue, red and orange. She moved through those lights and talked but Ludwik kept imagining she was walking alone. Proud and aloof. They could never communicate. Very often M. did not answer questions. Or would leave the room just as Ludwik was about to say something about art. In her presence Ludwik felt uneasy and protected himself with similar indifference, irony and inconsiderateness. He felt M. possessed a secret gift. Just as a magician's rod can detect water in unexpected places, M. detected in people their complexes and secrets. With one word she would uncover hidden and long buried resentments but she never passed judgment. She would smile and wave her hand casually. Sometimes she would say "Fool," "Swine" or "Idiot."

Ludwik disliked her also for ostentatiously turning away from weaknesses which accounted for the charm and attractiveness of the so-called fair sex. All attempts to broach the subject M. would cut short with a gesture of the hand.

At the same time Ludwik thought that M.'s presence was in some way an influence in his life. They met infrequently: once every few months. They would exchange a few words, sometimes limited to greetings and farewells. One evening, when the big glass doors of her studio were curtained, M. asked:

"Do you want to see the pictures?"

The question was unexpected. It was the first time Ludwik had heard M. suggesting an inspection of her paintings. The Master was also there. A silver haired poet with eyes of a village shepherd and the imagination of a Corbusier. The Master raised his index finger and said in an exalted tone:

"We have to teach Ludwik to look at paintings."

He laughed with his childish laugh. Then something unexpected happened. Ludwik shrugged his shoulders and replied rudely, even brutally:

"I am not going to look at anything. I'm not interested. . . ."

"Really, my dear friend. . . ." the Master raised his finger. M. did not speak. As if Ludwik wasn't in the room. She opened the door to the studio and all the guests went in. Soon voices could be heard.

"My God," thought Ludwik, that man is saying in all seriousness that the Sistine Madonna had transformed his sight. He heard the Voice of the Master . . . the same thing happened a hundred years ago to Mickiewicz who thought that sweet picture the greatest masterpiece of all time. But then Mickiewicz thought the "Maccabees" was a masterpiece too.

Ludwik sat alone in Gerwazy's room, thinking those in the studio were talking too much. The Master's commentaries on particular paintings were known to all by heart.

Then the door opened and M.'s head appeared in it. The black pullover reached high over her neck and her head was a little like those marvelous severed heads which addressed spectators.

"Swine," she said. At the same time her face brightened in a smile. It was a strange smile. As if a young boy was smiling through the lips of a mature woman. M.'s cheeks were almost red. A gleam came into her eyes, then faded. She closed the door. For several years after that evening M. did not speak to Ludwik about painting. She never showed him her paintings and never invited him to the studio. Ludwik behaved as if he knew nothing of M.'s pursuits. Naturally, he saw her paintings at exhibitions. But he did not talk about this to M. They both behaved as if they did not know about each other's work. Even so, they often talked in a lighthearted way. The irritation was hidden underneath. Gerwazy would remain silent. He alone knew how to be silent and behave loyally. He was loyal about love and friendship. But who would notice it in this world full of empty chatter? While everybody knew how to talk about anything, Gerwazy knew how to be silent. He was tolerant, even indulgent.

●   ●   ●

Before his flight Ludwik saw Gerwazy. Gerwazy said: "I hear M. spends whole days running about and gets tired and works at night. All the treatment will go to hell. You must explain that to her. . . ." And saying goodby he added: "Look after her over there."

"Look here old man, you know well enough she can't be looked after. You can just imagine her reaction if I were to tell her that I am to look after her. Tell me, did you ever succeed. . . ."

Gerwazy smiled helplessly.

Ludwik was now walking next to M. and thinking about Gerwazy's words. Naturally he gave no hint that he was supposed to be "looking after her." M. would probably have laughed so long and so genuinely that she would have drawn a crowd in the world's capital.

"Listen," Ludwik said cautiously, "aren't you spending too much time running about?"

"No."

Ludwik was silent. Samuel marched dignified in his light soiled mac but now and again he tried to roll up the frayed cuffs. He observed the women that passed by with great concentration, almost like a hypnotist. But the drawing power of his gaze must have been weak because they passed untouched by it as if at a fashion show. Ludwik was depressed. Samuel looked perplexed. M. was laughing: she poked fun at the worried and seemingly ashamed expressions of her companions. She was relaxed and appeared not to notice the handsome men, the beautiful women and the bearded youths.

What was she thinking about? . . . They bought tickets at the "Alhambra" and took seats on the balcony. The songstress with a bunch of black feathers growing out of her buttocks sang with a strong thick voice; she was shouting the text of her song. The rough and warm voice permeated the listeners' skins. Her body thrown like a spring on to the boards of the stage lighted up at the end of the show. Sweat covered the surface of this perfect human machine.

Ludwik felt the weight of his inside as if he had too many superfluous bones and too much fat. . . .

Samuel shrugged his shoulders.

"Not bad, but rather vulgar for my taste."

They said goodby to M. in front of her hotel.

"Give me a ring," she said, "By!"

It was after midnight when they sat down to supper.

Samuel was wiping his fat lips and hands with a handkerchief. He ate two sardines and wiped the oil in the tin with a piece of a roll. He turned on the tap and bending down he lapped the water. He did it every night. He did not drink tea.

Ludwik said:

"You'll be sick. Unboiled cold water on oil."

"It was worse in the camp," Samuel replied. He dried the water on his face and lay on his bed. He took out a thick exercise book and made notes.

"Fool! In the camp. You are in Paris, not a concentration camp. Try to understand. You are in Paris and it is Spring. You are here for the first and perhaps the last time. You are here to drink the nectar of pleasure and joy, the very froth of life!"

"It was worse in the camp," Samuel replied with philosophical calm. "I've got used to water. It is very healthy. Anyway, I shall probably go home before my time is up."

Ludwik nodded.

"Spent another half a day in front of a shoe shop, eh? He's got used to water in camp, the nit."

But Samuel made no reply. Then he closed the exercise book. He undressed and switched off the light.

"Good-night," he said wrapping himself up in an eiderdown.

"Listen," said Ludwik, "what's your opinion of M.?"

"A decent human being."

"Decent human being? But she's a woman."

"To me she is a painter. After all, she herself doesn't want to be a woman. A decent honest human being. And very talented, of course. But she's showing off. . . ."

"True."

"Good-night. I'm asleep."

"Sleep, sleep. The most faithful husband among husbands who have lived in this city and washed down oil with water."

"What's that?"

"Nothing."

"Good-night. We go to the Louvre tomorrow. Admission free."

"Let's sleep." Ludwik turned off the light on his night table.

Now in the dark he began to remember M.'s paintings. It was her first show after years spent in the "catacombs." A few of her paintings were hanging on a grey wall. Here in this foreign city Ludwik understood that she had laid herself bare in these pictures. They were her self-portraits. And she so unapproachable and masked. She painted the history of her organism. Hadn't anybody noticed that M. painted her hidden interior and the disease developing there? Those were paintings of tissues and cells seen through a microscope. No one had painted such nudes. Bodies resolved into cells, nerve fibres, blood vessels. They were like plates taken out of an unknown biology textbook or an anatomy atlas.

The cartoons displayed blood like a transparent pane. Human blood under the microscope. Red corpuscles. Slabs of blood. Black. Red. White. Yellow.

Other cartoons represented bones. Limpid, light, but designed to bear weights. Some bones were long, some short. Shoulder bones, metacarpus bones, finger bones. M. resembled a bird. Though the inside of her bones were filled with marrow. But the marrow had disappeared. Maybe her bones too were quite hollow inside and light like those of birds. In several cartoons the internal structure of bones as well as their external appearance was visible.

Ludwik felt that in these paintings the dead abstract form was feeding on its maker. What in the works of others had remained on the surface of the paintings—empty form, cold and perfect construction—acquired life in M.'s pictures. The form was nourished by her blood and bone marrow. It turned into a living organism capable of independent existence. At the same time M.'s own skeleton grew lighter. From a human skeleton it turned into a bird skeleton. It wasn't in the deliberations of critics (who as usual talked about dates, exhibitions and names of various groups, about the influences of various painters on M.'s work) that Ludwik could trace the origins of M.'s paintings. M. had returned to nature and was drawing upon it. She was a painter of the landscapes of her organism. A biology text-book explained her best. Human structure. A skeleton's structure. The structure of bones. Here was contained the most perfect definition of this work. ". . . The internal surface on the side of the bone cavity forms an arrangement of fine beams and fibres, the so-called spongy bone substance. Now it appears that these beams and bone fibres are placed parallel to the line of the greatest stress and pull. We observe the same principle in mechanics, for example in the construction of bridges and cranes, where the skilful placing of thin rails allows considerable pressure to be borne. This structure enables us to understand the staying power of long bones under pressure despite their hollowness inside. . . ."

M. wore a white ·blouse with short sleeves. Slender arms and sharply defined elbows. Hair cut short and lips painted lightly. She smiled faintly and stretched her arm to Ludwik. He held her cold hands in his and felt the tiny finger bones.

"Listen," he said, "you will be cold in that blouse."

M. did not reply. She cocked her head sideways and again smiled. He saw her lips for the first time. She was standing at an open window. There were poplars outside.

There was a scream. Ludwik opened his eyes. A man with his head thrown back and mouth open was lying on the other bed. His face shone beneath a green glaze. He breathed heavily as though he was lifting a huge stone on his breast. There was a bubbling noise and another snore-like cry in an unknown language escaped from his throat. He leaned over the floor.

"What are you doing?" Ludwik cried, "Wake up, do you hear?"

"What? What's up. . . ." Samuel raised himself on the bed. "What do you want?"

"You've been shouting."

"Me shouting?"

"Yelling like a slaughtered animal."

"Have I?"

"It's the water after the sardines in oil. . . ."

"Water is healthier than tea."

"Tell me, who was that cheerful blighter who caught you in the café? A school friend, I suppose."

"Oh, that one . . . no, not the school, it was the camp."

"And you recognized him just like that?"

"Me him? No. He recognized me. I didn't recognize him until now. Here. I recognized him here before I fell asleep."

"What was it he was telling you with such relish. He might have been trying to propose to you."

"What was he saying? He was glad we have met."

"I've heard 'a mountain and a mountain . . .' and so on."

"That's it."

"Say old man, do you feel like going out?"

"No . . . you can't go at this time."

"What time is it?"

"Three."

"I'm expecting a 'phone call from home at six. I'll have to reserve seats in LOT. . . ."

"In two weeks' time. . . ."

"I think I'll cut this stay short."

"Go tomorrow."

"Not tomorrow, but I shan't extend my stay for even an hour. I'm invited to dinner tomorrow."

"Who's invited you?"

"That chap from the café, Fiszel."

"Go. You wont be drinking water from the tap. Wine is healthier."

"If you wish, you can come with me."

"What an idea. I'm glad there is no one here wants to matter to me."

"Shall we sleep?"

"Let's. Don't yell."

"It's passed now. But it still comes sometimes. According to the wife I used to run away from bed clutching the eiderdown. Anyway, I don't count any more."

"Rubbish, of course you do."

"Look, we've got to eat these pots of jam tomorrow because we can't keep plates in the drawer."

"I'm going to the cinema tomorrow: there's a film with Ingrid Bergman. Won't you come?"

"I'll go to the cinema in Poland."

"You will go to the cinema in Poland, you will wash your feet in Poland, you will drink tea in Poland."

"I'm going to the Louvre tomorrow. And in the afternoon to dinner with Fiszel."

"Next week the English Queen will be here with her husband."

"Today, or rather yesterday, *mesyer* looked very disapproving. He reminded me that we have two plates and a fork in the drawer."

"We've got to buy shoe polish and a brush."

"I leave my shoes outside the door in the evening."

"You do, but they don't clean them."

"They do."

"You have a close look in the morning. Why should a tramp expect the French to polish his shoes? At such a price, too! We'll buy a brush tomorrow."

"Won't you come and dine with Fiszel?"

"No."

"Pride forbids you? God has placed the honor of the Poles in my hands. . . ."

"We are here incognito. . . ."

"But nobody knows that."

          •   •   •

They did not speak to each other. Ludwik did not say a word about his analysis of the paintings which he carried out in the night. There was no need because he had imagined it all to himself anyway: both his own words and M.'s reactions. She would listen silently making no reply and then break in with:

"Words, words. When literary men talk about painting they come up with this sort of tittle-tattle."

"So I am not allowed to talk about paintings," Ludwik replied provocatively, "Am I?"

"You are," replied M, "everyone is, but it is better not to. Waste of breath. You've added a whole literary edifice to a case which is quite clean."

"Then perhaps you will explain the composition's mysteries?"

"I won't."

"Why?"

"Because I don't feel like it."

M. would tighten her lips and fall into a long silence. Then she would ask suddenly:

"Where do you lunch? That cheese was good. . . ." Ludwik carried this excited conversation in his head. He asked the questions and provided the answers.

"Let's go and have some coffee," said M.

"No, I don't like coffee."

"Then have some wine."

"Wine gives me headaches. I'll go home."

M. did not reply. They were standing outside a café.

Ludwik disliked the thought of sitting at a table with her. After all, why should we irritate each other. We don't like each other.

"Take me to my hotel."

"We are going home in a fortnight's time," said Ludwik. "Samuel wanted to go home on the second day. Now he's got used to it a bit. He's also had a telephone from home this morning."

"I've been painting a lot during these months. I have quite a few pictures in the hotel. How are you spending your time?"

"Samuel goes to dinners with friends and I go to the pictures. We've bought a shoe brush. We go to the Louvre. How is the treatment?"

"I go to a clinic. Everything's all right."

"Gerwazy is coming in June."

"Pity he isn't coming in May. In the Summer everything's empty and stuffy."

"He's working."

"I know. He wrote to me. Let's have a coffee."

They were sitting at a table. M. lighted a cigarette.

"I met Z in the métro, he tried to hide but wasn't able. He invited me to his show. He's exhibiting landscapes, scenes of nature. . . . When I looked closely at him he began to sweat. I'm sure the Embassy had to subsidize that exhibition of trees and Polish skies."

"Shall we go there?"

"No, I would probably have to smack his mug."

"Why?"

"The insolence. Because of everything. He ought to be ashamed of being alive."

"I think you ought to buy yourself a blouse or a suit. Don't you ever buy yourself anything?"

"No."

"You always wear the same things. There is such a choice here . . . shoes or some lace pants to go with these trousers."

M. smiled.

"I haven't thought."

She sat stooping a little. In the black sweater and worn out jacket. Ludwik watched her hands. Motionless. "Does she see herself? What would she do if I were to offer her a bunch of violets? Maybe she would give them back to me. Nonsense. She might put them in her pocket together with her matches. For several years now I have been wanting to offer her flowers."

Once Ludwik bought her a small bunch of white forest flowers. He carried them in his briefcase. He even thought up a little amusing saying with which to offer the flowers to M. but the flowers stayed in the briefcase. After her departure Ludwik threw them away and repeated the saying for his own benefit. . . .

"You don't even want to talk about the sources of your paintings. You forbid people to talk about it. You say you are not interested in what 'people' say about your paintings, you say you don't paint for 'people.' And yet you have shows. So all this talk is 'intellectual gas' as Gerwazy rightly describes it."

"As for you and Gerwazy, you are supposed to have begun to understand people, but instead of writing for them, you write for fools. It is your good fortune that you are slightly more decent than the Warsaw literati. . . . That really is a crowd"—here she used a word too contemptuous to be preserved even in print.

"People are weak," said Ludwik, "you must understand." "You have no business to understand," M. had once replied. Ludwik felt she was right, that persisting in her mistake she was better than him and Gerwazy.

"You have too much goodwill. You've got to cut yourself off from those there instead of carrying on with them."

Only by rejecting talk about "people" could she do something for them and for herself. . . . She was paying for it. We did not help her during her worst time. It was she who helped us. Obvious. Yes. Gerwazy. What am I thinking about? I won't arrange to meet her again. I have no wish. I've got to cut myself off from her. She will spoil my whole stay. After all, she looks better than I do. This treatment must have been very good for her. She never looked so well. I'll waste my whole stay. She has been here six months, a year . . . and I've only got fourteen days. She has no right. She eats up my time. After all the specialist said she's got another ten years. Which one of us has been guaranteed ten years?

"I am going home," Ludwik said.

"Wait, I'll come with you."

"Do."

"This is a great favor: you've certainly turned into a boor in this place."

"Stop gassing. You know what Gerwazy told me?"

"I've heard it once."

"But I've got to repeat it word for word."

M. shrugged her shoulders.

"Tell my wife not to run about the streets too much. She should have her meals regularly and . . ."

"Tell my husband Mr. G . . ."

"Why all this sarcasm, this snorting: you are his wife and Gerwazy is your husband."

"And Samuel is his wife's husband and your wife is Ludwik's wife."

"She is, she is . . . you are not an exception. In a sense you are his property. . . ."

"Let's drop this."

"You *are* childish."

M. went on murmuring to herself. Ludwik brightened up.

"What's so funny?"

"That each one has his own wife or her own husband. And you too are a wife. Neither his ox, nor his ass, nor his servant, nor wife nor anything that is his. Farewell, I'm going this way. . . ."

"You certainly are a clown."

"You exaggerate."

"Wait, they're still open here," M. ran into a shop. She was back in a moment carrying a carefully wrapped parcel.

Further on the street grew empty. There were no shops. Only entrances to buildings and empty cars parked at the kerbs with their lights switched off. The glass in the hotel entrance was milky and opaque. Curtained windows of flats in grey walls of buildings. If you walked for another three hundred meters or took the métro you would find the city glowing and humming again. Here there was silence. Here things were dark and grey. These buildings were shut. They never opened up for tourists. Among these stood the hotel in which M. had been staying the last few months.

They stood outside the hotel doorway in silence. They had nothing to say to each other. At one moment Ludwik thought M. had gone. He thought he was alone on the pavement. He was looking at the barred window of a bank which was shut. There were no neons there, only walls, closed entrances, barred windows. A man standing on the kerb has nothing to say to other people. He does not even speak to himself. He is on a desert island. But a lost human being will not leave an impression in concrete and asphalt. People pass and leave no trail.

He shuddered when he heard a voice so close by.

Had M. been speaking for some time or were these her first words? Her words were clear. The words were clearly defined and sharp. Ludwik listened in the way one listens to small talk about the weather, prices and politics. . . .

"I don't feel well. . . . No, physically I am all right but I feel awful. Feel like jumping out of the window. I have such terrible moments when I want to jump out of the window."

She touched Ludwik's sleeve and added softly:

"Things are getting on top of me."

Ludwik said:

"Sleep it over, it will pass."

M. was silent. She stood her head bowed.

Ludwik added irritably:

"Words. Jumping out of the window. Suicide. Just for the sake of saying something. To the wind. Sheer waste of time."

"I am sorry," she said softly.

"Sleep well." He stretched his hand but did not feel the touch of her palm. She had turned away and quickly entered the hotel.

*   *   *

Beyond the Gothic steeple of St. James a knot of narrow streets. Women walk along these streets. They carry around their bodies, their wares, very ingeniously. Even experienced advertisers couldn't show their exhibits to better advantage. One of them not only had her legs raised on stiletto heels, but her bottom too seemed to be raised on a scaffolding. Gothic cathedrals, cars, pictures, Negroes, columns and shop windows were all at this moment mere decoration. All this was reflected in the shield of her behind. The buttocks of that girl were engaged in a dialogue. Full of significance, perfect. A mane of red hair of beaten copper promised an animal covered in red hair. A pearl of warmth. A rose-and-blue wave of light lifted and buoyed and rocked that fruit; the girl's behind was a tower, a siren and a ship. Ludwik sat over a piece of meat munching strange weeds and green leaves with oil and pepper. He drank cool wine. It was sour, it warmed and sharpened his inside. He felt the whole city in the roof of his mouth. He gobbled the city. The city spat him out. He had too little money. So he was satisfying his basic hunger. But the nourished body took vengeance on him. Yesterday in paradise a herd of beautiful naked women paraded round a golden tree. Veils fell from them. At last there were only green leaves and blue shells sparkling with sequins. They turned their breasts, bellies and faces. Now a whole bunch of buttocks was swaying rhythmically among the branches of the golden tree. There, nearer the stage were bald heads and raised eyes. Above the heads swayed naked innocent powdered bottoms.

Ludwik finished his wine. He leaned over the metal table and watched the steeple illumined by spotlights.

"But I can't go to her. I can't go to the hotel. I have nothing to say to her. I can't go to her with words of comfort. She might burst out laughing. Straight into my face. Fool. I couldn't sit there sad and bored. Was I supposed to kiss her . . . nonsense." Ludwik felt there was something unnatural in that thought. As if he were to kiss Gerwazy. An undefined heavy feeling rolled through Ludwik's body.

"No, no," he said aloud. The waiter who thought he was being summoned in a strange tongue, approached the table with his pad.

He walked along the Seine. In the electric light the pale chestnut leaves were silhouetted sharply against a black sky.

"She thought of jumping out of the window. She can't say things like that. Like a schoolgirl."

x   x   x

"What did you have for dinner?"

"Pity you didn't come. Fiszel was enquiring after you."

Samuel was lying on his bed writing up the impressions of the day.

"What did you have for dinner?"

"Quite a show, dear chap, quite a show. Fish. Crabs. Snails."

"I've never had oysters."

"One's got to try everything once."

"Rubbish."

"There were also bowls of water. I almost tried to drink . . ."

"You could have washed your feet . . . before returning to the Fatherland."

"We've had quite a chat. Has a pleasant wife. A daughter and a son. He took me back to the hotel in his Mercedes. We conversed in Polish. That wife of his looks at me, then at him and smiles, thinking we are talking about the 'sins' of youth. Smiles even rather coquettishly. And he talks and talks. Bored me stiff."

"Martyrology, eh?"

"Nothing but."

"You should have tried to wriggle out of it."

"Wriggle out of it! He held my hand as though I were his fiancée."

"You've stuffed yourself so you had to slave for it . . . Nowadays no one wants to hear about suffering and tortures . . . Bad luck. In Paris."

"I buried him, you know."

"Buried whom?"

"That Fiszel chap."

Ludwik was pouring out the tea which the chambermaid brought. "Listen, drink this. There will still be a whole cup left."

"I drink water."

"To hell with you."

" 'Don't you recognize me? You put me in the grave. I recognized you straightaway. Haven't you? I can see you don't recognize me . . .' Brother, didn't I just . . . I dragged him to the grave and placed his bullet filled corpse on top of the other bodies. He says he watched me all the time. That is true. First we carried, then others carried us. They didn't have time for me. Heaps were buried alive. Sometimes the earth moved, heaved up and down as if a thousand moles were burrowing, but those were the half-dead, the live ones. Earth breathed like a human. Fiszel talked about the camp and all that after dinner as though he were describing his first love. And that wife still quite attractive. There she was smiling at you. Wine and Mediterranean fruit. A little boy and a little girl . . . You know, we've been here too long."

"Nuts. What a conclusion."

"I've got to phone home."

"You do just that. Tell them we've bought ourselves a brush."

"And what did you do? Cinema?"

"I went for a walk with M. and took her home."

"How is she?"

"I don't know. Talks a lot of nonsense."

"They are decorating the place. There is a colored photograph of Elizabeth or the whole Royal family in every shop window. Philip is getting bald, she is quite a pet."

Ludwik was writing a card to Gerwazy.

"Dear Gerwazy. So we are in Paris. I've seen your wife. I passed on your message. She listened without reverence. She looks better than you do. She looks healthy and ruddy. Admittedly, she complains somewhat of 'the state of her soul' but that is psychological, artistic oversensitiveness, female tittle-tattle, etc. We shall be back in a fortnight. Cheers."

"There are two sardines for you in the tin," said Samuel. "I've been to the Louvre today. It was shut. They were bringing in boxes of flowers. Pots wrapped in pink tissue. They will probably festoon the Gallery in honor of the Royal pair."

"Surely, they are not going to put pots round the Nike."

"Oh yes they will. Nike and Gioconda and Venus and all the famous masterpieces. You don't know their bourgeois tastes," Samuel was moving the large toe of his left foot quickly up and down and jotting in his bulging notebook covered in oilcloth.

Ludwik took out an old newspaper from his case. He looked at his colleague with an inner serenity and even joy.

"I look at you, old chap, and think it's good it happened this way."

"What?"

"The fact that we are here together. Have you noticed that we never quarrel?"

"Between ourselves, your method of opening sardine tins leaves a lot to be desired."

"Find a better one."

"You mustn't turn the opener too quickly."

Ludwik closed his eyes, then smiled.

"Look, old chap, we are in Paris, aren't we?"

"There is no need to go on about it."

Samuel began cleaning his shoes.

"What's new in the paper?"

"This is an old one."

"Never mind, read it."

Ludwik read aloud.

"Rzeszow (PAP)

The body of a new-born baby was fished out of the San. The people of Przemysl have been shocked by the news. A small group of children bathing in the San saw a man throw a large jar into the river . . ."

II

M. was sitting on the floor. Her back to the window. There were sketches spread around her. She had been working all day. Now she was tired. She wore an old light jacket and sat head bowed, her hands round her knees. She wasn't attending the clinic regularly. The week before she had received a summons signed by the specialist himself. To have a blood test. They were reminding her she was ill. Engrossed in her work M. had forgotten about it. Now she was sitting with her eyes shut. She had not switched on the light. Rarely did she allow herself such moments of incomplete illumination. She hated "atmosphere."

"What are you trying to express by this? They ask what I want to express, they explain my paintings according to whatever comes to their heads. There is nothing I want to express." M. shook her head and her closely cropped hair bristled, "There is nothing I want to express, it is they that express me. These latest ones are clear and gay, but they have sucked light and life out of me leaving a marionette dressed in an old jacket and trousers baggy at the knees. I am in these pictures and not in this skin, these rags . . . The right thing for Gerwazy to do is to come to Paris and give me my supper."

She knew there were fruit, cheese and sausage on the table but she didn't feel like moving. She wanted him to hand her a fruit, she longed to touch his skin with her lips. That's how one feeds ponies in the circus, they get cubes of sugar on the palm of the hand for their difficult task, they create pure beauty in the nervous restless light of the searchlights. "Z is showing them landscapes of the Polish homeland. And my paintings, my colors, why did I have to defend them so strenuously? I was punished by not being allowed to eat, and yet these paintings *are really* very human and gay," M. laughed and shook her head. "Idiots," she said to those far-off people without a face, without a name. Who was it she was struggling with these last five years? That was Jacob's fight with an ass, an ass, not an angel. God, what idiots! She had not painted the trousers of the Bard, the beautiful trousers of the great classic of Polish literature.

M. went to the window. Below she could see a section of the pavement and the cobbles of the street. She looked down supporting herself on the window frame with her palms. There was nothing of special interest happening there. She leaned out and her fingers gripped the window frame in a hold that became tighter and tighter. The flesh under the fingernails went white, the blood flowed away.

From below there came a sound like someone striking metal against stone. It was an unexpected recurring sound. It cut across the continual hum of car engines. M. saw golden helmets. Riders were emerging from darkness into the light of a street lamp. Horseshoes were striking the granite, ringing. Scarlet plumes swayed above the golden helmets. An officer with white gloves and a drawn sword danced about on a black horse and there was a wave of riders behind him. Rounded cruppers glistened like black water. Bent silver swords, gilded trumpets, iron hammering against stone, the star of a stirrup on the patent leather boots of the last rider. Cold air blew in through the window. She heard the beating of horse-shoes on stone grow faint. She switched on the light. She picked her thick striped jacket off the floor. She looked at it and draped it round her shoulders.

x   x   x

Ludwik was looking through an old newspaper he had bought a fortnight ago. Once more he was reading the news about the new-born baby fished out of the San: ". . . the children immediately fished out that jar. To their indescribable surprise and terror they found the body of a hermaphrodite with two heads, one of them growing near the collar-bone."

He was again staring at those letters and words.

"Reading?" Samuel was standing at the window eating a roll.

"Mhm."

"What's new?"

"Nothing. They've fished out a newborn baby . . ."

"Have you seen the plaque on the house opposite?"

"Yes."

"Mickiewicz wrote *Pan Tadeusz* there."

"What else can you see?"

"An old boy is painting flowers and his wife has just brought him his breakfast. Now they've covered up the window."

"Stop spying."

"He's been painting that bunch of flowers for two weeks. Every day from eight to twelve and two to six."

Samuel lay down. Took his shoes off.

"My legs ache like hell. I've been tramping all day yesterday. So there was no telephone?"

"No."

"I've met a famous philosopher yesterday. Mr. Golde. He gave me his books."

"Those three fat ones?"

"Yes."

"What does he write? What are they about?"

"He's a philosopher. Well known in Parisian circles. Created a new philosophical system. Publishes in the most serious journals."

"You going to read them?"

"If only I find time."

"You better give them back to him. They won't go in your suit-case."

"I'll squeeze them somehow."

"And that system of his, what is its basis?"

"It's not clear."

"Not clear? Did he describe it to you?"

"No, he was telling me about his financial worries and his wife's illness . . ."

"You haven't got space for all the books. Baruch's also promised you his five-volume work on the sufferings of the Polish nation . . ."

"He may forget."

"Authors don't forget about such presents."

Samuel lay with his eyes shut.

There was a sharp knock on the door. M. knocks like that.

M. sat down in the armchair. She screwed up her face.

"It's stuffy in here—something stinks."

"We don't eat cheese."

"Socks."

Samuel lay with his eyes shut. There was a telephone on the wall above his head. Ludwik was washing plates in the sink. M. was reading French magazines and exclaiming melodramatically: *"Vive la reine!"* *". . . a vu la foule de Paris palpiter comme un grand coeur."* Suddenly she asked Ludwik:

"What's wrong with him?"

"Couldn't find a bra."

"A what?"

"You probably don't know what it is . . . it's a kind of a carrier for carrying breasts in."

"Listen. Listen to this: *"Vive Philipe . . . Comme il est grand!"*

"Samuel was looking for a strapless bra and couldn't find one. Spent a whole day looking . . . Paris is a dump, isn't it?"

"Please forgive me if I don't join in the conversation," Samuel said.

"Tummy ache?"

"Couldn't find a bra and had no telephone from home," Ludwik replied on Samuel's behalf.

"Telephone?"

"He's waiting for a telephone from home."

M. threw the papers at Samuel.

"Aren't you ashamed, you miserable old man?"

"I'll stay on this bed until I get the call. I've got a child and a wife . . ."

"When did you have the last call?"

"Last week."

"Fool," M. shrugged her shoulders.

"You always pretend," said Samuel. "You pretend you are not a mother and a wife, you pretend to be indifferent. This painting business is probably a pretense too."

"He is a cretin, isn't he, Ludwik?"

Samuel smiled brightly.

"I couldn't care less about the King and the Queen and this Paris of yours. I'm waiting for a phone call."

"Look," Ludwik shouted to M., "see what beautiful golden horns are growing on the brow of this ideal husband . . . his entire soul's hanging in a little slipper on a pin."

"I haven't anything else," Samuel replied quietly.

"You're shitting into a bamboo."

"And what are you doing in this place, have you seen anything interesting?"

Samuel closed his eyes and folded his arms on his chest.

"Ludwik's seen the Royal pair, let him tell you."

"I've seen one piece."

"Which piece?"

"I've seen one hand. The Queen's left hand in a long white glove . . ."

"And what else?"

"A hat. Then maybe it wasn't the Queen's hand. Hell of a crush."

"Perhaps it was Philip's leg," M.'s interest was roused.

"There was a hell of a crush. A hundred thousand. A sea of faces, as they say. Sellers of periscopes appeared in that sea. A forest of cardboard chimneys above a sea of heads. Made a terrible row. I didn't buy a periscope and I didn't climb a tree. In fact the Queen and I have not met."

"What about that hand?"

"I've seen a hand. Devilish squeeze. Two old geezers without a periscope. They stood on tiptoe, even climbed on my back. He in a lousy fur, she in a white lace kerchief on her head. Eyes glistening. Converse in Russian. They trod on my foot and "*pardon, pardon, pardon,*" and I, "*Nitchevo, babushka.*" And they "*Koroleva i korol uzhe prayekhali?*"* I took a look at the old grey children and let them stand in my place. I stood for a little while and then walked away into an empty side street. And they stayed there to see "koroleva" and "korol." They've now been waiting forty years. I went to a café."

"What did you eat?" asked Samuel.

"I drank *ven rooje ordeener*—pardon the pronunciation. The place was deserted. Cold and deserted. I sat there drinking wine. I wanted to get drunk."

"Why?"

"At the joyful thought that there is no longer any past. Everything begins anew . . . in Paris . . ."

---

* "Don't worry, old girl." "The Queen and the King, have they gone already?"

Samuel moved his leg.

"When he drinks wine he gets tummy ache and headache. He can't drink and he is no use anyway."

"I drank that wine until I drowned myself in it together with the Arc de Triomphe with inscriptions like Polotsk, Krasnoe, Ostrolenka ... with the *koroleva* and the *korol*. Red wine, red sea and thousands of cardboard periscopes above the waves ..."

Samuel reached for his notebook.

"The bard's improvising, he is seeing visions, must take it down."

"Do, I shan't repeat it."

"Spent much on that banquet?"

"Three hundred francs."

"And the waiter drummed on the table with his fingers expecting a tip," said Samuel.

"It wasn't a waiter, it was a waitress and she didn't drum."

"I know why he drank," M. said sarcastically.

"You don't know anything."

"I do, just as if I had been there with you."

"You don't."

M. stroked Ludwik's head.

"Poor little boy."

Samuel closed his eyes. "They are like children," he thought, "they know nothing. She paints her pictures, he sightsees. They know nothing. They do not know what water is. They do not know what air is. They do not know what bread is. Soup. They do not know what bed is, table, onion. They do not know what body is, song, flower, child. They know nothing and will know nothing. They laugh because I am waiting for a telephone, because they do not know it means salvation for me, that I have no other heaven. If I were to say to them: 'Save me, save me, I'm drowning' that would really raise a laugh. I can't tell them I'm dying since I am lolling on a bed after a good dinner and I'm seeing *Le mariage de Figaro* this evening. I have died and they do not see it. They will never know what a death crew is: we had leather belts with buckles which we fastened over the corpse's wrists. The ground was sandy, we had to pull the bodies out of the chambers and drag them as far as the graves. There was musical accompaniment when we dug the graves. What is music? Between the gas chamber and the graves a six-piece band usually played songs like *Es geht alles vorüber, es geht alles vorbei*. They played on violins and flutes. Was it true that 'cyclon' had enough strength to force blood out of the lungs and dung out of the rectum? Yes. *Sport machen. Mützen auf, antreten, wegtreten, rechts um, links um, ein, zwo, auf, nieder, rollen, hüpfen, hüpfen,*

Knie beugen, Augen rechts, ah, Mensch, Menschen Kind ... du Kerl, du Schlafmütze, du Drecksack, du Arschloch, dummes Zeug, Schwein-hund, links, links ein, zwo, drei, vier, links. Krematoriumsfleisch, alte Pipe, alte Hure, alte Latrine, du Pechvogel, links, links, ein, zwo, drei, vier, links."

Translated by ADAM CZERNIAWSKI

PART TWO

Poetry

MARIA KONOPNICKA*

Waiting

Once, and twice, the heavy plough
Through our land has riven now;
Black the cloven clods remain—
Waiting, sowing, waiting grain.
      Seedtime, sower, come, we plead!
      Do not tarry at our need.

Storms have awed the heart of earth;
Winds wail'd o'er with course of dearth;
Fruitful rain has fall'n from heaven;

Still we lack the sower's leaven!
      Nation's soul and prairie soil,
      Sower, wait thy vital toil!

With our fathers' bones each field
Hallow'd, grants an ampler yield;
Slow the sun dispels our shadows;
Roses tremble down the meadows.
      Sower, mankind supplicates you—
      Earth, the ancient, here awaits you!

(Watson Kirkconnell)

The River

Gleaming pool and rippling ford
Now are held in ice abhorr'd;
Gone are foam and living tide,
Hid in depths of frozen pride:

      Lost his spring-dawn's
      Ecstasy;
      Lost his journey
      Far to sea.

(* For biographical note see p. 75).

Dark, cold river, ice as king
Brings no new and fatal thing;
Every year the winter chains thee,
Every year the blizzard pains thee.

> Spring at last
> In buxom glee
> Sends thee dashing
> Far to sea.

Not for aye the sun hides deep;
Not for aye earth falls asleep;
Not for aye the flowers are furl'd;
Not for aye frost rules the world.

> Buxom spring
> Arrives with glee;
> Streams go dashing
> Far to seal

(Watson Kirkconnell)

Jan Kasprowicz

(1860–1926)

Jan Kasprowicz was born in Szymborz of impoverished peasant-stock. His hard childhood was later reflected in his work *From the Peasant Acre* (1891). Despite many difficulties, he acquired a secondary and then a higher education in philosophy and literature in Leipzig, Wroclaw and Lwow while he was doing social work in Silesia. He belonged to secret youth organizations and in 1888 was sentenced to a six-month term in prison by the Prussian authorities. In 1889 he settled in Lwow. He travelled to Italy and spent a great deal of time in the Tatra mountains, a region he celebrated in many of his poems, e.g., in his beautiful *The Wild Rose Tree* (1898).

Kasprowicz brought a new element to Polish poetry—the peasant world, touched by strong radicalism (*From the Peasant Hut*, 1889, *Christ*, 1890). His later works dealt with the dichotomy of the modern man, his faithlessness and his search for faith, his metaphysical quest and his preoccupation with destructive and liberating love (e.g., *Anima Lachrymans*, 1894, *Love*, 1895).

Kasprowicz is profoundly affected by the Promethean themes of Polish Romanticism; his dominant *motif* is suffering, not personal, but the cosmic anguish of mankind. Suffering and love, the two Shelleyan elements, fill his work. He is also concerned with religious themes, especially in his hymns *To the Dying World* (1902) which contains the well-known hymn "Holy God," *The Book of the Poor* (1916). His other important works are: *Ballad of the Sunflower* (1908), *Moments* (1911), *The Hill of Death, Napierski's Revolt* (1899) and *Herodias' Banquet* (1905).

Kasprowicz is also known for his translations of Greek, English and German literatures. He was professor of World Literature at the University in Lwow.

JAN KASPROWICZ

The Dreaming Mountains Fell Asleep

The dreaming mountains fell asleep
In purple veils of autumn mist;
The sunlight on the stubbled fields
Shone amber gold and amethyst.

Slow dust was settling to bestain
The birch-leaves' crimson oriflamme—
O melancholy hour of grief,
O melancholy autumn calm!

And I depart, for Time commands
Nor leaves a trace, my tale to tell.
O mountains, O bare harvest plain,
O silent Season of farewell!

(Watson Kirkconnell)

When Dusk Surrounds Me

When dusk surrounds me, and a gloom that presses
The human soul to earth in harsh assize,
There haste to rescue me from my distresses
Thy shining, gentle, and sagacious eyes.

Then evil, fleeing, draws off and regresses;
Its caravan of griefs in ruin lies;
A gaze like cherub-swords its fate assesses:
Thy shining, gentle, and sagacious eyes.

Cleansed and renewed in spirit I arise,
Ready to challenge life, since changed by seeing
Thy shining, gentle, and sagacious eyes,

Then clasp this charming treasure as my prize,
And kiss, with ardent rapture in my being,
Thy shining, gentle, and sagacious eyes.

(Watson Kirkconnell)

The Close of Day

Bending above my book,
I see no syllable;
But strain my weary ears
To hear if all be well.

To me no message comes
From rivers, crags, and peaks—
Only the traffic's roar
Importunately speaks.

To me no message comes
As sunset's flames depart—
Only the darkness floods
The desert of my heart.

Ah, but my mind breaks free,
And soars in eager flight
To find on sun-flush'd peaks
God's grace, before the night.

(Watson Kirkconnell)

Haycocks

Haycocks besprinkle the meadows,
The summits afar glimmer red.
The sun breaks suddenly forth,
A torrent of jewels to spread.

    Down under the rocky cliff
    The timeless Dunajec flows,
    Past the eye of the sentinel firs
    The murmurous river goes.

Just at noon, as the scorching sun
Flings widest its golden rays,
Hard by the river's edge
A figure of Longing strays.

Having shed the imprisoning hut,
She brushes her weary eyes,
And breathing the fragrant air,
Ponders the glowing skies.

    Then wrenches herself away,
    To be lost in the distant blue,

Or with eyes wide open to dream
And the whispering wavelets pursue.

But the folds of her wind-blown gown,
Yearning seizes with shuddering hand,
Sighing: how bitter to part
With the very soul of the land.

(Sigmund Sluszka)

The Baltic

From the sea we are, from the ocean!
O Baltic! Time's blade behold,
Raised o'er the fount of our glory,
The waters Polish of old.

From the sea we are, from the ocean!
From murmurous Baltic's space,
With vigor and freshness unceasing,
Renewing our Polish race.

From the sea we are, from the ocean!
From Baltic's enchanting strand.
Firm in the shore it caresses,
Each a true guardian shall stand.

From the sea we are, from the ocean!
On its banks let God shed his care!
We vow to defend them forever,
No foeman to threaten shall dare.

From the sea we are, from the ocean!
Far on its giant waves blown,
Already our prows cut its waters,
And sail to some happy unknown.

From the sea we are, from the ocean!
O Baltic! We are for thy might
A bulwark! Let danger but menace,
With sword lifted high, we shall fight!

(A. P. Coleman)

My Evening Song

Blessed be the moment
When the soul's evening hymn breaks forth!
When from the quiet fields,
From the stubble and the river bank,
The lanes and the fallow land,
The low-lying huts
And the weather-beaten barns,
The song of a lad comes, crying:
O play for me, little pipe!
Play for me, play!
I fashioned you from a willow branch,
Where flows the silver-blue river,
Where rises the murmuring grove.

Dew collects on the sleepy flowers,
On the meadows and dark wheat fields.
It rests on the lake's curving shore,
Does the soul of this far-spreading land,
And prayerfully stares in its depths.
Then it rises with mist-clouds on high,
O'er the silent, the praying waters.
It listens, and looks, and whispers
Perpetual prayers.
From the hamlets flow sounds of talking,
In the marshes the wild birds answer,
And far in a lonely corner, at a crossroad,
A single candle glimmers within some cottage.

(Charlotte Saikowska)

Antoni Lange

(1862–1929)

A short story writer, poet and critic, Antoni Lange did a great deal for Poland's poetic life by his translations of many works from foreign literatures, from Sanskrit to the French symbolists and Hungarian poets, and his critical articles on the contemporary poetry of Western Europe. He is considered as one of the most intellectual of modern Polish poets, and an innovator of the poetic form; thus, he introduced to Polish poetry assonance and new rhythms and stanzas.

His main works are: *Poems* (1895, 1898, 1899, and 1901); *Sonnets* (1910); the tragedies *The Weneds* (1909) and *Attila* (1910); and stories *The Funeral Repast* (1911) and *In the Fourth Dimension* (1912).

Although Lange's work reflects Western cultural influences, it also shows native Polish traditions, especially Neo-Romanticism. Thus, the slogan, "art for art's sake," is not necessarily a European import, in that it had been proclaimed also by the great Polish Romantics, who, however, qualified the dictum by combining it with Polish and universal Prometheism.

Lange's later work is reflective but he still continues to excel in lyrical poetry. He is also the author of several novels and dramas (*Elfryde, Crime, Tatters*).

ANTONI LANGE

Solitude

Eternal solitaries—human souls,
Solitaries blown astray;
Each wanders through the Milky Way,
Each in her finite circle rolls.

Like wandering planets they gaze
At one another in the sky's blue halls;
Each in her finite circle rolls,
But never from her orbit sways.

Across the skies each must gaze,
Yearning to reach the other's hand,

But never from her orbit sways;
Alas, one wave they never shall ascend.

Each solitary yearns to shake another's hand,
Each in her nebulae still rolls;
One wave, alas, they never can ascend,
Eternal solitaries—human souls.

(Adam Gillon)

Not for One Day

Not for one day alone thou sowest wheat,
But for to-morrow's famine, harsh and chary;
So, with thy land's black earth beneath thy feet,
Bend to thy plough across this fertile prairie—
Thus did the murmuring grain in song entreat.

Though hostile drought and tempest oft defeat,
With bloody sweat wear out thine adversary:
Let toil be not in vain, that man may eat—
Not for one day!

Nature's best song is ever bitter-sweet,
As if soft May should wed with January:
Diana slew Actaeon all unwary;
Dark, elemental powers are ill to meet;
Yet sow—in spite of hail and parching heat—
Not for one day!

(Watson Kirkconnell)

The Bridegroom

Virgins waiting long with sorrow,
Bring your boughs and precious gums—
Pleat a chaplet for to-morrow:
Lo, he comes, the bridegroom comes.

Many years you've waited, weeping;
Far he seem'd, you wish'd him near—

Suddenly, while you are sleeping,
See the godlike prince appear.

He has come, like dayspring shining—
Risen, living, robed in white.
Virgins, pain'd with long repining,
Have your lamps no oil to-night?

(Watson Kirkconnell)

Kazimierz Tetmajer

(1865–1940)

Kazimierz Tetmajer is an outstanding representative of the Young Poland movement and the most popular exponent of the ideas of the "decadent" generation at the turn of the nineteenth and twentieth centuries. Pessimism, disillusionment, mistrust of the world are characteristic features of his poetry which, on the other hand, expressed sensuality and eroticism. "Melancholy, nostalgia, sadness, discouragement are the essence of my soul" is a constantly recurring theme, but so is *Hymn to Love* and *The Birth of Aphrodite*. Although not an innovator, his voluminous poetic output is not devoid of fresh and original formulations, and excels in the rendering of mood.

In addition to being a lyrical poet, Tetmajer is also a playwright: *Husband-Poet* (1892), *Sphinx* (1893), *The Black Knight* (1901), *Revolution* (1906), *Judas* (1917). In the character of the "Poet" Wyspianski, another foremost representative of Young Poland, introduced him into his drama, *The Wedding*, in which the phantom of the "Black Knight" also appears.

Tetmajer's many novels are based on contemporary and historical themes, but special mention must be made of his tales connected with the folklore and past and present life of the colorful peasants of the region of the Tatra mountains: *In the Rocky Highlands* (five series, 1903–1910, a selection of which appeared in English as *Tales of the Tatras*, New York 1943) and *Tatra Legend* (1912) which deals with the legendary mountain brigand, Janosik, the "Polish Robin Hood." The poet's engrossment with the Tatras is also manifested by a whole cycle devoted to these mountains. These poems assure him an important place in the Tatra tradition of Polish literature.

KAZIMIERZ TETMAJER

In the Forest

With slow and dreamy motion,
In the clear blue withholden,
Go clouds of velvet glory,
Snow-radiant and golden.

Sometimes athwart the heavens,
The swallow, swart and slender,

Slips like a sliver'd arrow
Across the sun's bright splendor.

A silver frame encricles
The calm and shining meadow;
Along its brooks of opal
Float flakes of golden shadow.

Down through the dim green forest
Light streams in emerald lustres,
Or pierces through the branches
With rays in burning clusters.

On skies, green fields and forests
Its radiance suffusing,
The great sun drifts and gazes,
High in its blue path musing.

(Watson Kirkconnell)

Song of the Night Mists

Silently, silently slip we, where waves in their
        covert lie sleeping;
Nimbly we dance in the wind; through abysses of
        space we go sweeping. . . .
High round the moon, in a ribbon, we wrap us in
        amorous gesture,
And she, whose white body shines through, makes
        a rainbow of light from our vesture;
We catch the soft murmur of streams, their fresh
        life to the lake-deeps supplying;
We take the low moan of the cedar, the pine-tree's
        melodious sighing;
And we drink in the fragrance of flowers, that bloom
        on the breasts of the mountains:
Tuneful and tinted and fragrant, we soar in the
        blue heights like fountains.

Silently, silently slip we, where waves in their
        covert lie sleeping;
Nimbly we dance in the wind; through abysses of
        space we go sweeping. . . .

We hasten to catch in our arms the sad star that is
      falling from heaven,
And we weave a bright cross in the sky, as a sign
      that at last he is shriven;
We play with the down of the thistle, its white in
      the darkness revealing,
We brush the soft plumage of owls, that about in the
      shadows are wheeling;
We chase the dark bats, that are flying, as silent
      as we, in the night-time,
And we wind our invisible net round those gnomes
      in their flittering flight-time;
From peak to high peak we are flung; o'er the val-
      leys we hang like long bridges;
And stars, with their rays, clench the ends to the
      rocks of the pinnacled ridges;
There, for a space, the winds rest, and grow hush'd
      from the stress·of their roaming;
But the night wanes; we break; and in sport, they
      pursue us again in the gloaming.

(Watson Kirkconnell)

Stanislaw Wyspianski

(1869–1907)

Stanislaw Wyspianski was born in Cracow in 1869, son of a noted sculptor. He studied at the Academy of Fine Arts under the direction of the famous historical painter, Jan Matejko. He also studied abroad, especially in Paris, where he became familiar with the modern trends in art and literature. He began his literary career in Paris, and upon his return to Poland became artistic director of *Life* magazine in Cracow, in which his first dramatic works were printed. He was also active as a painter.

Wyspianski is known both as a poet and dramatist. His work combines the traditions of Greek tragedy, Shakespeare, Romanticism and Polish folklore. His early work, *The Legend* (1897; expanded version, 1904), drawn from the Polish legendary history, shows Wagnerian *motifs* (e.g., its "underwater" scenery as in *Rheingold*). Greek elements enter such works as *Meleager* (1898), *Protesilas and Laodamia* (1899), *Achilleis* (1903), *Return of Odysseus* (1907) and *The Ban* (1899).

His play, *The Wedding* (1901), is considered one of the most outstanding poetic dramas of Polish literature. Based on popular Nativity plays in its technique, it is actually a masterful social and political satire, although it is based on a topical event of a fellow poet's wedding with a peasant girl. The play lacks action in the conventional sense, but it abounds in suspense, musical effects, and it is a lively and symbolic discussion of personal and patriotic themes.

Although he was primarily a dramatist, Wyspianski was a most sensitive and imaginative poet, whose vision of reborn Poland proved prophetic. His achievement in art, drama and poetry is remarkable when one considers the fact that he died at the height of his powers, aged thirty-eight.

STANISLAW WYSPIANSKI

Invocation

Lord, through Thy Great Resurrection,
Thou hast waken'd from dejection
Every torpid, slumbering creature,
Granting life throughout all Nature.

Praise be Thine in songs of glory,
Praise be Thine in tempest's thunder:

Let them chant Thy Spirit's story,
Ris'n to life from graves hereunder.

Stand by us on that Great Morning,
God new-risen, Judah's Lion!
Let earth sing, Thy Throne adorning,
Praises of Thy heavenly Zion!

Trumpets play and bells are ringing,
Wind and thunder fill the height—
All today Thy praise are singing,
Resurrected God of Might!

(Watson Kirkconnell)

Funeral of Casimir The Great

Grimly, gravely they come,
The bells start a-tolling
From tower and steeple,
A-tolling a dirge
Funeral.

Grimly, gravely they come,
And bear in their hands
His crowns ceremonial,
That wrought though so finely,
Yet weigh as if leaden,
From tombs they come tarnished,
Sepulchral.

The bells are a-tolling
From tower and steeple,
A-flutter the pennons,
A-flap are the standards,
A-waving the streamers
Of mourning.

The bells are a-tolling
From tower and steeple,
Enormous and booming
To heaven.

And songs there above them,
Like wings of the angels,
Are swaying and mounting
Portentous.

Grimly, gravely they come
From each of the churches,
With banners and flowers
That, fragrant, in thousands
Are counted.

And peasants in smocks,
Great nobles in robes
And cloaks that are scarlet
And crimson.

And exquisite girls,
Young lordlings with curls,
Cheeks paler than those of the lily.
And grievous their treading,
And gravely they're stepping,
All through the long streets
Of the city:

And grievous their treading
And gravely they're stepping
Though blue are the skies
Without pity.

The scurrying clouds
Now enfold, now discover
The countless, slow-moving
Processions.

The shadows are writhing,
Now gleaming, now hiding,
Now gone in glimpse that was
Fleeting.

And grim they and grave,
The bells sadly tolling
From tower and steeple.

Are those untrodden meadows a-babbling,
Are the flowers they'd culled complaining?

Are the meadows and pastures a-bowing,
Or but bend they to the wind's pursuing?

And those woods on the hill—are they waving?
Are the wreaths of the fir-trees so fragrant? . . .
Are those forests of larches a-bowing,
Or but bend they to the wind's pursuing?

Are those meadows—that grey there behind them?
Comes that murmur from fields there behind them?
There behind them—do the forests be waving?
There behind them are those fir-woods now coming?
Are the bees in their thousands so humming,
There behind them—or the earth is it groaning?

     And grim they and grave,
     Mournful and sombre,
     The meadows so fragrant,
     The forests sky-tow'ring,
     Grandchildren of mine,
     The posthumous.

     And bells are a-tolling
     From tower and steeple,
     Enormous and booming
     Portentous.

(M. A. Michael)

Leopold Staff
(1878–1957)

Born in 1878 in Lwow, Staff was educated in this city and lived there till the outbreak of war. His first collection, *Dreams of Power* (1901), revealed an independent talent, destined to become a major literary voice in the country. Staff was one of the first to break with decadent influences in the "Young Poland" movement, advocating a somewhat Nietzschean concept of the will to power. But he was concerned with spiritual power rather than temporal, and persistently kept aloof from politics.

His next collections were *The Day of the Soul* (1903) and *The Victor*, in which he wrote of creative suffering, the inner conflict and the victory over oneself. A later work *To the Stars* displayed original linguistic innovations as well as an impressive vision of the universe. In his virtuoso treatment of rhyme and rhythm, Staff proved a poet's poet. His *Expiration* is a good example of his superb poetic craft; it is a collection of broken sentences representing a dying man's flow of thought. Staff's wide range of emotion, the wealth of tone, the compactness and originality of his imagery, the broad philosophical scope of his work—all these make him one of Poland's outstanding modern poets.

Staff's major achievement lies also in his having served as a bridge between the older Romantic poetry and the new poetry, especially that of the *Skamander* group. He was perhaps the only outstanding figure of "Young Poland," whose influence went beyond the confines of his period and profoundly affected a new generation of poets.

Throughout his long poetic career, Staff never lost his intense individualism, ignoring the political upheavals in the country. Some of his other major collections are: *To the Birds of Heaven* (1905), *The Blooming Branch* (1908), *The Smile of Hours* (1910), *In the Shade of the Sword* (1911), *The Swan and the Lyre* (1914), *The Needle's Eye* (1927), *Tall Trees* (1932). Staff also wrote poetic dramas, e.g., *The Treasure* (1904) and *Godiva* (1906).

LEOPOLD STAFF

Liberty

Straiten'd am I, O Lord, upon a pillar
Of lonely pride, with scarcely room to stand:
Stiff as a corpse long cabin'd in a coffin
    Are neck and knee and hand.

Beyond all else I thirst for greater freedom.
With prairies broad, I pray, my feet endow:
That I may kneel, and in the dust before Thee
    Press homage with my brow.

(Watson Kirkconnell)

To Love and Lose

To love and lose, to thirst and pity too,
To fall in anguish and rise up again,
To cry "Away!", yet longingly to woo—
Lo, this is life: mere vanity and pain.

Men traverse parching deserts for one gem;
For one great pearl, the ocean they explore;
Then die, and all that lingers after them
Is footprints on the sand and deep-sea floor.

(Watson Kirkconnell)

View on a Hill

Autumn weaves memories of youth's caress.
From the blue cloud, slow strands of silver stream
As spectral as the thought of nothingness.
Alas, was life no better than a dream?
We gaze upon the golden fields again,
On groves of peace, rare treasure of the years;
And all seems vaster, like the world of men
Seen through a sudden mist of human tears.

(Watson Kirkconnell)

Ave Aurora

Arise, my heart! For in the night's high plain,
That sullen over earth and thee hath lain,
At the first flashing of the dawn's bright sword
Hacked to dark, hostile shreds away
              The gloom is gone.

As in defeat the darkness takes to flight,
Greet the triumphant Sun! Exalt the Light!
New every morning let it be adored,
For still the spirit by its ray
                          To prayer is drawn.

Give praise, ye meadows fair, ye clouds and hills!
Sing out ye birds, yea, chant ye woods and rills!
And thou, my heart, join in with sweet accord,
For lo, in perfect grace of day
                          There comes the dawn.

                              (Watson Kirkconnell)

The Golden Elegy

Where is a golden goblet fill'd so deep
With golden wine as thou, in hue so bold,
O Earth, whom draughts of autumn lull to sleep
With all thy dreaming forests changed to gold?

To bud, and bear, and, after bounteous fruit,
To perish in surpassing pomp and splendor:
That were a fate serene and absolute!
My soul craves that last glory of surrender!

O Earth, our mother and our kindly nurse,
So meek in spring! But now that summer's done,
Thou hast become—while all else turns to worse—
A holy, golden sister of the sun.

Blest be the secret powers that here beget
Our dark existence with its zeal for duty—
Sending us toil and torment, blood and sweat—
If life can end in such a flame of beauty!

Then let my days in their dull series die,
Perish my yearning heart and all its pain,
If in their quiet autumn elegy
Only blue glory and gold grace remain!

Love gives thee back the tints that in its keeping,
O Earth, drew power from thy mighty breast.
Would that our hearts were fair as thou, here sleeping,
Could love like thee, and turn as brave to rest.....

(Watson Kirkconnell)

Boleslaw Lesmian

(1878–1937)

Boleslaw Lesmian (pseudonym of Boleslaw Lesman) was born in Warsaw in 1878, and was educated in Kiev. A poet's poet, Lesmian began his career with contributions to *Life*, the organ of the "Young Poland" movement and also in *Chimera*.

His first collection, *The Meadow* (1920), received critical acclaim, and his subsequent volumes were equally well received: *Shadowy Potion* (1936); *Sylvan Tale* (published posthumously in 1938). Lesmian was also a translator, and is responsible for the Polish version of several of Edgar Allan Poe's tales.

Lesmian's poetry is marked by singular refinement of the language, which is for him the main source of inspiration. The word is for him a concentrated summary of color, sound and the sensual experience. His artful visions are not marred by realism; the metaphorical conception of a thing is never brought into contact with the thing itself. His is a self-contained and dream-like world of imagination, filled with modernistic symbolism and expressed in a highly individual, beautifully wrought rhythm.

BOLESLAW LESMIAN

Brother

You rejected my hand ... The clouded dawn
Transformed the world.
And from the near-by bed you were drawn
By the call of a dying brother.

You ran, came back ... He was dead ... In the sky
Fate proclaimed its golden choice.
You whispered, "Now I am yours until I die."
Tearfully and in a broken voice.

Softly I asked, not looking in your face,
"He knew?" "Yes," you said.
Beyond the window a bird sped,
With a thought of distant space.

(Adam Gillon)

The Soldier

In spring the soldier came from the war,
Very crippled, dull and sore.

The bullet had whipped his legs and thighs,
With weary bounds his way he plies.

Now sad leaper of his sorry fate,
The crowd is amused by his anguished gait.

His woes and sorrow are belied
By merry capers, the pain that twists his side.

He plodded to his hut, his native soil;
They said: Away you clown from our toil.

To his pal he ran, knocked on his window pane,
The sexton chased him with a cane.

Off to his mistress then he trudged. She laughed,
Shaking her arms and hips in mirth, she scoffed:

I won't dance with him in bed—he quakes,
A third of him is flesh, the rest is shakes.

You think into your quivering arms I'll rush—
Oh, no, I shan't sleep on your moustache.

You are too jumpy, leap too bold,
Go some place else, don't curse, don't scold.

Hence to a wayside statue he dragged his feet.
Christ, all of pine, think you deep.

What mocking sculptor hewed your face?
He saved on wood and on the grace.

Your crippled knees give way under their load,
You sure must jump not walk, avoid the road?

You're such a wretch, such nothing come of air,
That all my hops you certainly can share.

Upon these words Christ downward slipped,
The carver of this God—his lid had flipped.

Both hands of Christ were left, both feet were right:
His pine-feet drilled the grassy site.

"Indeed, I am a wretched clod of pine,
I'll walk eternally on foot, it's fine.

"Together we will go on common sod,
A little of man, and a little of God.

"Our torment we will share: it must be shared.
To cripple us the human hand has dared.

"Some ridicule for me—and some for you,
Who first derides shall first love too.

"Your body shall support my own, I'll lay
My pine on yours, come what may."

They linked their arms, went off without delay:
Their legs a-stumble and grotesquely gay.

They marched to chimes of endless towers,
Where are those clocks to strike those hours?

The days, the nights had passed, that had to pass.
Unreal fields and bush and woods went thus.

And a storm arose and endless dark,
An absence of sun, terrible, stark.

What creature from the northern stormy whine
Appears so very human, so divine?

They are two cripples, pitiful and odd,
They limp into a world of God.

One not bereaved, the other walks in joy,
Bound in a love that cannot be destroyed.

God limped, man limped—their measure none too low.
What in them limped no man shall ever know.

They hopped so low and they hopped so high,
Until at last they reached the very sky.

(Adam Gillon and Ludwik Krzyzanowski)

Julian Tuwim

(1894–1953)

One of the great masters of the Polish language and a virtuoso of the written word, Julian Tuwim was born in Lodz, of middle-class Jewish parents. He was educated there in the Russian Gymnasium, and later studied law and philosophy at the University of Warsaw. His first collection of poems, *Lying in Wait for God* (1918), caused wide controversy, and made him the leader of the literary group *Skamander*. With each of the subsequent volumes Tuwim proved himself to be one of the most vibrant and fresh poets of his time. His collections *Dancing Socrates* (1920), *Poems, Volume 4* (1923), *Words in Blood* (1926), *Czarnolas Language* (1929), *Gypsy Bible* (1933) and others established his position as a leader of Polish Futurism, a discoverer of the exoticism of everyday life, and an original innovator of rhyme and meter. He was a poet of great lyrical power, capable of passionate eruptions, constantly searching for new forms, yearning for a fullness of life in all its manifestations—a poetry that defies critical or ideological isms. He was in turn conservative or extremely radical, his primary concern being with finding the source of the greatest emotion and an opportunity for the fullest self-expression. Thus, his attitude to many social problems was often purely instrumental. His reaction to them was one of an excited imagination rather than a case of ideological conviction.

Tuwim has sometimes been called the Polish Walt Whitman, because of his dedication to the expansion of the scope of Polish poetry so that it might include all the modern aspects of life—"everything under the sun." In *The Polish Flowers* (1949) he attempted to achieve this aim by encompassing the entire experience of modern Poland through a series of kaleidoscopic recollections and sketches of personal and historical events.

Tuwim was also an excellent translator from the Russian, and a man of wide interests: bibliophile, lexicographer of Bacchic terms, writer of children's verse, anthologist of "literary trifles." His translations from the Russian poetry include Pushkin and some of the modern poets, Balmont, Briusov, Mayakovsky.

JULIAN TUWIM

Life

Life?
     Relaxing, my arms I shall spread,
And fill my lungs with the morning breeze;

I shall humbly bow to the azure sky,
And shall cry, joyously cry:
How glad I am that my blood is red!

(Adam Gillon)

Woman

At times she will in rigid numbness freeze,
Horrid, immovable in thoughtless thought;
Dull apathy upon her soul will seize,
And fear, as if she saw a dead mouse rot.

With agony her glassy eyes are blind,
Of chaos full, and sad infinitude,
And crumpled thoughts come thick upon her mind,
And fields in madness throng, and deserts brood.

Wake her, and drunk with chaos she will start,
As though she had *returned*: yet hides much more,
For when she hoarsely speaks, her words impart
She has remained a savage, as of yore.

(Adam Gillon)

There Is No Country

There is no country whence I shall not yearn
In grieving anguish for the old, grey streets.
All cries of victory to sobbing turn,
And earth's wide wonder into nothing fleets.

There is no land where I have visited
Unhaunted by the old, grey memories.
No matter what the highway that I tread,
My inner eye the same horizon sees.

Nothing can solace to my heart provide;
Joyless is every vista I have scann'd;
Eternally above me opens wide
The old, grey welkin of my native land.

No travel helps, no road that I have trod,
Nor human crowds nor oceans bring relief;
Even upon the streets I pray to God,
While people gaze and listen to my grief.

No help in any wealth of language lies;
Nor savage hymns nor races foil despair.
For what it may avail, I face the skies
And raise anew my plain, old daily prayer.

I wail, I cry out in most desperate straits:
"Hearken, Jehovah, flash Thy sword to view!"
But yonder, in the streets, the Father waits:
The old, grey God my Polish boyhood knew.

(Watson Kirkconnell)

Old Folks

We sit and look at gutters
Through half-open shutters.

We kiss strange children's heads
And water little flower-beds.

Piously our fate we bear,
From calendars we pages tear.

(Adam Gillon)

The Two Winds

One wind—in the field he blew,
Another wind—in the garden grew:
Quietly and very lightly
He caressed the leaves and rustled,
Swooned . . .

One wind—a mighty swell,
Somersaulted, flatly fell,
Leaped, and surged, soared up high,

Upwards whirled into the sky,
Overturned and dropped pell-mell
Upon a soughing, drowsy garden,
Where so quietly and lightly
Now caressed the leaves and rustled
The other wind.

Off the cherry blossoms flew,
Laughter in all garden grew,
Brother took his twin for friend,
Now they cruise over the land,
Chasing clouds and birds in flight,
Rush into the windmill's stance,
And confuse its stupid arms,
Right and left they whistle, dance,
Blow their lungs with all their might,
Clowning in a frenzied riot!

The garden is so quiet . . . quiet . . .

(Adam Gillon)

Pursuit

I rush to your dwelling
With storm in my blood;
With thunders impelling
On the portals I thud.

A tempest blows through me,
It tears at the sills.
Come, open! Endue me
With calm! There pursue me
A legion of hills.

The plains in commotion
Like lions seek meat;
For me, a blind Ocean
Now roars in the street.

The universe rages
To catch me. Ah, stay!
For nothing engages
My life, save your sway.

Come, open and save me
And fence me about!
From the world you may crave me
As yours beyond doubt!

Vast powers are giving
My soul to the pit—
But Mother of Living,
Yea, Mother of Living,
Thou dost not permit! . . .

(Watson Kirkconnell)

You

You keep me on this earth,
And to the heaven draw near,
You are all to me on this earth,
Why go so far from here?

Today I know but you,
And only you have learned;
I understand no more,
I brushed aside the world.

Each step reveals new roads,
Each thought's a boiling abyss.
You alone reply
In words or a silent kiss.

I hear the blood of your heart,
I feel your misty breath,
And mad with love go on
With this life so full of death.

(Adam Gillon)

Request for a Song

If, O God, I have Thy splendid gift, the Word,
Cause my heart to beat with the wrath of oceans;
Give me the ancient poets' noble sword,
To strike at the tyrants with raging emotions.

No need for hymns to throng my head
To sing the wasted man, of an empty heart,
Ready to supplicate for a bit of bread,
Who for the king must play his menial part.

Give my angry words the flash of steel,
A fantasy and rhyme—well-aimed and strong,
So that the targets I shall hit feel
The sharp rapier of my glittering song.

(Adam Gillon)

A Prayer

I pray Thee O Lord
From all my heart,
O Lord! I pray to Thee.
With fervor and zeal,
For the sufferings of the humiliated,
For the uncertainty of those who wait;
For the non-return of the dead;
For the helplessness of the dying;
For the sadness of the misunderstood,
For those who request in vain;
For all those abused, scorned and disdained;
For the silly, the wicked, the miserable;
For those who hurry in pain
To the nearest physician;
Those who return from work
With trembling and anguished hearts to their homes;
For those who are roughly treated and pushed aside,
For those who are hissed on the stage;
For all who are clumsy, ugly, tiresome and dull,
For the weak, the beaten, the oppressed,
For those who cannot find rest
During long sleepless nights;
For those who are afraid of Death,
For those who wait in pharmacies;
For those who have missed the train;
—For all the inhabitants of our earth
And all their pains and troubles,
Their worries, sufferings, disappointments,
All their griefs, afflictions, sorrows,

Longings, failures, defeats;
For everything which is not joy,
Comfort, happiness, bliss—...
Let these shine forever upon them
With tender love and brightness,
I pray Thee O Lord most fervently—
I pray Thee O Lord from the depths of my heart.

(Wanda Dynowska)

Theophany

I feel you are coming, thunderous night,
Gigantic and red with a blazing hue.
You golden-strung vision, my holy light,
You are dawning, O Poetry New!

Though your face is yet unknown from which
Of ages hidden sense will gush with god,
I know, you will be mad, mysterious:
The soul to come, the future I laud.

Your name shall be the somber, grim "I am!"
Embracing all, tyrannical with dread!
You shall reveal yourself in this Fiery Creed:
"I am proudly come for the dream of the mad."

(Adam Gillon)

Jaroslaw Iwaszkiewicz

(1894–1980)

Jaroslaw Iwaszkiewicz (pseudonym: Eleuter) was born near Kalnik, Kievan Ukraine, in 1894. He was educated at home and at the University of Kiev, completing his law studies in 1918. After making his appearance as a poet in Kiev, Iwaszkiewicz moved to Warsaw, where he became one of the founders of the literary group *Skamander*. He is now the president of the Polish Association of Writers, editor of the respected literary magazine *Creative Work*, and an active participant in the country's political life.

His first volume of lyrics, *Octaves*, appeared in 1919. He was associated with the composer Karol Szymanowski, and wrote the libretto for the latter's opera, *King Roger of Sicily*. A widely traveled man (he was a state official in Paris, Copenhagen and Persia), Iwaszkiewicz has been called the Polish Oscar Wilde, because of his fine poetic sense and personality. His important early works are: *The Seven Rich Towns of the Immortal Kosciej* (1924) and *The Moon is Rising* (1925). His later works were: *Red Shields* (1934), an historical novel about the 12th-century Piast prince, Henry of Sandomierz; *The Maiden from Wilkohof* (1933); *The Mill on the Utrata, The Italian Stories* (1947); *Tales of Hearsay* (1954).

His novel, *The Passions of Bledomierz*, and his earlier novels are marked by decadence and disillusionment, but their fine style elevates them to works of art. His trilogy of novels, *Fame and Glory* (1956) presents the portrait of the Polish society in the period from 1913 to the present; other works are: *Ascension* (1959); *Sweet-flag* (1960) stories; *Icarus* (1960) stories. His plays are: *Summer in Nohant* (1936); *Masquerade* (1939); *Mr. Balzac's Wedding* (1960).

Several editions of his collected works appeared, among others, *Poems from Different Periods* (1952) and *The Trees of Autumn and Other Poems* (1954). Iwaszkiewicz's lyric poetry is subtle and refined in form and language, and he is generally considered a leading, contemporary Polish writer.

JAROSLAW IWASZKIEWICZ

A Message

I thank you for kindest of words you sent to us all,
I am human and the forest for the trees I fail to see,
And to rise upward is harder, ever harder for me.
Hence at times my song will be seasoned with gall.

But I always feel better, and see more clearly
When the words like yours arrive, the words of friendship.

(Adam Gillon and Ludwik Krzyzanowski)

The Brotherhood of Man

O Wanderer, if ever you approach the banks of river Seine,
the Place d'Alma in Paris,
you will observe a figure cut of bronze, standing upon a column.
The figure is not tall,
his coat is borne aloft by the breath of wind, and he extends his arm:
Thus stands, forever going somewhere, Mickiewicz—our prophet,
turned into a wind,
a wind that blows across the wastes.
It is our father, Adam,
who heralded to all the peoples of the earth eternal love
and brotherhood.
When tempests rage upon the ocean, and many-storied waves clap
against each other,
     emitting sounds like many thousands clapping hands,
     and toss ships and fishing boats against the rocks,
     and cast men .upon the waters of the sea, their heads bobbing
like wooden logs from shipwrecks—
     then suddenly the clouds are rent asunder, like grey curtains upon
the stage, and a solitary ray falls,
     like a gigantic arrow, or a chord that joins the sky with sea, and
the sea is calmed, and the vessels creep to their ports, lowering their
tattered sails,
     as a mother standing over her son's grave drops her arms.
     And the ray upon the turgid but already clearer wave
     draws the word: pax, pax, pax . . .
     Thus we too await for heavens to draw open and to give a sign
to all of us, to clasp our hands,
     and to exclaim as that ray of sun:
     pax.
     Why are you waiting, boys and girls? Why are you standing in
rows before the highstands? Why are your hearts pounding—and for
what reason? Why are all your eyes fixed on one spot, where the flag

is hoisted on the mast, climbing like a longshoreman? Why does the
sea of your heads fill the vast stadium in silence?
     Why

do you not shout all together, white, black, and yellow men:
pax, pax, pax?
I glance at you with fear. Perhaps there are those among you
whose bodies and souls are touched by the plague?
Perhaps there are those who hide their sharpened knives under
their white cloaks?
Or those who in their hearts still worship the serpents of hate,
those who wake up with malice,
those who are sworn
to vengeance?
Look, I draw the curtain
and show to you a flat and spacious land, a valley through which
flows Vistula, stretching her neck like a swan at night,
a valley which slumbers in autumn mists, and falls into the drifts
of winter snow,
and at times awakens, red with fiery sunsets,
the land covered with manifold grain
and forests—
The grain of this land is the hiding place for beasts and men, for
the man who grew among the tall rye,
and trod upon the poppies and corn-flowers.
The forests whose shadows covered the men who fought for
every harbor of peace, every anchor of hope, and every shred of life.
This is the brotherhood of Man!

You see those tall chimneys and the smoke above? Here are men
who burn other men, here the conquerors—
those who have no chance to fight even for a single breath.
No traitors' bodies hang from pear trees in the fields.
Judas, the conqueror, hangs upon the knotted trees those men who
couldn't even die.
The endless roads of this land
are trod by the iron heel of the trained rabble who trample human
brains and skulls, torn bowels, limbs; who trample on the cries and
thoughts of men, their lives and hopes, illusions and impatiences
and pain—
This is the brotherhood of Man!

Upon overgrown plateaux those who are dying of thirst groan
pitifully,
the blue tunics of soldiers press into the breadtree shadows,
and black corpses in the coffee groves
and green flies like leaven on faces
buzzing like poor fiddles
murmuring like water which isn't there, which isn't there.

The chieftains of fabulous lands—peeled mango fruits,
hang like ducks impaled on spits,
and soldiers with torn bellies
buzz with moans like flies!
In the thickets of lianas and roots, beneath the mangrove shadow
gleam the petals of orchids and victoria regia:
hearts ripped and dripping with blood,
eyes open and plucked with the knife of terror
from the festering orbs of ignorance.

Murdered man, murdered woman, murdered people, buried alive,
shot, killed, strangled, executed, knived, gassed—
This is the brotherhood of Man!

In the deserts, steppes, taiga, forests, jungles, icy expanse and
stretches of sand;
in hovels, houses, palaces, shelters, mud huts, cellars,
on all the earth,
fear now dwells and whispers into everybody's ear
ever more terrifying thoughts,
ever more gruesome visions:
eyes covered with sores, babies born like monsters, the flowers of
black death blooming in the armpits, dried blood on lips, vermin
feeding on living bodies
and on the bodies of the dead.
Fear for everything: the houses, gardens, souls, existence, for seas
lest they dry out, for mountains lest they cave in, for trees lest they
burn,
for children,
for our children, grandchildren and great-grandchildren.
This is the brotherhood of Man!

You, handsome, white, strong men! You who resemble the eternal
gods of Hellas! You, whose eyes and souls shine like sparks
when you stand thus
and when the swarm of your eyes flies like bees towards the spot
where the flag crawls up the mast like a sailor, when the sea of your
heads fills the gigantic stadium as black and white grapes fill a
wicker basket,
when you open your mouths, to give out the words of joy
like round balloons soaring into the sky,
like golden fish floating in dark-blue oceans,
like the fragrance of flowers borne by summer breeze,
think of all those who could not cry out before they died!

Think of those whose mouths were sealed with plaster, and of
those felled by bullets before they could cry out, of those whose eyes
were filled with blood and who could not cast a glance upon the sky,
as you look upon it now,
nor on the victorious banner,
because they died in degradation—
and think about the brotherhood of Man!

And if you cannot fight for man
and if you too take to swords and rifles
and kill your brothers—
mankind shall not attain salvation.

Think, think of this now.
Think of happiness and freedom.
For only the struggle for good can win goodness
and only the degradation of evil can elevate goodness
and only the brotherhood of man can raise upon the mast
the Olympic flag, great as the world.

Take each other's hand and sing:
pax, pax, pax—
To signify the brotherhood of Man.

(Adam Gillon and Ludwik Krzyzanowski)

Kazimierz Wierzynski

(1894—1969)

Co-founder of the *Skamander* poetic group, a surviving member of pre-1939 Polish Academy of Literature, Wierzynski has displayed throughout his prolific production a ceaseless search for fruitful new modes of expression and a rich diversity of subject-matter, attitude, technical approach, manner and tone. His poetry has been described on the one hand as rooted in the classical tradition, while on the other—as possessing a largeness and breadth characteristic of the Romantic school. Though his career has extended over more than four decades, he remains youthful and vigorous and the numerous new poems which continue to appear in émigré periodicals are evidence of his unflagging vitality and creative drive.

His collections of poems, starting with *Spring and Wine* (Warsaw, 1919), appeared with amazing regularity in the interwar period as well as during and after World War II. *Collected Poems,* brought out in London and New York in 1959, is an impressive volume of almost 600 pages bearing witness of the poet's evolution towards perfection and the wide range of his interests and themes. His most recent collections are *Tissue of Earth* (Paris 1961) and *With a Trunk on My Shoulders* (Paris 1964).

Wierzynski's early poetic volumes, filled with exuberant joyousness and affirmation of life, are a reaction against the "dolorisme" of Polish poetry in the period of partitions. *Olympic Laurel,* which celebrates the prowess of athletes in various kinds of sports, won for the poet the first international prize of the Ninth Olympic Games in Amsterdam in 1928. Social aspects are discernible in *Fanatic Songs* (1929), while moral and national problems are taken up in *Tragic Freedom* (1936).

After the catastrophe of 1939, Wierzynski made his way to France and then to Portugal and Brazil. He has been living in the United States since 1941. During the war and in the immediate postwar years he expressed in his poetry the innermost feelings of the Polish people in the face of the tragic fate of Poland, but he has never succumbed to despair.

Only a small selection of his poetry has so far been translated into English: *Selected Poems*, edited by Clark Mills and Ludwik Krzyzanowski (New York, 1959) and "New Selected Poems," *Literary Review,* Spring 1960.

Though first and foremost a lyrical poet, Wierzynski is also a prose writer of distinction: *Boundaries of the World* (1932) is a volume of short stories, *The Forgotten Battlefield* (English translation 1944) deals with the Nazi aggression against Poland, *The Life and Death of Chopin* (published in English 1949 before its publication in Polish and several other languages) has been widely acclaimed as an outstanding work of biographical interpretation.

KAZIMIERZ WIERZYNSKI

The Word

What waited my appearance here? The word,
branch cut from an ancient tree to which belongs
the violin I fashioned for my hands
to play the rustling ashtree of my songs.

What waits this moment with me still? The word,
in which my birth, as in a cradle, sways,
in which, as in a coffin of plain pine,
I lie, and tell my first and my last days.

What waits when I have disappeared? The word.
And my green roots explore the dark to learn
the language of the earth that utters me.
Born of the earth, to earth I shall return.

(Kenneth Pitchford)

The Compass Rose

I came upon an ancient map, new world,
Java, Sumatra: deep jungle, and strange beasts;
a hand-breadth island set in ocean vast.
Below, the star of winds, the rose unfurled.

From the flat trace of a world, from child-kept tales,
how quick the heart is touched, how often we
launch toward our own star, wrestling the sky,
asking the winds to tell us where to sail.

Far, without bound, in whatever flimsy hold,
under what sail, what storm, or trial of calm,
we yearn on, death urges us, we roam—
still failing of our shore, our mark, our fold.

Of what avail these launchings and our toil,
the search that only stares our eyes to pain?
The map yawns space; the compass arrow strains
and verges toward an iron, unknown soil.

Yet bless our wandering, compass rose; sigh deep.
Tell sunrise, sunset, and all winds' wide flight.
Give me to find, through plane and lone of night,
my handful island in the ocean's keep.

(Mary Phelps)

Nurmi

My pace, a dancer's tread—
      my steps beat like a heart;
clock-tower of breath, I hover
      in air, tall and apart.

My motion springs from motion
      —dial of an iron will,
I create living circles,
      ever unspent, unstill.

My rhythm, paced on earth,
      rings with a clear sound,
I drink up space, consume
      hemispheres, outward bound

beyond the tiered bravos
      and shouts, indifferent,
on to my goal: repose
      on a Greek pediment.

(Ludwik Krzyzanowski)

Cable

Spring moves about the house in moss-green slippers,
As tall birches strut outside in bark-glazed aprons,
And chestnut trees loom like pink-edged chandeliers.

In front the swallows flock, twittering operas
From wire perches, sending their flittering joy
On silhouette toes from line upon line of cables.

But please transform your green slippers into brown,
And launder your white apron, tie up your tossed hair—
For the useless chandelier will only go with the wind,
And the chestnut tree is really an old man, and not a light.

But the flocking swallows have noisily listened in,
To whittle their messages over alley, trees and house.
What do you say of this? What do you say?
There is nothing to say now. The time is summer.

(Harry Roskolenko)

Europe

O bitter, disconsolate love,
Europe, our Mother,
Among ancient stones I roam,
A wood of memories I comb,
One footprint after another.

I repeat your names,
I must wonder and admire
That despite the paltry human span
You did create some men
Like Bach, and Shakespeare's lyre.

A golden-pink façade
In Salamanca smiles with grace,
And your seductive spell,
Smiles at the Venetian shell,
The secret of your hand and face.

O lovely Mother, this rescues me,
To save you, too, my thought aspires,
Europe, the requiem for my closest deaths, you
Motherland of evening melody,
Of Parisian revelry,
Of Gothic rose-windows,
And holy spires.

(Adam Gillon)

Michelangelo

When Europe shuddered in her soul,
Michelangelo, under the dome
Painted chapel, fresco and wall,
On a mason's cradle swung
Nearer to God in Rome.

He gazed down at the brawling crowd
And at the bloody wars unfurled,
And from above spoke loud:
"Peace, men!
Or I'll throw down my brush, and then
Halt the Creation of the World."

(George Reavey)

Only for Happiness

Only for happiness, for happiness,
To thrill the heart, the breast, the eye, the ear,
Should we in humble prayer and yearning press,
Like gardens in the springtime of the year.

Nothing is changed. In legend we shall be
A loving echo of the living past;
And as smile finds with smile true harmony,
Soul shall embrace with kindred souls at last.

(Watson Kirkconnell)

To the Jews

You were picked again, for the countless time
Of man's progeny upon this earth,
To be destroyed and tortured in your prime,
And now to suffer scientific death—

Herded into the ghetto slums,
To be later driven in lime tumbrels

Out of your misery and ruins
By human butchers, to human shambles—

So that your David's Star deride
The sling that once the mighty laid
Upon their backs, so that you confide,
Till death, in promises of aid.

And, with a number on your back,
Deloused from a filthy, stinking stall,
Your bones in ovens thickly stacked,
Son of the same fathers, as we all.

So that your fate you might decry,
The early whipping and your fall,
Of heaven and earth demand: O why?
Son of the same mothers, as we all.

Thus aching, if you seek your neighbors
Among the ghosts, don't stare aghast;
They're brothers from gas chambers,
They shared your anguish to the last.

Thus, when in loneliness you call:
"Will no one see how great's my plight?"
Look whom they dragged through the empty hall,
Right near your home, on that same night.

Thus by the powerful betrayed,
Who for bullets sold the world like trash,
Look how in graves our kin were laid,
Today all mixed in a handful of ash.

When amid graves and phantoms you go,
And subdued by dark powers you stand,
Look what shame was sown by the foe
As he opened his Hell in our land.

So afflicted in Warsaw you rose,
At least to die, but finally free;
Look what remained of our temple to those
Who fought and earned their bloody fee.

Ah, thus selected of us all,
Look how Jerusalem we share,

You whom tears have frozen at the Wall,
Who for Messiah still prepare.

(Adam Gillon)

Tissue of Earth

Only the earth endures
before and after us
in the mute spring's ordered yield.
See the untarnished grain that pours
from the hand of the sower in the field
whose stride enlists us in the toil
under furrowed ranks of soil.

The furrows, tongued with dew,
gape like mouths to draw us
where the moist seeds dwell.
And deaf of a night, quickening, now,
beneath a gravid tissue's swell,
the painful labor mounts in cries
while our dazzled firstborn rise.

Green-haired now he grows,
straw-fingered, armed with spikes,
the universal grain.
A powdery breeze scatters and blows
his heavy pollen across the plain;
and soon, as thick as his green blood,
these crops flow from us in a flood.

The news fills every breeze
that June, July, and August,
those three great kings will ride
wreathed in a coronal of bees;
the coachman calls, whip at his side,
and in the field the sower stands,
potential harvest in his hands.

Hurry now, kings, for him,
that the soil may give us back
the breathing selves we gave;
Let the annunciation brim

into the blessed bread-bearing wave
for which wait strong arm, horse, and mill,
but which earth only can fulfill.

    Over the whole world, then,
    the tides of generation
    from furrowed ranks will creep;
And from the pollen-powdered plain,
from winds that promised we should reap
this uttered labor, we will claim
    the golden tissue of our life, like flame.

(Kenneth Pitchford)

The Fifth Season

A bird has flown across me—a bird
that left the door ajar.
In evening's penumbra, dead and living,
seasons have met in me.

One that I dream of, joyous, youthful, calls me
—laughter and emptiness, oh, the absurd!
Another, ardent, hot, touches me still
with its red mouth. A third, autumnal, and a fourth,
locked white in ice; and then the fifth season
at last, at last perpetual death.

                        Gathered,
they whispered in the evening's ear, whether
of bacchanalia, vespers, penance, I do not know.
Their song was too ambiguous. Time wandered,
a rivulet of changes, and I followed.
Yes, changes flowed about me on all sides
until their landscape trickled in my blood.

I banked myself with leaves, I uttered mountains—
in me the fires of shepherds burned. Under the trees,
dressed in their sackcloth, in the rain, they stood like ghosts.

In long grass, in clearings brimmed with sun
I slept. The dwarf pine rocked me on its branch
and does with knees like girls' awoke me,
leaping like fountains.

And out of Hungary the fat oxen, lowing,
followed the Jewish drover down the valley.
At noon the cowherds opened packs and bundles
and gnawed and drank in fragrant clouds of garlic.

Orchards lay russet, and the black plum jam
of peasants fumed and simmered, in brass kettles.
One with them all, in love like them, I shouted,
"Youth, give me wings!"

In winter through the forest-break the pines
crashed down to the snowy channel. Axes thudded,
their sound like groans on the bare skull, the summit.

The thaw came, and the Carpathian farmhand
wrestled them into the stream and bound them into rafts.
They floated down toward bread, down toward profit—
difficult, oh not easy, O my brother.

And springs and summers passed again slowly.
The wind shook down ripe apples and the plums,
pursued the clouds in fortune and misfortune,
the joyous and the wretched.

And transformations followed changes. Motion
of people, plants, the skins of animals,
temporal seasons and entangled time:
what was alive, and more.

Later from distances the dead arrived.
They leaned their elbows on the fir-forests
and looked about them, the expansive earth
as minute as an eyelash. The wind stood.
The roads were full of a white peace.
Spring crowded with swallows
lay at their feet outstretched
with owl-autumn, beechen summer, bearded winter.

And my father said to my mother
as he dispelled the noisome smell of war,
"Do not lose courage. Quiet will return
at time's end in the silences of death."

And the dead took me down, down to a mysterious
kingdom where nothing of the earth matters,

where spring, summer, fall and winter
were named in another tongue.
Innumerable changes and involvements
have been equated there within a single
and disentangled time that flows no longer,
but to resolve the arid, vacant ant-hill
after the tumult.

                                 All had been accomplished.
The fifth, the final season was at hand.
And now I hear what no one hears, and see
all things as if transparent, from below.
Death fills me as with calm. In me I hold
eternity, quite still and cool.

                                             I know.
My total death came to me long ago
and I endure now, elbow on the mountains.
Like others of my race, I lean, and I search
for my sons, and I wonder whether any
has heaped himself with leaves and burst with forests.
Does he now hover at a shepherd's fire,
at threshold of the trails that wind behind us,
who will repeat our gestures and our actions
as hot life poured through the whole skin,
leaped up in sunlight, walked out to the moon
—as in me my land's life circled
and in the mothers, milk, and resin in the pines.

My father said, "Oh, lead him still,
the human eyes in him pale with regret."
And then my mother, "There is nothing to regret,
for life and death are single."

And thus their speech, my consolation. And they tell me
that nothing has been lost, that they remember
how for a moment, quick, my shadow flickered in their country,
that I inherit an immense patrimony:
clearings and prairies, oxen from Hungary, blue winters
with tall pines, and poverty, in the Carpathians,
all the possessions fashioned out of people
and plants and skins of animals . . . They tell me more,
suddenly they remind me that a bird
that left the door ajar

to all my trees, my mountains, all my instances,
living and dead. Why does the bird not sing?

This my confession, my concern. I sing it
as if it were a peasant song. At dusk
the world slowly darkens, and I close
the windows, draw the blinds, and gather all
my evenings, and when the earth walks in
he will take off his heavy boots, knock dust from them,
the dust out of the fields, lie down and rest,
joyous, morose . . .

                              But let the apple roll
under the straw mattress, under the fecund bed.

                                        (Clark Mills)

Maria Pawlikowska

(1899–1945)

Often called "the queen of Polish lyricists and the Polish Sappho," Maria Pawlikowska (also known as Maria Jasnorzewska, née Kossak) was born in Cracow in 1899. She was the daughter of the noted painter Wojciech Kossak. Her poetry is aphoristic and lapidary, and she has brought the short, sensuous lyric close to perfection. Her talent for condensing sentences gives her work a unique character. She is not concerned with metaphysical anxiety or social problems, but mainly with the impressionistic effect of each poem, which she chisels to epigrammatic shortness.

She published many collections of poems, the most representative being: *Wool-Gathering* (1922), *Pink Magic* (1924), *Kisses* (1926) *Sylvan Silence* (1928), *Raw Silk* (1932), *The Sleeping Crew* (1935), *Ivy Ballet* (1935), *Crystallizations* (1937) and *The Rose and the Burning Forest* (1941).

Her early sophisticated poems were regarded as too aesthetic and too saturated with an atmosphere of the "salons"; but the total output of Pawlikowska is impressive even though her world is expressed in concentrated, short forms, in which psychological states are often combined with phenomena of nature. These forms have the perfection of a Japanese flower arrangement. Her poetic technique is rich, and her language is original without ever being obscure.

Pawlikowska was also a prolific dramatist. Her principal plays, not marked by any unusual depth or universality but popular at the time, are: *Chauffeur Archibald* (1924), *Egyptian Wheat* (1932), *The Airborne Wooers* (1933), *The Mother's Return* (1935), *Personal Evidence* (1936), *Literary Award* (1936), *The Ants* (1936) and *Hag's Marvel* (1939), a satire on dictators. During World War II Pawlikowska went to England.

MARIA PAWLIKOWSKA

La Precieuse

Your fur-clad figure now I see
In hesitation where a little puddle flows,
With Chinese poodle 'neath your arm, with parasol and rose ...
Is 't thus you'll step into eternity?

(Watson Kirkconnell)

Ophelia

Ah, long in glassy water shall I lie,
'Mid knotted water-plants, until to me 'tis proved—
And I believe the verdict with a sigh—
That, in plain terms, I simply wasn't loved.

(Watson Kirkconnell)

Love

It is month now since I saw you last.
Sure, it is nothing. I may show more care,
Lips very mute, a face of paler cast:
But it is hard to live, devoid of air!

(Watson Kirkconnell)

Sighs

Sad is the sea today. The sighs complain
At the shore o'ergrown with greyish-golden crest.
The waves like breasts arise and fall again.
The sea must sigh with waves. The earth with my breast.

(Adam Gillon)

Three Verses About Love

WHO LOVES TODAY...

For love today are thistles but no rose,
By no straight, easy highway shall she fare!
Who loves today, will never know repose,
Bread without husks, or day without its care. . . .

LOVE'S HEAVIEST BURDEN

Of bitter loves most bitter under the sun
Is not that first, which wakens with the Spring,

And strange illusions and deceits may bring,
But this, from care now dying: old though we may be
Love burns more ardently. . . .

I Shall Return No More

"I shall return no more! Now let God throw me
Far to the distant stars! Since unforgivably
This world afflicts me" . . . "Yes, but Love blooms here,
Love like an orchid strange and solitary . . .
Ah, will you not return?"

(Frances Notley)

Roses, Forests and the World

No time to regret the roses when the woods are burning—
No time to regret the forests when the whole world burns,
When the expanse of earth as one Sahara lies. . . .
No time to regret the world when Chaos now returns . . .

No one the hour knows or the day discloses,
When God, struck to the heart by earth's distracted sphere,
Fell, and rose up, a lion in his wrath!—
When every night is black with grief and fear. . . .

Yet for myself I weep and I regret the roses.

(Frances Notley)

A Girl Speaks

Listen, young soldier, you who passing by
Possessed me with a strange, distracted glance
Which I so swiftly caught—O, then I felt
A sudden flood of tender consciousness;
Pride and a sad reproach were in your eyes,
Blue, with black lashes sweetening them for love. . . .
Surely, I know what you would say to me:
"O to the war I go and I may perish . . .
Girl-woman, with your body's gift of life,
Sons you will bear for martial death. Weep then,
Weep in my mother's stead for me! O sigh

With helpless, unavailing tenderness!
Look, in my hands I bring flowers for farewell!"

And then to you my eyes would make reply:
"You move me, handsome lad. But pity me,
I beg you. We are comrades in this war,
You in the field as I am in the town.
One heavy shell will strike without compassion,
Will level us to earth and hurl us down,
Both equal then in common sacrifice.
For us one grave and one forgetfulness,
Or else one happy chance. Throw me your flowers!"

(Frances Notley)

Victory

Thou'rt like the Parian "Victory" from Samothrace,
O Love of mine, unsilenced by life's harms!
Though slain, you run the same all-ardent race,
And still hold out your bleeding stumps of arms. . . .

(Watson Kirkconnell)

Virtues

'Tis little, Lord, that I can see
In all the virtues men profess.
One virtue only I possess:
I love my enemy.

(Watson Kirkconnell)

A Bird

A dying bird seeks solitude to hide;
Far from the gaze of all it fain would flee;
And many a human heart has turned aside
In its last hour to die in secrecy.

(Watson Kirkconnell)

Poppies Will Grow Again

These battlefields, these fields of strife,
These fields of future legend,
Poppies, bursting forth in bloom, will cover rankly ...

Thou Nature, thou, before ourselves,
Were first, with pitying heart, to honor,
With the fire of radiant blooms,
The Unknown Soldier's memory.

(Irene Pyszkowska)

War Is Only a Flower

It is only the horrid flower
Of the plant that is Life;
It is but the eruption and color
Of thorny everyday creepers
Wildly and valiantly sprouting;

It is only the terrible flower
Of that which is—
Blazing, till eyes must ache,
Our eyes copiously weeping!

It must bloom until it fades
Losing its ghastly, purple shade,
Till it turns into rags of yellow papers,
And has accomplished its parade.

(Adam Gillon)

Kazimiera Illakowicz

(1892-   )

Born in 1892 in Wilno, Miss Illakowicz started to write poetry at the age of fifteen and attracted critical attention with her first collection of poems, *Icarian Flights* (1912). Her poetic evolution, marked by several collections, such as *Death of the Phoenix* (1922), reached maturity in *Fishing* (1926), and culminated in *Weeping Bird* (1927) and *Mirror of the Night* (1928). The same perfection is manifested in *From the Depth of the Heart* (1928), *Ashes and Pearls* (1930) and *Heroic Ballads* (1934). Her work is one of the richest and most prolific in post-World War I Polish poetry and is endowed with rare originality. Although a romantic her attitude to reality is based on sober, direct observation. The richness of her imagination and her predilection for the fantastic relate her to Tuwim, but she achieves a tone of her own. Her poetic world is filled with mysteriousness and suggestive qualities. She particularly excels in the form of the ballad which she handles in a fresh and thoroughly modern way. She worked out a poetic form characterized by great variety of meter and often bold assonances. Refined and sophisticated, with a wide range of emotion and the musical quality of her verse, she must be regarded as one of the leading figures of the Polish Parnassus of the inter-war period.

KAZIMIERA ILLAKOWICZ

Moth

It's not a blind and downy moth I see—
it's me.
Out of the dark I fly, emerge from ash-trees, lindens
and oaks, toward the glowing windows.
Of your window panes I miss none,
I break against every one,
I long for the lamp, for the candle I cry . . .
To death, to death, to my death I fly.

(Adam Gillon)

The Lithuanian Nightingale

Still, as in childhood days, a nightingale is swaying
On some bough in far-off Niemenland,
A canopy of hazel twigs above him, or a lilac cluster,
Sprigs, mayhap, of jasmine, just as then.

Not a breath is stirring, yet the leaves begin to rock:
It is the birds, gath'ring for flight or settling down to rest.
Drops of moisture fall from the trees. The song
Breaks off—the nightingale has cut his note in twain.

Cease not thy singing, nightingale, but sing, sing on
For me, and I your song will publish, as you sang
It then, inscribing, fresh and pure, each pearl
Of all your plaintive, questioning song.

Thy hymn of unremembered graves I will repeat,
And sunken crosses; sing of meadow roses, and a field,
Stream-bordered, hard by the forest rim; a footbridge,
And a two-haired lad, running amidst the flax.

The flax itself I'll sing that, crushed, is spun.
And woven into garments, fit for shroud or wedding gown;
Of cradles, gently rocked, and painted walls,
Of wormwood bitters and the healing yarrow leaf.

Sing ever more and more, O bird, sing out the full confessional
Of all who choke their longing back in sobs, for all
Who left the wilderness—themselves the wilderness's own—
Whose ways are foreign to the cringe of sycophant.

Sing for the ones who grit their teeth in curses,
Yet who pray—for all my people, and for me, O nightingale
Of Litwa: for us all, for ravaged boundaries, for us all,
Thou heart of us, O nightingale beloved!

(Julia Pruszynska)

Do You Remember . . .

The birch tree drooping white above the marshy road?
The rows of stunted pine trees,
Bent so low by winter's snow
That even spring could never lift them up?
Pools of blackish water near each cottage?
Do you remember?

The courtyard paved with cobbles,
The old church walls, the graveyard
Where the dead of all the village lay asleep?
The beggars' plaintive cry back there
Beneath the wall on holy days? The merry stalls,
And O! those riotous shawls!
And then the maidens, each with kerchief
Prettier than the rest, each one saucy, robust, fair,
As everything around was fair . . .
And each of them—thinking a little bit of you?
Do you remember?

(Julia Pruszynska)

Joseph Wittlin

Hymn to a Spoonful of Soup

Oh let me give you a spoonful of hot soup,
my brother, lying frozen in an alien land.
You, who dragged yourself through three cruel winters
and trudged through the windless desert of three summers,
on and on,
endlessly on and on,
sleeping in snatches on unfurrowed ground,
rotting in cattlecars,
eating decaying bread in ditches,
chewing tobacco cut from dung,
still trudging on,

---

* For biographical note see p. 181.

eaten alive by insistent lice
and chipped alive by iron bullets,
until thirsty death drank you dry.

Oh did death drink you dry
already parched by three Julys
till you became as arid as a pond
at evening's edge after the hour of sunset.
Oh let me give you a spoonful of hot soup:
it might wake you from your dreadful sleep,
your fatal vigilance in empty ditch
bypassed by the world's indifferent guard.

You must have fought for something, oh my brother,
been bitten for a purpose by the lice,
and felt a meaning in your ceaseless going,
your weedy hunger and infectious thirst.
If there was meaning there, we do not know—
perhaps some day God will tell us what it was.

But this I know:
that at the moment when death
fully equipped with all her frozen issues
came upon you quietly:
you did not ask for your mother,
nor for your father, nor for your wife,
but with your lips attacked by dying pain,
and your delirious legs and arms,
and with your eyes anticipating night,
and with your freezing blood, you asked:
Give me a spoonful of hot soup!
This I am trying to give you now—in vain.

(Paul Mayewski)

Psalm

Begetter of mornings, dawns and winds,
O Heavenly Father!

I, Joseph Wittlin, of the tribe of Judah,
stand before Thee in the bareness of my sins,
that my unworthy lips may stammer out Thy greatness.

Fearfully, I perceive my heart is sinking
toward the earth
which Thy foot so rarely touches now.
Before I am wholly consumed by earthly love,
I wish, with the remnants of my childhood,
to sing a psalm to Thee.
Let it remain with Thee, a hostage of my faith,
until the hour of my death.
And if I ever do deny Thee,
let it redeem me in Thine eyes.

Praised, praised be Thou,
Eternal Lord, be praised for ever and ever!
Be praised in the tongue of the living.
as Thou wert revered in the tongue of those that are dead.
Be Thou praised in Polish, in English, in German, in French,
in Hebrew, Arabic and Chinese,
and in the countless number of tongues to which Thou hast given
                                                            singularity
that day when Thou hast confused the only speech of man,
for the sin of the Babel Tower.

And be Thou praised with the lowing of cattle,
with the neighing of horses, the bleating of sheep, the barking
                                        of dogs, the mewing of cats,
and the drone of all insects.
And be Thou praised with the chirping of birds:
Let the lark warble to Thee in the heat of day,
let the nightingale trill to Thee on a tranquil night,
let the cuckoo and the turtle-dove sing Thee
on every day.
Let the stork rattle Thy glory on the 19th of March every year,
and let the woodpecker, true to our land all year, knock to Thee!
But to Thee let the raven croak over the soldier's corpse,
let him croak over the carrion of the disgraced man.
Be praised with the roar of wild animals and praised
with the silence of fish.

And be praised through all instruments,
created by the hand of man.
The plaintive violin and flute and oboe affecting the human voice
and the tender harp and the clamorous organ,
which are played in Thy houses,
let them ring deeply with Thy grandeur,
for into the musical instruments Thou hast set Thy own soul!

Everything on the earth that has a voice should sound
Thy beauty!
O Thou art fair in all the voices unheard by the deaf!

Therefore praised be Thou, praised,
praised be Eternal Lord through all colors:
The green hue with which Thou has painted the grass, adores Thee,
the white and the violet bow before Thee!
The gold and the silver, the fiery red and the purple of blood
bid Thee welcome,
and especially the sky-blue sweetly drawn from Thy heavens.
And be Thou greeted by color black which is sad,
for it arouses sorrow within us.
O, Thou art comely in all colors unseen by the blind!

Be Thou praised with all the odors which Thy earth produces.
All corn, which the poor want for their bread;
all plants, from the most precious herbs
to the meanest origin,
let them bow to Thee, sway for Thee, give Thee their fragrance!
And be Thou praised with the smell of sweat
of the man who bears the burdens of life,
and carries coal and stone
and hoists chests from ship to land!
O Thou art comely in all scents which will never
reach the nostrils of the prisoner.

And be Thou praised with all fruit, whose taste contains sweetness,
and with all weeds that issue bitterness
and a tart poisonous juice!
Be praised with the salt tears that stream from the eyes of man,
and with the acid vinegar with which they quenched the thirst of
Him that died on the Cross.
Praised, O praised be Thou Eternal Lord
with the taste of our daily bread and the taste of water and the
taste of wine,
praised be Thou with the flesh and blood of Thy Son
and praised with the bitterness and praised with the regrets
and praised with the despair and lament
of those that are hungry
and clamor that Thou art not!

Be Thou greeted with the grievance of widows,
and the wailing of mothers,
whose sons perished in the war.

Be greeted with the abandonment of orphans: therein an increase
of Thy great love.
Thus one day Thou hast also descended to me,
hast caressed me,
hast shaken hands with my sorrow,
and my sorrow has lived since in the shadow of Thy mercy!

O be Thou praised with the madness of men,
whom Thou hast ordered to be evil,
from whose eyes Thou hast extinguished light,
and they live and perish in darkness.
O be praised with health and disease,
and the sacred frenzy of poets:—
they bore Thy spark!

Be praised with all beauty that can be begotten by the souls
of unknown men,
whom Thou has not endowed with the pride of the artist,
O Lord of the meek!
Be praised, O praised with the beauty of works conceived by Thine
own hands!
The low whisper of the Nile, the holy murmur of the Ganges, the
sadness of the Jordan,
they stream with me down to Thy knees.
All rivers which I have never seen,
but only imagined in name,
proceed with me unto Thee.
O Thou Nameless, with a hundred names, named a hundred times,
O Thou Silent Ocean!

And knowest Thou who else praiseth Thee?
This little brook in Nagozhany, in that village where I spent my
childhood,
so little that it has not even a name among men!
But for Thee it has a name,
Thou knowest it, Thou canst hear its faint murmur,
as thou hearest my weak and wretched voice
that sings today Thy glory.

The two of us, that brook and I, stream toward Thee in the solitary
nook
of Polish land,
we call on Thee: Thou hast counted us too,
we trust Thee: Thou rememberst us,

we desire Thee: Thou shalt not leave us,
we cry to Thee: Hosanna!

Hosanna, Hosanna! For ever and ever, Amen.
Halleluiah, halleluiah! For ever and ever—Amen.

And be Thou praised with the prayer of those that believe not in Thee.

(Adam Gillon)

Antoni Slonimski

(1895–1976)

Antoni Slonimski was born in Warsaw in 1895, the son of a well-known Jewish physician; he was educated as a painter in Warsaw and in Paris, but in 1918 he gave up his painting, and turned to journalism and literature. He was one of the co-founders of the literary group *Skamander*, and his poems, novels, comedies, literary criticism and journalistic articles have earned him a reputation of fierce intellectual honesty, scatching irony and progressiveness. His poetry is far more restrained and intellectual than that of Tuwim. He has published many volumes of poetry. Some of these are: *Sonnets* (1918), *Harmonies* (1919), *Parade* (1920); *The Hour of Poetry* (1923), *Window without Bars* (1935).

One of the leading Polish pacifists, Slonimski wrote prolifically about the criminality of war, and the hopes for a better world. His poetry, however, is not didactic at all. It is strong and simple and sometimes, when Slonimski abandons the traditional poetic forms in metrics and stanzaic structure, it becomes experimental.

Slonimski's weekly *feuilletons* in Warsaw's *Literary News* made him famous as a fearless champion of the "little man's" cause. His satirical comedies have been compared with those of G. B. Shaw. They are: *The Warsaw Negro* (1928), *The Homeless Physician* (1931), *The Family* (1934).

In 1939 Slonimski fled to Paris, then to London, where he edited the monthly *New Poland*. He returned to Warsaw in 1946. In 1956, while serving as President of the Polish Writers' Union, he displayed singular courage during the October crisis. He is now living in Warsaw.

ANTONI SLONIMSKI

All

In Tolouse or Ankara, in Hungary or Scotland,
Lisbon, or Dakar or London, the wave is carrying us forward,
Further and further from our way back to our homes.
For what are we fighting, for what are we longing?
What treasures tremendous have we lost?
Not for glory nor riches are we wandering in pain,

For a greater and more sacred cause.
Not at world domination we aim; we dream of freedom

To enjoy the calm of big, old shadowy trees,
The peaceful hours of sunset in our dear village-home,
Lost in listening the soft humming of bees,
The neigh of horses grazing on meadows,
When the dark night is approaching . . .

We don't want to rule over others, we want to share bread
In all justice with our own people, at home,
We dream to walk freely through our well-known roads,
And look happily into the deep, starry sky
And sleep in peace under its blue vault
It's so little, and yet it's *all*.

(Wanda Dynowska)

He Is My Brother

This man, who his own fatherland forgets
When of the shedding of Czech blood he hears,
Who, as a brother feels for Yugoslavia,
Who in the pain of Norway's people shares,

Who with the Jewish mother wrings his hands
In grief and bends with her above her slain,
Who Russian is, when Russia falls and bleeds,
And with Ukrainian weeps for the Ukraine,

This man, with heart to all compassionate,
French, when France suffers in captivity,
Greek, when Greeks in cold and hunger perish,
He is my brother—man. He is Humanity.

(Frances Notley)

Warsaw

Christ on the cross died but once,
And two thousand cities are mourning,
Thrice over you the grave stone has closed,
Yet capitals of the world are silent.

Our Lord on the cross died but once,
And all the temples are covered with crosses;
Your blood has flown abundantly thrice,
Crucified you still are between villains two.

Christ but once was pierced by the shaft,
Once was His Passion insulted;
Hundred times were you by Peters denied,
Three times Pilate's hands were washed.

Your ruins will be covered by dust,
But out of your blood New Life will grow,
You will not be betrayed by Song alone
Which lightning's flash and angry storm carries.

(Maurice Frydman)

At Night . . .

A café deserted, dark.
A street empty and bare,
Only rain-drenched leaves, the spark
Of a street-light, and mist everywhere.

Only, afar to be heard,
The muted creaking of gates tight
Closing, nothing is stirred
Besides: alone, we two, with the night.

Only this hour, this one before dawn breaks pale,
When out of thy dreams thou hast hardly begun
To awake, do I find below its azure veil
Your face, O Warsaw, tendèr and young.

(Helen Sikorska)

Morning and Evening

Your dusky shadow at the window lingers,
    Alone and wakeful. Hidden amid tombs,
The ancient city sleeps. With listless fingers,
    You likewise sink to slumber in its glooms.

Somewhere, loud tramway-brakes gnash harsh on metal;
    The scream of factory-whistles wakes you not;
But soon the day and mounting din unsettle
    The timeless letter that your dreams begot.

Words voice their meaning vainly and obscurely;
    Thought oozes forth in speech like some slow juice;
By day and night the city roars obscurely;
    In dusk the livid brake-shoes flash abuse.

Actions and thoughts and persons without number
    Stride on in hostile rhythm night and day;
But still returns, returns that endless slumber
    When moon and peace and darkness held their sway.

Light floods the streets and shadows are departed;
    Colors return now, numberless and bright;
All things return, and drug us, drunken-hearted,
    Like fresh, sweet nosegays in the dusky night.

                               (Watson Kirkconnell)

Wladyslaw Broniewski

(1898–1962)

Broniewski represents the "proletarian" and "revolutionary" trend in modern Polish poetry. In the "poetic bulletin," *Three Salvoes,* he described his position "in the merciless struggle" of the proletariat against the bourgeoisie as decidedly "on the left of the barricade," and proclaimed the fight for a new social order as the supreme essence of his creative work.

This attitude produced such collections as *Windmills* (1925), *Smoke over the City* (1927), *Worry and Song* (1932), and *The Ultimate Cry* (1939). Influenced to some extent by Tuwim and contemporary Russian poets, especially Yesenin whose *Pugachov* he translated, and not an innovator but remaining within the framework of traditional language and meter, Broniewski manifests a great creative individuality and genuine artistry which won for him high praise, even from his political opponents, as one of Poland's most significant poets.

Ironically, Broniewski's "proletarian" convictions did not save him from imprisonment by the Russians after the invasion of Poland in 1939. Interestingly enough, an officially approved high school textbook relates this episode as follows: "The years 1939–1941 are the most tragic period in Broniewski's life. In the land of the revolution which the poet . . . eulogized with the greatest hope and trust, he was reached by the criminal hand of the falsifiers of the revolutionary idea. Like many other Polish revolutionaries, he was arrested and confined to prison until the Nazi attack on the Soviet Union and the conclusion of an agreement between the Soviet government and the Polish government-in-exile. Released from prison, Broniewski left the Soviet Union in General Anders' army and, together with it, he found himself in the Middle East."

After the years of wandering and decline in "ideological fervor," the poet was induced in 1949 to return to political poetry and produced several undistinguished if not downright tedious and pedantic works on Communist themes.

His earlier poetry however, reveals accents of tragic isolation and pure individualism. In fact, his personal poems are often considered to be on a higher artistic level than his best revolutionary poetry.

WLADYSLAW BRONIEWSKI

Bayonets Ready

When they come to set your house on fire,
The one in which you live—Poland,
When they hurl at you thunder, and kindle the pyre

Of iron-clad monsters of war,
And they stand before your gate at night,
And their rifle butts pound on your door,
Rouse yourself from sleep—fight.
Stem the flood.
Bayonets ready!
There is need for blood.

There are accounts of wrongs in our land
Not to be erased by a foreign hand.
But none shall spare his blood;
We shall draw it from our hearts and song.
No matter that our prison bread
Not once did have a bitter taste.
For this hand now over Poland raised
A bullet in the head!

O Firemaster of words and hearts,
O poet, the song is not your only stand.
Today the poem is a soldier's trench,
A shout and a command:

"Bayonets ready!
Bayonets ready!"
And should we die with our swords,
We shall recall what Cambronne said.
And on the Vistula repeat his words.

(Adam Gillon and Ludwik Krzyzanowski)

Ballads and Romances

"Listen, maiden! She does not hear . . .
It's broad daylight, a little town."
There is no town, there is no one here,
The naked Ryfka climbs atop debris,
A redhead of thirteen is she.

Fat Germans rode in tanks, iron-clad,
(Run for your life, O Ryfka, run!)
"Your Mom lies here, in camp your Dad . . ."
She laughed, and turned, was gone.

A friend from Lubartov came by.
"Take a roll, and be not sad."

She smiled, the roll did not deny.
"I'll bring it to my Mom and Dad."

A peasant came, a coin did spare,
A woman passed, and gave a penny;
Then others passed, so many, many,
Amazed she was red-haired and bare.

Lord Jesus passed, to anguish pledged,
To torture led by SS men,
Who stood them both at meadow's edge
And their rifles lifted then.

Listen Jesus, Ryfka, *sie Juden,*
For Ryfka's flaming hair, for Jesus' painful sigh,
His thorny crown, and for you both are naked,
Because we are so guilty—you must die.

And Allelujah rang in Galilee,
They stood like angels without fear;
The salvo boomed, distinct and dull,
"Listen, maiden! She does not hear . . ."

                                        (Adam Gillon)

My Homeland

O land of mine, more dear than all besides!
Amid each sleepless dream of mine abides
My memory, there childhood springs to life:
Idyllic, in its midst a modest home,
Where gardens smile, and low-built fences roam,
Where springtime's air with lilac scent is rife,
And lilies-of-the-valley freshly bloom
Each year my mother's name-day to adorn;
Where changless, through the ever-changing gloom,
An oak tree stands in prayer for man forlorn.
The Angelus of the Dominicans at eve—
Why does that bell my distant ears deceive?
I see the sun, its head in Wisla's stream,
A little lad . . . What further shall I dream?
Of daffodils? A thrush on pear alight?
Beats now the stroke of seven in what dome,

And every pear tree sheds its cloud of white.
Upon my paper her—that long lost home . . .
Arises . . . Why so sad, my soul, tonight?

(Loretta M. Bielawska)

My Native Town

The mid-point of my life I have not passed,
Yet now despair lurks ever in my years.
Of the far path that I have walk'd aghast,
Tell, O my heart, or break in bitter tears!

Pass in a moment to my babyhood
In a small garden I remember still. . . .
An old cathedral by the Wisla stood,
Grey-spired, upon a high Masovian hill.

There in the silent dusk the old bells rung
Their benediction to the dying day;
While the low sunset, with a crimson tongue,
Lapp'd at the crimson river where it lay.

Then o'er the plains, beside the dark shore there,
The musing of the forest-pines was born—
A grave, low voice that whisper'd everywhere;
And in the dark, the rooks replied forlorn.

Marvel, my heart, as you have done before,
At these old things now blending with the earth!
Although my road lay thither in the war,
I did not turn aside to know their worth.

Yet dear it were to me, on yonder spot,
To muse on time and life's indubious end;
For there it was this very speech I got
With which I love and suffer and contend.

Thanks, then, for every word, good people all,
Remember'd out of childhood days now flown—
Like those low forest-voices I recall,
That mark'd my heart for ever as their own.

(Watson Kirkconnell)

Jan Lechon

(1899–1955)

Jan Lechon (Leszek Serafinowicz), co-founder of the *Skamander* poetic group, was acclaimed as a poet of distinction at the age of nineteen. Despite a relatively modest output, Lechon is regarded as an outstanding contemporary poet. His prewar collections were *The Crimson Poem* (1920), *The Republic of Babin* (1921), *Silver and Black* (1924). Then came *Bekwark's Lute* (1942) and *Aria with Chimes* (1945). His *Collected Poems* were published in London in 1954, and this volume includes also *Marble and Rose*. His *Fable of One Little Boy and One Pilot* is a poetic excursion into children's literature. In addition to his poetic activity, Lechon edited the satirical weekly *The Barber of Warsaw* and translated Russian and French poetry and drama. He spent some years in Paris as a cultural Councilor of the Polish Embassy, later lectured at the Polish University in Exile in Paris in 1940. These and subsequent lectures formed the basis for his volume *On Polish Literature* published in 1946. Lechon also wrote a drama, *Hour of Warning* (unfinished), and a novel, *The Ball at the Senator's* (also unfinished) as well as a voluminous *Diary*.

Only a few of his poems are available in English translation. Noteworthy is Lechon's essay, *American Transformations* which is a penetrating interpretation of the role of America in the modern world.

During the forties, Lechon fled to Brazil and later lived in New York City where he was active as editor of *Polish Weekly* and directed the program on Polish art and culture produced by Radio Free Europe. He committed suicide in New York in 1955.

His early poetry established Lechon as a romantic in theme and a classical writer in technique—a painstaking search for the perfect poetic form. He combines pure lyricism with national motives. During the postwar years his work gained in volume and in scope and he emerged as one of the outstanding poets and essayists in contemporary Polish literature: a master of a delicately wrought short poem and a man of a brilliant intellect and personality.

JAN LECHON

Prayer

O Sower of the eternal stars on high,
O Lord alike of rains and burning heat,
Stoop from Thy silent vastness, we entreat,
And grant a draught of quiet from the sky!

Then drown us in Thy worlds of boundless light,
Gild us like stars, dissolve us like the seas,
Blend us with air in blue infinities,
And tune us like an echo in the height;

Mix us with morning, rising pale at dawn,
And with the cloud at noonday idly sailing;
Mix with night's veil across the dim earth trailing,
That we from self and soul may be withdrawn!

(Watson Kirkconnell)

Love and Death

You seek to know my life's essential theme?—
I answer: Love and Death are both supreme.
Love's eyes are blue, but Death's deep eyes are dark;
These are the twain that fire me with their spark.

Through skies unstarr'd across the black night cast,
They ride the interplanetary blast,—
That whirlwind whose great tides our lives enmesh
In endless grief of soul and joy of flesh.

Our days are ground in querns and sifted deep;
We dig in life for truth, with mine-shafts steep,
And find one changeless moral for our breath:
That Death in Love take refuge, Love in Death.

(Watson Kirkconnell)

Sarabande for Wanda Landowska

The wind slams at the window. Papers pirouette in air.
Let them! Poems and writing surfeit me! My need is music.
And I can see you dressed in write, who stroll the spacious garden
at leisure: tambouring, nightingale, sarabande attend you.

Where could we hang the Gobelins, or stand the candelabra?
Parquet constricts a shepherdess with staff and rose-filled basket.

Moon glitters like a chandelier. Blue gentians flood the vases.
The lawn, outside—here is the setting for your minuet.

On such an evening a concert could create itself!
Unseen, young spirits tune the instruments in perfect silence.
Nothing has spoken, not a note, no sound—yet in your ear
violins, flutes and oboes fill the wide nocturnal hush.

Each entity is wrapped already in the lunar haze.
In shadow, all things move, prepare—each accord, each note,
invisible to one who stares at written staves or books.
And these resound for senses focused straight into the night.

Listen! Narcissus whispers his whole love into the stream.
But wait now, wait until each leaf falls silent in the birches,
until the autumn-colored faun steals late across the meadow.
Oh wait, do not begin before his footfall's echo sounds.

Look, the acacia drops a white flower on the clavichord.
Venus engulfed in leafage stirs and shudders in her sleep.
What are the thoughts that rise out of the fragrant cloud of flowers
as the acacia bows to cherish the white rows of keys?

Already now, you tread the paths and soft grass, and you feel
harmony, number, fluid dream throbbing in your two hands.
They flower and must open wide, the ribbons of your bodice
will loosen as your fingers fall to meet the perfect moment.

As if among Greek temples, under poplar colonnades,
you pause and smile, apart, already quite sure of the whole.
And nymphs unbind their hair, to lie outstretched in music's vessel.
You are endangered only by the marble of perfection.

And now, like Saint Cecilia as she kneels, you bow your head,
aware of azure secrets to dissolve all wicked spells.
And the insensate white Carrara block glows and flashes
thousand-fold as your hand strokes Golatea's golden tresses.

Oh, what can contradict, when all things are within the music?
Together, oh together, all things trivial and eternal
hasten with roses and laurel in the tracks of vanished gods
and their bare feet graze over the white keyboard like a zephyr.

Now let our meditation tower and become a dream—
let it plunge down within the stream that splashes with the oars,
let it drop down, the plumb-weight that submerges all the net,
and float out from your hands like fair Ophelia, gowned in white.

Higher, lower, scatter notes and seeds along two rows
of flowers! Sowing is harvest—blossoms burst at once.
Lucid the sky, mists gone—the star floats higher, higher.
Joyous and beautiful, you play the clavichord at night.

(Clark Mills)

The Hills of Oytzouv

Something urges in me: "Harvest your life at last.
Wisdom should guide you now, beyond your youth."
I do not listen to that voice. Always to my surprise
I am aware of things I have not understood at all.

I see shadowy presences at the foot of every truth.
I hear in every stillness aftertones of cries.
Everything seems to me enigmatic and vast
Like the hills of Oytzouv when I was small.

(Clark Mills)

(from) La Mancha

His lance in his hand, enormous in his casque of steel,
His head tilted to heaven, at times, innoble pride,
One night de Gaulle crossed all of Paris on his charger
With Sancho Panza donkey-trotting at his side.

The Groom devoured the shop-displays, babbled of gowns
And perfumes headier with scent than large bouquets.
The Master, eye alerted for the apparition
Of Joan of Arc, Napoleon, or one of the Capets,

Reproved his Squire: "The Ancient Guardsman or the Maid
Will rise from their graves, now, and march across the sky.
If they did not, all things would vanish into mist,
The miracles of the Louvre, the magic of Versailles!

Never believe your senses! These delude us always.
Only the palm is prophetic—that, and the birds' flight."
And, spurs to Rosinante, he cantered far from the people
To challenge ultimate windmills past Paris in the night.

(Clark Mills)

Don Juan

The solid brass clangs in the dark,
Clatter of helmet and sword is harsh and hollow.
The unnecessary Colleoni rides,
Rides in and gusts of lunar brightness follow.

I stand at the window, laurel on my brow
As an adornment for the night.
Run! Run! The shadow there behind you
Raises its arm to blot the light!

Who was it cried, "It is time, already!"
The candle guttered. Is that a knock at the door?
O heavy tread, statue of the Commander,
Come, cross the threshold to depart no more.

I need the flourish of your cape more, now,
than wine and laughter, scrape of the guitar.
I wait alone, here, for the retribution
So as to recognize at last, you were and are.

(Clark Mills)

Manon

The storms threaten, they rage and swerve
Closer, and natural forces burst, and no man
Can be saved! We save all when we preserve
Our own storms, that keep us human.

Stare straight into destruction there,
See, the magnificent cities and the world on fire,
And if you glimpse hands, mouths, together and aware
Do not wring hands at that fulfilled desire.

Do you hear? what grew in centuries now falls
In bombed Verona, founders in huge flame
As Romeo Montague's nostalgia calls
Nightlong, nightlong, Juliet Capulet's name.

Ximena! Your scarf amulet of heroes, whom the hydra
Of wars cannot touch even when all is lost!
O Mary Stuart, Beatrice Cenci, O Phaedra,
Your sufferings endure now in the holocaust!
And you, constant only in indifference,
Your moods that shift like sunlight in a garden,
Look at me, Manon, for whose single glance
I shall forgive what none could ever pardon.

(Clark Mills)

The Death of Mickiewicz

They arrived for their usual orders, as every day.
Men stopped them, who were there to watch the dead.
"We cannot allow you to see him now," they said.
"In the terrible pestilence this man is taken away."

And they wept together like children and in their fear
Whispered, "Now the night looms ahead, so dark!
See, the moon rides above Stamboul, its mark
Other than moonlight on the Niemen, once so near."

Just then he thought: "It's here. And I am calm.
Listen, the songs they sang at the cradle for hours and hours.
These are the shores of Lake Switez, their leaves and flowers.
In the next moment I shall touch them with my palm."

(Clark Mills)

On the Death of Joseph Conrad

Your father, too, had a splendid, gloomy burial,
Followed by simple men and dignitaries.
Their boots like Greek cothurni struck the stones,
As he was led from bondage to eternal freedom.

The Poles addressed your father ruggedly,
In simple words, and silently they cried.
Like a soldier's cap they placed your Fatherland
Upon his grave; dispersed and fought again.

Now the Beyond envelops you as well,
And that sleepless, battered wanderer,
Your father, summons you with Polish speech
Where the same lighthouse brightens all the seas.

(Adam Gillon and Ludwik Krzyzanowski)

Stanislaw Balinski

(1899–   )

Born in 1899 in the district of Nowogrodek, Balinski published his first collection of short stories *City of the Moons* in 1924, excellently combining fantastic concepts of a romantic imagination with a realistic concretization of imagery. His first volume of poems, *Evening in the East,* appeared in 1928. He displayed high literary ability fusing a delicacy of tone and simplicity of structure with a typically romantic attitude toward the phenomena of the Orient. In a beautiful form leaning towards classicism the poet reveals the impressions of a modern traveler who, following the footsteps of Romantic poets, visits exotic "mysterious places."

A member of the Polish diplomatic service in the inter-war years, he held posts in Iran, Manchuria, China and Denmark and traveled extensively in other parts of the world. After the collapse of France he came to England and it is in London where his subsequent volumes of poetry appeared: *The Great Journey* (1940), *A Matter of Conscience* (1942), *The Other Shore of the Night* (1943), *Three Poems About Warsaw* (1945), *Complete Collected Poems* (1949). English translations of some of his short stories were published in *New Writing, Argosy* and *Nineteenth Century.* Balinski is also a translator of English poetry and special mention should be made of his Polish version of John Keats' *Odes.*

STANISLAW BALINSKI

The Two Loves

That one was fickle, all uncertainty,
She mocked your prayers, your pleading would not move her,
Yet, if you fled, she'd call you tenderly,
You could not like her, you could only love her.

This one will never change, she will not falter,
Her words are kind, her smile felicity,
Her you may trust, her loyalty will not alter,
Her word once pledged holds till eternity.

That one forsook me, she was not for me . . .
This one embraces me with all her heart,

From her all goodness, all security . . .
For that one I am sad and brood apart.

(Watson Kirkconnell)

Refugees

What have we done with life, alas, what have we done,
That which could be so fair, my friends, is now so strange,
That which could be so sweet, so sad has now become,
And I, I have no tears, for this we cannot change.

What have we done with life, alas, what have we done,
Search not these words, dear friends, for secrets there are none,
There are no depth—no purpose here lies hidden,
From the forgotten past returns to us unbidden
This simple melody, which with the night has grown . . .
A silver bunch of flowers, above the sleeping town.

Who weeps? In a strange hotel room nearby,
Some girl is sobbing, wild with grief. In vain
She tries to check her tears, herself constrain,
For on that self-same morn had reached her there
A telegram. O unappeasable despair!
Her love was dead—shot! O unending pain!

The last late stars now glimmer in the skies,
And the wind lightly brings the first cool thrill.
What have we done with life,
What do we still . . . ?
From the dark forest depths we look with eager eyes
To the new dawn, which flows from the old hands of Time.

(Watson Kirkconnell)

The Last Melody

On a day full of unwanted roses,
When Paris expired like a ghost—
I ran to the shop at the corner
To say, before all had been lost,

Good-by to the French midinette
With a face as fresh as Maytide
Who had dreamed that freedom and France
Were one country, that none could divide.

But I found the shop closed with a padlock,
Through the window I saw empty gloom,
In the distance came only echoing
March of the Germans like doom.

Someone had torn from a calendar
Half a leaf as they fled as from fire,
And with trembling fingers had written:
Fermé jusqu 'à la Victoire!

That leaf and its simple inscription
Pinned there in a silence of tears,
Have haunted me in my wanderings
And sound like a tune in my ears.

Paris arises behind us
Like that shop full of phantom desire,
With the notice, which someone had written
Fermé jusqu 'à la Victoire!

(Watson Kirkconnell)

Polish Landscape: 1933

How hard our land's peculiar charm to tell:
Its amber fields, its rosy hawthorn, and the breeze
That sings its way through starlit pines: the spell
Of crosses by the wayside, rowan shrubs, primeval trees.

How hard . . . for always when I start to paint
Its sky or sketch its scene my poem goes askew,
The rhythm becomes confused, the tone a plaint,
And what I write some strange, distorted view.

The dewy lilies and the lovers' grove change
Into battlefields in Europe's heart,
Toward yonder artist's hill great armies range
And out of fruitful meadows—trenches start.

That little *dwor* beyond the Warsaw line—
Remember in my early lyrics how it shone?—
Explodes in flames and, crumbling, leaves no sign
Save dust to show it was a home.

That silver stream of which we said, "How
Like the silver pen that Goethe's hand
Gave to Mickiewicz once in Weimar!", now
Becomes a line of last defense, of final stand.

And so my dream-born view is hid by cold
Reality: a grim design replacing my serene,
A blood-stained sun swift blotting out the gold,
A poisoned breath corrupting every scene.

Still stands, however, 'twixt my fading view
And that dread canvas which the fates unroll
For us this magic: courage—to renew
The fight and die, if death alone be life immortal's toll.

(Albina Kruszewska)

Of Nowogrodek Land . . .

Harken then: the Nowogrodek land is drear
And lonely: meadows, yield no bounteous fruitage here
Nor sparkle here Hutzulian or Podhalan handicrafts;
No stately harbors, mines nor golden draughts
Of oil are here; but only dreams: a silent shade
Of land, poor in the goods of industry and trade.

But still—it has a secret—no heresy
In this, a secret which like magic herbs springs
Nightly into life, to murmur and allure—'tis poetry,
That sighs in soft White Russian, and in Polish sings.

Mickiewicz first found out the land for us, then went away,
But could not live without it, so one day
Returned, to stay forever in the land he loves.
And now at night he treads her forest graves,
Her moonlit lanes of pine, to tarry wearily
At dawn, like pilgrim, on some gleaming balcony,

To whisper ancient stanzas, cherished still,
And watch the rosy mist each treetop fill.

And still remains in him the secret of that dream—
Enshrouded land, wrapt in the mist of that most verdant stream,
The green-hued Niemen, as it flows caressingly along
The border of that land of verse and song.

For hostile arms may trample it and burn
Its homes, may carry off its children, turn
Its meadows to a waste by some decree of hell.
But break its power,—never! Though a hundred times they fell
It, still a hundred times again 'twill spring
To life, to murmur in White Russian, and in Polish sing.

(Albina Kruszewska)

Mieczyslaw Jastrun

(1903–   )

Born in Korolowka, Mieczyslaw Jastrun (pseudonym of Mieczyslaw Agatstein) was educated at the University of Cracow. Working as a teacher, he made his literary debut in 1929 with a volume of poetry, *Meetings in Time*. Other volumes followed, e.g., *Other Youth* (1933), *History Not Grown Cold* (1935), *Brook and Silence* (1937), *Intermezzo* (1937–1939). During the German occupation Jastrun continued to teach in Underground schools, and contributed to the clandestine press. The collections of poetry *A Guarded Hour* (1944) and *A Human Matter* (1946) represent this period. A steady succession of poetic collections such as, among others, *A Poem About the Polish Language, Poetry and Truth, Hot Ashes, Bigger than Life* bear witness to Jastrun's unflagging creative effort. He is also the author of a biographical study of Mickiewicz, a collection of essays on poetry, *Between the Word and the Silence*. His autobiographical novel *The Beautiful Sickness* was published in 1961.

Jastrun is also a distinguished translator of French, German and Russian poetry.

MIECZYSLAW JASTRUN

Man

Well, then, he too had to die so
As no man ought to die.

This tree he chose already in his childhood.
It followed him.
The shadow of stretched-out arms followed him.

Here even a stone can see,
A blade of grass trembles with dread.

He was hanged to signify that murder has not changed its tools
   since time immemorial.

But tomorrow the roar of the radio station.
Night in the lustre of mourning fame,
And upon the ground a guarded silence,

Deeper than the hole
Into which they had thrown him in haste,
Looking back with terror,
Heaped upon him the earth heavy from millennia.
The idling engine drones on.
All windows and gateways closed.

No angel came, to dig up the grave.

The wind from the sea flutters the black ribbon,
A tiny ribbon, but it screams like a flag.
In the four walls an imprisoned whisper.
Between the garage and the prison,
Between the slaughterhouse and the bakery,
In the pavement each stone is seen,
The grass in the cracks, and the humid moss.

They killed a man,
They cut down a tree,
They trampled the grass.

History goes through the phases of the moon,
It goes with the bellow of deer into the forest of rut.

They cut down the forest,
They burned out the grass.

The desert shall triumph—
Until the day when
Upon the shame and the glory
Shall lay its mighty paw
The sea that chokes eternity.

Chaos that was before and after creation will start from the end in
nothing everything from beginning.

(Adam Gillon)

Funeral

The crematorium served as coffin,
with transparent lids of air,
and a wisp of smoke from a living man,
blown through the chimney of ages.

How should we honor your death?
How walk in your funereal train?
O homeless handful of ash,
scattered between heaven and earth?

How lay a wreath of green
on a grave dug in the air?
It is an ark cast to the world
under invaders' fire.

Your non-existent coffin
won't float down from the roaring guns;
the airy column alone
illumines your death with the sun.

And a terrible silence lies on the earth,
like a tattered, trampled flag,
in the stifling smoke of the dead,
in the crucified cry.

                                        (Adam Gillon)

Here Too As in Jerusalem

Here too as in Jerusalem
There is a gloomy, wailing wall.
Those who had to face it
Shall see it nevermore.

An empty night, an empty house;
From here they dragged the men,
Darkness remained, fear remained,
And the insides—the womb of death.

The houses in stony procession
Under the merciless sky
Resembled the funereal suit
Of a thousand mourning kin.

The Christians thrown to the lions
Knew well the cause of their death;
And you?—Behold your empty house,
With fire, its blind possessor.

There were none to cast some earth
On that mass grave of men.
You blessed by silence,
Free from the treason of words.

When your parched lips, like wounds
Were asking for a drop of water,
No one would bring it to you,
To the trains clad with wire.

The earth had escaped the cursed,
And Warsaw was drowned in smoke
When the sun on the panes of the windows
Exclaimed: It is dawn!

(Adam Gillon)

Elegy

Life, so short a life. I couldn't understand
My dying mother's words, "Shut the door!
The draft is killing me." The huge draft
That plunders us of all that we possess,
Carries us from year to year, from house to house,
Among the eyes dilated from the terror,
Among the eyes blinking from the light.

Always exposed, and covering our nakedness;
Only the beasts follow the call of their blood,
That is their whole destiny.
Silence alone is safe.
(The fish do not know the surface shine
Is changed into a knife's gleam.)

But that great one, do I know for sure he's great,
A budding musician, perhaps, barely grown from childhood,
Who cannot rule the madness he himself set loose,
So that the instrument plays on, no longer
In his hands, this one knows why

On lands, where blood courses in the horizons' veins,
In fresh or salt waters,

In the ocean, which is beginning and end,
In the ocean, where stars are voiceless visionaries,
In the air, which is a gift and a luxury,
In the enormous draft
Doors without keys are opened and slammed.

(Adam Gillon)

Alexander Janta

(1908–1974)

Alexander Janta was born in 1908 in Poznan. He was educated there and in Paris at the *Haute École des Études Sociales* and *École de Journalisme*. He made his literary debut at the age of twenty with a volume of poetry, *Death of the White Elephant* in 1929. An indefatigable traveler, he visited the Soviet Union, Japan, India and the United States and set down his impressions in several books: *Into the USSR* (1933), *I Look at Moscow* (1933), *Made in Japan* (1935), *The Capital of Silver Magic* (1936), *The Earth is Round* (1936), *The Discovery of America* (1936), *At the Confines of Asia* (1939). Janta's poetry published prior to World War II includes *Cry in the Circus* (1930), *White Train* (1932), *Ursa Major* (1935), *Heart Towards the East* (1938). Joining the Polish armed forces in 1939, he was decorated for bravery and also had the experience of a German POW camp, from which he managed to escape and which he described in *I Lied to Live* (New York, 1945), and *Bound with Two Chains* (1946). He was later sent as assistant to the military attaché in Washington, D.C. He established himself in the United States after the war and became a leader of a movement for cultural development in the Polish-American community. His visit to Poland in 1948 forms the subject of *I Return from Poland* (Paris, 1949). Some of Janta's poetry of the war and post-war period has been translated into English: *13 Polish Psalms* (London, 1944), and *Psalms of Captivity* (New York, 1947). He is also the Polish translator of American poetry including that of Robert Frost. Janta's autobiography, *Restless Spirit*, appeared in London in 1957, and a collection of studies and essays, *Destinies and People*, was published in New York and London in 1960. A volume entitled *Identity Tag* (1958) gives a representative selection of his poetry covering a period of thirty years.

ALEXANDER JANTA

Identity Tag

They carried him from battle, softly with care;
the road is long, each minute infinite.
Perhaps he will survive. First-aid point.
Pale-faced, he bites his lips. It hurts?
His side is bleeding, ah, poor boy, the doctor
bends over him, and gives the sign: no hope.

What else does Nurse in white desire?
The explosion ripped his hand off with his tag.
His name and home are still unknown.
Whom shall I notify when he is dead?
In vain they search his tattered tunic.
They find no papers, not a scrap.

He shakes his head, opens his dying eyes,
Why such darkness, why this strangling weight?
What do these strangers want of him again?
He gropes for words and bits of memory:
"What is your name? Your name—for mother's sake."

But when at last he grasps the meaning,
he wonders greatly—the wonder of the tide
that draws him into giant chasms of the beyond.
"Your name, for mother ..." Strange, since mother knows it.

(Adam Gillon)

Death

Velvet tiger. Greyish stripes.
His eyes stab with the pupils' edge.
Long he looks, while mourners,
Black butterflies, hover above.

(Adam Gillon)

An American Story*

The map-wide open wastes, a continental
wilderness lassoed by lean loops of rail
radiating silver bright and with no end
across a sunswept landscape of adventure
which covered wagons conquered going west
tenaciously to open the big trail

* Originally written in English.

Who wonders why
the heroes of those deeds fall back and die
forever unremembered and so clearly
extinct—mere casualties of a blunder
which places other glories far ahead
though here they had the guts to come and live
to fight it out to leave what now is left

Now we (the train, streamlined in aluminum
and with springs winging the weight of each journey)
move speeding through and under
or over so much memory and pain
and watchful strength which once upon a time
began to make a nation in this land

That movement measures distance while that speed
easily spans two oceans in two days
what once has challenged brave men's boldest mind
is tamed today by tracks timetabled for
effortless crossing and so we can have
an easy view from windows to partake
of the still restless rugged precedence
and wear an air of partners in adventure
who say it's great but scarcely care it's there

Administering high indifference
the passengers of our present tense
take in the shapes set sharp against the blue
which is electric over ardent sand

The privacy of summits unattained
will faithfully bear witness and no fruit
to those inhabitants who here inherit:
conquistadors riding in vista-domes
thoughtless, untroubled by ancestral deeds
insured against all risk and satisfied
basking in lazy boredom and in boast

Encased in pullman plush superior salesmen
of what they don't produce nor ever buy
smoke filter tips exchanging tips and talk
of what one makes to meet the coming payments

A couple bright with honeymoon and promise
a spinster never tired to be old
beaming with wrinkled charms and wagging words
a sailor going home, a priest, a book
that catches the eye with the sharp title *Murder*

A fat bald fellow solving crossword puzzles
A voice in white, the waiter comes to say
that lunch is being served. The dining car
is three cars to the rear. Mixed grill and coffee
are shaken down by happy vehemence
under the sky where storms brood low, the clouds
descend in avalanche with sudden night
over the mountain breeding deep the danger
of precipice and boulders and the bear

Such was the enterprise of men
who lived to leave a road of gleaming rail
across the ever wide open horizon
with distance multiplying and no mercy

This architecture of unbeaten tracks
inscribed in stone, tunneled by gorge and canyon
long waited for the steel and spanning bridges
which now we cover in triumphant thunder
of certainty, rolling on hundred wheels
strangers already to the recent story
riding already our own far faster.

Czeslaw Milosz

(1911–   )

Educated in Wilno and in France, Milosz is considered an "avant garde" poet. His two prewar collections of poetry, *Poem of the Frozen Time* (1933) and *Three Winters* (1936), attracted a great deal of critical attention. During the German occupation, Milosz was an active member of the Warsaw underground, and had an anthology of his poetry published clandestinely (*Independent Song*, 1942). Another collection appeared in 1945 (*Rescue*).

Milosz is a prolific translator of foreign poetry and also a literary critic and essayist. He has translated such authors as Milton, Shakespeare, Burns, Browning, Wordsworth, T. S. Eliot, Maritain, and Oscar Milosz (his uncle, a well-known French poet). His literary essays include studies of Defoe, Balzac, Gide, William James and Tolstoy.

In 1946 Milosz entered the diplomatic service of the then moderate Polish government. He was stationed in Washington and later in Paris. In 1951 he broke with the Warsaw government, and after a number of years in Paris came to the United States, where he is now professor of Polish at the University of California at Berkeley.

His book, *The Captive Mind* (English edition, 1953), is a disturbing portrait of contemporary spiritual slavery under a totalitarian regime. His novel, *Seizure of Power*, won the *Prix Littéraire Européen* in 1953. Other books are: The *Valley of Issa* (1955–1957), a novel of his Polish childhood, a critical study of Stanislaw Brzozowski (1962) and a new collection of poetry (1962).

CZESLAW MILOSZ

Campo di Fiori

In Rome, on the Campo di Fiori
baskets with olives and lemons
the pavement spluttered with wine
and broken fragments of flowers.
The hawkers pour on the counters
the pink fruits of the sea,
and heavy armfuls of grapes
fall on the down of peaches.

Here, on this very square
Giordano Bruno was burned;
the hangman kindled the flame of the pyre
in the ring of the gaping crowd,
and hardly the flame extinguished
the taverns were full again
and hawkers carried on heads
baskets with olives and lemons.

I recalled Campo di Fiori
in Warsaw, on a merry-go-round,
on a fair night in the spring
by the sound of vivacious music.
The salvoes behind the ghetto walls
were drowned in lively tunes,
and vapors freely rose
into the tranquil sky.

Sometimes the wind from burning houses
would bring black kites along,
and people on the merry-go-round
caught the flying charred bits.
This wind from the burning houses
blew open the girls' skirts,
and the happy throngs laughed
on a beautiful Warsaw Sunday.

Perhaps one will guess the moral,
that the people of Warsaw and Rome
trade and play and love
passing by the martyrs' pyres.
Another, perhaps, will read
of the passing of human things,
of the oblivion growing
before the flame expired.

But I that day reflected
on the loneliness of dying men,
on the fate of lone Giordano;
that when he climbed the scaffold
he found no word in human tongue
with which to bid farewell
to those of mankind who remain.

Already they were on the run,
to peddle starfish, gulp their wine;
they carried olives and lemons
in the gay hum of the city.
And he was already remote
as though ages had passed,
and they waited a while
for his flight in the fire.

And those dying alone,
forgotten by the world,
their tongue grew strange to us,
like the tongue of an ancient planet.
And all will become a legend—
and then after many years
the poet's word shall stir revolt
on the new Campo di Fiori.

(Adam Gillon)

Tadeusz Rozewicz

The Plains

Only in the rough embrace
of reality
does my heart beat
A stream of blood
the sun
it flows through the green tree
of my life
So thin is the air in my lungs
I shall open myself
like the plains
willing to accept movement and change
and be filled with

the ocean of life

Too long have I fed on the fields
of your graves You the dead

* For biographical note see p. 331.

turn from me
This matter is for the living
you soft lambs
you trembling twigs of light and dream
Go, be swallowed by a dark river
you soft lambs
with snouts so gently closed

the ocean of life

Thus must I walk
Walk with all years
pictures images lived seen
landscapes left behind
Walk with the Nazi hand on my brother's face
with all faces of the dead
all faces of the living
whose "eye sockets are rings
set in blind darkness
their precious stones torn out"

the ocean of life

so it is I must walk
Walk with all fruits
all colors of fruits
all words left unsaid
all black trees
on the snow
all nights to come
and one that already is

The scientists say that all words
said told since the world's beginning
that all voices from the world's beginning
have been are preserved in air
with all their warmth color taste

But in me are collected all images
unsaid
to which shape has not been given
color meaning

people with mouths glued by lime sulphate
Oh how it buds
grows within me
the silent seed
of dead fruit

It moves upward to light
thrusts through the blind clay
of my flesh
breaking inspiring my wooden tongue

In it are the words
of ten young poets
killed in Warsaw
They will not see
how the ribs of St. John's Cathedral
have healed
how the youngest cathedral in Europe
grows
still wet
a Gothic flower
beneath our clouded sky

In it is the whisper
of young girls
who will not dance
on a May night
under the tree crowns
Of girls
whose small bones and skulls
keep silence below earth

II

"A poet says that Orpheus
was pursued by trees, sea-waves and
stones . . ."
At night I lay
with my face in the darkness
the weight of your head
on my heart
the weight of an iceberg
or a bird that will fly away

I ask
Who walks behind me?
No one answers
Afraid I ask again
Who walks behind me?
I hear-Ringing quiet
Do I live in a huge
bell without heart
I ask for the third time
Who walks behind me?

I hear tears
shed at night
from closed eyes

All pictures I have seen
landscapes I have lived with
desert me

I am left with only one
alone
Under electric lights
I see people in long coats
of earth color
holding bowls tins
plates pots
Standing arms down
one against another
crowded standing into a suburban square
hedged by barbed wire
standing for nights and days silent
And then in the electric glare
I see them eating grass
eating roots
I hear the inhuman voice
In the daylight I see
a woman killed near the barbed wire
her spread-open fingers
from which bread has fallen
Under silent reflectors
I see the empty square
covered with lime white
At night people

heard wagons removing
the dead

This was how they destroyed
a camp of Soviet war prisoners
in one of our towns

It is not I who hold them
it is they who press
The Murdered
The Just
hold me with open hands

Having submitted
I do not escape
the defenseless

III

Down Zabia Street
in a Polish town
Rose walks
amid white feathers

It is no carnival night
Far the wind carries
feathers torn from the beds
of people who never will leave
their bodies' shape not even on cloud

who never will leave the shape of their heads
on May meadow grass
nor on snow
pierced by blue and gold swords
of sundown and sunrise
who never will leave the shape of their heads
on wave trembling darkly
over saffron fish fins
who never will leave the shape of their bodies
on hay
as over the threshing floor
black lightning swallows fly
chirping
who never will leave the shape of their bodies
on any bed

Down Zabia Street
in Poland
Rose walks
on uneven stones
passing houses marked with stars
passing windows barred with wood
she walks through a house of god
where wild cats
take shelter
she walks among shining feathers
on this black day

she walks your cities neutral Swedes
through your houses theaters churches
she walks your villages neutral Swiss
through your towns pure as clean tears
she walks leaving no trace on earth
as a cloud walks through the sky

I keep in me
the beating of her heart
the silence of her eyes
the warmth color of her mouth
pressure of intestines
escaping running away loins
in the shadow of love
the shape of her head
the red twilight of her falling hair

She walks like cloud
but why
the long unending shadow

IV

Now in my home
ten years after the war
I interrupt my poem
hearing the night steps
I live a moment's fear
Still they are after me
Still after fifteen years
I hear their breath
damp smelling

Smell of dead flesh
on May meadows

Boots creak
and black ropes creak
I put away my pen
hold my breath
I a man
marked death numbered
one of many
I wipe sweat from my forehead
hearing steps

I close eyes
that have seen too much—
the animal the beast
in the man's body

oh human flesh
most beautiful dust

V

In a Polish village
sleeping under autumn rain
seen only
through years' clear image of fields
rainbow of folklore
in a small Polish village
not heard of
by Morgan Dupont

Krupp Thyssen
not heard of
a village so small
that its name
appears only
on Wehrmacht maps

on an autumn night when wind blows
and black lupines glitter gold in the rain
and puddles are like dead eyes of the sky
on an autumn night they took him

from a room with a floor
hard walked on
by many generations
where the Byzantine face of Mother
dark above dried wreaths of plant
stood silent

Out from the circle of the oil lamp
on an autumn night they took him
a young man
in a linen shirt
from his supper

his wife opened her mouth
and touched her throat
when the three strange men
walked into the room taking him
asking to be shown the way

It happened outside

When he pointing
to show them the
One of the three
shot him between the eyes
through his clear forehead

He fell down in the mud
and stayed there
and those who had killed
walked into the darkness

The sky cleaned its black mouth
with rain
and the dark mother
placed her son's head on her bosom
pierced by swords
In the fields
on the roads
wooden crosses
kneel in the mud
in a small Polish village
where the wind blows
and black lupines glitter gold in the rain

This shot was not heard
this death not seen
by Morgan and Rockefeller
Krupp Cloy and Thyssen

VI

In me is a July night in an orchard
when the wind starts up and the rain peters out
in the middle of the night
we run to this garden
I and my dead brother

through wet grass
we run under trees
I see his face in a smile
and his hand holding fruit
half-eaten

I taste the rain
and the wind
The moon's enamel grows cold
on the dark pot of earth
after many years night comes
night the terrible night the long
night of the occupation
I see my brother
he goes Underground
gets killed

VII

In the country of forty-eight stars
they plan to build underground cities
they want to push life
underground
hide it from rays of H-suns

But there
below earth
are no forests no May meadows
what trees shall grow
what butterflies fly
what birds make nests

You can bury beneath earth's surface
iron cement stone
factory skeletons
of long dead cities
But you cannot bury mountain sea sunrise
or walking cloud

Where will the girl leave
her footprint
the girl who sprang into the sea
the girl like a pink cloud
who sings with joy
among green lights of foam

There beneath earth's surface
there are no orchards
where on July nights after storm
boys run
like a multitude
of black wet grass

Do not make your life there
below
Friends
Renounce renounce the laws
of fear of hate

Oh what a long way
your nation has come
from Whitman's human song
to the bellowing of Ezra Pound
He hides from the nation's anger
in an asylum
honored with laurels
in an asylum
The long dark way
of treason and mud
and at the end stands
Ezra Pound
traitor

Live in sun and peace
we hold out our arms to you

meeting meeting you on the way
In us is no treason no hatred
do not go below
Friends
do not go below

(Paul Mayewski)

Adam Wazyk

(1905-   )

Born in 1905, Wazyk was associated with the "New Art" movement which was the Warsaw branch of the Polish Avantgarde group originally centering around the literary periodical *The Switch* appearing in Cracow. His first volume of poems *Semaphores* (1924), was followed by *Eyes and Lips* (1925) and *Collected Poems* (1934). Of interest are his two surrealist novels, *The Man in the Drab Suit* (1930) and *The Lanterns Shine in Karpow* (1933). During the war Wazyk fled to Russia where in 1943 his collective poems, *The Heart of the Grenade*, manifesting Communist views, was published. A decade later it was hailed as "a document of splendid creative maturity of the poet's ideological conscience for whom the time of the war was the turning point of his political imagination and in his means of expression." After his return to Poland Wazyk was active as a writer, critic and literary historian. He was co-founder of the literary magazine *The Smithy,* propagating Socialist Realism, and, from 1950–54, editor in chief of the monthly *Creative Work.* New collections of poetry are *Postwar Garland, New Selected Poems,* and others, while his books *In the Direction of Humanism* (1949) and *Mickiewicz and the National Versification* (1951) are concerned with problems of literary art in a Socialist Realist interpretation. The fact that he was given the State Literary Prize in 1952 and the Polish Pen Club Award in 1953 is indicative of the standing he enjoyed in the Stalinist period. Thus, when on August 21, 1955, the literary periodical *New Culture* came out with Wazyk's "A Poem for Adults," this proved a veritable bombshell manifesting, as it did, the poet's disillusionment with and condemnation of the conditions brought about by Communist rule.

With bitterness and vehemence the poem denounces the brutality, poverty and hopelessness of the Polish people's life with a passion which can only result from an innermost feeling of outrage, shame and grief.

A Poem for Adults

SELECTIONS

I

When, by error, I jumped on a wrong bus
people in it, as usual, were returning from work
The bus rushed down an unknown street,
O Holy Cross Street, no longer Holy Cross,

where are your antique shops, bookstores, students?
Where are you, the dead?
The memory of you peters out
Then the bus stopped
on a dug-up square.
Old skeleton of a four-story house
anticipated the verdict of fate.
I got off in the square
in a working district,
where grey walls become silver, reminiscing.
People were hurrying home
and I did not dare ask them the way.
In my childhood, had I not come to this house?
I returned like a man
who had gone for medicine
and come home twenty years later.
My wife asked me where I'd been.
My children asked me where I'd been.
I said nothing and sweated like a mouse.

IV

From villages and little towns they come in carts
to build a foundry and dream out a city, dig out of the earth a new
    Eldorado.
with an army of pioneers, a gathered crowd,
they jam in barns, barracks and hostels,
walk heavily and whistle loudly in the muddy streets:
the great migration, the twisted ambition,
with a string on their necks—the Czestochowa cross,
three floors of swear-words, a feather pillow,
a gallon of vodka and the lust for girls.
Distrustful soul, torn out of the village soil,
half-awakened and already half-mad,
in words silent, but singing, singing songs,
the huge mob, pushed suddenly
out of medieval darkness: un-human Poland,
howling with boredom on December nights. . . .
In garbage baskets and on hanging ropes
boys fly like cats on night walls,
girls' hostels, the secular nunneries,
burst with rutting—and then the "Duchesses"
ditch the foetus—the Vistula flows here. . . .
the great migration building industry,

unknown to Poland, but known to history,
fed with big empty words, and living
wildly from day to day despite the preachers,
in coal gas and in slow, continuous suffering
the working class is shaped out of it.
There is a lot of refuse. So far there are grits.

XI

Speculators took her to a quiet hell
in an isolated villa—she escaped.
She wandered drunk all night
slept on cement till light.
They threw her out of art school
for lack of socialist morality.
She poisoned herself once—they saved her.
She poisoned herself again—they buried her.

XII

All this is not new. Old is the Cerberus of socialist morality.
Fourier, the dreamer, charmingly foretold
that lemonade would flow in seas.
Does it not flow?
They drink sea-water,
crying:
"lemonade!"
returning home secretly
to vomit.

XIV

They shouted at the ritualists,
they instructed,
enlightened and
shamed the ritualists.
They sought the aid of literature,
that five-year-old youngster,
which should be educated
and which should educate.

Is a ritualist an enemy?
A ritualist is not an enemy,
a ritualist must be instructed,
he must be enlightened,

he must be shamed,
he must be convinced.
We must educate.
They have changed people into preachers.
I have heard a wise lecture:
"Without properly distributed economic incentives
we'll not make technical progress."
These are the words of a Marxist.
This is the knowledge of real laws,
the end of utopia.
There will be no novels about ritualists,
but there will be novels about the troubles of inventors,
about anxieties which move all of us.
This is my naked poem
before it matures
into troubles, colors and odors of the earth.

(Paul Mayewski)

Konstanty Galczynski

(1905–1953)

Konstanty Ildefons Galczynski was born in Warsaw in 1905. At the outbreak of World War I, his family was evacuated to Russia; they returned after the war. Galczynski entered the University of Warsaw as a student of Classics and English, but he did not complete his studies. After a short term in the army, he joined the periodical *Kwadryga*, and became a member of a group of poets known by the name of the magazine.

It was while he stayed with this group that his poetic talent began to be recognized. Both his imagery and humor were strikingly original. A number of short verses of this period are already considered "classics."

When Germany invaded Poland, Galczynski was taken prisoner and remained incarcerated until freed by the advancing American Army. He spent some time in Paris, Brussels, and Rome before returning to Poland in 1946. He continued to write both satire and lyrics, but was regarded with suspicion by the government because he did not write socialistic verse. During the Stalinist period he wrote of "capitalist wolves," but he could never fit the working man into his poetry. He was officially censured by the party for his "decadent verse" and, despite his "Poem for a Traitor," on the occasion of Czeslaw Milosz's defection to the West, he failed to gain official recognition.

Galczynski managed to avoid both the "isms" and the different schools of poetry that abounded during the period between the two wars. He satirized both communists and capitalists, but his achievements as a lyrical poet will probably be the measure of his greatness. His poetry is chiefly concerned with nature and art. When a man enters it, he becomes merely one more part of the universal order. In "Of August" the poet walks down the "slanting street-light" not for any sociological or philosophical reasons. He remembers the moon over a power plant; he paints an order and a harmony beyond the reasoning power of man. His people are either generalized conceptions (mother, student, poet), or individuals who have become part of the national heritage (e.g., Wit Stwosz and Chopin). Like the American poet Wallace Stevens, he makes nature the real hero of his poetry. It is a system of order where "everything glows."

Since the upheaval of 1956, his works have gained great popular appeal. A record of Galczynski's recitation of his long poem "Niobe" shows him to be one of the finest oral interpreters of poetry in Poland. He is now recognized as one of Poland's most original and popular poets, but his work is virtually unknown in the West. Galczynski died in 1953.

Monument of a Student

In a certain Polish city—the truth must now be told,
A statue of a student stands, admired by young and old;

The monument is made of bronze, the base is bronze as well,
Of bronze is the story the allegories tell.

The student's books, a globe, a lamp, an owl in his prime,
All these the artist's craftsmanship captured for all time.

After that the artist called down a mighty curse—
His payment wasn't adequate to fill his slender purse.

But that's no matter now—for us the monument's the thing:
A student stands upon the base, around him tatters cling;

His well-worn coat is full of holes, the wind blows freely through,
It's held together by a pin, but this is broken too.

The bottom of his overcoat, which should be quite concealing,
Is decorated with a hole—a little too revealing!

But his lips are parted in a smile, his hands prepare to clasp
A greatly needed scholarship just within his grasp.

Written on the pedestal we see this dedication:
THIS MONUMENT WAS CAST IN BRONZE, ERECTED BY THE NATION

IN HONOR OF HER DEAREST CHILDREN, THOSE FORGOTTEN STUDENTS
WHO BECAUSE OF IGNORANCE—PERHAPS THEY CALLED IT PRUDENCE—

FOR MANY REASONS NOW UNKNOWN (POSSIBLY THE FEES)
DID NOT COMPLETE THEIR STUDIES, WERE GRANTED NO DEGREES.

A student who's alive will be the cause of sad laments,
But—it's the truth—we Poles will always cherish monuments.

(Margaret Dunn)

Poem about Crows

In the glittering air
crows are sitting on a tree,
supported by a limb.

They are content to sit
because snow has begun to fall,
shutting them off, as by a wall.

Nearby there's a field
with a winding brook,
a township looms, industrialized.

But the mad eyes of the crows
in a wholly crowy manner
look only upon each other.

If they could be changed into notes
played on but one string,
those notes would still ring.

Stiff and erect, they will sit
for the glory of crowdom
till kingdom come.

The night sky blossoms.
Everything glows:
night, wind, the tails of crows.

Go to sleep, you winding brook,
Branches, sleep tight.
Crows, good night.

(Victor Contoski)

Of August

1

Stars stood under my window
like village musicians.

Green-eyed August
danced through the orchard.

The orchard, kissed
by the moon,
was moved to tears.
Light as a gypsy dance
was the dance of August.

Once the gold in the tree bark
trembled, frightened by shadow.
People blinked.
Night opened her eyes.

2

The pines turned dark.
Above each a star.
Like you, the night embraces
and grows cloudy.

The light of far-off dawn
is like a far city
shining on the hill
in starlight.

The tears which fall from your eyes
tell the earth of our sorrows.
Let's go for a walk.
Our tears will dry on the road.

Don't be ashamed of your tears.
In this night we wander:
a sparkling night,
a singing night,
a night without end.

Reeds sleep in the water.
Motionless dawn.
The wind has died.

Silver-shouldered stars
are beaming; each one has
his own pine tree.

3

Hold out your hat: stars fall,
gilded like Christmas ornaments.
Hold out your hat: maybe you'll
catch one for your true love.

And when they lie to you, that
she's out or sick or something,
you throw the star back to heaven
and your cap goes back on your head
at an angle.

4

Rustling.
The wind is rustling.
The eternal wind, blowing
without pity,
ceaselessly.

August has expanded gardens,
filled them with dreams and warmth.
The wind is blowing.
In the rustling of the wind
I am lost in love.
Once more I will try,
once more in the green August night . . .

The green bird of August
alighted
on the black tower of night.

A silver window in the tower.
August flaps his wings,
turning his head.

5

Look. How many stars in the sky tonight,
each as warm as a mother's smile.
The wind blows, and August shines in Poland.
A man must dream long before he falls asleep.

6

You say: "Don't go there.
It's a slanting street—night.
Why do you go down that slanting street?"

I answer: "You're a silly girl.
I go because I then remember
a certain street with the moon
over a power plant.

7

I came back as if from a journey
through the streets, the winding alleys.
Yes, it's here—the moon so big.
Yes, it's here—the gate and the picket fence.
My mother came with her wrinkled face
displeased. She looked at me.
'My son,' she said, how old you have become.
You were a falcon, now you're gray, like a dove.'"

(Victor Contoski)

Zbigniew Herbert

(1924–   )

Zbigniew Herbert was born on October 29, 1924 in Lwow. He graduated from the Academy of Commerce in Cracow and also studied law in Torun and philosophy in Warsaw. His debut as a poet came in 1950 in the Catholic weekly *Tygodnik Powszechny*. Twenty of his poems were included in an anthology published in Warsaw in 1954. His first individual volume of poetry bore the title *A Chord of Light* (1956). It was followed by two other volumes, *Hermes, Dog and Star* (1957), and *The Study of an Object* (1961). Herbert was also the author of a very well received book of essays, *A Barbarian in the Garden* (1963), and a number of plays, including *The Philosophers' Den* (1956), *The Other Room* (1958), and *Lalek* (1961). His plays have been performed on the stage and on radio, and one has been televised. Herbert has also established a reputation as an art critic, collaborating mainly with the monthlies *Creative Writing* and *The Bond*.

English translations of Herbert's poetry have been published in the London *Observer* and in the literary journal *Encounter*, and have been broadcast on several occasions over the BBC which also presented two of his plays *The Other Room* in 1962, and *The Philosophers' Den* in 1963. The English translation of *The Philosophers' Den* appeared in an anthology of contemporary Polish writings, *The Broken Mirror*, published in New York in 1958.

Zbigniew Herbert is undoubtedly one of the outstanding poets in Poland today. His first volume of poems was enthusiastically received by critics and readers alike. In their reviews the critics stressed the philosophical quality of Herbert's poetry, and observed that he was at the same time extraordinarily sensitive to the political problems of our epoch. Herbert seeks a definition of his times by probing in his poetry the problem of authority and the problem of man entangled in the "progress of history." His deeply humanist approach tinted by his slightly sceptical humor never appears as anger or contempt for a human being. He prefers to direct his irony against superficial truths but never against man. In his love poems the tone of self-irony and humor also dominate the intensity of his feeling. His poetry, simple but at the same time difficult, compels the reader to return to it time and time again.

When his poetry was introduced in England, critics there acclaimed Herbert as "one of the most original and impressive young poets in Europe." His verse has been described as classical—disciplined and lucid. A. Alvarez in *The Observer* in an introduction to Herbert's poems says that the qualities of his poetry "together with his extraordinary independence and intellectual range make for maturity which is more or less unique among his generation of poets on either side of the Iron Curtain."

An Episode

We are walking by the sea
holding tightly in our hands
two ends of an ancient dialogue
—do you love me
—I love you

with closely knit eyebrows
I compress the whole wisdom
of two testaments
of astrologists prophets
of philosophers from the gardens
and philosophers from the monasteries

and it sounds almost like this:
—do not cry
—be brave
—look: everybody

you purse your lips and say
—you should have been a preacher
and angrily you walk away
one does not love moralists

what am I to say on the shore
of a small dead sea

the water slowly fills in
the shape of feet which disappeared

Maturity

What has passed is good
what is coming is good
and even the present
is good

In the nest weaved of flesh
lived a bird
it fluttered its wings against the heart
most often we called it: anxiety
and sometimes: love

in the evenings
we went to the rapid river of sorrow
you could see yourself in the river
from head to foot

now
the bird fell to the bottom of the cloud
the river sunk in the sands
helpless like children
and experienced like elders
we are simply free
that is ready to depart

At night a nice old man comes
with a pleasant gesture invites
—what is you name—we ask afraid

—Seneca—so say those who went to school
and those not knowing Latin
call me: dead

I Would Like to Describe

I would like to describe a simplest emotion
joy or sorrow
but not as others do it
reaching for rays of rain or sun

I would like to describe light
which is born in me
but I know that it is not similar
to any star
because it is not so bright
not so clear
and uncertain

I would like to describe courage
without dragging behind me a dusty lion
and also anxiety
without shaking a glass full of water

in other words
I will give all metaphors
for one expression
peeled out from my chest like a rib
for one word
which is contained
in the limits of my skin

but I suppose it cannot be done

and in order to say—I love
I run about madly
picking armfuls of birds
and my compassion
though it is not of water
asks water for a face

and anger
different from fire
borrows from it
an outspoken tongue

it's so mixed
it's so mixed up
in me
that which grey haired men
divided for ever
and said
this is the object
and this is the subject

we go to sleep
with one arm under the head
and the other in a heap of planets

and our feet leave us
and taste the earth

with small roots
which in the morning
painfully we break off

Apollo and Marsyas

Apollo's actual duel
with Marsyas
(absolute hearing
versus enormous scale)
takes place towards the evening
when as we know
the judges
.granted the victory to god

well tied to a tree
with carefully peeled off skin
Marsyas
cries
before the cry reaches
his tall ears
he rests in the shadow of that cry

shaken by shivers of disgust
Apollo cleans his instrument

only apparently
the voice of Marsyas
is monotonous
and consists of a single vowel
Ah

in fact
Marsyas
tells
inexhaustible wealth
of his body

bald mounds of liver
white digestive ravines
whispering forests of lungs

sweet hills of muscles
joints gall blood and spasms
winter winds of bones
by the salt of memory
shaken by shivers of disgust
Apollo cleans his instrument

now the choir
is joined by the spine of Marsyas
basically the same Ah
only deeper with added rust
this is beyond the endurance
of god with man made fibre nerves

by a gravel path
lined with privet
the victor departs
wondering
whether from Marsyas' howls
will emerge in time
a new branch
of art—say—concrete

suddenly
at his feet drops
a nightingale turned to stone

he turns round
and sees
the three to which Marsyas was tied
is white

all over

The Silkiness of a Soul

Never
did I talk with her
either of love
or of death

only a blind taste
and a dumb touch
ran between us
when immersed in ourselves
we lay close together

I must
look down her
see what she wears
inside

when she slept
with open mouth
I peeped
and what
and what
what do you think
I saw

I expected
boughs
I expected
birds
I expected
a home
by huge silent waters

but there
on a glass slab
I saw a pair
of silk stockings

my God
I'll buy her those stockings
I shall

but what will appear then
on a glass slab
of that small soul

will it be something
which cannot be touched
even with fingertips of dreams

A Study of an Object

1

the most beautiful object
is that which does not exist

it is neither used to carry water
not to hold the remains of a hero

it was never embraced by Antigone
a rat never drowned in it

it has no opening
it is completely open

it can be seen
from all sides
that means just about
sensed

the hair
of all its edges
combines
into one ray of light

neither
blindness
nor
death
will tear away the object
which does not exist

2

mark the place
where the object stood
the one which does not exist
with a black square
it will be
a simple elegy
on the beautiful absent

a manly regret
enclosed
in a quadrangle

3

now
the whole expanse
swells like an ocean

the hurricane hits
the black sail

the wing of the storm circles
over the black square

and the island sinks
into the salty swell

4

now you have
an empty space
more beautiful than the object
more beautiful than the space it occupied
it is an ante-world
a white paradise
of all possibilities
you can enter it
and cry out
vertical-horizontal

into the naked horizon
a perpendicular thunder will drop

we can leave it at that
you already created the world

5

listen to the advice
of the inner eye

do not yield
to whispers mutterings gurglings

it is the non-created world
thronging by the picture gates

the angels offer
pink fluff of the clouds

the trees poke everywhere
untidy green hair

the kings recommend purple cloth
and tell the trumpeters
to gold plate

even a whale begs for a portrait
listen to the advice of the inner eye
don't let anybody in

6

take out
from the shadow of the object
which does not exist
from the polar space
from raw dreams of the inner eye
a chair

beautiful and useless
like a cathedral in the wilderness

put on the chair
a crumpled tablecloth
and add to the conception of order
the conception of adventure

let it be a proclamation of faith
in the face of the vertical wrestling with the horizon

let it be
more silent than the angels
more proud than the kings
more true than the whale
let it have the countenance of the final things

we beg you speak out of chair
the bottom of the inner eye
the iris of necessity
the pupil of death

(Magdalena Czajkowska)

PART THREE

New Poetry

Czeslaw Milosz

(1911–   )

Even before winning the 1981 Nobel Prize, Milosz had gained wide recognition in the English-speaking world with the following books translated into English: *The Captive Mind, Postwar Polish Poetry, Native Realm, The History of Polish Literature, Selected Poems, Emperor of the Earth: Modes of Eccentric Vision, Bells in Winter, The Valley of Issa.* Milosz won the 1978 Neustadt International Prize for Literature; he was also awarded the degree of Doctor Honoris Causa by the Catholic University of Lublin in 1981. See also pp. 447–449.

Incantation

Human reason is beautiful and invincible.
Neither bars nor wire nor book-burning
Nor the verdict of exile can touch it.
It lays down the principles of the language,
And guides our hand, thus we write in capital letters
Truth and Justice, and in small: a lie and a wrong.
An enemy of despair, a friend of hope,
It raises what should be, above what is.
It doesn't distinguish Jew from Greek, slave from master,
Making us share the management of our world.
From the obscene uproar of tormented words
It saves rigorous and lucid sentences.
It insists all is new under the sun,
And opens the clenched fist of the past.
Philo-Sopia is beautiful and very young,
As poetry is, allied with her in the service of Good.
Nature celebrated their birth just yesterday,
The unicorn and echo brought the news to the mountains.
Their friendship will be famous, their time knows no end.
Their enemies have delivered themselves to destruction.

(Grazyna Drabik and Austin Flint)

You Who Have Wronged *

You, who have wronged a simple man,
Bursting into laughter at his suffering,
Keeping around a crew of clowns
To confound good and evil,

Even if all bowed down before you
Ascribing to you virtue and wisdom,
Forging gold medals in your honor,
Content to live through one more day,

Do not feel safe. The poet remembers.
You may kill him—a new one will be born.
Deeds and talks will be recorded.

A winter dawn would be better for you,
And a rope and branch bent under the burden.

(Michael J. Mikos)

---

* This poem, written in Washington, D.C., in 1950, appeared in *Daylight*,
the first collection of Milosz's poetry published in exile in 1953.
   Lines taken from this poem were inscribed on a monument unveiled in
Gdansk in December 1980 to commemorate the anniversary of the workers'
massacre of 1970.

Krzysztof Baczynski

(1921–1944)

Krzysztof Baczynski was born in Warsaw and died in Warsaw during the August Uprising. His first poetic efforts date from as early as 1936, but his first publication was a typescript of seven poems which was distributed clandestinely in the summer of 1940. His first book, *Selected Poems,* appeared in 1942 in a mimeographed edition of ninety-six copies under the pseudonym of Jan Bugaj. In 1943 Baczynski published *Jan Bugaj's Poetic Sheet.* In 1942 he enrolled in the underground university. In 1943 he became a cadet in the Home Army's officer training school, and he remained faithful to his soldier's duty until his untimely death during the Warsaw Uprising. Baczynski's works were printed in full only posthumously.

I will open a golden sky for you,
make a white thread of silence weave
like a nutshell of sounds so huge,
which will crack in order to live
upon the green little leaves,
with the music of dusk, the songs of lakes,
until a milky kernel appears
a bird-like dawn.

I'll change the hard soil of meadows
into a dandelion flight, soft and fluid;
from things I will draw their shadows,
make them arch, as cats do it;
they'll roll up all, their fur aglow
into leaves' hearts and hues that flow
from storms into gray braids of rain.

And the trembling streams of air, for you,
as smoke rises from an angel's cottage,
I'll transform into long avenues,
into a singing sway of birches,
until they sound as violas do
a plaint—and then one sees
pink rising lights, the hymn
played by the wings of bees

Krzysztof Baczynski

Only from my eyes take the galling
painful glass—the days' flood
which pictures white skulls rolling
across the burning greens of blood.
Only change the cripple's time,
cover the graves with the river's coat,
wipe off my hair the battle grime,
the black dust afloat
with those angry years.

June 15, 1943

(Adam Gillon)

Stanislaw Baranczak

(1946–   )

Stanislaw Baranczak was born in Poznan. A poet, essayist, translator, and a scholar, Baranczak is also a prominent member of the Polish opposition movement. He taught Polish literature at the University of Poznan until he was discharged from this duty for political reasons. As a poet he began his career in 1968 with the volume *The Correction of a Face*. He was able to publish two more books of poems and several volumes of literary criticism. Thereafter, his books were banned in Poland. Thus, he has published them in the Polish *samizdats* and émigré presses: *I Know That This Is Unjust* (Paris, 1977), *Artificial Respiration* (London, 1978) and *Triptych of Concrete, Weariness, and Snow* (Paris, 1981). In 1981 Baranczak was allowed to leave Poland and he has assumed the post of professor of Polish literature at Harvard University.

In One Breath

In one bracket of breath closing a sentence
in one bracket of ribs closing like a fist
around the heart, like a net around slender fish, in one breath
to close all and to enclose myself, in one
shaving of flame whittled off the lungs
to scorch the walls of prisons and to take that fire
behind the bony bars of the chest and into the tower
of the windpipe, in one breath, before you choke
on a gag of air thickened from
the last breath of the executed, the breathing of hot
barrels and blood steaming on concrete,
air in which your voice resounds
or dissolves, you, the swallower of swords,
these side-arms, bloodless yet bloodily
wounding brackets, among which
like the heart in the ribs and like the fish in the net
a sentence flutters stammered out in one breath
till the last breath.

(Grazyna Drabik and Austin Flint)

It Does Not Concern Me

It does not concern me, this severe
coolness of a barrel touching someone's nape
it does not concern me, does not belong to me
neither this head, nor this hand with a gun, nor
the judgment as to who is right and on whose side lies
the shovel with which a pit was dug, you, do not bother
my shaven head, thinking about it doesn't stir my hand
neither this one in a uniformed sleeve nor
that one tied with a wire, it does not concern me
(and yet I feel that though it's so unimportant,
it still
insults me);

I repeat to myself: it does not concern me, does not touch
me the index finger of a club, it is not my head
covered with hands, I have nothing in common
with this beaten man besides an irrefutable fact
that I too am a man, and this, after all,
means so little, besides they don't beat
for no reason, I am to be sure free of prejudice,
but even if they beat someone without a warning, I know
that he himself bears the blame, it does not concern me
(and yet I feel that though it's so little
it still
constrains me);
once more: it does not concern me, I do not feel offended
when I have to whisper my confession through grids
of questionnaire columns, with relief I write in large
letters DOES NOT APPLY when they ask me about
past, present and future opinions,
I absolve myself, I give my word
that I will not get involved in anything, that I will not say a word
more than necessary, for the last word
in any case belongs to the stronger, it does not concern me
(and yet: though it permits me nothing
it still
does not relieve me)

(Grazyna Drabik and Austin Flint)

Miron Bialoszewski

(1922–   )

Miron Bialoszewski was born in Warsaw, where he studied Polish philology and journalism at the underground university during the time of World War II. His first volume of poetry appeared in 1956 and was entitled *The Revolution of Things*. Other volumes are: *Calculus of Whims* (1959), *Misdirected Sentiments* (1961), *There Was and There Was* (1965). His autobiographical novel, *Memoir of the Warsaw Uprising* (1970), attracted a great deal of attention (also in an English translation by Madeline Levine, published by Ardis Press, Ann Arbor, Michigan).

"Oh! Oh! Should They Take Away My Stove . . ." My Inexhaustible Ode to Joy

I have a stove
like a triumphal arch!

They're taking away my stove
like a triumphal arch!!

Give me back my stove
like a triumphal arch!!!

They took it away.
All that's left
       is a grey
            gaping
               hole
     a grey gaping hole.

And that's enough for me:
grey gaping hole
grey-gaping-hole
grey-ga-ping-hole
greygapinghole.

(Andrzej Busza and Bogdan Czaykowski)

To—

Suddenly you are cut out
from the confused shapes of the street
with the convexity of legs
face

You approach—half of you
you pass by—half of you

How I miss
that always hidden side
you walk away—half of you
the movement of others
cuts you into smaller and smaller pieces

Suddenly
I am left with nothing of you

(Andrzej Busza and Bogdan Czaykowski)

Adam Czerniawski

(1934–   )

Adam Czerniawski was born in Warsaw where he lived until 1941. After prolonged wartime wanderings, he settled in England and completed his studies. He had his literary debut as a translator in 1951, and as a poet in 1953. His first poem "Odysseus's Return" was published in the Polish journal *Youth* in London. Czerniawski was editor of various literary periodicals, such as the monthly, *The Continents*. He earned his living as a teacher in Ealing Technical College and then in Medway College of Design in Rochester; thereafter he worked as an insurance agent, still publishing his works in Polish and émigré presses. In 1966 he received the five-year grant of the Abraham Woursell Foundation for young people, which enabled him to continue his studies, creative works, and translation projects. In 1967 his poetry was awarded the prize of the Association of Polish Writers Abroad. He is the author of several volumes of poetry: *The Hunt of the Unicorn* (1956), *Interior Topography* (1962), *Dream Citadel, Copse* (1966); a collection of short stories, *The Parts of a Lesser Whole* (1964), and many valuable translations from Polish into English.

Knowledge

Someone told me what mother is
Someone said this is a house
Kingdom, crisis, ceremony and hemorrhage
That's why I know today
Later on I understood the meaning
of dread bitterness rubble and game
of brain tongue liver and sex
now I know
what cannot be
described

(Adam Gillon)

A Cry and a Definition

The sky is cloudy
It is quite cold
perhaps it will rain
behind the hedge-row of bitter alder I hear voices:
but how to get there what day is it
What year?
If it's May and the signs in the sky, the empire is already imperilled
but there are no medicines for consumption
and people still don't realize they're the co-creators
of the class struggle
If on the other hand we're in the 9th century before our era
there's no point to ponder the constancy of common truths
or to strain one's love of one's neighbor

But whence these speculations about "our" epoch?
For perhaps it may be the year 1974 which
does not belong as yet to our era nor to any time
of old, and our decision shall not be rendered easy
by this gust of wind or the pigeons' cooing
which turned now into the cry of quarrel

(Adam Gillon)

Anna Frajlich

(1942–   )

Born in Soviet Central Asia, Anna Frajlich grew up in Szczecin, studied philology in Warsaw, and continued her studies at New York University. Her first poems appeared in 1958, but her first collection of verse was published in London in 1976, under the title *To Paint the Wind.* Another volume, *Only the Earth,* appeared in 1979.

I am separate
the leaf which drops for me
falls at my feet so unusually
nobody sees it with my eyes
I am separate—
no part of a system
nobody's property
nor a cog in a machine
separately I measure the hills on the moon
I breathe dust into the only lungs in the universe
I may stop functioning—I may
suddenly stop
I may fall in love—may
suddenly reject
and dying sanctify with my lips
the separate name of a separate God.

December 1973

(Adam Gillon)

To Paint the Wind

With a drop of rain you're still reclining
on my lips
under the heavy lid the dream remembers you still
but I no longer watch the roads
my threads are entangled
I'll not know how close
you're so far
I will only cry out within your blood
With a sudden pain I'll be slammed like a door open
To paint the wind—one must know the reed
so upright in silence and in a storm—
bent down.

March 1974

(Adam Gillon)

Henryk Grynberg

(1936–   )

Born in Lodz, Grynberg is one of the few survivors of the Holocaust of Polish Jewry. He decided to leave Poland after the so-called cultural pogrom of 1968. He had by then established himself as a well-known prosaist and poet. His publications include a volume of short stories, *Antigone's Crew* (1963), novels, *The Jewish War* (1965), *Ideological Life* (1975), *Private Life* (1979), *Everyday and Artistic Life* (1980); and poems: *The Holiday of Stones* (1964), *Anti-Nostalgia* (1971), *Poems from America* (1980).

In the World of Fireflies

I was born in a world of fireflies
in a little world of glow-worms
filled with the murmur of insects, smells and
the muttering of domestic animals.

I was born among the fireflies
which appear only when they are dimmed
I'm alive, alive and I watch
how they leave me behind dying, and vanish
into the world beyond the lights

I'm alive, alive, and constantly learn worse things
thus I also turn worse and worse
and all the while it is getting late
and more and more I am seized by fear
that I won't have time to explain
to the star of Jerusalem's spirit
and to the Bethlehem road
my David-like aloneness
and my Czarnolas * speech

* Czarnolas: literally "Darkwood," a small estate of Jan Kochanowski (1530–84), greatest Polish Renaissance poet, where he composed his greatest masterpieces (e.g., *Laments, Psalter*); hence the symbol of Polish utterance suggesting poetic inspiration and excellence.

So I turn to the glowing star
of an evening in July

(Adam Gillon)

An American Fable

We were enticed by Baba Yaga **
to the fabulous land of adventure
and she is feeding us
to eat us

In the bosom of this breeder cannibal
fed upon our flesh lady
of the fertile cemeteries
we fall asleep listening to the beautiful
and terrifying tale of life
for a good-night

and we pray that someone after us
might wake and go on listening

(Adam Gillon)

** The wicked witch of the Polish equivalent of the tale of Hansel and
Gretel.

Zbigniew Herbert

(1924–   )

Herbert is the author of several volumes of poetry, plays, and essays, and the recipient of numerous international literary awards. His major works are: *The String of Light* (1956), *Hermes, Dog and Star* (1957), *The Study of An Object* (1966), *Inscription* (1969), *Collected Poems* (1971), *Mr. Cogito* (1974). He also issued a volume of *Dramas* (1970) and a collection of literary essays, *Barbarian in the Garden* (1962). Some of the recent English translations are *Selected Poems* (Penguin Modern European Poets, 1968) and *Selected Poems* (Oxford University Press, 1977). Also see pp. 470–480.

Journey

1

If you plan a journey let it be a long one
a traveling seemingly aimless a groping wandering
that you might learn the roughness of the earth not merely looking but
    touching
and challenge the world with the skin of your body

2

Make friends with a Greek from Ephesus a Jew from Alexandria
they will lead you across the drowsy bazaars and
cities of treatises cryptoporticoes *
there over the burnt-out philosopher's stone
sways an emerald-studded board with
Basileus Valens Zosimus Geber Filalet * *
(gold had evaporated wisdom remained)
past the lifted curtain of Isis
corridors mirror-like framed with darkness
silent initiations and innocent orgies
mines now deserted of myths and religion

* The ancient cryptoporticus—a long vaulted underground passageway.
* * Basil, Valens, Zosimus—two emperors and a historian of the Byzantine period. Geber and Filalet are obscure, at least to this translator.

you will reach the naked gods deprived of dead symbols
that means eternal in the shade of their monsters

3

And if you already acquire the knowledge keep it silent
relearn the world again like the Ionian wiseman
taste the water and fire the air and the earth for
they will remain when everything transpires
and the journey too will remain though yours no longer

4

Then your fatherland will appear smallish
a cradle a boat tied to a branch with the hair of your mother
if you mention her name no man seated round the fire
will know beyond which mountain it is lying
what trees its soil is growing
being so tiny it requires tenderness
before you fall asleep repeat the sounds of speech so funny
that—whether—to
before you fall asleep smile at the blind icon
at the charlocks of the stream at the footpath and the brood
the house has passed
there is a cloud above the world

5

Realize the evanescence of speech the royal power of gesture
the uselessness of ideas the purity of vowels
whereby we can express all joy all wonder wrath
but have no anger
accept all things

6

Pou vrikomaste tora ***—what is this town this bay street or river
the rock that grows in the sea doesn't ask to be named
and the earth is like heaven
the signposts of wind high lights and low ones
the little boards have crumbled into dust
the sand the rains and grass have levelled recollections
names are like music meaningless transparent
Kalamba Orchomenus Kavalla Levadia ****

*** *Pou vrikomaste tora*—translated roughly it seems to mean in modern
Greek: "Where are we now? Where do we find ourselves now?"
**** These place names are all to be found in modern Greece.

the clock has stopped and now the hours are black or white or azure
absorb the thought that your face is losing its features
when the sky has implanted its stamp on your head
what response can a graven inscription give to the thistles
return the empty saddle without regret
return the air to another one

7

So if there is a journey let it be a long one
a real journey from which no traveler returns
a world repeated an elementary journey
a talk with the elements a question with no answer
a pact enforced after a battle
                    a great reconciliation
                              (Adam Gillon)

Waclaw Iwaniuk

(1915–)

Waclaw Iwaniuk belongs to that generation of Polish writers who were beginning their careers on the eve of World War II. His first poems were published in 1934 in the monthly *Camenae* and *The Vicinity of Poets*. His first volume, *Fullness of June*, appeared in 1936. During the war Iwaniuk fought on many fronts. After the war he settled in Canada, and there his poetic volumes regularly appeared in the Polish *émigré* presses: *Song of Songs* (1953), *Silences* (1959), *Selected Poems* (1965), *Dark Time* (1968), *Mirror* (1971), *Nemesis Travels the Empty Roads* (1978). An English translation of his poems, *Dark Time*, appeared in 1979 in Canada (Hounslow Press).

Après le Déluge

In our world even the innocent birds
are swept from their nests by the raging storm.
Turning towards the sky a harmless dove
will soon become a ruse of propaganda.
The artist sells his soul for any slogan
and art is measured by the empty word.
Time drops towards darkness.
The moon escapes earth's apparition.
Dreaming of Ararat
we wait for the dove to bring to us
swiftly the laurel leaf.

What is salvation if those who survived
hurry to be devoured again by night.
Bathed in the rising dawn, impatiently
we wait for the approaching night.
Our garden lies untended,
the canary sleeps
and our lips cannot utter a word.
With a sack on our backs, and not salvation,
we carry with us our cemeteries.
Preferring chaos, though order is better,
preferring hell, though heaven is nearer.

We measure God again with silver pieces
and Christianity with cybernetics.
Temple in our time does not mean temple,
nor Bible Bible.

(Gustaw Linke)

Paraphrases

I darken along with the night
With the star torn from the sky
With the moon washed to the bone
With my word (I have no other)
Bitter like bitter wormwood.

I have sown myself
It took root—
So what of it.

Oh my earth
Don't move from under my feet
I cannot fly
I am only a man
My wing is my word.

My poem shines
When light is extinguished
Its rays have
Their own trajectories
And the cosmos is spacious.
Light is extinguished
When my poem
Is shining still.

I feed on word as a rabbit on leaves
I feed on word as a bee on honey.

My poem stubbornly waits
Surrounded by silence
Like a soul gone astray
Looking for the body.

To live only on bread and salt
What kind of a life is it
Death—this is nourishment
For us—who survived.

And I around the poem
Like this ring on the finger
Around life
Without beginning
Without an end
Around the word.

The gilded wing of a butterfly
Does not burn in the fire
It is undone by its gossamer flight
And by the voracity of neighbors.

I stumble over a darkness
At noon
Over a shadow
Over alien graves
Which I carry within me.

Our backbones do not creak in vain.

(Adam Gillon)

Tymoteusz Karpowicz

(1921–   )

Tymoteusz Karpowicz, born in a remote village near Vilna, was a member of the underground resistance movement during the German occupation. After the war he studied Polish philology at the Wroclaw University, obtained his Ph.D. degree, and became a university professor. In 1948, he published his first volume of poetry, *Living Dimensions*. Since then he has issued eight volumes of poetry and has written about twenty plays, numerous articles, and a book of literary criticism. He has been an editor and contributor to such Polish literary magazines as *New Signals, Straight from the Shoulder, The Oder* and *Poetry*. At present Karpowicz teaches Polish literature at the University of Illinois Chicago Circle.

Wind from the Sea *

To *Lech Walesa*
  Lech Badkowski
  and all carriers of sunshine

APPEAL
TO ALL WHO ARE SCATTERING IN THE PANIC OF LIVING
PIECES OF "GUERNICA"

this poem I will never end
because I never began it
it was given in the breath of native soil
from her always and as long as earth exists
nothing ever ended on it
seemingly long ago dead Heidegger
continually meets me in the morning and says
straightening his Marburg necktie gifted
to him on Zeus' nameday by Heraclitus:
"die Welt ist nie sondern weltet"
and today's ant rotates a white
rounded little egg in the anthill

* An excerpt from a longer poem.

before Noah too will never end
the light of my August and yours
our nation's and mankind's
in a thousand years Faulkner will return again
and will write a new chapter to his
old novel "Light in August"
the reverend and wise Jan Dlugosz * * will stand
by me once more and correct my errors
in the ortography of the word "Poland" and Descartes
in the expression "mankind"
and whatever we talk about henceforth
or write will always concern
stretching one's arms in the morning
and greeting the sun which unfastens
the wrap from the hips of Aphrodite
and the cloth from the loins of Eros not to let them hide
parts of their beauty before the world
and the sun will always bind our hands
with the stole of light and the stole of freedom in order
to bring together those who
will never sleep with Aryman
no matter what the night
(even Paskiewicz's * * * night)
because such is the law of the beginning
that there cannot be an end of mankind
in the middle of the pride of man

and so I will still long write this poem
a living testimony of one dawn
I will write it even after my death
with the pen of a poet being born today

(Frank Mocha)

** Jan Dlugosz (1415–1480), Archbishop of Lvov and the first Polish historian, tutor of the King's sons.
*** Ivan Paskiewicz (1782–1856), Russian Field Marshal, who suppressed the 1830–31 Polish Uprising; Tsar's governor of the Kingdom of Poland, famous for his persecution of the Polish citizenry.

Ryszard Krynicki

(1943–   )

Ryszard Krynicki is one of the leading poets of his generation. He took his degree in Polish literature from Poznan University and there in 1966 he published his first poems in the monthly journal *The Current.* Krynicki's volumes of poetry appeared first in Poland: *Birth Certificate* (1969), *Collective Organism* (1975). But following the author's involvement in the political dissident movement, the publication of his works in Poland was banned. His next volume, *Our Life Is Growing*, was published in Paris in 1978. Krynicki is also a translator of contemporary German poetry, in particular that of Bertold Brecht, Ivan Goll and Hans Magnus Enzensberger.

Tongue, this Wild Meat

for Zbigniew Herbert and Mr. Cogito

tongue, that wild meat growing in a wound,
in an open wound of the mouth,
      the mouth that feeds on deceitful truth,
tongue, this bared heart beating outside,
      this naked edge
that is a defenseless weapon, this gag suffocating
the defeated uprisings of words, this beast
                        day by day tamed
by human teeth, this inhuman thing growing in us and
surpassing us, this beast fed with the poisoned meat
                        of a body,
this red flag which we swallow and spit out
                        with blood, this
divided something that encircles us, this real life
                        that seduces,

this child that teaching the truth, truthfully lies

(Grazyna Drabik)

Caute

He leaves after him several dozen books,
some copperplates, a green coat, one quilt,
seven shirts and several other objects.

—Leszek Kolakowski

Cautiously you open the palm, it is
blind and mute. Shameless, naked. Impressed,
identified
and put in records. There are no more friends of
Spinoza, nor those who denied him,
nor those who preyed on his still warm corpse,
nor worms foddered on his flesh,
nor his enemies,
nor inquisitors of his time,
nor clouds crossing the borders of his time,
also the causes of his death stopped being topical,
his coat, quilt and shirts
do not cover anybody, new books are in new bookstores,
exiles are in exile, fingerprints
in files, watch-towers on borders, files in albums,
customs officers at the end, inhabitants in apartments,
                                        juries on benches,
typescripts in drawers, smiles in mouths, blood
in veins, workers at work, soldiers in uniforms, potatoes
in bellies, citizens in the country, uniforms
                        in warehouses, identity cards
in pockets, help in need, entrails inside,
hands in gloves, foreign countries outside, tongue
behind teeth, prisoners in prisons, meat in cans, teeth
on sidewalks, sputniks in space, the dead in graves, sun
in the day, graves in the earth, dreams in the night,
                        earth in the universe
(that contracts and expands), a gap in biography,
the past in the present, temperature in degrees,
                                        everybody
in his place, lifeline in a drawer, heart
in the throat, the sky in clouds, any questions

thank you, I don't see any

(Grazyna Drabik)

Ewa Lipska

(1945–   )

Ewa Lipska was born in Cracow, where she still resides. She studied at the Academy of Fine Arts in Cracow, and she has been publishing poetry since 1966. Some of her recent works are: *The Home of Tranquil Young Age* (1979), *The Living Death* (poetic prose), *Such Times: Selected Poems* (1980), published in English in Canada. In 1979 Lipska received the prestigious Robert R. Graves Award of the Polish P.E.N. Club.

Testament

After God's death
we shall open the testament
to find out
to whom the world belongs
and
this big trap
for people.

(Adam Gillon)

Holidays in a Hotel

The hotel drags on like a freight train
the shabbiest hotel in the world.
One can live through despair and holidays in it,
It's increasingly more difficult to write in it—
the poems later get paralysis.
In this train I have lived for many a year.
The years have long since overtaken the train.
They're close by. They make port,
Their boats filled with madness.
A draft within rattles the small cabins
Everything that is concealed
in the planetarium of the human skull
lies before them like a map.

Knowledge in an orthopedic boot
takes a forward step.
Nearby the moods of the regimes. The East and the West.
Statesmen with ribbons in their lapels
Marie-Antoinettes starting their race toward guillotines.
The records of crimes.
Close by, my sister dashing off into life
with a knapsack on her back. Islands
of Christmas plates swimming crawl-style
upon square tables. A Babylonian
harvest with central heating.
Love in embroidered corsets and
in black stockings. Beautiful like geometry.
Nearby everybody
succumbing to the illusions
that history will err. Documents
will perish. The witnesses will be burned.
Remembrances grown old will burst of heart attacks.

I am lying
in a hotel room. There is
no one near me. No one
to whom I might say that my God
my God in whom I find it hard to believe
is very sad and travels
as we do
in the same freight train.

(Adam Gillon)

Anna Swirszczynska

(1909–   )

Anna Swirszczynska was born in Warsaw where she completed her
schooling and has lived all her life. Her literary debut took place in 1936
when she published a volume entitled *Verses and Prose.* During the
German occupation of Poland. Swirszczynska participated in the resistance
movement, notably in the Warsaw Uprising. After the war she made a
name for herself as poet and playwright. Two of her last volumes, *I Am a
Female* (1972) and *I Was Building the Barricade,* (1974) brought her
wide acclaim among Polish readers and were translated into English.

He Chews Raw Rye

He never looks out the window,
never goes down to the shelter,
he chews raw rye,
from dawn to dawn he writes
a book.

When someone knocks now and then,
he hides the book in the oven.
The oven may burn along with the house,
houses are on fire all around,
he curses the uprising.

At night he went down to the cellar,
creeping like a thief,
he buried the book in the earth,
on top piled
a mound of coal.

He went back happy,
he had saved his life.
Now
they can go ahead and shoot him.

(Magnus J. Krynski and Robert A. Maguire)

Wislawa Szymborska

(1923–   )

Wislawa Szymborska was born in Kornik near Poznan, but she has lived in Cracow almost all of her life. She made her debut soon after World War II, publishing her first volume of poems, *That's Why We Live*, in 1952. Another volume, entitled *Calling Out to Yeti* (1957), brought her enormous popularity in Poland. Her subsequent books have established her as one of the foremost poets in the country: *Salt* (1962), *A Million Laughs* (1967), *There but for the Grace* (1972), *A Great Number* (1976). Her work has appeared in numerous foreign editions, including English translations. The most recent of these are *Sounds, Feelings, Thoughts: Seventy Poems*, translated by Magnus J. Krynski and Robert A. Maguire, published in 1981 by Princeton University Press.

Psalm

Oh, how porous are the boundaries of man-made states!
How numerous the clouds that float unpunished over them,
how numerous the desert sands that shift from land to land,
how numerous the mountain pebbles that go rolling into alien domains
provocatively hopping!

Must I here enumerate how bird flies after bird,
or how it just now lights on the lowered barrier?
Be it but a sparrow—its tail is now abroad,
though its beak is still at home. Moreover—what a fidget!

From insects numberless I'll mention just the ant,
which between the left and right boot of the borderguard
to the question: from where to where?—disclaims all response.

Oh, to see all this chaos all at once in detail,
on every continent!
For is it not the privet on the opposite bank
that smuggles its umpteenth leaf across the river?
For who, if not the cuttlefish, brazenly long-armed,
violates the sacred sphere of territorial waters?

In general can one talk of any kind of order,
if even the stars cannot be so arranged
for each to know which shines for whom?
And add to this, the reprehensible spread of the fog!
And the billowing of the dust over all the steppe's expanse,
as if it were not cut in half at all!
And the echoing of voices along the obliging waves of air:
of summoning squealings and suggestive gurgles!
Only that which is human can be truly alien.
The rest is all mixed forests, the burrowing of moles, and wind.

(Magnus J. Krynski and Robert A. Maguire)

Utopia

An island on which all becomes clear.
Here you can stand on the solid ground of proof.
Here are no points of interest except the point of arrival.
The bushes fairly groan under the weight of answers.
Here grows the tree of Right Conjecture
with branches disentangled since all time past.
The dazzlingly simple tree of Comprehension
hard by the spring that's named It's Just That Easy.
The deeper into the woods, the wider opens out
the Valley of the Obvious.
If doubt exists, it is dispelled by the wind.
Echo unevoked sends forth its voice
and eagerly explains the secrets of the worlds.
Off to the right a cave wherein lies Reason.
Off to the left the lake of Deep Conviction.
Truth breaks off from the bottom and lightly floats to the surface.
Towering over the valley stands Unshakable Certainty.
From its peak emerges the Crux of the Matter.
For all its charm, the island is uninhabited,
and the faint footprints seen along the shore
point without exception in the direction of the sea.
As if this were a place just for the leaving
and for immersion in a depth with no return.
In a life that's not for comprehending.

(Magnus J. Krynski and Robert A. Maguire)

Stanislaw Wygodzki

(1907–   )

Born in Bedzin, Wygodzki published several volumes of poetry and prose before the outbreak of World War II. During the war he was first in the ghetto and then in the concentration camps of Auschwitz, Oranienburg and Dachau. After the liberation, Wygodzki published numerous volumes of short stories and poems, e.g., *A Diary of Love* (1948), *Silence* (1958), *A Concert of Wishes* (1960). In the late 60's he emigrated to Israel, where he is still writing and publishing in Polish. His major works include novels: *Pieskin Became an Author* (1973), *Detained Until Case Cleared,* (1968), and poetry volumes: *The Tree of Darkness* (1971), *A Winter Journal* (1975).

Before we start from here
tempests will rush through the house;
before we leave this place
who will come across this floor?
Later, when we are gone,
who will slam the door?

(Adam Gillon)

To the Memory of Jan Palach

There, in darkness rain is falling,
there, in darkness, snow is falling
there, in darkness, carts are moving,
now they crossed the other bank;
a sullen wind is tugging
at the soaked bridles.

There, in darkness, singing stopped,
there, in darkness, a cry was stifled;
the wheels are clattering all night,
they're in formation now,
the sullen wind is tugging—
who will call?

There, in darkness, shuffling feet,
there in darkness, doors are shut;
the prison gates are fastened tight,
the hand is shackled, the body bleeding and
the sullen wind is tugging at
the empty skies.

(Adam Gillon)